Britain and the World

Series Editors
Martin Farr
School of Historical Studies
Newcastle University
Newcastle Upon Tyne, UK

Michelle D. Brock
Department of History
Washington and Lee University
Lexington, VA, USA

Eric G. E. Zuelow
Department of History
University of New England
Biddeford, ME, USA

Britain and the World is a series of books on 'British world' history. The editors invite book proposals from historians of all ranks on the ways in which Britain has interacted with other societies from the sixteenth century to the present. The series is sponsored by the Britain and the World society.

Britain and the World is made up of people from around the world who share a common interest in Britain, its history, and its impact on the wider world. The society serves to link the various intellectual communities around the world that study Britain and its international influence from the seventeenth century to the present. It explores the impact of Britain on the world through this book series, an annual conference, and the *Britain and the World* journal with Edinburgh University Press.

Martin Farr (martin.farr@newcastle.ac.uk) is the Chair of the British Scholar Society and General Editor for the Britain and the World book series. Michelle D. Brock (brockm@wlu.edu) is Series Editor for titles focusing on the pre-1800 period and Eric G. E. Zuelow (ezuelow@une.edu) is Series Editor for titles covering the post-1800 period.

More information about this series at
http://www.palgrave.com/gp/series/14795

Philip Payton · Andrekos Varnava
Editors

Australia, Migration and Empire

Immigrants in a Globalised World

Editors
Philip Payton
College of Humanities, Arts
and Social Sciences
Flinders University
Adelaide, SA, Australia

Emeritus Professor of Cornish
and Australian Studies
University of Exeter
Exeter, UK

Andrekos Varnava
College of Humanities, Arts
and Social Sciences
Flinders University
Adelaide, SA, Australia

Honorary Professor of History
De Montfort University
Leicester, UK

Britain and the World
ISBN 978-3-030-22388-5   ISBN 978-3-030-22389-2   (eBook)
https://doi.org/10.1007/978-3-030-22389-2

© The Editor(s) (if applicable) and The Author(s) 2019
This work is subject to copyright. All rights are solely and exclusively licensed by the Publisher, whether the whole or part of the material is concerned, specifically the rights of translation, reprinting, reuse of illustrations, recitation, broadcasting, reproduction on microfilms or in any other physical way, and transmission or information storage and retrieval, electronic adaptation, computer software, or by similar or dissimilar methodology now known or hereafter developed.
The use of general descriptive names, registered names, trademarks, service marks, etc. in this publication does not imply, even in the absence of a specific statement, that such names are exempt from the relevant protective laws and regulations and therefore free for general use. The publisher, the authors and the editors are safe to assume that the advice and information in this book are believed to be true and accurate at the date of publication. Neither the publisher nor the authors or the editors give a warranty, expressed or implied, with respect to the material contained herein or for any errors or omissions that may have been made. The publisher remains neutral with regard to jurisdictional claims in published maps and institutional affiliations.

Cover credit: World History Archive/Alamy Stock Photo

This Palgrave Macmillan imprint is published by the registered company Springer Nature Switzerland AG
The registered company address is: Gewerbestrasse 11, 6330 Cham, Switzerland

In Memory of Eric Richards, 1940 to 2018, doyen of emigration historians.

Acknowledgements

This book grew out of the First Eric Richards Symposium in British and Australasian History, held at Flinders University in Adelaide, Australia, from 31 January to 3 February 2017. Acknowledgement is due to Flinders University, for so readily supporting this international conference, and to Tony Nugent and Dr. Ella Stewart, for their sterling work on the organising committee which made it happen. Eric Richards, in whose honour the symposium was conceived, was enthusiastic about the resultant book and set about writing his own chapter, based on his keynote address. Sadly, Eric died suddenly and unexpectedly before the chapter was completed, and it fell to Dr. Robert Fitzsimons—with the assistance and permission of Eric's wife, Professor Ngaire Naffine— to retrieve Eric's writings and help in the marshalling of the composite chapter, based almost entirely on Eric's original work, that appears in this collection. It is fair to say that, without Robert's diligence and commitment, it would not have been possible to complete Eric's contribution, and we are deeply indebted to Robert for his assistance.

Philip Payton
Andrekos Varnava

CONTENTS

1   **Australia, Migration and Empire**   1
Philip Payton and Andrekos Varnava

2   **British Emigrants and the Making of the Anglosphere:**
Some Observations and a Case Study   13
Eric Richards

3   **Emigrant Choices: Following Emigrant Labourers**
on the Cusp of the Age of Mass Migration   45
Heidi Ing

4   **Why Single Female Emigration to New South Wales**
(1832–1837) Was Doomed to Disappoint   69
Melanie Burkett

5   **Squatter-Cum-Pastoralist or Freeholder?**
How Differences in Nineteenth-Century
Colonists' Experiences Affect Their Descendants'
Historical Consciousness   93
Skye Krichauff

CONTENTS

6   Distress in Ireland 1879–1880: The Activation of the South Australian Community   119
Stephanie James

7   'Yet We Are Told That Australians Do Not Sympathise with Ireland': South Australian Support for Irish Home Rule   151
Fidelma Breen

8   Cornish Miners in Western Australia 1850–1896   181
Anthony Nugent

9   Bal-Maidens and Cousin Jenny: The Paradox of Women in Australia's Historic Mining Communities   207
Philip Payton

10   Mary Booth and British Boy Immigration: From Progressivism to Imperial Nationalism   229
Bridget Brooklyn

11   The Memorialisation of Hector Vasyli: Civilisational Prestige, Imperial Association and Greek Migrant Performance   253
Andonis Piperoglou

12   Dealing with Destitute Cypriots in the UK and Australia, 1914–1931   277
Andrekos Varnava and Evan Smith

Index   313

Notes on Contributors

Fidelma Breen is a native of Co. Armagh, Northern Ireland, and a graduate of Magee College at the University of Ulster, the University of Leicester and the University of Adelaide. Her Ph.D., entitled 'Contemporary Irish migration to Australia, 2000–2015: Pathways to permanence' received a Dean's Commendation for Research Excellence and won the 2018 John Lewis Silver Medal for Geography from the Royal Geographical Society of South Australia. Her research focusses on Irish migration to Australia, Australia's immigration system and its underlying policy, settlement processes, mental health and social media as a platform for support in the migration process. Her interest in migration, particularly the global movement of the Irish, stems from a lived experience of repeat and frequent migration.

Bridget Brooklyn is a lecturer in the history and political thought discipline in the School of Humanities and Communication Arts at Western Sydney University. Her research interests are late nineteenth- and twentieth-century Australian social and political history, women's political history and eugenics. She is currently researching the life and work of conservative activist and eugenicist Dr. Mary Booth. Recent publications are 'Claiming Anzac: The Battle for the Hyde Park Memorial, Sydney', *Melbourne Historical Journal* 45, no. 1 (2017), and '1954: Did Petrov Matter?' in *Elections Matter: Ten Federal Elections That Shaped Australia*. ed. Benjamin T. Jones, Frank Bongiorno and John Uhr (Monash University Publishing, 2018).

xii NOTES ON CONTRIBUTORS

Melanie Burkett completed her Ph.D. at Macquarie University with the support of the International Macquarie University Research Excellence Scholarship and under the supervision of Tanya Evans. Burkett's research interests focus on migrants within the British Empire in the nineteenth century. Her dissertation is a cultural history of the first government-assisted emigrants to New South Wales. She completed her M.A. in history at North Carolina State University and also holds degrees from Duke and Ohio universities.

Heidi Ing is a Ph.D. candidate with Flinders University working under the supervision of Prof. Philip Payton and Prof. Don DeBats. Heidi completed an honours thesis on the German language in South Australia's colonial schools and a master's thesis on South Australia's Institute libraries. Her Ph.D. research investigates the career mobility of immigrants who arrived in South Australia in 1836 and follows the geographic and occupational mobility of their children and grandchildren.

Stephanie James' passion for Irish-Australian history is rooted in direct links with the strength of her Irish descent. The direction of both her M.A. on the early Irish in the Clare Valley region of South Australia and her Ph.D. examining issues of Irish-Australian loyalty during imperial crises can be seen in this context. Her research interests have also been reflected in publications looking at the Irish-Catholic press in the diaspora, Irish South Australia on the eve of World War One and parallels in the treatment of German and Irish-Australians during that war. Most recently, she co-edited and contributed to a 2019 volume which explored *Irish South Australia: New Histories and Insights.*

Skye Krichauff is a historian and anthropologist who is interested in historical cross-cultural relations and understanding the enduring legacies of colonialism. She has convened courses on Australian history, colonial history and Aboriginal-settler history at Flinders University, worked as a history researcher for an Aboriginal community organisation and as an expert ethnohistorian on the successful Kaurna Native Title Claim. Her first book *Nharangga Wargunni Bugi-Buggillu: A Journey Through Narungga History* (Wakefield Press, 2011) examines cross-cultural relations on nineteenth-century Yorke Peninsula, South Australia. Her second book *Memory, Place and Aboriginal–Settler History* (Anthem Press, 2017) is a place-centred ethnography which investigates the absence of Aboriginal people in settler descendants' historical consciousness. Skye is currently a Visiting Research Fellow at the University of Adelaide.

Anthony Nugent is a Ph.D. candidate at Flinders University working under the guidance of principal supervisor, Professor Philip Payton. He arrived in South Australia from Cornwall in 1978 and spent many years in the science faculty at Flinders University. In 2015, after successful completing both an undergraduate and an honours degree (first class) in International Studies, he was awarded a Ph.D. scholarship. His Ph.D. thesis concerns the Cornish contribution to Western Australia 1850–1930.

Philip Payton is a professor of history at Flinders University, South Australia, and Emeritus Professor of Cornish & Australian Studies at the University of Exeter, UK, as well as Hon. Fellow of the Australian Academy of the Humanities. He is the author/editor of more than fifty books. His recent volumes include *The Maritime History of Cornwall* (ed. with Alston Kennerley and Helen Doe, 2015), *Australia in the Great War* (2015), *One and All: Labor and the Radical Tradition in South Australia* (2016), *Emigrants and Historians: Essays in Honour of Eric Richards* (2016), *Cornwall: A History* (2017), *A History of Sussex* (2017), *'Repat': A Concise History of Repatriation in Australia* (2018), *More than the Last Shilling: Repatriation in Australia, 1994–2018* (2019), and *The Cornish Overseas: A History of Cornwall's Great Emigration* (2019).

Dr. Andonis Piperoglou grew up on Ngunnawal country and has Cypriot and Castellorizian cultural background. He is a historian who focusses on migration, race and settler-colonialism in the early twentieth century. He completed his dissertation at La Trobe University in 2017. His thesis explored how Greeks were positioned in Australian racial imaginings while also investigating how Greek people articulated a sense of settler-colonial belonging. In 2018, he was a recipient of the AHA/Copyright Agency Early Career Mentorship Scheme, co-founded the Australian Migration History Network, and was elected a member of the International Australian Studies Association Executive Committee. Currently, he lectures at the Australian Catholic University and is a Research Associate in History at Flinders University, where he is a Primary Investigator on the Australian Research Council Discovery Project 'Managing Migrants and Border Control in Britain and Australia, 1901–1981'.

Eric Richards held a professorial chair in history at Flinders University in Adelaide, South Australia, since the early 1970s, and was Emeritus Professor at the university until his untimely death in September 1918. He was a specialist in the history of Scotland, colonial Australia, and in Australian, British and international migration history. His most recent monographs were: *The Genesis of International Mass Migration* (Manchester University Press, 2018); *Destination Australia: Migration to Australia Since 1901* (University of New South Wales Press, 2008); *The Highland Clearances: People, Landlords and Rural Turmoil* (Birlinn, 2008); *Debating the Highland Clearances* (Edinburgh University Press, 2007); and *Britannia's Children: Emigration from England, Scotland, Wales and Ireland Since 1600* (Continuum, 2004). In 2003, he received the Australian Centenary Medal for 'Services to the Arts and Australian Society'. In 2009, he won the New South Wales Premier's Literary Prize, and in 2014, he was the Carnegie Trust Centenary Professor in Scotland, when he was based at the University of the Highlands and Islands.

Evan Smith is a research fellow in history in the College of Humanities, Arts and Social Sciences at Flinders University, South Australia. He is part of the ARC Discovery Project, 'Managing Migrants and Border Control in Britain and Australia, 1901–1981'. He has published widely on the history of immigration, anti-racism and political extremism in Australia, Britain and South Africa. His latest book is *British Communism and the Politics of Race* (Haymarket, 2018).

Andrekos Varnava FRHistS, is an associate professor in imperial and military history at Flinders University, South Australia, and an Honorary Professor at De Montfort University, Leicester. He is the author of three monographs: *British Cyprus and the Long Great War, 1914–1925: Empire, Loyalties and Democratic Deficit* (forthcoming, Routledge 2019); *Serving the Empire in the Great War: The Cypriot Mule Corps, Imperial Loyalty and Memory* (ManU Press, 2017; ppbk 2019); and *British Imperialism in Cyprus, 1878–1915: The Inconsequential Possession* (ManU Press, 2009; ppbk 2012). He is the editor/co-editor of seven volumes, the latest being *Comic Empires: The Imperialism of Cartoons, Caricature and Satirical Art* (ManU Press, forthcoming 2019), and *The Great War and the British Empire: Culture and Society* (Routledge, 2017). He has published numerous chapters in various books and peer-reviewed articles, including in *Journal of Modern History* (2018), *English Historical Review* (2017), *The Historical Journal* (2014), *Historical Research* (2014 and 2017) and *War in History* (2012, 2015 and 2016), and has others forthcoming in *Social History of Medicine* (2019) and *Contemporary British History* (2020).

LIST OF FIGURES

Fig. 5.1	A tribute to the pioneers, Snowtown and district 1878–1978	111
Fig. 5.2	Detail of the Snowtown centenary plaque	112
Fig. 5.3	Dedicated to the pioneers of Redhill, on the occasion of the centenary celebrations 1969	112
Fig. 11.1	Hector Vasyli Memorial, 1918, Brisbane (*Source* John Oxley Library, State Library of Queensland)	262
Fig. 11.2	'Mr Paul Cominos Ancient Greek Display', *The Queenslander Pictorial*, supplement to *The Queenslander*, 4 January 1919, 25 (*Source* John Oxley Library, State Library)	266

LIST OF TABLES

Table 7.1 Catholic and Irish percentages of population of each electoral district in 1881 and 1901. The Irish-born numbers for 1891 are also given to aid comparison 160

Table 7.2 Comparative wealth of the colonies, 1889 171

CHAPTER 1

Australia, Migration and Empire

Philip Payton and Andrekos Varnava

In the great narratives of Britain and the World, migrants feature routinely, although the sheer diversity of their experience has not always been fully recognised. Migrants played a major role in the creation and settlement of the British Empire and the wider 'Anglosphere' and established global mobility as a defining feature of the Empire's life. Most often this was outward movement, from Britain and Ireland to the far-flung destinations of emigrant settlement, not least to Australia, the focus of this volume. But there were also counter-flows, often distinctive and not always welcome, from the Empire back to Britain itself, establishing pockets of immigrants in the Imperial homeland long before the better known large-scale Commonwealth immigration of the post-colonial era.

P. Payton · A. Varnava (✉)
College of Humanities, Arts and Social Science,
Flinders University, Adelaide, SA, Australia
e-mail: andrekos.varnava@flinders.edu.au

P. Payton
Emeritus Professor of Cornish and Australian Studies,
University of Exeter, Exeter, UK
e-mail: philip.payton@flinders.edu.au

A. Varnava
Honorary Professor of History, De Montfort University, Leicester, UK

© The Author(s) 2019
P. Payton and A. Varnava (eds.),
Australia, Migration and Empire, Britain and the World,
https://doi.org/10.1007/978-3-030-22389-2_1

1

Likewise, despite the numerical and cultural dominance of British-Irish emigrants in Empire settlement, the complexity of global movement had attracted other European migrants to Britain's Imperial project, creating new avenues of loyalty and identity. Contact between settlers and Indigenous peoples was similarly complex, in Australia as in other Imperial destinations, the nature of cross-cultural relations informed by the diversity of migrants' backgrounds, ethnicities, religious affiliations and other factors. This, in turn, alerts us to the fact that British-Irish migrants were by no means the homogenous group often assumed by historians, especially in the Australian context. Despite their shared experiences of migration and settlement, not to mention the primacy of the English language, these migrants nonetheless often exhibited distinctive cultural identities, ones that could be deployed for community, political or economic advantage. In the same way, gender could be a powerful determinant of attitudes and behaviour, overlapping issues of ethnicity and class to influence ways that immigrant women in Australia and the wider Imperial world understood their role and purpose.

This volume is designed to address each of these considerations, using Australia as our example in illuminating the complexity and diversity of the British Empire's global immigration story. Eric Richards, in his chapter, sets the scene and establishes many of the themes elaborated in the book. He alights upon the mass emigration from the British Isles to the Empire and wider 'Anglosphere', noting especially its sudden acceleration in numbers and intensity during the 1820s, an unprecedented surge that underpinned the fundamental relationship between migration and Empire. It was an outstanding outrush, a new dynamic force unleashed upon the world. But the first stirrings of this 'great emigration' had been noticeable in previous centuries, especially after 1770, and the outward movement from Britain and Ireland remained significant until at least the 1950s. Eventually about 19 million left the British Isles and they re-populated three continents—North America, South Africa and Australasia—creating the Anglosphere and acting as the spear carriers or foot soldiers of the greater Empire narrative. But there were discontinuities, as new destinations for potential emigrants appeared, and within the British Isles there was a fundamental disparity between the trajectories of Ireland on the one hand and Britain on the other. Within this dichotomy, there were also significant regional variations, such as the distinctive emigration regions of Ulster and Cornwall, and identifiable shifts in population from localities such as Scotland, Wales and various parts of England.

Within the grand narrative of a globalised Anglosphere, there were, as Richards notes, the sub-narratives of specific destinations. South Australia, he explains, forms a significant case study. The newly proclaimed colony began recruiting immigrants at the very moment emigration from the British Isles acquired its mass characteristics, entering the migrant market in 1835–1836 and offering special incentives to intending migrants who could meet the criteria. In this way, South Australia was successful in diverting some migrants away from more 'mainstream' destinations within the Anglosphere. Yet, as Heidi Ing shows in her chapter, among the early intending migrants to South Australia who had already applied for assisted passages and had been accepted, there were those who after all did not embark in the ships bound for the new colony in 1836. Some had become disillusioned by the seemingly interminable waiting and delays. Life-changing events—such as marriage, pregnancy, the birth of infants—also served to change people's minds or lead to eleventh-hour alterations of plans. Some of these people may have merged back into the general population but many eventually chose competing destinations in the Anglosphere, such as New South Wales, Van Diemen's Land, Canada and the USA, which lured potential emigrants away from the South Australian scheme. As Heidi Ing demonstrates, these individuals and families can be 'hunted down' by using techniques to interrogate online-digitised databases to identify their varied outcomes, and she employs such forensic methods to discover the fates of those early applicants for assisted passage to South Australia. Thirty-year-old Joseph Dennis, for example, was scheduled to emigrate to the colony in 1836, along with his wife, two sons and daughter, but instead the family headed for New South Wales in 1837. John Garread, meanwhile, abandoned plans to go to South Australia—a long and potentially hazardous journey of some four to five months—deciding upon the alternative destination of New York. His wife was pregnant, and they had a three-month-old son as well as an eighteen-month-old daughter, so the shorter trip across the Atlantic no doubt appeared a safer and more attractive option.

Emigration to early South Australia, then, was not quite as straightforward as its founders had hoped, and, despite the special attractions of the new colony, including incentives, not all intending migrants took the plunge, many ending up eventually in more 'mainstream' destinations within the British Empire and wider Anglosphere. Likewise, the seemingly attractive plan devised by the British government in the 1830s to encourage single female emigration to New South Wales was met with unanticipated opposition. Designed to address the acute gender imbalance in New South Wales, thought to be the source of all manner of social and moral evils in the colony, the single female emigration programme was seen by the British government as an 'improving' device. However, as Melanie Burkett explains in her chapter, the plan was viewed as anything but improving in the colony itself, especially among its elite. Still smarting from its reputation as a 'convict colony', New South Wales was alert to any development that might further damage its reputation. The prospect of a flood of single women, mostly from working-class backgrounds (with lives and socio-economic characteristics not unlike the convicts themselves), filled many with horror. The potential female immigrants were seen, not as models of acceptable (middle-class) femininity and 'respectability', but rather as a potential new threat to the moral fabric of New South Wales. This was a theme taken up in the colonial press, the plan's vociferous detractors often motivated by their own political agendas, the emerging debate linking the proposed single female immigration explicitly to the convict 'problem' and highlighting the stark disconnect between British and colonial expectations of the programme. As a result, as Melanie Burkett concludes, 'the single female immigrants were doomed to disappoint'.

Meanwhile, as potential migrants from Britain and Ireland mulled over the relative advantages and disadvantages of competing destinations, and as British emigration schemes sometimes met colonial resistance, so the new waves of emigrants intruded upon the traditional owners of 'new' land ostensibly only now being opened up for settlement. Again, South Australia is our case study. Skye Krichauff, in her chapter, focusses on the agricultural mid-north of South Australia. Initially, in the years after 1836, the mid-north was pastoral country, where the 'squatters-cum-pastoralists' ran large herds and flocks across extensive leases. During this period, the Aboriginal population outnumbered the new arrivals, and there were numerous opportunities for, and instances of, cross-cultural contact, sometimes violent. By the 1870s, however, the pastoral leases had given way to the freeholder farmers of the wheat frontier, a time of much closer settlement with fewer opportunities for cross-cultural contact, the European settler population now larger and the numbers of Aborigines already much diminished.

It is in this historical context, argues Skye Krichauff, that one can begin to explain the relative absence of Aboriginal people in the historical consciousness and oral narratives of those farming families today in South

Australia's mid-north descended from the nineteenth-century settlers. Conventional explanations for the absence of Aborigines in the historical consciousness of such descendants have ranged from 'denial' to 'averted gaze', a collective conspiracy (almost) to perpetuate what William Stanner famously labelled 'the great Australian silence'. Skye Krichauff, however, calls for a more nuanced understanding of the phenomenon, pointing out that Aboriginal and non-Aboriginal people's experiences of colonialism were diverse across Australia and often specific to particular eras and areas, with a range of factors, including geography, topography and resources, affecting cross-cultural contact. In the case of South Australia's mid-north, she shows that settler families today, far from exhibiting the discomfit of the 'averted gaze', express genuine ignorance and sometimes surprise when asked to consider the erstwhile Aboriginal owners of their land. Moreover, the same lack of historical consciousness extends to an absence of knowledge regarding the earlier 'squatters-cum-pastoralists', the oral narratives of today generally going back no further than the arrival of a descendant's first forebears on the land. If the traditional Aboriginal owners of the land are forgotten, then so too are the 'squatters-cum-pastoralists' who predated the freeholders.

Memory of a different sort helps explain the otherwise puzzling role played by South Australia in responses to the 'Distress in Ireland' in 1879–1880. Although, as Eric Richards once observed, South Australia was for the nineteenth-century Irish immigrant, 'the most alien corner of the new continent', the colony retaining its overwhelmingly Protestant flavour well into the twentieth century, there had been a significant arrival of Irish, particularly after 1850. Irish settlement was on a smaller scale than in the eastern colonies, and although their numbers were relatively low, the Irish formed a visible minority within the South Australian settler population, even to the extent of attracting the anti-Irish sentiment observable elsewhere in Australia. Moreover, many of those who had arrived in the colony in earlier years had experienced or remembered the great Irish Famine of 1845–1851, and when news broke of the renewed dearth and distress in Ireland in 1879–1880, they were moved to do something about it. As Stephanie James observes in her chapter, the actual extent of this response is at first sight surprising, given the modest size of the Irish community. Yet South Australia led the continent in initiating the relief movement. As she explains, the rapid and largely seamless mobilisation of South Australia's population—Irish and non-Irish—in raising funds for the

'Irish Distress', when prejudicial opinion was broadly put to one side, was mainly due to the fund-raising energy and public relations flair of the Fund's enigmatic Honorary Secretary, Irishman M.T. Montgomery. Although Adelaide's Lord Mayor, E. T. Smith, was pivotal in launching the official response to the appeal, it was Montgomery who systematically engaged local government to support the establishment of colony-wide relief committees. Subscription lists demonstrated the breadth of community generosity, and extensive newspaper coverage revealed the range of fund-raising events and activities, which garnered more than £8000 in just three months. It was not all plain sailing, as Stephanie James shows, and there were very public disagreements, with Montgomery emerging as a somewhat divisive figure. Nonetheless, South Australians pulled together in a remarkably efficient and well-organised campaign to rise to the challenge of the 'Irish Distress'.

Significantly, as Fidelma Breen argues in her chapter, the relatively small Irish population was likewise able to make its influence felt in the wider South Australian community during the debate over Irish Home Rule. Between 1883 and 1912, envoys from the Irish Parliamentary Party visited South Australia at the behest of its Irish population, engaging in fund-raising and enhancing the reputation of the Irish (in the absence of a coherent Orange opposition to Home Rule) through favourable press treatment of Irish issues. It is clear that the assumed assimilation of the Irish into the broad 'Britishness' of the colony was misplaced, and that during the Home Rule debate they were increasingly politicised. But it is also clear that the Irish were successful in reaching out to other components of South Australian society, garnering strong support for the Home Rule cause in a colony where the majority of the population was neither Irish nor Catholic. Paradoxically, in marked contrast to the eastern colonies, where the Irish proportion of the populations was much larger but with fractured loyalties, including a structured Orange opposition, in South Australia the size, unity and nature of the Irish nationalist voice were complemented by the colony's natural affinity with the notion of self-government and through the fraternal bonds moulded by issues of land ownership and control. Indeed, while fund-raising was the prime object of the series of visits to Australia by Irish MPs between 1883 and 1912, acceptance of the Irish claim for Home Rule among Australians in general proved equally important. As Fidelma Breen concludes, despite the relatively small Irish community in South Australia, the colony contributed generously to the Home

Rule cause, attracting widespread involvement from non-Irish and non-Catholics alike.

As Eric Richards has shown, among the distinctive emigration regions of the British Isles was Cornwall. In the period from 1815 to 1914, perhaps as many as 250,000 people left Cornwall for overseas destinations (with a similar number bound for other parts of the UK), many in response to the demand for Cornish skills and technology on the rapidly expanding international mining frontier. Cornish miners—'Cousin Jacks'—were much sought after for their practical experience and their ability to improvise in seemingly unpromising conditions, and they turned up across the Anglosphere and beyond in often remote locations. In 1867, for instance, as Anthony Nugent describes in his chapter, Captain Samuel Mitchell and a group of Cornish miners arrived near was is now Geraldton in Western Australia to take over the management of the Geraldine Lead Mine. Mitchell was considered the epitome of the 'practical mining man' and went on to carve out a varied and successful career in the mining industry and in parliamentary politics in Western Australia, as did other notable Cornish mine managers in the colony.

Yet, as Anthony Nugent shows, these eminently practical Cornish miners were increasingly the butt of criticism from scientifically trained mining engineers and geologists who objected to what they saw as the 'rule-of-thumb' and 'old school' methods of the Cousin Jacks. An early detractor was the Irish-born and Dublin-educated Edward Townley Hardman, and his criticisms of the Cornish were echoed forcefully by the American college-trained Herbert Hoover, who arrived in Western Australia in 1897. By then the Cornish had already secured their dominance in the newly developed Eastern Goldfields of the colony. However, Hoover agitated for the appointment of scientifically trained mining engineers in their stead, and Cornish hegemony was correspondingly diminished in the years ahead. Yet, as Anthony Nugent shows, the Cornish were by no means as untutored as their detractors claimed (several leading Cornish mine captains in Western Australia having authored technical and scientific papers). Moreover, their departure from the Eastern Goldfields in the late 1890s was not so much evidence of their managerial failings but rather a function of the growing attraction of the South African goldfields, increasingly the focus of British capital investment. Some 5000 Australian miners moved from the Eastern Goldfields to the Rand during the early 1900s, and among them a goodly number of Cousin Jacks, deploying their globalised information networks to identify preferred destinations, in this case South Africa.

The story of Cornish emigrants overseas is often a male-oriented narrative. But among the early applications for assisted passage to South Australia were two single 'female mine workers'—'bal-maidens' in Cornish parlance—Sukey and Jane Fletcher, who hailed from Wheal Butson, near St Agnes, in Cornwall. Not long after, bal-maidens were observed at work, sorting and grading the ore brought to surface, at the newly discovered Wheal Gawler silver-lead mine, near Adelaide. However, despite this early visibility, women soon found themselves excluded from employment in the rapidly expanding mining industry across Australia, an exclusion that—until very recently—has been reflected in the historiography of Australian mining itself. Increasingly criticised as unfeminine in the British press, female mine workers were encouraged to retreat to the domestic sphere, a critique that was echoed in the Australian press, not least in mining districts such as the goldfields of Victoria, where there was by now general resistance to female employment in the mining industry. Insofar as women were allowed a space in the narratives of Australian mining communities, it was in supportive roles which emphasised their 'civilising' qualities and their ability to bring order and domesticity to otherwise rough and ready mining camps. As Philip Payton explains, this was an important component of the 'myth of Cousin Jenny', part of the story that the emigrant Cornish told about themselves, asserting the superiority of such women on the international mining frontier. Moreover, despite the desired confinement to the domestic sphere, there is evidence that female agency could on occasion play a decisive role in the life of Australian mining communities, not least in strikes and industrial actions, such as the significant interventions by women on South Australia's northern Yorke Peninsula and at Broken Hill in New South Wales from the 1870s until the turn of the twentieth century and beyond. Today, a memorial at Broken Hill commemorates the role of women in the city's long history of industrial struggle. But behind the sentiment lies the reality that, despite their earlier prominence, women at Broken Hill were increasingly marginalised by the male-dominated trade unions who sought to confine them to the domestic sphere, or at least to clearly delineated areas of 'women's work' outside the mining industry itself.

Yet there were professional spheres, beyond the mining industry, where women were active in Australia by the early twentieth century. Dr. Mary Booth, for example, a feminist and adherent of the American-inspired reformist 'Progressivist' movement, was a successful childcare specialist and practitioner. During the First World War, she shifted her humanitarian gaze, as did many women of her class and background, to voluntary support services for soldiers and their dependants, notably her extremely successful Soldiers' Club in central Sydney, opened in 1915. A primary aim of this Club was to preserve the health of the 'British race' in Australia by protecting the purity of new recruits from 'the bush' from the evil temptations of the city. In the aftermath of the war, the Club eventually closed in 1923. By this time, as Bridget Brooklyn demonstrates in her chapter, Mary Booth was already moving her attention to providing wholesome accommodation for 'British boy' immigrants. Migration programmes after the First World War targeted British youth—for example, some 18,000 young farm workers were enticed to Australia between 1922 and 1930—these youngsters being seen as the epitome of British vigour and racial purity. Here was a continuity of Booth's eugenic preoccupations from her Soldiers' Club days, but her 'Progressivist' ideas were increasingly wedded to a politicised Australian Imperial nationalism. She ran unsuccessfully for parliament in New South Wales in 1920 and did not try again. But, as Bridget Brooklyn concludes, Mary Booth's active engagement in a variety of causes all pointed towards her embrace of an 'Empire nationalist' political vision, one which incorporated the eugenic and Imperial values of her profession, class and generation, but also offered practical and sympathetic support to those she saw as carrying the promise of British Australia.

Despite the 'British race' dimension of Australian Imperial nationalism, there was room for others within the often carefully constructed world of Australian Empire loyalty. An intriguing insight into this process is provided by Andonis Piperoglou in his discussion of the fate of Hector Vasyli, an eleven-year-old schoolboy of Greek background. On 9 June 1918, Hector Vasyli was walking along a road near the southern end of Victoria Bridge in Brisbane to join a group of children who were cheering Australian soldiers returning from the First World War. These soldiers were travelling in a convoy of motor cars from South Brisbane railway station to the Military Hospital at Kangaroo Point. Suddenly, one of the cars veered to the side and struck Hector, killing him. In the outpouring of grief that followed, negotiations between the Hellenic Association of Queensland, the Returned Sailors' and Soldiers' Imperial League, and South Brisbane Council led to the erection of a memorial in honour of Hector's patriotism. When the memorial was unveiled in early December 1918, the President of the Hellenic Association of

Queensland, Christy Freeleagus, delivered a rousing speech in which he outlined the civilisational prestige and trans-imperial association of Greek settlers in Australia. In Freeleagus' account, Hector Vasyli, and his unexpected death, epitomised Greek settler pro-British loyalty in Australia. Freeleagus extolled the supposed historical, trans-imperial and racial affiliations between Britain and Greece, while the memorialisation of Hector Vasyli served to emphasise and validate early Greek settler ties with Australia, a permanent physical manifestation of cross-cultural interaction. Thus the memorial stood as a sombre moment of public recognition and unanimity that seemed to entrench forever the prestige of Greek civilisation within Brisbane and in Australian society more generally.

Hellenic Empire loyalty was one thing; disreputable Cypriot immigrants quite another. In 1928, the exasperated Australian authorities told the British government that they would no longer allow Cypriots into Australia because of the widespread destitution of those already in the country. In their chapter, Andrekos Varnava and Evan Smith take a comparative approach to understand the problem of Cypriot immigrant destitution, which was also endemic within the UK as well as in Australia. They explore how both the British and Australian authorities attempted to deal with the issue of destitute Cypriots, those who had emigrated abroad before, during and immediately after the First World War. The problem was complex, not only as a result of the destitution itself, but because many had not acquired British Cypriot nationality at the time of British annexation of the island in 1914, having been absent overseas. Indeed, emigration from Cyprus to various parts of the world had become noticeable before the outbreak of the First World War and, although the British prohibited the emigration of men of military age in 1916, it restarted again as soon as the restriction was lifted after the Armistice in 1918. Recent research has shown that the British authorities had considered the London Cypriots a deviant community by the 1930s, both for their perceived criminality and their communist activity. Andrekos Varnava and Evan Smith, however, shift the focus to the preceding period and adopt a broader context (Australian as well as British) to focus on how Cypriot destitution was handled from before the First World War up to 1929.

Although Australia enjoyed a renewed surge of British and Irish immigration after the Second World War, by the 1950s, as Eric Richards has noted, the first signs of the beginning of the end of the long emigration from the British Isles to the Anglosphere were already observable. Indeed, many of the defining characteristics of *Australia, Migration and Empire* had been in place long before 1939, ranging from the early emigration schemes of the 1830s that had coincided with the sudden upsurge of British and Irish migration, through the complex issues of Aboriginal displacement and settler memory, to the impact of transnational identities such as the Irish and the Cornish. Although there remained throughout a commitment to 'British race' identification, which was subsumed within an emerging Australian Empire nationalism, there were opportunities for other immigrant groups to demonstrate their worth as loyal members of the (White) Australian community, although there were notable exceptions which demonstrated the limits of this inclusivity. Over the long period since 1788, the propensity of the populations of Britain and Ireland to emigrate to Australia has varied widely, not least due to the attractions of alternative destinations in an increasingly globalised world, but what is most noticeable perhaps is that, behind its often homogenous façade, British and Irish emigration to Australia has been remarkably diverse in character and impact.

CHAPTER 2

British Emigrants and the Making of the Anglosphere: Some Observations and a Case Study

Eric Richards

Eric Richards was eager to contribute to this volume and had intended to offer a chapter on the peopling of the Anglosphere, with South Australia as a case study. At the time of his death, in September 2018, it was not ready for publication. In its place, Robert Fitzsimons and Philip Payton have drawn on Eric's unpublished writings to produce the chapter that follows. It is a composite piece but the text is almost entirely in his words. Editorial additions have been kept to a minimum, but some have been necessary to achieve better coherence and narrative fluency. The more substantial intrusions have been placed within curly brackets, thus { }

E. Richards (✉)
Late of Flinders University, Adelaide, SA, Australia

© The Author(s) 2019
P. Payton and A. Varnava (eds.),
Australia, Migration and Empire, Britain and the World,
https://doi.org/10.1007/978-3-030-22389-2_2

I

Long Trends in British Emigration Since 1600[1]

In William Boyd's novel *The Ice Cream War*, Gabriel Cobb, a soldier of Britain's remote West African empire, says to himself that 'maps should be banned. They gave the world an order and reasonableness which it didn't possess'. This is also the demographic historian's hazard and is especially the case with the British Diaspora, that is, the spread of people from the British Isles since 1600. The emigrants were not nearly so neatly regimented as the lines stretching across the globe in the maps in my book *Britannia's Children* suggest: there has always been an untidy, uncontrolled and indeed chaotic dimension to emigration, which is one of its intellectual attractions.[2]

Over the past four centuries, departures from the British Isles have been exceedingly uneven. There have been times of widespread and sustained emigration at high and concentrated levels. Some of these exoduses have been so large that the country as a whole took such a fright at the loss of its bone and sinew that the government was urged to intervene to staunch the flows.[3] At other times, the outflows from the British Isles have been slight and even negative, and the recruiters of migrants abroad sought other human supplies to compensate for the deficits. These fluctuations, these surges and retreats, are one of the most intriguing aspects of the history of British migration—the more so because emigration was often regarded as a barometer of the health of the home nation. When people left the country in large numbers, it was natural for social commentators to think that something was wrong with the body politic or body moral. On the whole, however, the British have been more anxious about immigration than emigration, though both are accompanied by severe statistical problems.

The 'British Diaspora' has been crucial in the demographic development of large parts of the modern world. A large proportion of the population of the United States, Canada, South Africa, Australia (including South Australia, as we shall see) and New Zealand trace their origins to the British Isles. In the second and third centuries of international migration out of Europe, the British Isles were the leaders of mass emigration and remained so until the end of the nineteenth century.[4] They constituted a *völkerwanderung*, much celebrated in Victorian literature.[5]

But the measurement of its extent, composition and range is extremely difficult.

The most striking and significant statistic of international migration in the long run relates to the extraordinary precocity and dominance exerted by the British Isles in the so-called Great Age of Emigration. This refers to the long nineteenth century (1825–1930). The best estimate is that about 52 million people left Europe. The British Isles constituted about 10% of the Europe's population at that time but contributed about 36% of the European exodus.[6] Within this broad proposition, there were further disproportions—such as the very large contribution of Ireland to the total.

The purpose of this chapter is to depict the broad flows of people out of the British Isles at various moments in the past 400 years, initially as a panoramic overview, and then presenting as an exemplar a case study of South Australia. The chapter is also concerned with the trends in the propensity to emigrate over that period, expressed as a proportion of the population leaving each year. Establishing authentic migration data, even in the most recent times, is notoriously problematic. Until the late nineteenth century, systematic data were simply not collected. Even in the twenty-first century, the statistics of immigration and emigration are fraught with difficulties of definition, provenance and reliability. Many of the data for this paper are derived from population reconstructions from fragmentary and fragile sources. Moreover, migration is often derived as the final residual calculation at the end of a chain of estimates of total population change and the relationship between birth and death rates. Migration is therefore almost always expressed in *net* terms— essentially because the actual data for inflow and outflow simply do not exist. Consequently, many of the assumptions underpinning the data are, at best, heroic.

Nevertheless, the long perspective on migration trends is a matter of great significance not only for a measure of the vitality of the British Diaspora, but also for the internal demography of the British Isles. Thus, as a simple example, it is clear that in 1630, when the population was a mere six million, the country had a much higher propensity to emigrate than when the population was more than 60 million in 2001. It is also transparent that some parts of the British Isles passed through different chronologies: thus, for example, most of Ireland had a different emigration history from most of rest of the British Isles. By the mid-twentieth century, some demographers announced 'the end of the British Diaspora'.[7]

The notoriety of migration data does not abate with time and technology. As every demographer knows, current measures of movements across international borders are as dubious as they were in 1900 and little better than in 1800. The problems of registration, reporting, deception, informality, changing of minds, re-categorisation, category-jumping and definition remain largely unresolved. Meantime, both the scale and the complexity of such movements have multiplied and even computerised systems are stretched to their limits.

Fluctuations in migration over time are matched by a great unevenness in the origins of British emigration. Sometimes, certain regions have dominated the exoduses—the Scottish Highlands and Ulster were remarkably prominent in the mid-eighteenth century, and less so in the following century. Sometimes, England has been a great donor, sometimes much less generous. This unevenness charts the shifting structure of the nation at large. The regional disparities in emigration run parallel with the changing fortunes of the component parts of the economy, and it is tempting to read special significance into these flows—such as the high outflows from industrial Scotland in the late nineteenth and early twentieth centuries.[8]

Convict transportation, which had nourished the American colonies (to 1776) and then the new Australian settlement from 1788, aroused severe criticism at home and abroad by the 1820s. By 1840, the convict flows were largely brought to a halt. Thereafter, the outflows from the British Isles comprised, overwhelmingly, individuals and families travelling volitionally to a widening array of destinations within and beyond the formal empire.

The maps and tables presented here gather together several current estimates of the flows of British emigration over the long run. Despite the great scholarly investment in recent times devoted to the demographic history of England and Wales since 1570, the emigration dimension has not been settled. Until the late nineteenth century, there was no official and systematic registration and categorisation of movements of passengers into and out of British ports.[9] The problem of distinguishing authentic emigrants from all other travellers is perennial and has been exacerbated by the greatly increased flows of international traffic in recent decades.

For the pre-statistical age, and even into the twentieth century, most estimates of emigration are normally derived as the residual graph once other calculations, notably birth and death rates, have been established. Constructing graphs of emigration (gross or net) for long periods is necessarily an exercise in speculation, producing rough sketches only. Ideally, we would construct annual maps of the regions of expatriation, their intensities and destinations, and chart the sequence of regional shifts over the decades and centuries—which would, for instance, expose the remarkable careers of Ulster or Cornwall in the patterns of change since 1600. In reality, few specific studies or estimates exist, though Ireland in the era of the famine is better served than most.[10]

II

Maps[11]

The first two maps collect aggregated data from modern estimates for the first two centuries of emigration from the British Isles (the seventeenth and eighteenth centuries, respectively); the subsequent maps employ data for individual years: 1840, 1880, 1920 and 1970. They show the changes in the relative scale and direction of British emigration.

Map 1: The Seventeenth Century

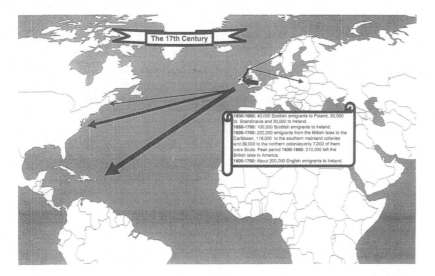

It is conventional to regard the start of English oceanic emigration as the voyage of the 'Pilgrim Fathers', who constituted forty-one of the 102 passengers on the *Mayflower* voyage of 1620 to New England. In reality, there were precursors over the previous forty years though, in comparative terms, it is clear that the English were slow in their engagement with American colonisation, lagging well behind Portugal and Spain and even France. This changed radically in the period 1620–1640 with the so-called Great Migration in which the English suddenly flooded across the Atlantic—beginning 400 years of mass emigration. The Scots and Irish were slower to make their move across the Atlantic.

There were other significant flows, for example the extraordinary number of Scots in Poland and Northern Europe. But the most common form of mobility continued to be the movement of people within the British Isles: these encompassed the usual short- and long-term internal mobility patterns within England which, some historians believe, provided much of the preparation and impetus for external migration.[12] A crucial internal movement, politically and demographically, was that of large numbers of Scots and English into Ireland which was quantitatively as large are the English flow to North America in the seventeenth century. In some respects, the invasion and colonisation of Ireland were a precursor of emigration to America.

The first map also indicates the preponderance of Caribbean destinations among American destinations in the seventeenth century, though this was beginning to shift by the 1680s, reflecting the remarkable growth of sugar/tobacco economies on the mainland colonies of the mid-Atlantic. New England absorbed a relatively smaller population. In the background were two large secular trends which may have been connected—one was the diminishing propensity of English people to emigrate by the end of the seventeenth century; the other was the swift expansion of slave migration into North America by the 1670s.

Map 2: The Eighteenth Century

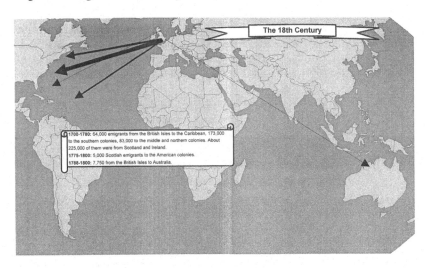

For most of the eighteenth century, in comparison with the earlier transatlantic surge, the vigour of English emigration was not sustained. Significant compensation was, however, provided by the parallel rise in Scottish and Irish emigration (the latter overwhelmingly from the north east of Ireland) and also some German migration to the British colonies. Within the British Isles, the incursion of Scots and English into Ulster had ceased, and far larger numbers of Scots and Irish were now beginning to head for England (especially London).

There were other significant structural shifts in the direction of British emigration. The Caribbean became much less attractive to English emigrants—and there was a wholesale displacement of white labour in the plantations by slave labour—indeed producing an outflow from the sugar islands to the American mainland. Most British emigrants—mainly under indenture contracts—headed for the middle and northern colonies, the flows recurrently disrupted by war and the American Revolution. The transatlantic migrations included about **50,000** convicts from Great Britain whose transportation ceased after **1776**.

In 1788, the stream of expelled convicts was diverted to New South Wales, making it a new far-distant destination for British emigrants, though of small importance for many decades to come. More significant was the sojourner migration of British personnel to India and to the Cape of Good Hope, but these were not registering in terms of settlement at this point.

Map 3: 1840

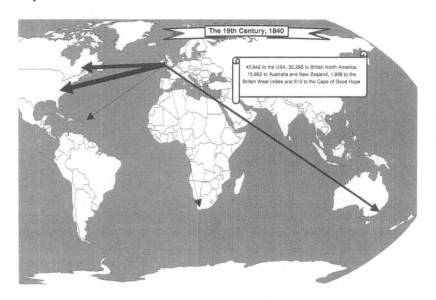

Individual years (such as 1840) demonstrate the relative scale and direction of British emigration across the globe. When the age of mass emigration dawned, Great Britain remained far from clear about the meaning and purpose of its exodus of people. In London *The Times*, observing the convict and pauper elements in British emigration, exposed a nerve when it declared:

> We have no right to cast out among other nations, or on naked shores, either our crime or our poverty. This is not the way in which a great and wealthy people, a mother of nations, ought to colonize.[13]

Great Britain might be the mother of colonies, even of nations, but much of its supply of people came from its gaols and from the least fortunate of its masses. By 1815, new currents were now at work. The great stream of indentured labour which (with convicts) fed the North American labour markets for 200 years had now virtually terminated.

Large annual outflows emerged in the late 1820s, overwhelmingly to the United States, which was the cheapest and best-serviced destination. In the 1830s, the Australian colonies began providing systematic assistance to selected British emigrants and began to secure rising numbers of non-convict workers. South Africa remained a small possibility; despite governmental preference for the Canadas, most British emigrants headed for the United States. Emigration from southern Ireland rose rapidly in the years 1815–1845, ahead of the deluge associated with the Great Famine (1847–1851).

Map 4: The Year 1880

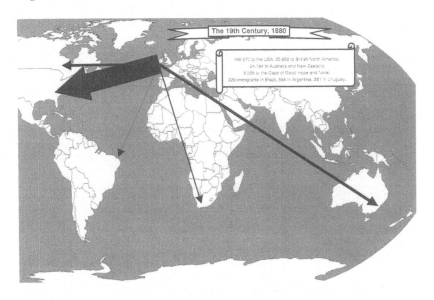

By the 1880s, the flow of emigration from the British Isles was in spate and had greatly widened. There were British communities across the globe, from Peru to Dunedin, from Patagonia to St Petersburg. But the most significant aspect of the story was the overwhelming attraction of the United States. Even those migrants going to Canada often proceeded on to the United States. Australian numbers remained modest, especially when the immigration boom associated with the gold rushes of the early 1850s rapidly subsided. Assisted immigration was imperative to these flows and the Irish took up a disproportionate share. In the 1870s, British and Irish emigration remained high (and rising) despite the onset of improved living standards, even in Ireland.

Map 5: The Year 1920

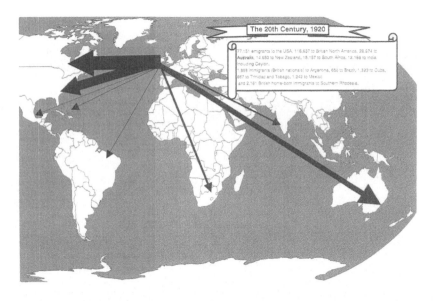

Having risen to an extraordinary peak in 1911–1913, British emigration in the 1920s was relatively disappointing in terms of volume, and despite heavy investment in migration propaganda by the Dominions. The United States was introducing immigration quotas, but the relatively generous allocations made to prospective British and Irish migrants were not taken up. More significant was the redirection of British emigrants, which had been developing since 1906. This entailed a swing away from the United States towards Dominion countries, especially to Canada, but also to a lesser degree to Australia, New Zealand and South Africa. The traditional dominance of the United States as a destination for emigrants from the British Isles was brought to an end—though the reduced number of Irish still continued to flow mainly to the United States. To a large extent, the Dominions were able to use persuasion and subsidies more effectively than before—even though the annual emigrations (even in the empire) remained less than anticipated throughout the 1920s. After 1929, Britain became a net immigrant country for most years before the Second World War.

Map 6: The Year 1970

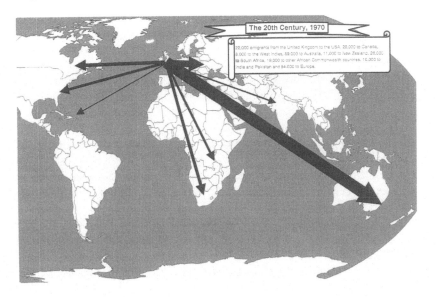

Towards the end of twentieth century, in 1970, British emigration continued the shift identifiable at the start of the century. Now, the United States was a relatively minor destination for British emigrants; moreover, Canada had diversified its intake. The great campaign to stimulate migration to Australia, New Zealand and the African colonies had succeeded, perhaps against a diminishing inclination among the British to emigrate after the 1960s. Meanwhile, of course, each of these destinations was looking beyond the British Isles for immigrants. The great surge on demand for immigrants in the long boom, after 1947, was subsiding at a time when the propensity to emigrate from the British Isles in traditional mode of permanent settlement was itself fading. Australia appeared to succeed especially well, though it may seem like an artificial resuscitation of a declining flow.

III

Observations on Net Emigration Totals from England and Wales[14]

Net Emigration Totals: England and Wales 1600–1870
As explained above, emigration statistics are based either on brave (and often contested) estimates, or else elaborate deductions from reconstructed population data (drawn from samples of parish registers, usually in fragmentary form). They are based on decennial annual averages and show that the broad shape of English and Welsh migration was clearly subject to large periods of relative dormancy. The shape of the seventeenth-century exodus was influenced by the considerable outflow to Ireland and, more particularly, by the so-called Great Migration of the 1620s and 1630s to the new American colonies. After the English Civil Wars, emigration did not pick up and remained relatively low (the net graph affected by inflows from Scotland and Ireland) until the late eighteenth century. The American War of Independence in 1776 and the wars against France from 1796 seem to have broken the upward trend which was fully revived by the early 1830s. This was the true break of trend—the beginning of mass emigration by the mid-nineteenth century.

The story is more complicated when the *rate* of emigration is considered. During this long stretch of time, the country had passed through crucial demographic phases—a rising home population until about 1640, then stability and even some decline until about 1750, after which the population grew at unprecedented and cumulative rates. The propensity to emigrate (per 000) was therefore very high at the time of 'The Great Migration' after which it fell significantly until the 1750s/1760s and declined again until the 1820s. The data suggest strongly that emigration out of England and Wales was seriously uneven and possessed its own history.[15]

Net Emigration Totals: England and Wales 1850–2001

By the late nineteenth century, the British government made more systematic efforts to register inward and outward movements of people. Complicating factors were evidently at work throughout: for instance, increasing volumes of commercial and tourist travel made authentic emigration difficult to differentiate; short- and long-term departures and entries had a similar effect; there was also a substantial and variable quantity of return and re-return emigration. According to one authority, almost 40% of British emigrants in the decades 1861–1913 returned home.[16] In more recent times, the sheer volume of international movement has been overwhelmingly greater than actual emigration and the methods used to measure genuine resettlement are widely regarded as imperfect.

Nevertheless, the broad trends in British emigration are relatively clear and open to interpretation. The impressively rising trend in Victorian or Edwardian times was broken by the decline in the 1890s coincident with a prolonged depression in the British economy (and also in some of the colonies). The propensity to emigrate rose in periods of unambiguous improvement in British living standards in the 1870s and 1880s and also in the peak time before the First World War. Throughout these many decades, the emigration of English/Welsh people was, at least in part, compensated by continuing high immigration, primarily from Ireland, but also to a lesser degree from Scotland and the Continent. The inter-war years were sluggish (and negative after 1929) in terms of net emigration and the general trend, despite some revival after 1947–1979, was downward. The long trend was a decline in the rate of net emigration (notably in oceanic migration) and was amplified by the growth of immigration at the end of the twentieth century. Although about 200,000 British people were leaving the country per annum in the 1990s, the inflow was generally greater. Here, it is imperative to emphasise the point that the precise status of both emigration and immigration had become much more ambiguous.

In 1950, Charles Carrington had announced the end of the English Diaspora.[17] His assertion was perhaps premature—especially in the light of the revival of Dominion emigration (primarily to Australia) in the 1950s and 1960s. But the long trend indeed appears to vindicate the idea by the turn of the new century. The rich modern industrial country, with a population of 60 million, was now exporting a much smaller proportion of its people than when it had been a very small pre-industrial nation.

Net Emigration from Ireland Since 1880

Ireland, and especially Catholic Ireland, experienced a demographic history radically different from most of the rest of the British Isles. Capturing this difference in graphs and statistics is difficult because, in the case of Ireland (and indeed of Scotland), there is no equivalent of Wrigley and Schofield's population reconstructions.

It is well known that there was extraordinary emigration from Ireland during the Famine of the 1840s. Other accounts of the pre-famine and famine emigration have produced a relatively clear account of Ireland's demographic history. Thus, there was considerable transatlantic emigration from the north of Ireland to America from as early as 1720, though less so from the remainder of the island. Emigration from Ireland to England and Scotland was becoming significant from the mid-eighteenth century. Ireland's population doubled between 1780 and 1830 and expanded fastest between 1780 and 1821 and continued until the catastrophe of the Famine in 1847–1851.

It is now relatively clear that emigration from Catholic Ireland was rising very swiftly in the 1820s and 1830s: it is very likely that this emigration helped to diminish some of the devastation wrought by the Famine in 1847–1851. Rates of emigration, of course, reached phenomenal levels in the Famine years and continued at reduced but nevertheless very high levels through the remainder of the century. Net emigration was greater than natural increase in the Irish population, and consequently, the Irish population declined continuously until the late twentieth century.

The rate of Irish emigration (now encompassing the west and south of the island) undoubtedly rose rapidly in the 1820s, well ahead of the Great Famine of the 1840s. It was probably up to 3 per thousand as early as 1820 with an average of 7 per thousand for the years 1815–1845. In the first year of the famine, about 100,000 left Ireland—about 12 per thousand. It then rose to the awful crescendo of 35 per thousand in 1851 and remained well above 10 per thousand throughout the 1850s. The average for the years 1846–1850 was well over 25 per thousand; for the longer period 1850–1870, it was close to 20 per thousand throughout.[18] Irish emigration rates therefore followed a high but falling trend. The total emigration numbers were also falling—in part because the cumulative depletion of the Irish population left fewer in each generation to maintain emigration totals. Nevertheless, for many generations, emigration was a common expectation for a very high proportion of the Irish people.

The long-established Irish emigration tendencies seem to have run their course until, by the 1970s and 1990s, Ireland was beginning to register years of net immigration—a reversal of 200 years of the Irish Diaspora. The very long-run trend seems to have been broken and this signalled an alteration in Ireland's demographic relationship with the rest of the world. Emigration from Northern Ireland followed a path between that of the rest of Ireland and that of England and Wales. The rates of emigration, while higher than in England and Wales, remained much lower than in the Republic. Each part of the British Isles eventually entered the parallel declines in the late twentieth century which made up the shrinking Diaspora, the diminishing supply of people outward from the British Isles.

Scottish Emigration, 1861–2001
Scottish emigration before 1861 was notable for an early engagement with transatlantic movements in the eighteenth century, with substantial involvement of the Highlands (which accounted for half of the Scottish population before industrialisation in the early nineteenth century). During the century before 1850, there was also a drift of people towards central Scotland, which altered the distribution and balance of the Scottish population.

Though Scotland experienced the fastest and most spectacular transition to industrialisation, it maintained relatively high rates of out-migration, much of it to England but also to the rest of the British world. Though mostly lower than the rate of Irish emigration, the Scots actually overtook the rate of Irish emigration at the start of the twentieth century. Some Scottish nationalists and historians saw the high propensity to emigrate as 'haemorrhaging' and looked for special Scottish problems to explain the losses. The Scottish rate remained much higher than that of England but declined in parallel, so that, by 2000, Scotland was beginning to experience population growth—and, most remarkably, in the Highlands.

More Recent Migration Levels from the UK, 1964–1998
Most of the graphs have depicted *net* movements into and out of the British Isles, that is the differences between inward and outward movements. The actual totals of these movements are highly flexible. Even in the most recent decades, much of the data relating to emigration have been derived from self-reporting by travellers, whose numbers have

increased much faster than those of authentic settler migrants. Despite the fragility of the evidence, it seems that the tendency of British emigration had been quietly downward, the rate per thousand falling quite decisively since the 1960s. But at a reported rate of about 200,000 per annum at the turn of the century, it still remains somewhat premature to declare an end to British emigration. However, these considerations relate to a total population far greater than in any previous century of the British Diaspora.

Meanwhile, levels of immigration—the subject of fierce political controversy—seem to have been trending upwards. Moreover, the gap between emigration and immigration which, traditionally, has been slight has in more recent years widened appreciably. But it is still not much more than 150,000 per annum. The greatest caveat to this, of course, is that the status of both 'immigration' and 'emigration' remains highly questionable.[19]

IV

A Corner of the Anglosphere: The Foundation of South Australia[20]

Over the long time period dealt with in this chapter, the average propensity to emigrate from the British Isles has fluctuated substantially. By identifying these long trends, it is possible to periodise the history of British emigration and to see this remarkable phenomenon in its wider historical perspective. At the same time, however, it is also possible to examine emigration to specific destinations within this broader historical context, furnishing micro-histories or exemplars that illuminate the complexity and diversity of the long emigration from the British Isles. South Australia is one such case study. This colony was formally established in 1834, almost fifty years after the colonial beginnings at Botany Bay, and now in the first decade of mass migration from the British Isles.[21]

The Australian immigration story was improbable from the start. Australia was an immense distance from any other British settlement and extremely difficult to reach. Its peopling from the British Isles was achieved by its access to layers of the British and Irish populations made suggestible in the 1830s and beyond—critical years at both ends of the migration system. In the process, the Australian colonies slew off the negative image of the original convict colonisation and generated new lines of immigration. South Australia is especially interesting because, by design, it was aligned with the question of migration in Britain: its planners inaugurated a 'systematic' mechanism to scientifically recruit and employ certain sorts of recruits in Britain. Its founders combined piety, capitalism and a theory of colonisation designed to demarcate the new colony from all previous colonisation enterprise—most of all, it would introduce immigrants in a manner which was synchronised with the sale and utilisation of land.

{'This, then, is the people for private enterprise... Emigration is in vogue: out go swarms of colonists, ... each by himself, and at his own arbitrary and sudden will'.[22] So wrote John Henry Newman in March 1855—in the heyday of empire—from his residence in Birmingham. Although rarely cited by migration historians, Newman was a significant observer and his remarks are of particular interest in relation to the colonisation of South Australia. An Act of Parliament of August 1834 erected South Australia into a 'British Province'. Its first colonists arrived in 1836 and its growth was rapid: by 1855 the colony had a population of 97,000.[23]}

{The founders of the new colony have been described as an 'alliance of Dissenters, reforming Whigs and secular "Benthamite" radicals'.[24] Commentators typically drew attention to certain 'peculiar' features of the original blueprint for the colony,[25] noting especially its provision that 'no person convicted in any Court of Justice in Great Britain or Ireland or elsewhere, shall at any time, or under any circumstances, be transported as a convict to any place within the limits' of the new Province.[26] Emigration to South Australia was to 'partake as much as possible of the family character', wrote Cardinal Moran in 1895: 'It was to embrace only those who bore a respectable character, and had sufficient means to purchase one or more blocks of land'.[27] Richard Whately, Church of Ireland Archbishop of Dublin, was one of the notable public figures attracted by many features of the 'projected new settlement'— despite the planners' intention that there was to be no State Church. In an open letter addressed to Earl Grey, in January 1834, Whately quoted at length and approvingly from the prospectus of the South Australian Association.[28] Its proposals accorded with his vision, outlined in an earlier letter: 'A colony so founded', he said, 'would fairly represent English society, and every new comer would have his class to fall into, and to whatever class he belonged he would find its relations to the others, ... much the same as in the parent country'. An emigrant to the new country would find 'little more revolting to his habits and feelings' than if he had 'merely shifted his residence from Sussex to Cumberland or Devonshire'.[29] Whately's views were by no means exceptional in the 1830s. It is pertinent to ask to what extent they were realised in the ensuing history of the colony.}

The original plan derived from Edward Gibbon Wakefield and was meant to solve various problems associated with colonisation and emigration.[30] It would render the colony attractive to investors and migrants (mainly because it eschewed all notion and taint of convictism); it would synchronise land sales and the availability of labour; it would form the basis of civic society in advance of other colonies—with its aspirations towards freedom of religion and democratic institutions. These were important selling points for the colony—and, more to the point, significant elements in this extension of the Anglosphere.

The new colony of South Australia was designed specially to recruit emigrants across the British Isles with assisted passages—on tight criteria for the selection of working people, chosen by age, gender balance, occupation and good character. A large fund was established, together with facilities for recruitment and the delivery of migrants. It was a particular test of the availability and propensity to migrate, early in the Age of Migration, but relatively late in the continuing transformation of British society. The colony sought rural labourers and domestics most of all—to provide the foundation labour force of the very distant new colony which was expected to be a rural society with the prospect of primary production eventually to export. But the first call was to set up farms in the destination. The assistance system allowed the colony to reach deeper into the prospective migrating population—people who were otherwise too poor to be able to emigrate. The range was widened. But it did not mean that the colony recruited the worst sorts of emigrants, because the selection procedures were stringent and the barriers were higher so that the more literate tended to be selected or self-selected.

Special factors affected recruitment: the distance and the obvious finality of the decision; the untried character of the colony; the supposed (but erroneous) association with convictism. All were balanced against some favourable terms on offer: free passages, freedom of movements for employment, a guarantee of employment, and liberal conditions of government and religion. It was, most of all, a test of the availability of people prepared to leave Britain and Ireland. Some of the resulting initial population of South Australia seem to indicate basic features in the emigrant market.

There was a clear bifurcation among emigrants to South Australia: Young Bingham Hutchinson on the *Buffalo* in September 1836 made the distinction between 'the gentlemen emigrants' and the 'emigrant labourers'.[31] Investors bought land and some were prepared to send younger sons and poor relatives to the colony—'into a rural exile', according to Douglas Pike.[32] They were also able to persuade tenantry and retinues to depart, collectively in some cases. Institutional recruitment also worked: the South Australian Company recruited 250 labourers in the first shipments to the colony. Recruiting agents—with the full apparatus of persuasion, including itinerant lecturers—were distributed unevenly. Their distribution was skewed towards southern England. London was predominant; Cornwall was well represented, while Ireland was notably under-represented.

Assistance and recruitment were critical. Agents recruited 14,000 emigrants of whom 12,300 were assisted, and quite a few of these possessed capital.[33] The Home Counties predominated, which suggests that funding and information were critical—and sufficient in the first phase to meet requirements. But young married couples without children were actually difficult to recruit. The first recruitment was successful—and only 360 were paid for by parishes—so there was little suggestion of 'shovelling out paupers'. To put a human face on these statistics: William Kelly and his young wife emigrated from the Isle of Man in 1838, soon after getting married. They obtained an assisted passage and Kelly was designated as 'sheep keeper or shepherd'. He possessed a few sovereigns with which to make a start and soon had purchased a few cows and headed for the Adelaide Hills—at first squatting at Cudlee Creek. There he established his family in a bark hut and was able to employ a helper. His older brother followed in 1839, and Kelly had gained freehold in 1842. The family raised potatoes and other crops and by 1844 had 1200 sheep and thirty cultivated acres. Kelly had thirteen children, of whom nine survived. He effectively became the model yeoman migrant imagined by the Wakefield scheme; his sons eventually moved north to land at Riverton.[34]

The scheme demonstrated the possibilities of channelling migration, of arousing interest in exotic destinations, and the willingness of many different classes to take up opportunities. The potential emigrants were certainly a mixed bag—receptive to the idea of higher wages and plots of land. Further, there is evidence that labourers were motivated by the possibilities of small subsections of land—and were enticed by the prospect of social and economic independence. People with capital also obtained free passages and they jumped into the land market on arrival in South Australia. The whole system was oversubscribed—which again suggests a pent-up demand for emigrants. There seems to have been a susceptible population in the 1830s reasonably easily persuaded of the advantages of emigration to this new colony.

South Australia is a significant case study because it began recruiting immigrants at the very point of the rise of mass emigration in the British Isles.[35] It entered the migrant market in 1834–1836, offering special incentives to migrants who could satisfy their criteria. Agencies were activated, but the catchments were skewed by the net employed by the commissioners. The impact of their intervention exposes the state of suggestibility and prior mobility in the system as it existed in the 1830s. Ireland may have been under-represented at the start, but it made significant early contributions. For example, in 1840, Sir Montague Chapman, who had bought land in the colony, persuaded 213 tenants and labourers to go to South Australia, in a party organised by the agent Hervey Bagot: the Chapman estate had been executing clearances which chimed in nicely with the emigration plans. Such migrations were driven by individual landowners taking initiative and investing quite heavily: the emigrants begin to look like rural refugees out of Ireland.[36]

The recruitments for South Australia were biased towards London, the south-east of England and the south-west, areas probably benefiting from their proximity to the planning offices of the colony. About 12,000 'poor persons' were selected: 7% from Ireland, 9% from Scotland, 8.5% from the north of England—thus 65% were from a line south of Bristol to London. In the period 1836–1847, it was highly localised. Further, in 1838–1841, George Fife Angas financed the emigration of 800 German immigrants, and in the years 1841–1850, some 5400 came from different parts of Germany.[37] The German recruitments were curious and odd and were determined by special factors. But they were themselves part of the coinciding exits out of Europe.

There was a sudden crisis in the colonial economy in 1841 which caused an equally sudden hiatus: the colony turned off the tap of migration until a strong recovery occurred in 1845, mostly associated with the discovery of copper at Kapunda and Burra and the extension of farming and grazing to produce an export-driven recovery. The expansion was accompanied by a rapidly rising demand for immigrants, not least for Cornish miners and their families who arrived in large numbers after

1845, bringing new skills to the colony. Many were Methodists, enhancing the colony's Protestant nonconformist flavour.[38] But conditions in England generally were less propitious: railway construction seems to have dampened demand for emigration. Leading colonists began to think of seeking Chinese labourers to come to Adelaide—indeed, £2000 was subscribed but the plan was vetoed by Governors Robe and Grey.

By 1847, all the immigration systems had returned to full function: there was £100,000 in the Emigration Fund, much publicity and the end of the railway boom in England. Now, the number of applicants rose rapidly—as Douglas Pike noted, there were almost too many.[39] And in the years 1847–1851, South Australia received 35% of all emigrants to Australian destinations. Free passages were given to 20,262 emigrants (34% males and 39% females, over 14 years of age); there were 13,000 fare-paying emigrants, and 4000 Germans. They had many different motivations. Further, some 12,000 migrated from other colonies, making a total immigration of more than 50,000.

{George Grey, governor of the colony, recorded a telling vignette of its capital, Adelaide, at the beginning of 1845:

> The European population are collected from almost all parts of the world… You meet Scotchmen in kilts and plaids, Irish women without bonnets and their cloaks thrown over their heads, Germans in their national costumes, … Chinese with their wide trousers, Indians in different costumes, natives with kangaroo skin cloaks, … London dandies, all mixed on our streets.[40]

Colourful and perhaps exciting as this sketch might seem, Grey also made a more serious observation: these folk were 'accustomed to different laws and usages, all ignorant of one another, of the country into which they have come, of its seasons, of its soils'. Ignorance of the seasons and soils would lead to grave disasters in some areas of settlement.[41]}

Synchronising the inflows of immigrants with local needs was never easy, and there were periodic over-supplies and sudden shortages. However, the South Australian experience, as a case study, suggests that the system of assisted migration was generally able to arouse adequate numbers which were then synchronised by close attention to the details of the regulations—'tinkering with the rules' to get the right results. Bearing in mind the time differences from the source countries, this required heavy intervention from time to time to produce the desired results. Much emphasis was given to the introduction of single female immigrants to serve as domestic servants. In some years, this recruitment was channelled by way of English and Irish workhouses. The first 200, in 1848, were easily engaged in employment. In 1849, there were 1600, mainly from workhouses. There were many different distressed females from philanthropic bodies, including the National Benevolent Society. In 1850, the London Females Colonization Society sent 400 girls from Holborn and Westminster to South Australia. The Highlands and Islands Emigration Society was involved in 1852–1853. Unemployed railway workers arrived after working in Belgium and France. There was a special intake of unemployed weavers from Calais.[42]

From time to time, there was an over-supply of recruits. The mechanisms were adjusted to meet these exigencies—modifying the regulations usually affected the contributions required of immigrants to adjust the flows and there were moments when the cost became as much as that of the transatlantic passage. Another development was that of nomination schemes, which entailed the participation of earlier emigrants in the recruitment of relatives and friends in the homeland.

As noted above, Cornish people began to arrive in large numbers after 1845, responding to land and mining opportunities. By 1850, the Irish proportion began to rise very rapidly, mainly because recruitment in England was too laggard, suggesting levels of prosperity. This then raised the question of the ethnic composition of the colony. The prevailing idea was to achieve the representative population of the home countries, but this was never likely to be achieved.

By the early 1850s, the net had widened across the British Isles and there was an increasing recourse to Ireland, especially for female recruits as domestic servants. There was still a Home Counties bias and very few emigrants from the Midlands or the north of England; the Irish component was carefully monitored to prevent it overwhelming the colony, though there was never a real danger of this happening. There was a local panic in 1854–1855 when 5500 orphan and pauper girls were sent from London and Ireland, and temporarily deluged the labour market in recession. Thereafter, Ireland was the most reliable source of immigrants and their number rose to as much as 20% of the intakes at various times in the later century.

The Irish element had begun early, however, and at the start, there were specific recruitments.[43] Colonel Robert Torrens, who was himself

Irish, had been keen to recruit Irish capital and investment in South Australia and, beginning in 1837, four agents were appointed to Ireland (there were fifty in England). This was the earliest stage for the colony. Torrens began advertising in Ireland (his son Robert Richard Torrens and Thomas Pope Besnard, of Cork, were helping) and pressed the case as a means 'to relieve the impoverished agricultural population'. Torrens junior talked of the 'absolute dispauperisation of the Irish working classes' and their relief 'by the instrumentality of an extensive and judicious system of emigration'.[44] He promoted the new scheme enthusiastically and had obtained emigrants by June 1840. The *Mary Dugdale* sailed from Dublin and the *Birman* from Cork in the summer of that year. The Chapman, of Killua Castle in Westmeath, bought a £400 land order which allowed them to nominate 300 emigrants. Chapman toured Munster and Leinster in early 1840 and recruited 224 emigrants, although the transit of these emigrants from Irish estates was delayed by the crash of 1841. Sir Montague Chapman himself did not emigrate to South Australia until 1852.

There were 700 Irish among the 15,000 early colonists who had arrived in South Australia before recruitment was halted in December 1840, and most of them were Protestant. In 1837, the South Australia Protestant Emigration Community, founded in Dublin, appealed directly to 'emigrating Protestants'—an opportunity to 'retire in peace and comparative comfort from strife and agitation and impending distress, which hang over this beautiful but ill-fated island'.[45] They were promised a first-class voyage with a clergyman and a surgeon, and the construction of an Episcopal Church in the colony. The shareholders were required to declare 'unreserved loyalty and individual allegiance' to the king, and other forms of religious worship were forbidden to this community's members. They appear to have raised £100,000 and began plans for 1000 emigrants. Recruitment proceeded. However, the scheme collapsed and it obtained the reputation of being operated by 'bigoted Orangemen'. Nevertheless, some of its prospective migrants found their way to South Australia through more conventional channels—making a contribution to the Protestant Irish emigration of 1836–1841. Within Ireland, some of the Tory press was critical of the losses from the Protestant lower class, since they threatened to weaken the 'Protestant Ascendancy', and blamed their landlords for their oppressive tenancy arrangements. Ireland—especially Protestant Ireland—should keep its capital and its people.[46]

The official version of the South Australian experiment, authored by William Harcus, was published in 1876.[47] It made great play of the separation of Church and State and extolled the principle that 'no form of religion should be distinctively recognised by the State' and all religion was on an equal footing.[48] It acknowledged the fine work of all denominations, including the Catholic Church (not least the Jesuits), as well as the Dissenters and the Jews. Yet immigration was designed to 'maintain the proportion of the nationalities – English, Irish and Scotch – according to the proportion in the United Kingdom'.[49] The agenda here was transparently conservative: to resist any disproportionate growth of Catholicism. Forty years from the start of the colony, the practical realities had become evident and accommodating: 'The principle is not very steadily adhered to; nor is it necessary. It is found that all classes, as a rule, make good immigrants; and the Irish, who half starve at home, become well-to-do colonists when they get a fair start here'.[50] Similarly, it was said, the Germans did well because of their industry and thrift.

South Australia at its foundation was to be a place of refuge for pious Dissenters from Great Britain.[51] George Fife Angas certainly persuaded many to come. Indeed, the most blatant intervention was by Angas (1789–1879), a wealthy investor who became the biggest landowner in the new colony and was therefore able to sponsor the most immigrants.[52] He shaped the pattern of immigration in South Australia's early years. Angas was a zealously evangelical nonconformist, with dogmatic views on Sabbath keeping, gambling and horseracing, yet he was perfectly philanthropic. Not only did he sponsor emigrants from Britain but also from Germany. It was Angas who, hearing of the plight of a band of Lutherans in Prussia (they refused to adopt a new form of Church Liturgy made compulsory by the King of Prussia), met with their leader, Pastor Kavel, in Hamburg and funded their emigration to South Australia. Some 250 came to South Australia from Hamburg in 1838 and then 187 and 596 in two other vessels—a thousand emigrants in all.[53]

Angas strenuously opposed immigration from Catholic Ireland—especially the migration of poor women. In the long run, however, all this was reversed when South Australia ran dry and had recourse to the Irish. {William Harcus reported, in 1875, that 85% of South Australia's population was Protestant. The Roman Catholic minority comprised about 15% of the total population.[54] This corner of the Anglosphere, South Australia, remained predominantly Protestant until the second half of the twentieth century. It had a much larger proportion of Methodists than any other Australian state. Despite the positions taken by Angas and others, there is strong evidence to suggest that, throughout the nineteenth century, Catholics and other minority religious groups (e.g. the Jews) experienced wide toleration in South Australia. In the years 1862–1868, South Australia had Australia's first Roman Catholic Governor, Sir Dominick Daly, a native of County Galway. It was claimed that Daly's appointment was the 'first practical recognition by the Downing-street authorities of the fundamental principle of religious equality upon which this colony is founded'.[55] Daly became popular; some observers considered him the best of the colony's early governors.[56]}

Nonetheless, religion skewed the pattern of immigration to South Australia, and the Wakefieldian system gave it the means. It affected Irish immigration but this bias was ultimately defeated by the practical realities as they applied to the new colony. It also affected the attraction to Dissenters. South Australia was a heavily Protestant endeavour and London-based: alongside the predominantly Methodist Cornish and other nonconformists who were attracted to the colony, and 'onerous regulations favoured the literate, well connected, "respectable" or better-off Irish who were mainly Protestants'.[57]

CONCLUSION

The South Australian case illustrates how the intervention of a scheme to subsidise migration and to channel labour incentives worked out in practice, using recruiting agencies (and premiums) to stimulate flows to the colony. The scheme operated in tandem with private initiatives which also helped to activate special responses. But these stimuli were probably secondary to the general shifts of population which sped thousands from Britain and Ireland towards far-distant destinations, mostly to America. South Australia was successful in diverting at least some away from more 'orthodox' streams in the Anglosphere. In this, South Australia touched the outer edges of the several great diasporas of the nineteenth century— British, Irish, German—and the colony's immigrants came especially from the high-emigration zones of the British Isles. Its access to Cornish and Irish emigration was to prove particularly fortunate.[58] Yet the South Australian experience, instructive as it is, with its particular defining features, was but one part of a 'Great Migration' from the British Isles to an increasingly far-flung Anglosphere that had lasted for some 400 years, and only now seems to be running down, perhaps permanently, a

38   E. RICHARDS

demographic shift first signalled and anticipated as early as the mid-twentieth century—for instance by Forsyth, Hancock and Carrington.[59] Such predictions are hazardous but the long profile of British and Irish emigration, as attempted in this chapter, offers evidence that it has indeed reached its term.

NOTES

1. Parts of this paper were originally prepared, but not published, as an appendix to Eric Richards, *The Genesis of International Mass Migration: The British Case, 1750–1900* (Manchester: Manchester University Press, 2018). I wish to thank Robert Fitzsimons and Jan Schmortte for their assistance.
2. See Eric Richards, *Britannia's Children: Emigration from England, Scotland, Wales and Ireland Since 1600* (London: Hambledon and London, 2004), pp. 53, 71, 121, 179, 211, 237.
3. See Richards, *Britannia's Children*, chap. 6.
4. For a useful international comparison, see Dudley Baines, *Emigration from Europe, 1815–1930* (1991), chap. 1.
5. A fuller narrative is provided in Richards, *Britannia's Children*.
6. Some of the disparities over time and region within the British Isles can be seen in the estimates of Baines, *Emigration*, p. 10: these are overseas emigrants per 000. In the 1840s, the decade of the Great Famine, the disparities between Ireland and the rest were even greater.

	England and Wales	Ireland	Scotland
1851–1860	2.6	14.0	5.00
1861–1870	2.8	14.6	4.6
1871–1880	4.0	6.6	4.7
1881–1890	5.6	14.2	7.1
1891–1900	3.6	8.9	4.4
1901–1910	5.5	7.0	9.9
1913	7.6	6.8	14.2
1921–1930	2.7	5.9	9.2

7. See Richards, *Britannia's Children*, chap. 12.
8. See T. M. Devine, *The Scottish Nation, 1700–2000* (London: Penguin Books, 1999), passim.
9. See N. H. Carrier and J. R. Jeffery, *External Migration* (London: HMSO, 1953).
10. See, for instance, David Fitzpatrick, *Irish Emigration, 1801–1921* (Dublin: The Economic and Social History Society of Ireland, 1984), pp. 12–13.

11. It is important to note that, in the migration maps, the size of the arrows is not uniformly comparable across all four centuries. The arrows in the seventeenth- and eighteenth-centuries maps are directly comparable, because the same multiplier was used to produce the sizes of the arrows. This is also true of the arrows in the nineteenth-century or twentieth-century maps with regard to their representation of the sizes of the movements. But the arrows in the first two maps are not comparable with that for the later two centuries.

12. See, for instance, Bernard Bailyn, *The Peopling of British North America* (New York: Knoft, 1986), passim.

13. *The Times*, 27 May 1844, quoted in Philip Payton, *The Cornish Overseas: A History of Cornwall's 'Great Emigration'* (Exeter: University of Exeter Press, 2015), p. 52.

14. The tables follow James Horn's heroic effort to depict the rates of emigration from England from 1601 to 1861. See James Horn, 'British Diaspora: Emigration from Britain, 1680–1815', in P. J. Marshall (ed.), *The Oxford History of the British Empire*, vol. 2 (Oxford: Oxford University Press, 1998), pp. 28–35.

15. These graphs may be compared with that of James Horn, 'Net Migration from England, 1601–1861', in P. J. Marshall (ed.), *Oxford History*, p. 30. Horn probably based his graph on similar sources to those used in the present study.

16. See Baines, *Emigration*, p. 39 especially, but also Richards, *Britannia's Children*, pp. 169, 214, 267.

17. See Richards, *Britannia's Children*.

18. Irish emigration (even including the flow to England) remained relatively slight until the 1820s. In the period 1770–1815, the national figure seems to have been less than 1 per thousand per annum. The slowness of most of Ireland to take up the emigration option is made clearer by the well-known fact that until about 1815 most Irish migration originated from a particular province, namely Ulster which had a tradition of emigration to North America dating from the early eighteenth century. The figures in the text are much higher than those depicted in Baines' account (see above note 5) essentially because his data excluded movement from Ireland to Scotland and England. Baines' figures are confined to overseas movement but they show the declining (though fluctuating) level of emigration per thousand in the 1870s and after 1900. By 1900, there appears to have been an emigration of about 50,000 per annum out of a population of 4.39m which gives a rate of 11.38 per thousand. See especially David Fitzpatrick, in W. E. Vaughan (ed.), *A New History of Ireland: Ireland Under the Union*, I, V (1989), p. 565; Cormac O'Grada, *Black '47 and Beyond* (Princeton, 1999), chaps. 1 and 3; Joel Mokyr, *Why Ireland Starved* (London: George Allen & Unwin, 1983), chap. 3; Kerby

40　E. RICHARDS

Miller and Liam Kennedy, 'Irish Migration and Demography, 1659–1831', in Kerby Miller, Arnold Schrier, Bruce D. Boling, and David N. Doyle (eds.), *Irish Immigration in the Land of Canaan: Letters and Memoirs from Colonial and Revolutionary America, 1675–1815* (Oxford, 2003), pp. 656–659.

19. See Richards, *Britannia's Children*, chap. 12; C. A. Moser, 'Statistics About Immigrants: Observations, Sources, Methods and Problems', *Social Trends*, 3 (1972), 20–30 and subsequent issues of this journal to the end of the century.

20. See also Eric Richards, 'Migrants in the Mature Colony: South Australia c.1840–c.1977', *Journal of the Historical Society of South Australia*, no. 45 (2017), 1–16.

21. See Brian Dickey and Peter Howell (eds.), *South Australia's Foundation: Select Documents* (Adelaide: Wakefield Press, 1986).

22. J. H. Newman, 'Who's to Blame?' (1855), reprinted in Newman, *Discussions and Arguments on Various Subjects* (London, 1872), pp. 336–337. The quotation comes from a series of essays by Newman, arguing that Britain was 'not wise' to engage in the Crimean War.

23. Wray Vamplew et al. (eds.), *South Australian Historical Statistics* (Kensington, NSW: Australia 1788–1988: A Bicentennial History, 1984), p. 14.

24. David Hilliard and Arnold Hunt, 'Religion', in *The Flinders History of South Australia*, vol. 1 (1986), p. 195.

25. See, for example, Patrick Francis Moran, *A History of the Catholic Church in Australasia* (Sydney, 1895).

26. Brian Dickey and Peter Howell (eds.), *South Australia's Foundation: Select Documents* (Adelaide: Wakefield Press, 1986), p. 49. Quoted in Moran, *History*, p. 497. See also P. Sendziuk, 'No Convicts Here', in R. Foster and P. Sendziuk (eds.), *Turning Points: Chapters in South Australian History* (Kent Town: Wakefield Press, 2012), pp. 33–47.

27. Moran, *History*, p. 497.

28. Richard Whately, *Remarks on Transportation; and on a Recent Defence of the System; In a Second Letter to Earl Grey* (London, 1834), pp. 168–170, 92.

29. Richard Whately, 'On Colonization', in *Thoughts on Secondary Punishments: In a Letter to Earl Grey* (London, 1832), pp. 197–198. Quoted in Moran, *History*, p. 497.

30. See Eric Richards, 'Wakefield Revisited Again', in Carolyn Collins and Paul Sendziuk (eds.), *Foundational Fictions* (Adelaide: Wakefield Press, 2018), pp. 28–42.

31. Y. B. Hutchinson, 'Journal of His Majesty's Ship "Buffalo" from Portsmouth to the New Colony of South Australia … Kept by Bingham

Hutchinson, Emigrant passenger', Entries of 13 September and 20 September 1836. State Library of South Australia.

32. Douglas Pike, *Paradise of Dissent: South Australia 1829–1857*, 2nd ed. (Carlton, VIC: Melbourne University Press, 1967), p. 148.

33. See Pike, *Paradise of Dissent*, p. 517.

34. See W. S. Kelly, *Remembered Days* (Adelaide: Rigby, 1964); C. R. Kelly, *Merrindie: A Family's Farm* (Adelaide, 1988).

35. Eric Richards, 'Migrants in the Mature Economy: South Australia c.1840–c.1877', *Journal of the Historical Society of South Australia*, 45 (2017), 5–18.

36. This section draws upon Peter Moore, 'Half-Burnt Turf: Selling Emigration from Ireland to South Australia, 1836–1845', in Philip Bull et al. (eds.), *Irish Australian Studies: Papers Delivered at the Sixth Irish-Australian Conference, July 1990* (Melbourne: LaTrobe University, 1991), pp. 103–119. See also Susan Arthure, Fidelma Breen, Stephanie James, and Dymphna Lonergan (eds.), *Irish South Australia: New Histories and Insights* (Adelaide: Wakefield Press, 2019), especially chap. 1; Dymphna Lonergan, 'G.S. Kingston and Other Pioneer Irish in South Australia', pp. 1–11.

37. See David Schubert, *Kavel's People: Their Story of Migration from Prussia to South Australia*, 2nd ed. (Highgate, SA: H. Schubert, 1997).

38. Payton, *Cornish Overseas*, pp. 161–200; Philip Payton, *One and All: Labor and the Radical Tradition in South Australia* (Adelaide: Wakefield Press, 2016), pp. 55–74. See also Wray Vamplew et al. (eds.), *South Australian Historical Statistics* (Kensington, NSW: Australia 1788–1988: A Bicentennial Project, 1984), pp. 139–140.

39. Pike, *Paradise of Dissent*, p. 310.

40. George Grey, letter to his uncle, 16 January 1845. Letter of George Grey D7063/8 State Library of South Australia. Quoted in Max Carter, *No Convicts There* (Adelaide, 1997), p. 247.

41. See Janis M. Sheldrick, *Nature's Line: George Goyder, Surveyor, Environmentalist, Visionary* (Kent Town: Wakefield Press, 2012).

42. Richards, 'Migrants in the Mature Economy', p. 12.

43. Moore, 'Half-Burnt Turf', pp. 103–119. Robin Haines describes such projects as "Gentry-led Emigration Societies". See Robin F. Haines, *Emigration and the Labouring Poor* (Basingstoke: Macmillan, 1997), pp. 93–101.

44. Moore, 'Half-Burnt Turf', p. 110.

45. *Dublin Standard*, 13 June 1837. Quoted in Moore, 'Half-Burnt Turf', p. 106.

46. Moore, 'Half-Burnt Turf', p. 114.

47. William Harcus, *South Australia: Its History, Resources and Productions* (London and Adelaide, 1876). Harcus states, in his dedication, that the work had been 'prepared at the request' of the Government. See also the article 'Harcus, William', in *Australian Dictionary of Biography*.
48. Ibid., p. 80.
49. Ibid., p. 76.
50. Ibid.
51. See Hilliard and Hunt, 'Religion'.
52. See article on Angas in *Australian Dictionary of Biography*.
53. See Schubert, *Kavel's People*.
54. Harcus, *South Australia*, p. 229. See also Vamplew et al., *Historical Statistics*, pp. 137–192, esp. pp. 139–140.
55. Editorial, *South Australian Register*, 2 March 1868, p. 5.
56. 'We never had a wiser, better, or more popular governor'. Editorial comment in *South Australian Advertiser*, 2 March 1868, p. 3.
57. Moore, 'Half-Burnt Turf', p. 116.
58. Richards, 'Migrants in the Mature Economy', p. 16.
59. See W. D. Forsyth, *The Myth of the Open Spaces* (Melbourne: Melbourne University Press, 1942); W. K. Hancock, *Survey of British Commonwealth Affairs*, vol. II, Pt. 1, p. 157; and C. E. Carrington, *The British Overseas: Exploits of a Nation of Shopkeepers* (Cambridge: Cambridge University Press, 1950), pp. 1021–1031.

BIBLIOGRAPHY

Baines, Dudley E., *Migration in a Mature Economy: Emigration and Internal Migration in England and Wales, 1861–1900* (Cambridge University Press, 1985), p. 61.

Ferenczi, Imre, *International Migrations, Vol. I: Statistics* (New York: Arno Press and The New York Times, 1970).

Gemery, Henry A., 'Emigration from the British Isles to the New World, 1630–1700: Inferences from Colonial Populations', *Research in Economic History*, 5 (1980).

Gemery, Henry A., 'Markets for Migrants: English Indentured Servitude and Emigration in the Seventeenth and Eighteenth Centuries', in P. C. Emmer (ed.), *Colonialism and Migration: Indentured Labour Before and After Slavery* (Dordrecht: Martinus Nijhoff Publishers, 1986).

Horn, James, 'Introduction', in Ida Altman and James Horn (eds.), *"To Make America": European Emigration in the Early Modern Period* (Berkeley, CA: University of California Press, 1991).

Price, Charles, 'Immigration and Ethnic Origin', in Wray Vamplew (ed.), *Australians: Historical Statistics* (Sydney: Fairfax, Syme and Weldon Associates, 1987).

Smout, T. C., N. C. Landsman, and T. M. Devine, 'Scottish Emigration in the Seventeenth and Eighteenth Centuries', in Nicholas Canny (ed.), *Europeans on the Move: Studies on European Migration, 1500–1800* (Oxford: Clarendon Press, 1994).

Vaughan, W. E., and A. J. Fitzpatrick (eds.), *Irish Historical Statistics: Population, 1821–1971* (Dublin: Royal Irish Academy, 1978).

Williams, R. M., *British Population*, 2nd ed. (London: Heinemann, 1978).

Woods, Robert, *The Population of Britain in the Nineteenth Century* (London: Macmillan, 1992).

Wrigley, E. A., and R. S. Schofield, *The Population History of England, 1541–1871: A Reconstruction* (Cambridge: Cambridge University Press, 1989) (first published 1981).

CHAPTER 3

Emigrant Choices: Following Emigrant Labourers on the Cusp of the Age of Mass Migration

Heidi Ing

This chapter investigates intending emigrant labourers who applied and were accepted to receive assisted passage to the proposed colony of South Australia. These potential emigrants did not embark on the colonising ships which left London in 1836 but chose instead to follow other paths. From the perspective of social history, these individuals, couples and families would merge back into the general population of Great Britain, but by using online databases of digitised, transcribed and indexed resources these potential emigrants can be hunted down to discern their varied outcomes. Some chose competing destinations, such as New South Wales, Van Diemen's Land, Canada and the United States, which lured emigrants away from the South Australian scheme. Marriage, pregnancy and infants delayed or halted emigration plans, while the lives of others ended tragically. This research follows

H. Ing (✉)
Flinders University, Adelaide, SA, Australia
e-mail: heidi.ing@flinders.edu.au

© The Author(s) 2019
P. Payton and A. Varnava (eds.),
Australia, Migration and Empire, Britain and the World,
https://doi.org/10.1007/978-3-030-22389-2_3

45

the diverging paths of intending emigrants who appeared in the public record seeking opportunity or adventure through emigration and examines where their choices led them.

Emigration schemes which supported labourers in Great Britain to access the far-flung Australian colonies have been well documented, with great efforts put into recording the 'voices, movements and characteristics' of emigrant labourers.[1] In *Leaving England*, Charlotte Erickson investigated emigration from Great Britain to the United States in 1831 and found that, 'the English who chose to emigrate to the United States were probably not people expelled by need or absolute hardship but people able to make rational and conscious choices'.[2] When discussing the 'Settler Revolution' and accelerated demand for new lands in which to spread, James Belich highlighted movement motivated by perceived benefits and expectation, where 'rational choice' pulled people in their search for higher wages and opportunities.[3] Similarly for Australia, Robin Haines investigated passage-assisted emigrants from the United Kingdom who 'appear to have been well-informed, self-selecting, literate individuals with initiative who shrewdly took advantage of a number of private and official agencies to enable them to finance their deposit, outfit of clothing, and travel to the port of embarkation'.[4]

The accelerating demand for emigrant destinations was one of the results of an industrialising economy, increasing unemployment and a displaced rural workforce. Transformative agricultural practices were combined with rapid population growth to create a surplus population in Great Britain, particularly in rural areas.[5] Rates of emigration out of the UK increased rapidly in the early 1830s. Emigration out of England rose from 27,174 individuals per annum in 1829 to 99,211 in 1832.[6] Between 1827 and 1832, the amount of people arriving in the United States increased fivefold.[7] Eric Richards pointed out that an excess in population could only result in emigration 'where there exists a receptive destination'.[8] It is doubtful that the Indigenous owners of the land comprising Britain's far-flung colonies could be described as 'receptive', but it was their land that provided an outlet for this overflow of population. In particular, Upper and Lower Canada, the Cape of Good Hope, and on a smaller-scale New South Wales, Van Diemen's Land and Swan River on Australia's west coast were presented as colonial destinations for potential emigrants seeking profit, employment or a change in fortunes in the early 1830s.[9]

Societal changes in Great Britain in the nineteenth century demanded public and political attention, and emigration was put forward as a strategy for population relief. Migration journeys were funded through a variety of government, private, philanthropic or parish schemes which proliferated in the United Kingdom from the 1820s onwards.[10] When the Australian colonies entered the arena to compete as emigrant destinations, the cost of passage and associated travel expenses were significant obstacles. The entire cost of passage for an adult to travel the three- to four-week journey to the United States was comparable to the additional expenses charged on top of cost of passage for the longer four- to five-month voyage to Australia.[11]

Labourers, who relied on financial assistance to fund their emigrant journey, have been shown to have had the capacity and the agency to choose their destination and labouring emigrants utilised their available resources and networks to meet the costs associated with travel.[12] Funds were sourced from friends and family, their community or parish, local charities or emigration societies.[13] In order to qualify for parish and government assistance schemes, potential emigrants needed to be without sufficient capital to cover their costs of passage and to meet conditions for age, gender, marital status, health, social standing and skill or occupation.[14] If assessed as suitable, their journey could be partially or fully funded through the applicable scheme. As demand increased, the shipping industry and private enterprise experimented with techniques to provide the desired service. As Eric Richards demonstrated, the high cost of passage to the antipodes was beyond private enterprise in the 1820s, but by the mid-1830s the cost of passage had reduced.[15] Government, private and philanthropic subsidisation schemes brought the cost of passage within reach of enterprising and ambitious people of all classes, and the Australian colonies became increasingly within reach as an emigration destination.

In 1827 economist Colonel Robert Torrens MP, later associated with emigration to South Australia, spoke in parliament in support of emigration as a strategy for population relief and promoted New South Wales as a viable destination. Torrens warned that mechanised farming practices and land consolidation was soon to be implemented in heavily populated rural Ireland, which would result in a flood of farm labourers from Ireland to join those already fighting for employment in England.[16] In his 1827 speech, Robert Torrens emphasised colonial land speculation as a strategy to increase emigration. He called attention to the rise in land values experienced in the United States as the amassing population rapidly spread westward into newly appropriated lands. He called for the British government to replicate in the Canadian colonies the land profiteering being experienced 'on the American side of the lake' in the regions of the Ohio, Mississippi and Missouri Rivers.[17]

The government of Great Britain had experimented with population relief through the relocation of paupers to appropriated land in Canada. A scheme, promoted by Robert Wilmot Horton as a humanitarian measure to offset the rising unemployment, was implemented on a small scale as a trial in 1823 and 1825. A 'pauper' was defined as a temporarily redundant worker who was 'unable to maintain themselves or a family at a minimum subsistence level'.[18] Selected pauper families were provided with free passage, provisions and access to land in Canada, with an option to purchase the land in five years.[19] This effort was judged to have had mixed results. The outcomes were positive from the perspective of the immigrants, but too many did not retain their allocated land and were lost over the border into neighbouring United States.[20] The scheme was deemed too expensive to replicate on a scale large enough to effectively reduce population pressure in the United Kingdom.[21]

When the colony of Swan River was proposed in 1829, potential emigrants demonstrated their hope for the provision of free passage. Swiftly after publication of plans for the new colony, the Colonial Office received numerous applications for free passage, despite there being no emigration fund available or promoted as being available.[22] As a potential new Australian colony, Swan River was stated to have many advantages over New South Wales; better soil and climate, a more favourable geographical position for trade, and no history of convict transportation. Swan River was promoted as having the potential for 'a rapid growth like that of Singapore', which in the previous decade had grown from initial foundation to a significant trading post and British colony.[23]

An example of emigrants attracted to the Swan River endeavour was the Henty family, landowners in West Sussex. Private letters within the family demonstrate that they had considered emigration to India, New South Wales and Van Diemen's Land before deciding on the west coast of Australia.[24] This large family continued to explore alternative destinations, and most branches eventually settling in Portland in the Port Phillip district, now Victoria.[25] As funded passage to Swan River had not been provided for labourers without capital, other strategies such as indentured servitude had to be used to bring over a labour force. When the eldest Henty sons sailed for Swan River, they travelled with labourers and servants, which consisted of five couples with young children, one young newly married couple and six single men, all selected from their local area of West Tarring and 'nearly all old employees of the family'.[26] These labourers were signed on to serve 'as dutiful servants for five years in return for a free passage, twenty pounds a year, fuel, and board'.[27] This system of indentured servitude had been used to fund emigration from the United Kingdom to the United States, but was not frequently seen as a method to support labour migration to Australia.[28]

It was against this backdrop of competing colonial destinations that a plan to colonise the southern coast of Australia was initiated. A scheme, which came to be known as 'systematic colonisation', began in Newgate Prison where Edward Gibbon Wakefield and his brother William were serving three-year sentences for the abduction of a fifteen-year-old heiress, with whom the thirty-year-old Edward Gibbon had eloped. Edward Gibbon Wakefield had narrowly missed a sentence of transportation to Australia and his European career prospects were removed through the scandal. Perhaps with this motivation, Wakefield threw himself into an analysis of colonial planning and emigration schemes.[29] Two of the many publications which resulted from this jail sentence were the 1829 pamphlets *Sketch of a Proposal for Colonizing Australasia* and *A Letter from Sydney, the Principal Town of Australasia*.[30] Both of these pamphlets were also released as serial newspaper articles and proposed a scheme where land in Australian, which had been claimed for the crown and labelled 'waste', would be sold for a sufficient price to fund the passage of an associated labour force.

A combination of land sold in concentrated settlements and the marketing of the colony to 'respectable middle-class capitalists' made Wakefield's systematic colonisation plan attractive to a wide range of British society.[31] Wakefield aimed to remove the negative stigma associated with emigration. His essays on systematic colonisation claimed that concentrated settlement would result in a 'civilized colony from the beginning', attracting ambitious colonists, the 'uneasy' middling class, and those who may not wish to become 'a backwoodsman in Canada, a convict driver in New South Wales, or a bush-man at the Swan River'.[32] In early 1830, the National Colonisation Society was formed, inspired by Wakefield's *Letters from Sydney*, and they soon published *A Statement of the Principles and Objects of a Proposed National Society for the Cure and Prevention of Pauperism by Means of Systematic Colonization*.[33] This Society sought a place where their theoretical concepts could be put into practice, with Australia, Canada and South Africa put forward as candidate destinations.[34] Their initial publication described the demand for labour and opportunities and compared their plans with previous experiments in the United States, especially Massachusetts, New York and Pennsylvania.[35]

South Australia was chosen as the preferred destination for this scheme after receiving news that Charles Sturt had travelled down the Murray River to its mouth on the land of the Ngarrindjeri people in early 1830.[36] By 1831, a Land Company had been formed and a plan submitted to the Colonial Office to propose a new colony on the southern coast of Australia.[37] Philosopher and social reformer Jeremy Bentham had previously written against colonisation, calling it an 'agreeable folly', but he was apparently won over by the golden tongue of Edward Gibbon Wakefield.[38] Bentham was an influential advocate and wrote his 'Colonization Company Proposal' as a commentary on the *Sketch of a Proposal* publication. In his commentary, Bentham emphasised that the aim, or 'special end', of a colonisation scheme was the transfer of individuals 'in an unlimited multitude' until the 'Australasian Continent contains a population as dense as the European'.[39] The colonial planners who promoted South Australia set about attracting 'colonists' who had capital to invest in appropriated land and 'emigrants' to act as labourers for the new colonial endeavour.

According to the colonial promoters, applicants both with and without capital were not in short supply and eagerly awaited the formation of the new Australian colony. As early as May 1832, it was reported that 'families and individuals of a superior description' intended to emigrate and that many families were 'waiting in the most painful suspense for a decision'.[40] The pace of promotion and ambition exceeded the practicalities of the plans. The *Morning Chronicle* reported in September 1832 that the planned province of South Australia had lost 'a body of settlers with a combined capital of more than £200,000' who, 'unable to go to South Australia, emigrated in disgust to Canada and the United States'.[41] Canada was seen as a prominent competitor to South Australia and promoters combatted the loss of emigrants through propaganda, focusing particularly on climate. Promoters compared their scheme's destination to Canada, where the 'frosts of winter' were 'hard and protracted, lasting for months, and covering the earth with heavy snows'.[42] In his 1835 publication on colonisation Charles James Napier, who had been considered for the position of Governor for South Australia, chose scare tactics, or possibly comedy, to discourage emigrants from choosing Canada by stating,

To be sure there is Canada – but Canada is cold, and full of agues! One's fingers and toes keep continually dropping off during winter, and nothing is so common as to pull off your nose in blowing it: ... Who, after learning these things, and having the least regard for his digital ornaments, will go to Canada?'[43]

One family who had intended to travel to South Australia, but instead chose Canada was twenty-two-year-old bricklayer Charles Stafford, along with his twenty-four-year-old wife and five-year-old son.[44] This couple delayed emigration while they expanded their young family, instead immigrated to Canada with three sons and a daughter. By the 1851 Canadian census, they had two more children, born in Canada in 1848 and 1850 in the relatively mild area of Ontario on the border with Vermont.[45] Canada was also the chosen destination for a pauper emigration scheme of the 1830s, funded through the local patronage of an 'immensely wealthy philanthropist', George Wyndham, Earl of Egremont.[46] Wyndham was responding to the rural crisis in his local area in West Sussex with the 'Petworth Project', which involved the transfer of about 1800 local labourers to Canada.[47] Like previous pauper emigration schemes, it was largely motivated to relieve local parish funds of their support.[48]

The article in the *Morning Chronicle* in 1832, which had lamented the loss of colonists to Canada, also discussed six thousand labouring class emigrants who had applied for free passage but had been 'plunged again into unrelieved wretchedness' by delays in the establishment of South Australia.[49] These emigration applicants from 1832 cannot be identified as their application forms are not known to have survived. Some of these individuals may have been amongst the applicants registered in 1836. It is unknown whether the labourers who applied for free passage in 1832 waited for the South Australian plans to be finalised, or if they pursued other options.

In 1834, South Australian promoters again called for pity for the waiting emigrants, reporting that they had applications from more than 5000 labourers.[50] Emigration Agent John Brown attempted to hurry parliament by relating the urgency felt by the colonists and emigrants waiting to embark.[51] One of the South Australia's initial colonial planners, Robert Gouger, attempted to motivate government by provided a first-hand account of his experiences with the waiting emigrants and the 'daily painful and anxious enquiries' he had been subjected to.[52] Promoters attempted to convince parliament that the South Australian project was not a 'speculative land venture' but a scheme based on philanthropic principles.[53]

For this purpose, colonial planners of the new colony of South Australia presented the applicants for free passage as paupers in a desperate state.[54] This was motivated by a desire to impart a philanthropic depiction of the colonial venture. Suspicion that the aims of the organisation were predominately motivated by financial gain continued to impede their progress through parliament until the Duke of Wellington, Prime Minister from 1828 to 1830, was won over to the South Australian cause in 1834.[55] Gouger had convinced Wellington that the South Australian project was not a company land grab but a systematic scheme with humanitarian intent.[56] Under Wellington's guidance, the South Australian Act passed with little debate and was granted Royal Assent on 15 August 1834.[57]

Government instability and changes in personnel in the Colonial Office were also a cause of delays and frustrations. From the time that the southern coast of Australia was designated as a destination in 1831, to the embarkation of emigrants and capitalists in 1836, Great Britain had changed Prime Minister four times.[58] When Prime Minister Sir Robert Peel left office in April 1835 to be replaced by William Lamb, 2nd Viscount Melbourne, the Emigration Agent for South Australia John Brown lamented, 'So endeth the fourth Colonial Secretary that had to do with our project'.[59] In March 1835, Robert Gouger, South Australia's first Colonial Secretary, emphasised that some emigrants, 'perhaps unwisely & imprudently', had begun to make their preparations to sail when the Act of Parliament had passed in August 1834.[60] Some emigrants had disposed of their assets and were drawing on their resources while waiting to embark, resulting in 'the greatest distress and anxiety' and were reportedly 'quite ruined by the delay'.[61] Gouger recorded despondently in his diary and letters that intending emigrants had scattered in both 1832 and 1834.[62]

The research behind this chapter focuses on those intending emigrants who scattered in 1836. The resource used for this research, the 'Register of Emigrant Labourers applying for a Free Passage to South Australia', was initiated in January 1836.[63] This was a register of applicants who had been certified and accepted as suitable to receive free passage to South Australia. The format of the applications has been preserved, but unfortunately, no completed application forms are known to have survived.[64] The form that the potential emigrant labourers needed to complete required four signatures; two from 'respectable householders' who were well acquainted with the applicant and could verify that the applicant was honest, sober and industrious, another from a magistrate or clergyman of the local district and another from a physician or surgeon to certify that the applicant was not 'seriously mutilated or deformed' or 'afflicted with any disease'.[65] This certification process may have persuaded the majority of applicants to be truthful, but ambition and human nature prevailed. The remarks column of the 'Register' occasionally included a warning that the signatures on an application were all in the same handwriting.[66] Emigration Agent John Brown's diary records that an applicant was accepted and registered as a single male, but a wife and children came forward after his ship had already sailed.[67]

Through the 'Register of emigrant labourers applying for a free passage to South Australia', we have a long list of individuals, couples and families who considered emigration to South Australia with serious enough intent to have completed the application process. This chapter involved an analysis of the first 200 applicants for free passage to South Australia to be entered into the 'Register' and found that just over half of the first 200 registered emigrants, 101 of these applicants, did not to travel to South Australia.[68] This leaves us with the question, what was the outcome for these potential emigrants? Were those who did not embark 'plunged again into unrelieved wretchedness' as reported in the *Morning Chronicle* in 1832?[69] Approved applicants were not obliged to embark if other opportunities took their attention elsewhere, or if they simply changed their mind. Bernard Bailyn discussed the impact of emigrant choices on late eighteenth-century emigration agents, who discovered their recruited labourer force had pursued other opportunities when it came time to embark.[70] The investment by and in these people had been substantial. They had been reached by promoters through agents or public presentations, word of mouth or published material. Time had been taken not only to complete the application process, but also to assess, select, register the applicant and contact them as the time for embarkation drew near.

Those registered applicants for free passage who did not choose to emigrate have not been examined to date. From a social history point of view, these people are absorbed back into the general population, no longer emigrants waiting to embark but incorporated into those who remained. This research seeks to identify any available patterns in the behaviour of those who stayed. By mining the rich data available through online genealogical database, brief appearances in obscure historical documents are able to locate an individual, couple or family at a place and time. A name search, together with other known identifying data such as approximate age and place of birth, can locate an individual within the English censuses, passenger lists, church records, civil registration records, and workhouse and hospital records. This capability to link historical records to particular individuals makes tracking emigrants from cradle to grave progressively more plausible, as microdata provided through granular datasets brings to light identifying documents.[71]

The research for this chapter made use of the digitised, transcribed and indexed resources provided through commercially available online databases created primarily to support genealogical research. This research was conducted using subscriptions to Ancestry www.ancestry.com, My Heritage www.myheritage.com, FindMyPast findmypast.com and registered access to Family Search familysearch.org. The 'Register' provides clues for the hunt; first, last and occasionally middle names, age, occupation, gender, address on application, marital status, age of wife and ages and genders of children. The remarks column provides the occasional tasty titbit which aids investigation, such as that for William Moore, a twenty-nine-year-old married brickmaker who 'wishes his sister aged 19 to go', or widowed seaman George Baker Clark who 'left four children in England'.[72] These additional elements provide added fuel for the chase.

Information such as age, location and occupation cannot be treated as reliable identifying data. Locations and occupations potentially change often over the course of a lifetime and ages are frequently rounded and adjusted to suit the situation. When applying for assisted passage to South Australia, it was in the applicants' best interests to provide information suited to the selection criteria. There was a clear temptation to adjust ages when preference was given to applicants under thirty.[73] Thirty-one-year-old labourer, Robert Sherlock was entered on the register as travelling with his wife and twenty-one-month-old daughter, but a note in the remarks column indicated that his thirty-five-year-old wife was 'too old' and the family did not receive assisted passage.[74]

Occupations were potentially altered to suit the needs of emigration agents. An individual named Andrew Churcher was entered on the 'Register' in 1836 as a single twenty-eight-year-old carpenter living in Acton, east of London.[75] Carpentry and all building trades were sought-after occupations which attracted assisted passage.[76] The only potential match identified for this individual was an Andrew Churcher born on 14 July 1807 and baptised 3 January 1808 at Westminster St James in Piccadilly.[77] In the 1841 census, we can find an Andrew Churcher, single, living in Clapham and working as a hairdresser.[78] An Andrew Churcher whose occupation and father's occupation were listed as 'hair manufacturer' married Elizabeth Challis in 1842.[79] Through the subsequent censuses in 1851, 1861, 1871 and 1881, we can follow Andrew Churcher working as a hair worker and living in Lewisham, London with his wife Elizabeth, son George and daughter Elizabeth.[80] Andrew Churcher died in April 1886 in Lewisham at the age of 79 years.[81] The link between Andrew Churcher the carpenter and Andrew Churcher the hairdresser is a tenuous, based on first and last name and age, but a search of online databases provided no other potential match either living in or emigrating out of England.[82]

By using the known identifying data and moving backwards and forwards in time, it is possible to chart individuals from cradle to grave and to paint, in a mixture of pointillism and the broadest of brushstrokes, a picture of the course of their lives. This has previously been the case for society's most notorious or notable, but through the granular and immense datasets now available, the place where an individual's life briefly touches the public record can become visible. The first registered applicant who did not embark to South Australia was entry number two, twenty-one-year-old cook and confectioner Charles Booty who applied with his twenty-two-year-old wife.[83] Through consecutive census and hospital records, we find that Charles Booty enlisted with the 16th Lancers in 1837 and was discharged in 1862 as a Chelsea Pensioner.[84] While he may not have journey to Australia, as a private with the 16th Lancers Charles Booty may have seen action in central Afghanistan in 1839 during the First Anglo-Afghan War.[85]

Of the 101 registered applicants investigated in this research, 48 applicants could not be positively identified in documentation with enough certainty to warrant inclusion in the study. Almost all of the unlinked individuals had common names, such as William Jones or James Day, producing too many results with matching variables, and the majority were single men who lacked the corroborating details provided by a wife and children.[86] In order to establish a longitudinal link between documents for individuals, couples or families and the identifying data (first and last name, approximate age and place of birth, marital status, age of wife and ages and gender of children) needed to match subsequent documentation.[87] Links were ranked using a three-level confidence scale, but even the most supported link between primary source documentation cannot have guaranteed certainty. There are cases of people born in the same town, in the same year, with the same name and who follow similar paths in life. When making use of large datasets of resources, we are reliant on those sources which have been selected for digitisation and have been provided online, the accuracy of the transcription, search functionality and the researcher's use of search terms.[88]

After removing those who could not be identified with confidence, only 14 of the 101 applicants investigated could be found identified as emigrants to other destinations. The most prevalent destinations were New South Wales and New York, but it must be noted that this could be a result of the quality and quantity of the available datasets. Amongst the datasets searched for New York were: the *New York, State and Federal Naturalization Records, 1794–1940* containing almost three million records, the *New York, Passenger and Immigration Lists, 1820–1850* with 1.6 million records and the enormous *New York, Passenger and Crew Lists (including Castle Garden and Ellis Island), 1820–1957* containing over 82 million records. Also relevant is the quality of the transcriptions of the original digitised record. Details such as age, place of birth, occupation and marital status must not only be present in the document but transcribed accurately in order to appear in search results and be linked to individuals. Amongst the datasets for New South Wales was the *New South Wales, Australia, Unassisted Immigrant Passenger Lists, 1828–1896* with almost 8.5 million records and the *New South Wales, Australia, Assisted Immigrant Passenger Lists, 1828–1896* with half a million records. The New South Wales list of assisted immigrants includes not only age, place of birth and usual occupation, but names of parents and other biographical details regarding marital status, perceived character, health, religion and 'probable usefulness'.[89] This level of detail leads to positive identification and links to a sought individual. With datasets of this volume and detail, it is unsurprising that positive matches with individuals from the 'Register' make an appearance on passenger lists to both New York and New South Wales.

Thirty-year-old shoemaker, Joseph Dennis, was entered on the 'Register' as an applicant with his wife, two sons and a daughter.[90] Instead of travelling to South Australia in 1836, he and his family arrived in New South Wales in December 1837 as bounty immigrants on the ship *Alfred* at a bounty of £45.[91] The bounty system, commonly used as a means of assisted passage to New South Wales and Van Diemen's Land, was operated by approved bounty operators who were paid on arrival in the colony. The bounty payment was only provided if the selected immigrants met the approval of an immigration officer; if a selected bounty immigrant was rejected on arrival as unfit, or died during the voyage, the bounty was refused, and the cost had to be met by the shipowner or bounty operator.[92] Another applicant for free passage to South Australia who ultimately appeared in New South Wales was twenty-one-year-old baker William Cambridge.[93] He had been accepted as a registered emigrant to receive free passage to South Australia but was instead transported as a convict to New South Wales in January 1837, to serve a fourteen years term as punishment for stealing cloth.[94]

A family who emigrated to New York was that of John Garread, who had been entered on the 'Register' in February 1836 as a gardener with a wife, an eighteen-month-old daughter and three-month-old son.[95] This couple chose the much shorter passage to the United States, where another son was born in New York in 1837.[96] With a pregnant wife and an infant son, the passage of three- to four-weeks contrasted starkly to a four to five-month voyage to South Australia. Their fourth child, a daughter, was born in New York in 1840.[97] John Garread died in 1880 aged 73 years and was buried in Brooklyn with his wife Harriet, who had died in November 1846 at the age of 45.[98] Her death may have been associated with childbirth, as their youngest daughter, also named Harriet, had been born in late 1846.[99] The prevalence of digitised records for the city of New York enables the progress of this family to be tracked with regularity.[100]

Marriage, pregnancy and the care of infants appear to have impacted on the timing of emigrant journeys as couples and young families made the decision to stay or to go. Emigration programs to Australia initially sought young labouring couples before they had had their first child.[101] Women were required to balance the sexes in the new colonies, and their emigration as young brides would provide them with both a chaperone and respectability.[102] Emigrant agents were instructed to seek young couples without children as the most 'cost effective emigrants' for assisted passage, as young couples were cheaper to fund on the long voyage to Australia and both the husband and the wife would provide the colony with labour before childbirth took the mother out of the labour market.[103] The ambition to attract young couples did not prove to be a realistic aim. Young couples without children were not prevalent amongst the applicants, and many chose not to embark when the ship was ready for sail.

Couples without children represented approximately ten per cent of applicants, but an analysis of the first two hundred applicants finds that childless couples represented a mere two per cent of applicants who decided to embark for South Australia. Marriage and first pregnancy were impediments to emigration plans. Emigration Agent John Brown records that in March 1836 seven labourers arrived from Gosport to embark on the *Cygnet*.[104] These labourers had been entered onto the Register as a group in February 1836 and were young single men between 18 and 24 years.[105] Only one of the Gosport labourers, a twenty-year-old tailor by the name of John Moon, was annotated with the comment 'engaged to be married'.[106] John Moon did not receive an embarkation number and was listed on the 1841 census as married and living in nearby Winchester with his wife Mary and son Henry, who had been born in 1837.[107]

Of the 36 applicants on the 'Register' who were identified as remaining in Great Britain, 17 were found with one or more children on the 1841 England census. Twenty-one-year-old single labourer Edward Lucas was amongst fourteen labourers from Acton, then a rural area west of London.[108] This group was entered on the 'Register' on 13 January 1836 and almost all sailed to South Australia on the *John Pirie* in February 1836.[109] Edward Lucas was one of the few from this region who did not leave for South Australia. He could be found on the 1841 England census still in Acton, married, with a five-year-old son.[110] A more unfortunate outcome from the Acton applicants is that of seventeen-year-old labourer Joseph Dearn.[111] Joseph died on 5 February 1836, two weeks before the *John Pirie* sailed, and was buried in Harrow, ten kilometres north-west of Acton.[112]

The tendency to avoid emigration while a family is experiencing pregnancy or has an infant child is reasonable. Colonial Secretary Robert Gouger travelled to South Australia with his new wife during their first pregnancy in 1836. Robert Gourger was an experienced colonial agent in the 1830s who assisted labourers to emigrate to Canada and Australia and arranged passages to and from India for East India army agents.[113] He had been involved with the planning of South Australia from its inception in Newgate Prison, where he also served a two-week sentence for debts incurred while promoting the scheme.[114] It was not until Gouger had been awarded his five per cent commission on South Australian land sales that he had been in a financial position to marry.[115] The family of his fiancé Harriet Jackson discouraged the young couple from emigrating, but Harriet had taken an active interest in the plans for South Australia.[116] The couple sailed on board the *Africaine* in late June 1836 and arrived in early November 1836.[117] Harriet Gouger was thirty-two years old when she gave birth to their son Henry Hindmarsh Gouger on 29 December 1836, the day after the Proclamation of the colony of South Australia by Governor Hindmarsh.[118] Both Harriet and her son Henry died two and a half months later in March 1837.[119]

This research finds that the emigrant labourers who did not embark for South Australia had varied outcomes. Far from being the plunged into 'unrelieved wretchedness', they can be found setting out for alternative destinations or staying local, starting families and settling down. Of the 'Register' applicants who could be positively identified, only two could be found in the workhouse, one in the infirmary for illness and the other listed as 'partially disabled' in 1854.[120] While these two applicants identified in workhouse records represent a small proportion of those investigated, it is possible that other applicants attended the workhouse at some stage over the course of their life. The digitised and transcribed London workhouse records include over ten million records.[121] Despite the size of this dataset, it cannot be considered exhaustive. Also, those with common names were not linked with confidence to records. It is possible that any or all of the individuals that were listed as 'not found' within this research may have made an appearance in workhouse records.

Social history research conducted through data mining benefits from the creation and expansion of enormous databases of digitised, transcribed and indexed information. Through the provision of these datasets, the lives and choices of people from all facets of society can be uncovered and examined. The labourers who considered emigration to South Australia and applied for free passage in 1836 represent people exploring their options and taking advantage of potential opportunities. Their decisions appear to be based on rational choice, in support of Robin Haines's finding that,

> Labourers weighed the costs and benefits of imminent departure and made decisions based on the best available information and on their most auspicious immediate prospects.[122]

To investigate the outcomes of these choices, researchers need to be able to locate and identify the precious few relevant references left behind for each individual. Through continued efforts in digitisation and the construction of population databases, these brief moments in time where the lives of individuals touch the public record will be increasingly brought to light and illuminate the path for social history research.

NOTES

1. Haines, Robin. "'The Idle and the Drunken Won't Do There': Poverty, the New Poor Law and Nineteenth Century Government Assisted Emigration to Australia from the United Kingdom." *Australian Historical Studies* 28, no. 108 (1997), p. 2.
2. Erickson, Charlotte. *Leaving England: Essays on British Emigration in the Nineteenth Century.* Ithaca, NY: Cornell University Press, 1994, p. 157.
3. Belich, James. *Replenishing the Earth: The Settler Revolution and the Rise of the Anglo-World, 1783–1939.* Oxford: Oxford University Press, 2009, p. 132.
4. Haines, Robin. "Indigent Misfits or Shrewd Operators? Government-Assisted Emigrants from the United Kingdom to Australia, 1831–1860." *Population Studies* 48, no. 2 (1994), p. 246.
5. Richards, Eric. *The Genesis of International Mass Migration: The British Case, 1750–1900.* Manchester: Manchester University Press, 2018, Chapter 5: 'The discontinuity'.
6. Erickson, *Leaving England*, p. 132.
7. Richards, *The Genesis of International Mass Migration*, p. 76.
8. Ibid., p. 276.
9. For a break-down of numbers by colony see Haines, Robin, and Ralph Shlomowitz. "Immigration from the United Kingdom to Colonial Australia: A Statistical Analysis." *Journal of Australian Studies* 16, no. 34 (1992), p. 45.
10. For a thorough description of the funding schemes, see Richards, Eric. "How Did Poor People Emigrate from the British Isles to Australia in the Nineteenth Century?" *Journal of British Studies* 32, no. 3 (1993), p. 250–279; Richards, Eric. "Emigration to the New Worlds: Migration Systems in the Early Nineteenth Century." *Australian Journal of Politics and History* 41, no. 3 (1995), p. 391–407.
11. Haines, Robin. "'The Idle and the Drunken Won't Do There': Poverty, the New Poor Law and Nineteenth Century Government Assisted Emigration to Australia from the United Kingdom." *Australian Historical Studies* 28, no. 108 (1997), p. 4.

12. Examples of emigrant agency can be found in Haines, Robin, Margrette Kleinig, Deborah Oxley, and Eric Richards. "Migration and Opportunity: An Antipodean Perspective." *International Review of Social History* 43, no. 2 (1998), p. 235–263.
13. Haines, 'The Idle and the Drunken Won't Do There', p. 5.
14. For more on selection criteria see Nance, Christopher. "Making a Better Society? Immigration to South Australia, 1836–1871." *Journal of the Historical Society of South Australia* 12 (1982), pp. 104–122.
15. Richards, Eric. *The Genesis of International Mass Migration: The British Case, 1750–1900.* Manchester: Manchester University Press, 2018, pp. 269–270; Richards, Eric. "Emigration to the New Worlds: Migration Systems in the Early Nineteenth Century." *Australian Journal of Politics and History* 41, no. 3 (1995), p. 398; and Richards, Eric. "British Poverty and Australian Immigration in the Nineteenth Century," in *Poor Australian Immigrants in the Nineteenth Century.* Canberra: Division of Historical Studies and Centre for Immigration and Multicultural Studies, Research School of Social Sciences, Australian National University, 1991, fn 6, p. 4.
16. Torrens, Robert. *Substance of a Speech Delivered by Colonel Torrens in the House of Commons, 15th February, 1827: On the Motion of Sir Robert Wilmot-Horton, Bart., for the Re-Appointment of a Select Committee on Emigration from the United Kingdom.* 2nd ed. South Australian Facsimile Editions No. 38. Adelaide: Public Library of South Australia, 1962, p. 40.
17. Torrens, *Substance of a Speech*, pp. 53–54.
18. Haines, Robin. "'The Idle and the Drunken Won't Do There': Poverty, the New Poor Law and Nineteenth Century Government Assisted Emigration to Australia from the United Kingdom." *Australian Historical Studies* 28, no. 108 (1997), p. 7.
19. Mills, R. C. *The Colonization of Australia (1829–42): The Wakefield Experiment in Empire Building.* London: Dawsons of Pall Mall, 1968, pp. 31–33.
20. Mills, *The Colonization of Australia*, p. 37.
21. Ibid., pp. 38–40.
22. Ibid., p. 59.
23. Ibid., p. 58, quoting *Quarterly Review*, April 1829. For an overview of the foundation of Singapore see Sim, T. Y. H. "Through a Glass Darkly: A Fresh Look at the Stories of the Foundation of Singapore." *Kemanusiaan* 20, no. 2 (2013), p. 1–14.
24. Richards, *The Genesis of International Mass Migration*, pp. 57–58; Bassett, Marnie. *The Hentys: An Australian Colonial Tapestry.* Oxford: Oxford University Press, 1954, Chapter 4: The Spirit of Emigration, pp. 32–38.

25. Bassett, *The Hentys: An Australian Colonial Tapestry*, Part VI: Launceston to Portland Bay, 1834–1837.
26. For a list of the emigrant labourers accompanying the Henty family see Bassett, *The Hentys: An Australian Colonial Tapestry*, p. 40.
27. Ibid.
28. Bailyn, Bernard. *The Peopling of British North America: An Introduction.* London: Tauris, 1987, pp. 63–64; Richards, "Emigration to the New Worlds", p. 391.
29. Pretty, Graeme, L. 'Wakefield, Edward Gibbon (1796–1862)', *Australian Dictionary of Biography*, National Centre of Biography, Australian National University, http://adb.anu.edu.au/biography/wakefield-edward-gibbon-2763/text3921, published first in hardcopy 1967, accessed 20 January 2019.
30. Wakefield, Edward Gibbon. *Sketch of a Proposal for Colonizing Australasia.* London: Printed by J. F. Dove, 1962; Wakefield, Edward Gibbon. *A Letter from Sydney, the Principal Town of Australasia: Together with the Outline of a System of Colonization.* Edited by Robert Gouger and Edward Gibbon Wakefield. London: Joseph Cross, 1829.
31. Richards, Eric. "Wakefield Revisited Again," in *Foundational Fictions in South Australian History*, edited by Collins Carolyn and Paul Sendziuk. Mile End, South Australia: Wakefield Press, 2018, pp. 35–36.
32. Wakefield, Edward Gibbon. *The New British Province of South Australia, or, a Description of the Country, Illustrated by Charts and Views: With an Account of the Principles, Objects, Plan, and Prospects of the Colony.* London: Printed for C. Knight, 1834, pp. 79, 123.
33. Wakefield, Edward Gibbon and Provisional Committee National Colonization Society. *A Statement of the Principles and Objects of a Proposed National Society for the Cure and Prevention of Pauperism by Means of Systematic Colonization.* Statement on Systematic Colonization. London: J. Ridgway, 1830.
34. Pike, *Paradise of Dissent*, p. 55.
35. Wakefield, *A Statement of the Principles*, p. 38.
36. Wakefield, Edward Gibbon and South Australian Association. *South Australia: Outline of the Plan of a Proposed Colony to Be Founded on the South Coast of Australia: With an Account of the Soil, Climate, Rivers, & c.* London: Ridgway and Sons, 1834, p. 10.
37. South Australian Land Company. *Proposal to His Majesty's Government for Founding a Colony on the Southern Coast of Australia.* Edited by George Sutherland. London: Nicol, 1831.
38. This is according to the testimony of Wakefield. While no correspondence exists between Wakefield and Bentham, Bentham is recorded as calling Wakefield 'a most valuable man', stating that he, Bentham, had

'thrown my mantle over him and shall turn him to good account'.
Bentham, Jeremy. *Writings on Australia: VII. Colonization Company Proposal.* Edited by Tim Causer and Philip Schofield. The Bentham Project, 2018, pp. iv–v.

39. Bentham, *Writings on Australia*, pp. 6–7.
40. Wakefield, Edward Gibbon. "England and America: Appendix III," in *The Collected Works of Edward Gibbon Wakefield*, Edited by Muriel F. Lloyd Prichard. Glasgow, London: Glasgow, London, Collins, 1968, p. 632.
41. *Morning Chronicle*, 24 September 1832, in Pike, Douglas. *Paradise of Dissent: South Australia 1829–1857.* 2nd ed. Melbourne: Melbourne University Press, 1967, p. 63, note 57 on p. 523.
42. Stephens, John. *A Facsimile of the First Edition of the Land of Promise.* Adelaide: Gillingham Printers, 1988, p. 85; also see section 'Comparative capabilities of Australia and Canada' in Torrens, Robert. *Colonization of South Australia.* Adelaide: Public Library of South Australia, 1962, pp. 148–174.
43. Napier, Charles James. *Colonization, Particularly in Southern Australia: With Some Remarks on Small Farms and Overpopulation.* New York: A. M. Kelley, 1969, p. 46.
44. Colonial Office Records, 'Register of Emigrant Labourers Applying for a Free Passage to South Australia', *CO386: Land and Emigration Commission (South Australian Content),* Australian Joint Copying Project, Reel 874, Part 149, Entry Number 42.
45. 'Charles Stafford, Bricklayer, Stormont County' in *Census of 1851 (Canada East, Canada West, New Brunswick, and Nova Scotia).* Ottawa, ON: Library and Archives Canada. Retrieved from www.ancestry.com.
46. Richards, *The Genesis of International Mass Migration*, p. 63.
47. For more on the Petworth Project see Cameron, Wendy. *Assisting Emigration to Upper Canada: The Petworth Project, 1832–1837.* Edited by Mary Maude. Montreal: McGill-Queen's University Press, 2000.
48. Richards, *The Genesis of International Mass Migration*, p. 65.
49. *Morning Chronicle*, 23 September 1832; Wakefield, Edward Gibbon. 'England and America', p. 635.
50. Pike, *Paradise of Dissent*, p. 96.
51. Brown, John. *Transcript of Diary of John Brown, Emigration Agent, with Index.* Adelaide, SA: Flinders University Library, Special Collections, 1835, p. 12.
52. Brown, *Transcript of Diary of John Brown*, p. 13.
53. Pike, *Paradise of Dissent*, pp. 72–73.

54. For example: quoting George Grote, "colonization, and colonization alone... affords the means of providing for the industrious and operative classes a lot better and more promising in every respect than that which awaits them here" 'New Colony of South Australia', *Morning Chronicle*, 1 July 1834; also Wakefield, Edward Gibbon and Provisional Committee National Colonization Society. *A Statement of the Principles and Objects of a Proposed National Society for the Cure and Prevention of Pauperism by Means of Systematic Colonization*. Statement on Systematic Colonization. London: J. Ridgway, 1830.
55. Pike, *Paradise of Dissent*, pp. 72–73.
56. Ibid., p. 73.
57. Great Britain, Parliament. *An Act to Empower His Majesty to Erect South Australia into a British Province or Provinces, and to Provide for the Colonization and Government Thereof: 15 August 1834*. Foundation Act 1834 (UK). London: Printed by George Eyre and Andrew Spottiswoode, 1838.
58. Prime Ministers between 1831 and 1836 were; Charles Grey, 2nd Earl Grey (Whig 1830 to 1834), William Lamb, 2nd Viscount Melbourne (Whig 1834 to 1834), Arthur Wellesley, 1st Duke of Wellington (Acting Prime Minister, Tory 1834 to 1834), Sir Robert Peel 2nd Baronet (Conservative 1834 to 1835), William Lamb, 2nd Viscount Melbourne (Whig 1835 to 1841).
59. Brown, *Transcript of Diary of John Brown*, p. 19.
60. Ibid., p. 13.
61. Ibid.
62. Gouger, Robert. *The Founding of South Australia: As Recorded in the Journals of Mr. Robert Gouger, First Colonial Secretary*. Edited by Edwin Hodder. London: Sampson Low, Marston, and Company, 1898, p. 42 & pp. 87–93.
63. Colonial Office Records, 'Register of Emigrant Labourers Applying for a Free Passage to South Australia', *CO386: Land and Emigration Commission (South Australian Content)*, Australian Joint Copying Project, Reel 874, Part 149.
64. For examples of the application form see Gouger, Robert. *South Australia in 1837: In a Series of Letters; with a Postscript as to 1838*. Adelaide: Public Library of South Australia, 1962, pp. 111–112; Button, Pat. *A Free Passage to Paradise?: Passenger Lists of United Kingdom Emigrants Who Applied for Free Passage to South Australia. 1836–1840*. Adelaide: South Australian Genealogy and Heraldry Society Inc., 1992, p. 124.
65. Gouger, *South Australia in 1837*, p. 112.
66. Colonial Office Records, 'Register', Entry Number 238, 'James Horn'.

67. Brown, *Transcript of Diary of John Brown*, p. 110.
68. For more on embarkation numbers and discerning who stayed and who left see Button, *A Free Passage to Paradise?*, pp. 9–14.
69. *Morning Chronicle*, 23 September 1832.
70. Bailyn, Bernard. *Voyagers to the West: A Passage in the Peopling of America on the Eve of the Revolution*. Edited by Barbara DeWolfe. New York: Knopf, 1986, p. 306.
71. Baskerville, Peter, and Kris Inwood. 'Introduction' in Baskerville, Peter, and Kris Inwood. *Lives in Transition: Longitudinal Analysis from Historical Sources*. Montreal: McGill-Queen's University Press, 2015.
72. Colonial Office Records, 'Register of Emigrant Labourers Applying for a Free Passage to South Australia', Entry Number 128, 'William Moore' & 234 'George Baker Clark'.
73. Gouger, *South Australia in 1837*, p. 109.
74. Colonial Office Records, 'Register', Entry Number 227, 'Robert Sherlock'.
75. Colonial Office Records, 'Register', Entry Number 18, 'Andrew Churcher'.
76. The occupations listed as meeting the requirement for free passage to South Australia were, 'Agricultural labourers, shepherds, bakers, blacksmiths, braziers and tinmen, smiths, shipwrights, boat-builders, butchers, wheelwrights, sawyers, cabinet-makers, coopers, curriers, farriers, millwrights, harness-makers, boot and shoe-makers, tailors, tanners, brick-makers, lime-burners, and all persons engaged in the erection of buildings.' Gouger, *South Australia in 1837*, p. 109.
77. *London, England, Church of England Baptisms, Marriages and Burials, 1538–1812*. London: London Metropolitan Archives, Reference Number: DL/T/090/004. Retrieved from www.ancestry.com.
78. *Census Returns of England and Wales, 1841*. Kew, Surrey: The National Archives of the UK: Public Record Office, 1841. Retrieved from www.ancestry.com.
79. *London, England, Church of England Marriages and Banns, 1754–1932*. London: London Metropolitan Archives, Reference Number: p95/tri1/111. Retrieved from www.ancestry.com.
80. *Census Returns of England and Wales, 1851, 1861, 1871 & 1881*. Kew, Surrey: The National Archives of the UK: Public Record Office, 1851, 1861, 1871, 1881. Retrieved from www.ancestry.com.
81. *England & Wales, Civil Registration Death Index, 1837–1915*. London: General Register Office. Retrieved from www.ancestry.com.
82. Online databases searched were Ancestry www.ancestry.com, My Heritage www.myheritage.com, FindMyPast, findmypast.com, and Family Search familysearch.org.

83. Colonial Office Records, 'Register', Entry Number 2, 'Charles Booty'.

84. 16th Regiment of Lancers, Regimental Number 1063, *Royal Hospital Chelsea Pensioner Soldier Service Records; Census Returns of England and Wales, 1871*. Kew, Surrey: The National Archives of the UK: Public Record Office, 1871. Retrieved from www.ancestry.com.

85. Cannon, Richard. *Historical Record of the Sixteenth Regiment or the Queen's Regiment of Light Dragoons, Lancers Containing an Account of the Formation of the Regiment in 1759 and of Its Subsequent Services to 1841*. London: John W. Parker, 1842, p. 111.

86. Colonial Office Records, 'Register', Entry Number 114, 'William Jones', 184 'John Taylor' or 187 'James Day'.

87. For a review of historical data linking methodology see Massey, Catherine G. "Playing with Matches: An Assessment of Accuracy in Linked Historical Data." *Historical Methods* 50, no. 3 (2017), pp. 129–143.

88. Efremova, Julia. et al. (2015) "Multi-Source Entity Resolution for Genealogical Data," in *Population Reconstruction*, edited by Bloothooft Gerrit, Christen Peter, Mandemakers Kee, and Schraagen Marijn. Springer, pp. 130–132.

89. New South Wales Government. *Persons on Early Migrant Ships*. Series 5310, Reel 1286. State Records Authority of New South Wales, Kingswood, New South Wales. Retrieved from www.ancestry.com.

90. Colonial Office Records, 'Register', Entry Number 90, 'Joseph Dennis'.

91. New South Wales Government. *Persons on Early Migrant Ships*, 'Joseph Dennis, Arrival Date: 31 December 1837, Vessel Name: *Alfred*.' Retrieved from www.ancestry.com.

92. Haines, Robin. "Indigent Misfits or Shrewd Operators?" p. 228.

93. Colonial Office Records, 'Register', Entry Number 109, 'William Cambridge'.

94. Home Office: *Criminal Registers, Middlesex and Home Office: Criminal Registers, England and Wales; Records Created or Inherited by the Home Office, Ministry of Home Security, and Related Bodies*, Series HO 26 and HO 27; The National Archives of the UK, Kew, Surrey, England; Home Office: *Settlers and Convicts, New South Wales and Tasmania;* (The National Archives Microfilm Publication HO10, Pieces 5, 19–20, 32–51); The National Archives of the UK, Kew, Surrey, England, 'William Cambridge, Arrival Date: 1837, Vessel: *Charles Kerr*.' Retrieved from www.ancestry.com.

95. Colonial Office Records, 'Register', Entry Number 67, 'John Garread'.

96. *Census of the State of New York, for 1855*. Microfilm. Various County Clerk Offices, New York. 'George Garreade, 18, Male'. Retrieved from www.ancestry.com.

97. *Census of the State of New York, for 1855.* 'Susanna Garreade, 15, Female'. Retrieved from www.ancestry.com.
98. *Brooklyn, New York, Green-Wood Cemetery Burial Index,* The Green-Wood Historic Fund. Retrieved from http://www.green-wood.com/burial_search/. 'John Garread' & 'Harriet Garread'.
99. *Census of the State of New York, for 1855.* Microfilm. Various County Clerk Offices, New York. 'Harriet Garreade, 8, Female'.
100. For example, *U.S. City Directories, 1822–1995; U.S. IRS Tax Assessment Lists, 1862–1918; New York, State and Federal Naturalization Records, 1794–1940.* Retrieved from www.ancestry.com.
101. Pike, *Paradise of Dissent,* p. 57.
102. Rushen, Elizabeth A., and Perry McIntyre. *Fair Game: Australia's First Immigrant Women.* Spit Junction, New South Wales: Anchor Books, 2010, p. 2.
103. Pooley, Colin G., and Jean Turnbull. *Migration and Mobility in Britain Since the Eighteenth Century.* London: UCL Press, 1998, p. 277.
104. Brown, *Transcript of Diary of John Brown,* p. 113.
105. Colonial Office Records, 'Register', Entry Number 46–52.
106. Colonial Office Records, 'Register', Entry Number 50, 'John Moon'.
107. *Census Returns of England and Wales, 1841.* Kew, Surrey: The National Archives of the UK: Public Record Office, 1841. Retrieved from www.ancestry.com.
108. Colonial Office Records, 'Register', Entry Number 7, 'Edward Lucas'.
109. Colonial Office Records, 'Register', Entry Numbers 5–15.
110. *Census Returns of England and Wales,* 1841. Kew, Surrey: The National Archives of the UK: Public Record Office, 1841. Retrieved from www.ancestry.com.
111. Colonial Office Records, 'Register', Entry Number 12, 'Joseph Dearn'.
112. *Board of Guardian Records, 1834–1906* and *Church of England Parish Registers, 1813–2003.* London: London Metropolitan Archives, Reference Number: dro/003/a/01/018. Retrieved from www.ancestry.com.
113. Robson's London Directory 1833 and 1834 quoted in Pike, *Paradise of Dissent,* p. 100.
114. Pike, *Paradise of Dissent,* p. 53.
115. Ibid., p. 100.
116. Brown, *Transcript of Diary of John Brown,* p. 45.
117. Pike, *Paradise of Dissent,* p. 101.
118. Jaunay, Graham. *South Australia Pre-civil Registration Births.* Adelaide, SA: Gould Genealogy, 2005.
119. Jaunay, Graham. *South Australia Pre-civil Registration Deaths.* Modbury, SA: Gould Genealogy, 2005.

120. Colonial Office Records, 'Register', Entry Number 35, 'George Illsley' & 60 'Duncan Grant'.
121. *London, England, Workhouse Admission and Discharge Records, 1764–1930.* London: London Metropolitan Archives. Retrieved from www.ancestry.com.
122. Haines, "Indigent Misfits or Shrewd Operators?" p. 230.

SELECT BIBLIOGRAPHY

Baskerville, Peter, and Kris Inwood. *Lives in Transition: Longitudinal Analysis from Historical Sources.* Montreal: McGill-Queen's University Press, 2015.

Belich, James. *Replenishing the Earth: The Settler Revolution and the Rise of the Anglo-World, 1783–1939.* Oxford: Oxford University Press, 2009.

Erickson, Charlotte. *Leaving England: Essays on British Emigration in the Nineteenth Century.* Ithaca, NY: Cornell University Press, 1994.

Haines, Robin. "Indigent Misfits or Shrewd Operators? Government-Assisted Emigrants from the United Kingdom to Australia, 1831–1860." *Population Studies* 48, no. 2 (1994), 246.

Haines, Robin. "'The Idle and the Drunken won't Do There': Poverty, the New Poor Law and Nineteenth-Century Government-Assisted Emigration to Australia from the United Kingdom." *Australian Historical Studies* 27, no. 108 (1997), 1–21.

Mills, R. C. *The Colonization of Australia (1829–42): The Wakefield Experiment in Empire Building.* London: Dawsons of Pall Mall, 1968.

Richards, Eric. *The Genesis of International Mass Migration: The British Case, 1750–1900.* Manchester: Manchester University Press, 2018.

Richards, Eric. "How Did Poor People Emigrate from the British Isles to Australia in the Nineteenth Century?" *Journal of British Studies* 32, no. 3 (1993), 250–279.

Richards, Eric. "Emigration to the New Worlds: Migration Systems in the Early Nineteenth Century." *Australian Journal of Politics and History* 41, no. 3 (1995), 391–407.

CHAPTER 4

Why Single Female Emigration to New South Wales (1832–1837) Was Doomed to Disappoint

Melanie Burkett

At the beginning of the 1830s, the British colony of New South Wales had a problem: a highly lopsided sex ratio. In 1833, men over the age of twelve outnumbered women of the same age by three-and-a-half to one.[1] Colonial commentators blamed the disproportion of the sexes for rampant prostitution, bachelors lusting after their neighbours' wives, and women immodestly proud of the amount of male attention they received.[2] A problem in most contemporary colonies (due to differential emigration rates)[3] and exacerbated by convict transportation (which saw significantly higher numbers of men than women exiled to New South Wales), the sex imbalance was widely thought to form 'the principal barrier to the advancement of this colony in wealth, morals, and population'.[4]

Also at the beginning of the 1830s, Viscount Goderich, the British Secretary of State for War and the Colonies, enacted sweeping changes to land policy in New South Wales. The new policies discontinued

M. Burkett (✉)
Macquarie University, Sydney, NSW, Australia

© The Author(s) 2019
P. Payton and A. Varnava (eds.),
Australia, Migration and Empire, Britain and the World,
https://doi.org/10.1007/978-3-030-22389-2_4

69

colonial land grants and instead decreed that all land in the colony be sold at auction with a set minimum price. The proceeds from the land sales would fund working-class emigration to the colony (so-called assisted emigration). This would provide the colony much-needed workers and alleviate pressure on the British labour market with its high unemployment caused by industrialisation and the end of the Napoleonic wars. Goderich also saw the potential for the new scheme to address the sex ratio and, accordingly, ordered the engagement of a ship dedicated to conveying single women to New South Wales. In April 1832, this pilot ship of single female emigrants, the *Red Rover*, left Ireland for Sydney.[5] Eight more ships would follow in the next five years, bringing over nineteen hundred single women to New South Wales.[6]

Given the concern about the sex imbalance expressed in the colony, one might think that the colony's social leaders would have welcomed the Colonial Office's efforts. Instead, the scheme was condemned and the women themselves were said to be immoral, 'in most cases absolute curses – increasing the stream of depravity almost beyond the power of control'.[7] These complaints should not be taken at face value for they existed within the context of larger political battles surrounding assisted emigration and the new land policy.[8] At the same time elite colonists mourned the loss of their land grants, the immigration fund *they* had created via *their* land purchases (at least in their eyes) was 'wasted' on 'immoral' women instead of the male labour the growing pastoral industry so desperately needed. According to colonial rhetoric, the poor 'quality' of women sent was proof that British authorities could not be trusted to act in the best interests of the colony. In many ways, the single female ships became a scapegoat for colonial frustrations with Goderich's policies.[9]

This chapter, however, focuses not on that political posturing, but rather on the impact of the negative rhetoric on the construction of gender in New South Wales. Gender and morality are both socially constructed and, like all such constructs, are shaped by discourse. In New South Wales, the single female immigration scheme of 1832–1837 spurred such discourse as the perceived character of these women and their assessed worth to the colony was discussed at length in the colonial public sphere, including in pamphlets, government reports and the colonial press. The condemnation of these women—according to a standard they failed to meet—worked to crystallise gender norms, solidifying a developing British middle-class ideal in a colonial context. The impact of this articulation of gender norms was long lasting, as the complaints made about the single female immigrants of the 1830s resurfaced around similar efforts to bring single women to the Australian colonies in the latter half of the nineteenth century.[10]

The morality of this first group of single female immigrants was so easily condemned due to a combination of factors: classed and sometimes inherently contradictory ideals of femininity which stood in opposition to the immigrants' experiences as working-class women and as migrants, tactics which linked the immigrants to convicts, and a disconnect between the expectations for the women held by policy makers in Britain and those held by colonial commentators. These factors overlapped and created contradictions that proved impossible to resolve. Morality was conflated with middle-class femininity. The ideal of middle-class femininity stressed purity and left no room for redemption. The process of emigration itself was believed to endanger purity. If a woman did not achieve the middle-class ideal, she was deemed no better than a convict. Class and gender were constituted together. Caught in the middle of this web of meanings were the single female immigrants themselves. Single female immigration was doomed from the start.

The Scheme and Its Context

In order to qualify for an assisted passage, a woman had to be between the ages of eighteen and thirty, unmarried or widowed, and 'of good health and character'. The emigration application required consent from the woman's parents or family and signatures from a magistrate or clergyman as well as two parochial officers. Finally, before embarking, each woman had to pass a health inspection.[11] Despite such strict criteria, colonial condemnation of the women often blamed the selection process for disappointing 'quality'. The New South Wales Legislative Council's 1835 Committee on Immigration declared that 'a great number [of the women were] ... very different in character from what they appear to have been represented to the Committee in London, and quite unsuited to the wants of the colonists'.[12]

Historians have long repeated these negative impressions of the single female immigrants. Writing in 1937, R. B. Madgwick concluded that the scheme 'undoubtedly merited the criticism it received'.[13]

A. J. Hammerton was one of the first to reassess the scheme in the 1970s.[14] He judged the criticisms to be overblown, the result of natural missteps in the early stages of a new process that were corrected over time. Historians who have followed him have worked to rescue the women's reputations. Elizabeth Rushen and Perry McIntyre have painstakingly tracked the individual women on many of the ships through police reports, newspapers and birth, marriage and death records.[15] Together, they have shown that the women were not all 'absolute curses'.[16] Some disappointed, but a large majority of them fulfilled their intended purpose: to work as domestic servants, get married and help populate the continent.

The aim of this chapter is to build on—not to repeat—work that has already been done. What follows is not an assessment of the women's relative worth to the colony. Instead, the goal is to examine what the expectations for and complaints about these women revealed about developing gender norms. The existing historical work on the single female immigrants of the 1830s has tried to move beyond negative representations and to discover 'reality'. However, representations help construct an alternate reality, a social reality. Cultural concepts such as 'morality' and 'respectability' are shaped by public rhetoric. And, as we will see, the standard of 'respectability' that these women were publicly derided for failing to meet was fundamentally at odds with their class backgrounds and the roles they were expected to fill.

The early nineteenth century was a time when British gender norms shifted as the bourgeoisie solidified, when complementary standards for men and women evolved. Men were to occupy the competitive world of commerce, engage in politics and support their families financially. A balance to their husbands' highly public lives, women were to devote themselves to motherhood and the home and to support their families morally. Women were not to work, but to remain dependent, passive, fragile and pure.[17] Though this ideal of 'separate spheres' would be nigh impossible for working-class families (and even some lower-middle-class families) to attain,[18] it nevertheless created real constraints on the actions of both men and women. These gender norms did not merely impact the daily lives of those in Britain; gender shaped all aspects of Empire and, conversely, colonial rule created new understandings of gender.[19] These exchanges occurred, in part, through migration and migration policy. Britain's evolving gender norms travelled from Britain to the Australian colonies[20] and that transfer was facilitated by the single female immigrants, whose arrival set off a flurry of rhetoric around acceptable femininity.

The Tension Between Emigration and Ideal Femininity

Unfortunately for the single female immigrants, they would help transmit gender norms not as exemplars of respectable femininity. Rather, they would help establish the female ideal via their perceived flaws—not via their virtues—an outcome made possible by the paradoxical nature of the gender norms themselves. Women were expected to be at once the guardians of morality within the family *and* susceptible to corruption. The resolution of this contradiction was to argue that their moral status depended on 'separation from disorder in the public world'.[21] Women were to concern themselves with domesticity, maintaining a safe space to which men could retreat from the competition of the working world and the public sphere.[22] As the separate spheres ideology became more entrenched, the physical movement of women was increasingly constrained. When women left the domain of the home, they struggled to find 'respectable' accommodation and were expected to be accompanied, even when travelling within the British Isles.[23] Emigration, naturally, multiplied these hurdles for women. By contrast, contemporary ideals of masculinity connected to the process of emigration in a much different way. Men were praised for independence, hard work, courage, assertiveness and tenacity, all attributes which the act of emigration required.[24] Emigration was itself a masculine activity.

Colonial rhetoric exploited this contradiction between the feminine ideal and the realities of emigration by arguing that the women's 'respectability' was endangered at every step in the process, and, therefore, the women who arrived in the colony were most probably 'disreputable'. The first unforgivable mistake these women committed was relying on a philanthropic institution before they left Britain. The *Sydney Monitor* complained, 'Women of lewd habits and immoral bringing up, and of wasteful habits, cast out of the … Refuges for the Destitute … are the sort of people which England is vomiting on our ill-fated shores'.[25] In reality, only a small proportion of the assisted women came directly from institutions for the poor. Of the nearly five hundred immigrants on board the *Bussorah Merchant* and the *Layton*, only thirty came from institutions—arguably, not a large enough proportion to count as 'vomiting' inappropriate women onto the colony.[26] Furthermore, such institutions existed 'to reclaim women … of whose Reformation there is a reasonable prospect'.[27] The men who ran these institutions fully trusted their own abilities to discern the 'deserving' from 'undeserving' poor. They believed (or at least claimed to believe) the women they nominated were not beyond the hope of redemption and that emigration would offer these women a second chance.[28] Nevertheless, according to colonial rhetoric, a stay in such an institution equated to poor character.

The second mistake was emigrating on a ship where amorous activities occurred or were rumoured to have occurred. Press coverage painted a picture of floating brothels, expressed shock over single women arriving pregnant, and lamented the mixing of 'good' women with the 'bad' on board.[29] Though such complaints conceded that at least some of the women *were* 'good', in practice, the entire ship was condemned. 'The names of *Red Rover, Bussorah Merchant*, and *Layton*, are in a majority of cases equivalent to those of rogue, vagabond, and worse', declared the *Sydney Gazette*.[30] Whether an individual woman participated in the alleged disreputable activities or not, the name of the ship became a derisive shorthand for the entire group.

If an individual woman managed to make it to the colony without succumbing to the bad influence of her shipmates, she most likely would be corrupted by the 'vicious society' into which she had arrived, one (reportedly) replete with crime, drunkenness and lasciviousness.[31] Such assertions implicitly critiqued the colony itself, and yet, a fall from grace would often be blamed on the weakness of the woman's character rather than conditions in the colony: 'well-conducted emigrant females will always meet with encouragement and respect in this colony … if they will only resolutely resist the designing influence of the low, vulgar, and dishonest herd who are sure to beset them on landing'.[32] 'Encouragement and respect' were reserved for those who resisted temptation.

Eventually, as the complaints against the single female immigrants became increasingly shrill, the conclusion was reached that a truly virtuous woman would never have emigrated in the first place. A virtuous woman would presumably never consider travelling 'unprotected'—alone, without family—and she would never willingly leave her family behind. According to this logic, the fact that a single woman came at all proved that she was unacceptable. In a public speech, Presbyterian minister J. D. Lang noted, 'For although the spirit of adventure may be as strong in some females as it is in most men, we cannot suppose ... that it is the most virtuous of their sex who would undertake a voyage of 16,000 miles'.[33] Those who did leave must have possessed an unfeminine 'spirit of adventure'. Once again, emigration was considered an inherently masculine activity.

PRODUCTION AND REPRODUCTION

Once in the colony, the women's fitness for their intended roles—production and reproduction—was questioned. Recruitment circulars in Britain explicitly named these opportunities for women. For example, the 1833 'Notice to Young Women' proclaimed, 'In New South Wales and Van Diemen's Land there are very few Women compared with the whole number of People, so that it is impossible to get Women enough as Female Servants or for other Female Employments'.[34] Likewise, an 1834 circular told prospective emigrants that they 'may look forward in a Country where the disparity between the sexes is so great, to marry under circumstances of respectability and comfort far beyond what they can hope for in the crowded population of Great Britain'.[35] The policy makers and, presumably, the women themselves expected the immigrants to enter into domestic service for a time before marrying and starting a family.

To impugn the women on these fronts, colonial rhetoric tactically linked the female immigrants to the much-despised convict women, who were denigrated as the most debased group in colonial society.[36] An advice pamphlet produced for new female arrivals clearly designated convict women as the 'other' against which the free immigrants would be judged: 'The difference between you and them, does not so much lie in the names emigrant (that is, free) and convict, as in the difference of your conduct as compared with theirs'.[37] This seemingly simple advice for the immigrants to differentiate themselves from convict women was not so simple, however. First, convicts and free immigrants had similar backgrounds,[38] most especially in terms of occupation[39] and age.[40] Second, the free immigrants were, in many respects, treated similarly to convicts during the emigration process. Ship charters for emigrant women were based off the template provided by charters for female convict ships and captains and surgeons were chosen specifically for their experience with transporting convicts.[41] The emigrant women's freedom of movement on board was greatly curtailed, to what could best be termed a 'virtual imprisonment'.[42] On arrival, the prison-like atmosphere continued, as efforts—including the use of a watchman—were made to prevent women from 'absconding' from the temporary accommodation provided.[43] The women were paraded off the ships before large, sometimes jeering crowds[44] and, as has already been described, often became indelibly associated with their ship of arrival, a practice begun with convicts of both sexes.[45] All these seemingly small linkages with convicts were nevertheless significant as they revealed an underlying preconception of the women as no better than convicts. The women were told to differentiate themselves from convicts, yet the logistical arrangements for their travel and their reception once arrived did little to create any distinction.

Similarly, immigrant women's primary economic role—domestic service—had heretofore been performed by convict women. A common complaint against convict domestic servants was the lack of skill they brought to the job.[46] This same complaint arose about the free immigrants, who reportedly possessed 'a perfect ignorance of domestic and household work'.[47] No voices urged patience. None reasoned that the women needed time to learn their jobs before they were condemned. These women were expected to be better workers than the convict servants and they were not (or at least they were not perceived to be).

The female immigrants were also expected to be more obedient and loyal than the convict women. Dissatisfaction with the obedience of workers, however, is a pervasive theme in the history of domestic service. The intimate nature of the relationship between the servant and the family she attended paired with the mistress's need to assert authority over her servants created tension.[48] Thus, the complaints about the single female immigrants were more reflective of workplace dynamics than of any character failings of the women themselves.[49] Additionally, convict women were actually seen to be *better* than immigrant women in one way: employers held more control over convicts than they did over immigrants. If an employer was dissatisfied with a female convict servant, the employer could send the convict back to the government and receive a replacement. However, with free immigrants, this power dynamic was reversed. After the women had been in the colony a while—after they had figured out the geography of the place, the social hierarchy and the exact level of wages they might reasonably expect—they might leave their initial placement for another position. This freedom of movement did not sit well with employers, who lamented the loss of control over their servants: 'prisoners are under the subjection that free females can set at defiance, and thus it is, that emigrants of bad character are worse than convicts'.[50]

Of course, one reason a woman might leave her service would be to get married and, indeed, as we have seen, this outcome was both intended and advertised as a real possibility in Britain. This use of single female emigration as a corrective for the moral failings of New South Wales showed great faith in the institution of marriage, an institution which was the cornerstone of the developing middle-class ideal of respectability. Though companionate marriage was a key component of how the middle class conceived of *them*selves and of the superior morality *they* strove for, in this case, British authorities intended to bequeath the institution unto the lower classes. By giving a labouring man a wife (and eventually children) who was dependent on him, 'marriage [acted as] a restraint from evil, and an incitement to frugality and perseverance'.[51] These merits of marriage were believed to be so obvious that once more partners were available to the men in the colony, they would undoubtedly choose to marry. Marriage, in and of itself, would improve the habits and character of those joined in matrimony. By providing the marriage partners, the single female emigration scheme would improve the morality of the colony.

Colonial condemnation of the female immigrants on moral grounds, however, precluded the realisation of this vision. Since the separate spheres ideology deemed women the site of morality within the family, the single female immigrants—the intended wives—bore the bulk of the responsibility for the moral improvement of the colony. The colonists were the objects in need of improvement; the women the instrument through which that would occur. When the colonial elite branded the single female immigrants as a group immoral, however, it rendered them unsuitable for the task. Instead of viewing marriage as the path to improved morality of the community overall, the marital destiny of the immigrant women strengthened class distinctions. The aforementioned advice pamphlet stressed that, though they were expected to marry, not just any marriage would be deemed acceptable:

> Beware how you enter the married state ... when any one proposes marriage to you, enquire if he be a sober man, and a man of good repute;

and if you learn that he is given to drinking, or keeps company with men of loose and desolute [sic] habits, refuse his offer, however plausible and engaging he may be in his manners, and however many fine promises he may make to you.[52]

The pamphlet did not acknowledge in any way the civilising influence the policy makers in Britain expected the women to exert. Rather, it warned women to choose their husbands carefully, for a poor choice would irrevocably taint a woman's reputation. The women were expected to marry, but only certain men would be suitable. The women were expected to improve the morality of the colony, somehow without associating with the immoral people. The power of marriage to improve virtue was in doubt. The policy makers and the colonial elite held different opinions on the possibility of redemption.

The types of men the immigrants were supposed to avoid—the 'drunkards' and 'thieves'—were allusions to convicts and freed convicts, the very men cited as in need of both wives and moral improvement. In many cases, those were precisely the men the single female immigrants chose to marry. Of the women on the first ship, the *Red Rover*, sixty per cent of the women who married, married freed convicts.[53] Such matches were vocally disdained.[54] In testimony before the Legislative Council's Committee on Immigration, wealthy landowner Robert Scott proclaimed, 'The disproportion of the sexes exists only among the Convict class, and it would be worse than a waste of the fund to import women fit to consort with them, and propagate a race it was policy to get rid of'.[55] According to this logic, providing wives for the convicts was a waste of money. Carried a step further, this method of reasoning denied that the sex imbalance was worthy of concern, for it only existed among the convicts.[56] As in the case of domestic service, the women were deemed unsatisfactory by colonial rhetoric even when they fulfilled the role intended for them by policy makers in Britain. Furthermore, those perceived failures had the effect of tying them to the convict class in terms of social status.

Part of the problem with these two roles—production and reproduction—was the paradox between the two in relation to class distinctions. Domestic servitude was for the working classes and the 'virtuous wife' was a middle-class role. The intractability of this difference was unrecognised by authorities in Britain. The imagined outcome of the scheme would have created a gendered society in which middle and working class alike would reap the civilising benefits of marriage anchored by the virtue of the wife. The working classes could use a middle-class ideal, not necessarily to raise their status, but rather to live more moral lives. However, from the colonial point of view, 'respectable' marriages had to be reserved for unquestionably 'respectable' people. Had these women been accepted into both roles, the effect would have been to weaken class distinctions. Instead, colonial rhetoric condemned them on both fronts.

'Damned Whores'?

Single female immigrants provoked such condemnation even when they performed the roles they were expected to fill. When they were thought to be entering a less respectable occupation, colonial ire grew proportionately. Engaging in prostitution was a complaint often levied against the single female immigrants.[57] The 'streets of Sydney' were allegedly 'swarming with free emigrant prostitutes!'[58] It may be impossible to know exactly how many of the immigrants turned to prostitution, but the newspapers were not shy about offering estimates. According to the *Monitor*, one-third of the *Red Rover* women were 'living in concubinage and prostitution' and the *Colonist* claimed that forty of the *Canton* women resided in 'houses of bad fame'.[59] Whether these complaints of widespread prostitution were hyperbole, accurate, or—what is most likely—somewhere in between, they were used to condemn not just the actions of individuals, but the single female emigration scheme, as a whole. The complaints also had the net effect of clearly delineating what was and was not acceptable feminine sexuality.

Feminist historians have approached the study of prostitution in a variety of ways. One strategy is to reveal the structural forces that left women with few choices besides prostitution. Here again, the single female immigrants had more in common with female convicts than with the middle-class women they were expected to emulate. Both groups had to contend with a disproportionately male population that rendered sexual services in high demand.[60] Indeed, the sex imbalance was the impetus behind the entire single female emigration scheme. Additionally, women of all statuses lacked access to more 'respectable' forms of employment; under the middle-class gender ideals of the day, there were not many jobs that were acceptable for women to do at all. Women were condemned for turning to prostitution when they were unemployed, while at the same time, gender conventions made them largely unemployable.[61] Domestic servitude was the only widespread choice[62] and the unique nature of this occupation created an additional challenge for the immigrants should they leave/lose their employment: sudden homelessness. If an immigrant woman left her service placement, she had no place to go.[63] Condemnations of both convict and immigrant prostitutes largely ignored these structural issues that might lead women to turn to prostitution. Instead, women presumably made such a choice as a result of poor character.

Other feminist historians look beyond the structural issues that might drive women to prostitution and insist upon agency. They examine prostitution as a viable economic choice.[64] Descriptions of 'prostitutes dressed in the best apparel, and faring sumptuously every day' suggested that it, in fact, was.[65] Though difficult to prove, it was very likely given the disproportion of the sexes in New South Wales (which was highlighted in advertisements directed at single women) that there were at least some unapologetic prostitutes in Britain who saw the colony as a fertile market for their services and, therefore, chose to emigrate. Immigrant women who engaged in commercial sex were not necessarily driven to it by pure desperation; engaging in prostitution may have been a shrewd business decision. Furthermore, the women themselves may not have felt the expected shame at their occupation given different attitudes towards sexuality among the lower classes.[66] Among the 'respectable' classes, however, such entrepreneurship would have never been deemed acceptable. The *Gazette* was indignant over a supposed agreement made among several women on board the *Duchess of Northumberland* to open a brothel upon arrival.[67] In the middle-class feminine ideal, sexual virtue was inextricably linked to respectability. Immigrant prostitutes were neither chaste nor economically dependent on husbands—the only acceptable paths for 'respectable' women.

Occasionally, though, a voice in the press took a more pragmatic stance. The *Monitor* was willing to concede that, even if the incoming women were not 'reputable', they were still better than no additional women at all.[68] This rationale was linked to the laws of supply and demand:

> That a good deal of dissoluteness should be the effect of the several importations of females already had, was but a natural consequence of the great sexual disparity in respect of numbers ... but still there was a likelihood

when the supply had adjusted itself in some measure to the demand, that profligacy would have attained a sort of equilibrium.[69]

Such statements acknowledged that there was a market for sex. An influx of prostitutes—while still morally repugnant—would help equalise the market by making that line of work less lucrative and therefore less attractive. In essence, the colony needed some sacrificial lambs to stabilise the sex trade.

Though women were condemned for selling sex, men were not likewise held to account. The sex imbalance was used as an excuse for men's drinking to intoxication, visiting brothels, and 'being intimate with neighbours' wives'.[70] It seemed that such behaviour in men was to be expected given the sex imbalance; the use of prostitutes was understandable:

> Until the free and freed people of this Colony can get virtuous and industrious free wives, what would you have them to do, so long as they retain their sex? Would you convert them into pious men? ... But if you cannot do this, had you not better tolerate concubinage than grosser immorality? Is not prostitution a less evil than crimes of another dye?[71]

Hidden within this assessment was the condemnation of homosexual practices, obliquely referred to in the public sphere as 'moral pestilences' or 'worse crimes even than rape and adultery'.[72] In the colony's current state, even prostitution was 'a less evil than crimes of another dye'. According to this rationale, female sexual propriety could be sacrificed for men's.

Even with these admissions of the necessity of commercial sex, the fact that some of the single female immigrants turned to prostitution was still used to condemn the group as a whole. The net effect of these criticisms and cautious concessions was to articulate the social standard for respectable sexuality. As the arrival of the single female immigrants catalysed public discussion, imperial policy—and the reception of that policy—helped construct sexuality. The motivation for and marketing behind the scheme situated acceptable feminine sexuality within the institution of marriage. Even though *some* voices in the colonial press were willing to concede that prostitution was *somewhat* necessary, marriage was laudable and prostitution was not. Thus, an effective way to condemn the women—and, therefore, the policy—was to brand the women prostitutes.

The Scheme's End and Its Aftermath

The complaints against the single female immigrants were loud, relentless, and seemingly unresolvable. The clash between the feminine ideal and the nature of emigration along with the disconnect between British and colonial expectations for the women rendered their situation hopeless. In 1835, the New South Wales Legislative Council convened a committee to assess the first few years of assisted emigration, which concluded that there was 'a difficulty bordering upon impossibility of procuring the emigration of single females, combining all the requisite qualities of moral character and useful requirements'.[73] Ironically, when the London Emigration Committee—the board of volunteers responsible for organising the single female ships on behalf of the Colonial Office—attempted to defend itself against the complaints, it used the same argument. From the London Committee's point of view, it *was* nearly impossible to find suitable women, but not because they did not exist. Rather, the negative press had made acceptable candidates unwilling to go: 'the unwarranted imputations cast on them by the Colonial press, (which are copied & circulated in this hemisphere) render it impossible for the Committee to select a number of young women of unexceptionable character from any particular class'.[74] One side argued that suitable women did not exist, the other that suitable women were scared off by bad press. In either case, the women who arrived in the colony were *un*suitable. Both sides disparaged the women themselves. Eventually, the London Emigration Committee gave up. In July 1836, the Committee informed the Colonial Office that it would no longer send women to New South Wales.[75] The last ship, the *Lady Macnaghten*, set sail in November, after which the Committee officially disbanded. The practice of sending single female emigrants on dedicated ships was over—for now.

The sex imbalance remained and, as one historian put it, 'idylls of colonial bachelors in the bush awaiting willing wives ... died hard'.[76] Accordingly, throughout the second half of the nineteenth century, various schemes to bring large numbers of single women materialised.[77] Such schemes were made possible by slowly changing attitudes in Britain towards women and emigration,[78] altered attitudes which made it more socially acceptable for middle-class women to migrate and even, by the end of the century, which held women to have an important role to play in the peopling of the Empire.[79] Nevertheless, in the colonies, the familiar complaints persisted: it was nearly impossible to provide female immigrants adequate 'protection'; British agents could not be trusted to select suitable emigrants; women who came were either bad workers and changed services frequently or else they were prostitutes.[80] Colonial criticisms of the first scheme were not forgotten and, in fact, created a confirmation bias against future schemes.

Conclusion

The vehemence with which the colonial elite attacked the single female immigrants was politically motivated. The elite were unhappy with the loss of land grants and wanted the colony—not Britain—to control immigration. But, at the same time, the rhetoric used was not invented solely for political purposes; it reflected and heightened cultural assumptions about class and, especially, gender. Disparate conceptions of the acceptable roles and behaviour of men and women enabled the public sphere to demonise the single female immigrants. Male immigrants were also criticised for their work ethic and lack of skill, but no one questioned the propriety of men making the journey alone. Licentiousness on single female emigrant ships was blamed on the superintendent's failure to control the women,[81] yet no one criticised the superintendent for failing to control the crew. Prostitutes were condemned, but not the men who patronised them. The exalted position of women under the middle-class gender ideals of the day set up the working-class single female immigrants for a massive fall. As they protested the new land and emigration policies, the colonial elite could easily use these perilous gender norms to discredit the single female immigrants.

This was possible because the separate spheres ideology was self-contradictory. Those contradictions, in turn, helped explain the disconnection between the expectations held by British officials and by the colonial elite. Women were thought to be both the moral centre of the family *and* susceptible to corruption. Relying on the first part of the ideal, policy makers in Britain intended the immigrant women to redeem the colony morally. However, the second part of the ideal clashed with the nature of emigration itself. From the colonial perspective, the women's virtue was under threat at every stage of the emigration process and, once their virtue was compromised, the women were forever categorised as 'disreputable'. The policy makers and the colonial elite actually deployed the same standard of middle-class femininity, but to opposite effect.

The classed nature of the separate spheres ideal provided another opportunity for the colonial elite to condemn the immigrant women. In order to be judged 'reputable', the single female immigrants had to be the opposite of convict women. However, the free immigrants often came from similar backgrounds to the convicts and the procedures used to convey the women to the colony mirrored those used for convict ships. Furthermore, the policy makers intended the women to work in the same jobs as convict women and become wives to convict and freedmen. In those roles, according to British logic, the women might provide models of virtue for the colony's debased population. According to colonial logic, however, association with convicts irredeemably corrupted. Once again, British intentions and colonial expectations clashed. This association with convicts was only strengthened by the presence of some immigrant women in the sex trade. To the colonial elite, this proved the immigrant women were no better than convicts. The demographic, economic and structural factors that forced or encouraged both groups to turn to prostitution did not matter; sex work was still used to condemn the women who engaged in it and, by extension, the group of single female immigrants, as a whole. All of these factors grouped the assisted immigrants with the convicts according to social class and prevented them from achieving the middle-class ideal.

The qualities these women were expected to possess—and were derided for *not* having—constituted an impossible standard. Impossible, because the standard was not only class-based, but also deployed in order to maintain class distinctions. The middle-class separate spheres ideal equated femininity with morality. As working-class women who chose to emigrate, single female immigrants failed to meet both the class component of the ideal and the moral standard of the woman whose virtue was constantly protected and never questioned. Simultaneously, the structure and intended outcomes of the single female emigration scheme linked the immigrants to the unquestionably depraved (at least according to the colonial rhetoric) lower-class, female convicts. Thus, the connection between class and morality (or, in this case, *im*morality) strengthened. Assisted emigration provided the social moment for this mutual construction of class and gender/morality. Subsequently, the single female immigrants found themselves the unlucky subjects of the ensuing flurry of condemnation and mudslinging. Caught in the middle of paradoxical gender norms and differing expectations for the scheme in Britain and in New South Wales, these women were doomed to disappoint.

Acknowledgements This chapter is derived from my Ph.D. thesis, which was supported by the International Macquarie University Research Excellence Scholarship. I would like to thank the participants of the 2017 Writers Retreat (sponsored by the Macquarie University Department of Modern History, Politics and International Relations) for their valuable feedback on this chapter.

NOTES

1. Australian Bureau of Statistics 2014, *Australian Historical Population Statistics*, 'Table 2.2: Population, Age and Sex, NSW, 1833–1846', data cube: Excel spreadsheet, Cat. No. 3105.0.65.001, accessed 30 September 2016, http://www.abs.gov.au/ausstats/abs@.nsf/mf/3105.0.65.001.
2. 'Wisdom of the "Of-No-Sect"', *Sydney Monitor*, 31 October 1832, 2.
3. Charles Tennant, *A Letter to the Right Hon. Sir George Murray, &c. &c. &c. on Systematic Colonization* (London: James Ridgway, 1830), 27.
4. *Sydney Gazette*, 2 June 1832, 2.
5. House of Commons, *Emigration: Report of Commissioners*, 1832, CO 384:27, PRO 4101, Mitchell Library, State Library of New South Wales, Sydney, 4–5. (The Mitchell Library is hereafter referred to as 'ML'.)
6. Number compiled using Hammerton's appendix along with Rushen and McIntyre's number for the *Red Rover*. A. J. Hammerton, '"Without Natural Protectors": Female Immigration to Australia, 1832–36', *Historical Studies* 16, no. 65 (1975): 562–565; Elizabeth A. Rushen and Perry McIntyre, *Fair Game: Australia's First Immigrant Women* (Spit Junction, NSW: Anchor Books Australia, 2010), 42.
7. 'American and Australian Female Emigrants', *Sydney Gazette*, 3 March 1835, 2.
8. A note on terminology: Migrants leaving a particular location are referred to as '*emi*grants'. Once they arrive at a destination, they are then '*immi*grants'. The colonial press in the 1830s, however, inconsistently used the two terms and most often defaulted to 'emigrant'. The policy/practice itself was almost always referred to as 'assisted *emi*gration'.
9. As I argue in my upcoming Ph.D. thesis.
10. Lisa Chilton, 'Single Female Immigration and Australia's Early National Identity', *Australian Studies* 20 (2005): 209–232; Janice Gothard, *Blue China: Single Female Migration to Colonial Australia* (Carlton South, VIC: Melbourne University Press, 2001).
11. 'Emigration of Females in New South Wales and Van Diemen's Land' circular published by the Refuge for the Destitute (dated 9 June 1832) included as an enclosure to Forster to Goderich, 30 March 1833, CO 384:32, PRO 4102, ML.

12. New South Wales Legislative Council, *Final Report of the Committee on Immigration* (Sydney: Stephens and Stokes, 1835), Q304.894041/5, ML, Sydney, 6.
13. R. B. Madgwick, *Immigration into Eastern Australia, 1788–1851* (London: Longmans, Green, 1937), 110.
14. Hammerton, 'Without Natural Protectors'.
15. Elizabeth A. Rushen, *Single and Free: Female Migration to Australia, 1833–1837* (Kew, VIC: Australian Scholarly Publishing, 2003); Elizabeth A. Rushen and Perry McIntyre, *The Merchant's Women* (Spit Junction, NSW: Anchor Books Australia, 2008); Rushen and McIntyre, *Fair Game*.
16. 'American and Australian Female Emigrants', *Sydney Gazette*, 3 March 1835, 2.
17. Sonya O. Rose, *Limited Livelihoods: Gender and Class in Nineteenth-Century England* (Berkeley: University of California Press, 1992); Leonore Davidoff and Catherine Hall, *Family Fortunes: Men and Women of the English Middle Class, 1780–1850*, rev. ed. (London: Routledge, 2002).
18. Rose, *Limited Livelihoods*, chap. 1.
19. See Tony Ballantyne, 'Colonial Knowledge', in *The British Empire: Themes and Perspectives*, Sarah Stockwell, ed. (Malden, MA: Blackwell, 2008), 7–37; Angela Woollacott, *Gender and Empire* (Hampshire, UK: Palgrave Macmillian, 2006).
20. As Penny Russell's work on 'genteel femininity' in the colonies has shown. Penny Russell, *A Wish of Distinction: Colonial Gentility and Femininity* (Carlton, VIC: Melbourne University Press, 1994).
21. Ibid., 60.
22. G. R. Searle, *Morality and the Market in Victorian Britain* (Oxford, UK: Clarendon Press, 1998), 157.
23. Davidoff and Hall, *Family Fortunes*, 404.
24. John Tosh, *Manliness and Masculinities in Nineteenth-Century Britain: Essays on Gender, Family, and Empire* (Harlow, UK: Pearson Longman, 2005), 177.
25. *Sydney Monitor*, 21 September 1833, 2.
26. Rushen, *Single and Free*, 11, viii.
27. Forster to Elliot, 13 February 1832, CO 384:30, PRO 4101, ML.
28. Davidoff and Hall, *Family Fortunes*, chap. 10; Searle, *Morality and the Market in Victorian Britain*, chap. 8.
29. See, respectively, Amicus [pseud.], 'Queries Addressed to a Member of the Emigration Committee in London', *The Colonist*, 15 January 1835, 2; 'Female Emigration. More Work for Mr. Marshall!', *The Colonist*, 19 February 1835, 1; *Sydney Gazette*, 1 November 1834, 2.

30. *Sydney Gazette*, 30 October 1834, 2.
31. *Sydney Gazette*, 3 March 1835, 2.
32. *Sydney Gazette*, 8 November 1834, 2.
33. John Dunmore Lang, *Emigration; Considered Chiefly in Reference to the Practicability and Expediency of Importing and of Settling Throughout the Territory of New South Wales, a Numerous, Industrious and Virtuous Agricultural Population; Being a Lecture Delivered in the Temporary Hall of the Australia College Sydney, 9th May 1833* (Sydney: E. S. Hall, 1833), 14.
34. Edward Forster, 'Notice to Young Women Desirous of Bettering Their Condition by an Emigration to New South Wales,' 26 February 1833, SAFE/D 356/17, ML.
35. Printed circular included as an enclosure to Forster to Hay, 24 February 1834, CO 384:35, PRO 1039, National Library of Australia. (National Library of Australia hereafter referred to as 'NLA'.)
36. Joy Damousi, *Depraved and Disorderly: Female Convicts, Sexuality and Gender in Colonial Australia* (Cambridge, UK: Cambridge University Press, 1997); Anne Summers, *Damned Whores and God's Police: The Colonisation of Women in Australia*, new ed. (Sydney: NewSouth Publishing, 2016), chap. 8.
37. Reprinted as 'Advice to Free Females Arriving in the Colony Under the Auspices of His Majesty's Government', *Sydney Gazette*, 25 August 1832, 3.
38. Deborah Oxley and Eric Richards, 'Convict Women and Assisted Female Immigrants Compared: 1841—A Turning Point?' in *Visible Women: Female Immigrants in Colonial Australia*, Eric Richards, ed. (Canberra: Division of Historical Studies and Centre for Immigration and Multicultural Studies, Research School of Social Sciences, Australian National University, 1995), 1–58.
39. Two-thirds of the convict women had been domestic servants before transportation, the very occupation single female immigrants were recruited to fill. Raelene Frances, *Selling Sex: A Hidden History of Prostitution* (Sydney: University of New South Wales Press, 2007), 10.
40. Both groups were overwhelmingly in the fifteen-to-thirty age range— prime working and child-bearing years. Single female immigrants of the 1830s were, in fact, required to be within this age range. Convict data from Oxley and Richards, 'Convict Women and Assisted Female Immigrants Compared', in Richards, ed., *Visible Women*, 45.
41. Conveying large numbers of emigrants was a new endeavour for British officials. Accordingly, they relied on tried-and-true processes. Burnett to Dawson, 28 March 1835, CO 384:39, PRO 1040, NLA; Rushen and McIntyre, *The Merchant's Women*, 20.

42. A. James Hammerton, 'Gender and Migration', in *Gender and Empire*, Philippa Levine, ed. (New York: Oxford University Press, 2004), 164.
43. Rushen and McIntyre, *The Merchant's Women*, 47.
44. For descriptions of various arrivals, see 'The Free Females by the *Red Rover*', *Sydney Monitor*, 15 August 1832, 2; *Sydney Herald*, 19 December 1833, 2; *Sydney Gazette*, 8 November 1834, 2.
45. Babette Smith, *A Cargo of Women: Susannah Watson and the Convicts of the Princess Royal*, rev. ed. (Dural, NSW: Rosenberg, 2005), 35.
46. Deborah Oxley, 'Female Convicts', in *Convict Workers: Reinterpreting Australia's Past*, Stephen Nicholas, ed. (Cambridge: Cambridge University Press, 1988), 85–97.
47. *Sydney Gazette*, 1 November 1834, 2.
48. A task complicated by the fact that the mistress herself was a woman and, therefore, according to gender norms, was supposed to be submissive. See Victoria K. Haskins and Claire Lowrie, eds., *Colonization and Domestic Service: Historical and Contemporary Perspectives* (New York: Routledge, 2014), 42.
49. Oxley and Richards, 'Convict Women and Assisted Female Immigrants Compared', in Richards, ed., *Visible Women*, 35.
50. *Sydney Gazette*, 30 October 1834, 2.
51. *Sydney Gazette*, 18 August 1831, 2.
52. Reprinted as 'Advice to Free Females Arriving in the Colony Under the Auspices of His Majesty's Government', *Sydney Gazette*, 25 August 1832, 3.
53. Rushen and McIntyre were able to find marriage records for two-thirds of the women on the *Red Rover* and of the two-thirds they confirmed, sixty per cent married freed convicts. Rushen and McIntyre, *Fair Game*, chap. 7.
54. For example, see *Sydney Herald*, 13 October 1836, 2.
55. Robert Scott testimony in New South Wales Legislative Council, *Report of the Committee on Immigration, 1835*, 55.
56. Philalethes [pseud.], 'To the Editor of *The Colonist*', *The Colonist*, 26 February 1835, 4; *The Australian*, 9 October 1835, 2.
57. Here, I'm using 'prostitution' in the sense of commercial sex, while acknowledging that the word itself was often used to describe any kind of extra-marital sex.
58. 'Mr. Marshall's Pamphlet', *The Colonist*, 21 January 1836, 3.
59. 'State of the Female Factory', *Sydney Monitor*, 8 May 1833, 2; 'Mr. Marshall's Pamphlet', *The Colonist*, 21 January 1836, 3.
60. Frances, *Selling Sex*, chap. 2.
61. Rita S. Kranidis, *The Victorian Spinster and Colonial Emigration: Contested Subjects* (New York: St. Martin's Press, 1999), 6.

62. Though Cath Bishop and Desley Deacon revealed that there *were* other select employment opportunities open to colonial women via small businesses and bureaucratic employment (respectively), these opportunities became more constricted as the separate spheres ideal became more entrenched. Katrina Alford convincingly argued that, overall, women were not valued as economic actors. Catherine Bishop, *Minding Her Own Business: Colonial Businesswomen in Sydney* (Sydney: NewSouth Publishing, 2015); Desley Deacon, *Managing Gender: The State, the New Middle Class and Women Workers 1830–1930* (Melbourne: Oxford University Press, 1989); Katrina Alford, *Production or Reproduction?: An Economic History of Women in Australia, 1788–1850* (Melbourne: Oxford University Press, 1984).

63. Upon arrival, immigrant women were initially housed in a makeshift camp at the Lumber Yard. By 1836, after the Lumber Yard had been torn down, the women were temporarily housed in a ballroom at Government House. These facilities were only available until all the women had obtained initial employment. If a woman left a position without having her next 'situation' arranged, she could not return to the government-supplied accommodation.

64. Judith R. Walkowitz, 'The Politics of Prostitution and Sexual Labour', *History Workshop Journal* (2016): 188–198.

65. 'Female Immigrants,' *Sydney Monitor*, 15 June 1836, 2.

66. In Britain, it was not unheard of for working-class women to turn to prostitution temporarily during hard times. Anna Clark, *The Struggle for the Breeches: Gender and the Making of the British Working Class* (Berkeley: University of California Press, 1995), 50; Frances, *Selling Sex*, 26–27.

67. 'Emigration', *Sydney Gazette*, 10 November 1836, 2.

68. 'The Female Emigrants by the "David Scott"', *Sydney Monitor*, 5 November 1834, 2; 'Female Immigrants', *Sydney Monitor*, 15 June 1836, 2.

69. *The Australian*, 13 December 1836, 2.

70. 'Wisdom of the "Of-No-Sect"', *Sydney Monitor*, 31 October 1832, 2.

71. 'Fearful Scarcity of Labour', *Sydney Monitor*, 7 December 1836, 2.

72. Respectively, C. Lushington, 'Emigration to New South Wales', *Sydney Monitor*, 8 December 1832, 2; 'Fearful Scarcity of Labour', *Sydney Monitor*, 7 December 1836, 2.

73. New South Wales Legislative Council, *Report of the Committee on Immigration, 1835*, 8.

74. Forster to Hay, 1 July 1835, CO 384:38, PRO 1040, NLA.

75. Forster to Grey, 22 July 1836, CO 384:41, PRO 1041, NLA.

76. Hammerton, 'Gender and Migration', in Levine, ed., *Gender and Empire*, 160.

90   M. BURKETT

77. Including schemes to bring Irish orphan girls (see Harling), distressed needlewomen (see Hammerton), and middle-class spinsters (see Hammerton and Kranidis). Jan Gothard provided a thorough examination of the schemes after 1860. Gothard, *Blue China*; Philip Harling, 'Assisted Emigration and the Moral Dilemmas of the Mid-Victorian Imperial State', *The Historical Journal* 59, no. 4 (2016): 1027–1049; A. James Hammerton, *Emigrant Gentlewomen: Genteel Poverty and Female Emigration, 1830–1914* (London: Croom Helm, 1979); Kranidis, *The Victorian Spinster and Colonial Emigration*.

78. Chilton, 'Single Female Immigration and Australia's Early National Identity'; Hammerton, *Emigrant Gentlewomen*, chap. 4.

79. Hammerton, 'Gender and Migration', in Levine, ed., *Gender and Empire*, 156–180.

80. Gothard, *Blue China*, especially chaps. 2 and 7.

81. Forster to Hay, 25 July 1834, CO 384:35, PRO 1039, NLA.

SELECTED BIBLIOGRAPHY

Alford, Katrina. *Production or Reproduction? An Economic History of Women in Australia, 1788–1850*. Melbourne: Oxford University Press, 1984.

Chilton, Lisa. 'Single Female Immigration and Australia's Early National Identity'. *Australian Studies* 20, nos. 1–2 (2005): 209–232.

Damousi, Joy. *Depraved and Disorderly: Female Convicts, Sexuality and Gender in Colonial Australia*. Cambridge, UK: Cambridge University Press, 1997.

Davidoff, Leonore, and Catherine Hall. *Family Fortunes: Men and Women of the English Middle Class, 1780–1850*. Rev. ed. London: Routledge, 2002.

Frances, Raelene. *Selling Sex: A Hidden History of Prostitution*. Sydney: University of New South Wales Press, 2007.

Gothard, Janice. *Blue China: Single Female Migration to Colonial Australia*. Carlton South, VIC: Melbourne University Press, 2001.

Hammerton, A. J. '"Without Natural Protectors": Female Immigration to Australia, 1832–36'. *Historical Studies* 16, no. 65 (1975): 539–566.

Kranidis, Rita S. *The Victorian Spinster and Colonial Emigration: Contested Subjects*. New York: St. Martin's Press, 1999.

Levine, Philippa, ed. *Gender and Empire*. New York: Oxford University Press, 2004.

Richards, Eric, ed. *Visible Women: Female Immigrants in Colonial Australia*. Canberra: Division of Historical Studies and Centre for Immigration and Multicultural Studies, Research School of Social Sciences, Australian National University, 1995.

Rose, Sonya O. *Limited Livelihoods: Gender and Class in Nineteenth-Century England*. Berkeley: University of California Press, 1992.

Rushen, Elizabeth A. *Single and Free: Female Migration to Australia, 1833–1837.* Kew, VIC: Australian Scholarly Publishing, 2003.

Rushen, Elizabeth A., and Perry McIntyre. *Fair Game: Australia's First Immigrant Women.* Spit Junction, NSW: Anchor Books Australia, 2010.

———. *The Merchant's Women.* Spit Junction, NSW: Anchor Books Australia, 2008.

Searle, G. R. *Morality and the Market in Victorian Britain.* Oxford: Clarendon Press, 1998.

Summers, Anne. *Damned Whores and God's Police: The Colonisation of Women in Australia.* New ed. Sydney: NewSouth Publishing, 2016.

Tosh, John. *Manliness and Masculinities in Nineteenth-Century Britain: Essays on Gender, Family, and Empire.* Harlow, UK: Pearson Longman, 2005.

Walkowitz, Judith R. 'The Politics of Prostitution and Sexual Labour'. *History Workshop Journal* 82, no. 1 (2016): 188–198.

CHAPTER 5

Squatter-Cum-Pastoralist or Freeholder? How Differences in Nineteenth-Century Colonists' Experiences Affect Their Descendants' Historical Consciousness

Skye Krichauff

INTRODUCTION

Aboriginal people are largely absent in the historical consciousness of settler descended residents of mid-northern South Australia. When analysing this absence, an understanding of the concrete workings of memory and a recognition of historical contingencies—in particular the timing of arrival of a descendant's forebear and, inseparably, the nature and extent of this forebear's relations with Aboriginal people—are essential. Referring to British migrants who occupied land in South Australia's mid-north in the nineteenth century, this paper draws attention to differences in the experiences of squatters-cum-pastoralists and freeholders. Drawing on interviews and site visits conducted with both pastoralist and

---

S. Krichauff (✉)
University of Adelaide, Adelaide, SA, Australia
e-mail: skye.krichauff@adelaide.edu.au

© The Author(s) 2019   93
P. Payton and A. Varnava (eds.),
Australia, Migration and Empire, Britain and the World,
https://doi.org/10.1007/978-3-030-22389-2_5

freeholder descendants between 2010 and 2013, this chapter demonstrates how these differences in experience transfer through the generations to shape current generations' consciousness and oral narratives of the colonial past.

* * *

Numerous scholars from a variety of disciplines are interested in understanding settler descended Australians' consciousness of the colonial past and, in particular, how historical injustices suffered by Aboriginal people are remembered.[1] However, I suggest that such studies do not pay adequate attention to the concrete workings of memory; the multitudinous ways through which the past is known and, significantly, the *relationship between* these different ways of knowing the past are neither ethnographically examined nor evaluated. Another problem is the tendency to conflate and homogenise aspects of the colonial past and current rural experiences. This is done by: referring to all who occupied land in rural districts during the colonial period under the homogenous term 'settlers'; understanding sparsely settled rural regions distant from the capital cities in the colonial period as 'the frontier'; assuming those who have generational connections with rural districts are closer to the violence of the frontier than other non-Aboriginal Australians; and assuming that people living in rural areas are more likely to have contact with Aboriginal people than people living in urban areas.[2] However, Aboriginal and non-Aboriginal people's experiences of colonialism were diverse and specific to the era, area, invaders and inhabitants of the land occupied; contingencies such as geography, topography, vegetation and availability of water and other natural resources affected colonial cross-cultural relations, as did differences between Aboriginal groups and types of colonists. With regard to colonists, their place of origin, previous experiences and social and economic position require consideration. For example, were the new arrivals novices to the act of colonising or did they come from other Australian colonies or other parts of the British Empire? Were they practical people? Did they have farming or labouring backgrounds or were they entrepreneurs keen to make a quick fortune? This chapter demonstrates how, when making sense of setter descended Australians' consciousness of the nineteenth century past and the process of colonisation, there is a need for nuanced histories that recognise diversity in colonial experience.

This chapter is divided into four sections. The first outlines findings regarding the presence or absence of Aboriginal people in mid-northern settler descendants' historical consciousness. These findings, drawn from fieldwork conducted between 2010 and 2013, are compared with those of other scholars who are similarly interested in non-Aboriginal Australians' consciousness of Australia's colonial past and contemporary race relations. The second section argues for the significance of experience in shaping what aspects of the past are remembered and recalled through the generations. The third section draws on archival records to differentiate between the experiences of nineteenth-century colonists. It proposes that squatters-cum-pastoralists can be crudely divided into three broad groups and that the nature and extent of relations with Aboriginal people varied between these groups. It subsequently differentiates between freeholders and squatters-cum-pastoralists and their relations with Aboriginal people. The concluding section demonstrates how these differences between nineteenth-century settlers' experiences transfer through the generations to shape the way current descendants understand and remember the colonial past.

SETTING THE SCENE

In the concluding session of the inaugural Eric Richards Symposium, keynote speaker Alison Bashford summarised the diversity and scope of papers presented over the four-day conference. Bashford deduced that Australian humanities scholars were currently preoccupied—'obsessed even'—with the topic of settler colonialism. In twenty-first-century Australia, themes of colonial violence and its repercussions are explored in a variety of ways in popular culture—through television series, documentaries, theatrical productions, museum exhibitions and literary outputs. It is currently standard for public events to open with an acknowledgement that the event is being held on Aboriginal land and a statement that current descendants' cultural and spiritual links with that land have not been broken.

However, this seemingly widespread fascination with the Aboriginal–settler past is not ubiquitous throughout Australia. Between 2010 and 2013, I conducted a series of qualitative interviews and went on site visits with over fifty settler descendants from the mid-north of South Australia. I also surveyed the public spaces of twenty-two mid-northern towns and the extensive collection of local histories held by the State

Library of South Australia. (It is worth noting that most of these written histories were produced in the 1970s and 1980s to celebrate the centenaries of the founding of various towns and districts.) Among those I interviewed and in the public spaces I examined, I found an overwhelming absence of knowledge and information about Aboriginal people. The currently accepted names of the traditional owners—Ngadjuri, Nukunu and Kaurna—did not appear on public signs in any of the towns I surveyed, and, during interviews, it was clear that these words were unfamiliar to local residents. There was no mention of 'Aboriginal' or 'Indigenous' on any of the information boards or commemorative plaques with one exception; in Crystal Brook's central pedestrian strip, under the theme 'exploration', Aboriginal people are mentioned once, under the first heading 'footsteps'. Regarding the written histories, *if* Aboriginal people are mentioned, it is generally as a precursor or footnote to the main story or as an obstacle pastoralists had to contend with. These centenary histories are respected and referred to sources of information about the colonial era for local residents. Three local histories published in the 1990s were the only indication that the centenary histories have been added to or amended in accord with contemporary understandings evident at the national and state levels.[3] The lack of reference to Aboriginal people was equally pronounced in the memories and oral narratives of those I interviewed; one man succinctly summarised local sentiment when he stated 'it felt like we were the original owners, had been forever'.[4] A liberal-minded, tertiary-educated business woman who has lived most of her adult life in Sydney and Adelaide was amazed it had 'never occurred' to her (before our conversation) 'that Aboriginal people were here [her family's property near Riverton] before us'.[5]

The lack of recognition that Aboriginal people lived on and owned the land prior to the arrival of Europeans and the absence of Aboriginal people in non-Aboriginal Australians' consciousness of the colonial and twentieth century past is not confined to the geographical area or the social group that were the focus of my study. In 1968, Bill Stanner interpreted this absence as a silencing when he famously drew attention to the 'great Australian silence'. Other scholars have interpreted this absence in a variety of ways—as a 'forgetting' or, drawing on psychoanalytical theories, as symptomatic of disavowal, repression or denial.[6] However, although compelling, such explanations are not necessarily universally accurate or useful. They assume pre-existing knowledge that is denied. However, my mid-northern interviewees genuinely *didn't know* or had *never thought* about the historical presence and experiences of Aboriginal people. In this, my findings align with those of Peter Read who found that rural people living 'out-West' of Sydney have a 'historical and contemporary *ignorance* of Aboriginality'.[7] Likewise, in an article aptly titled 'What settler Australians talk about when they talk about Aborigines: Reflections on an in-depth study', Anthony Moran concludes that 'Aborigines still stand outside many people's social worlds both physically and imaginatively' and for many 'thinking of Aboriginal issues involved a difficult imaginative leap'.[8]

This ignorance is not due to a lack of information; as Ann Curthoys and Mitchell Rolls have pointed out, at least since the late 1960s and steadily increasing since then, numerous papers and books expressly concerned with Aboriginal people have been published and reissued, policies concerning Aboriginal people have been debated in parliament, and the actions of Aboriginal advocacy groups and their non-Aboriginal supporters have been (and continue to be) well reported in the media through newspapers, journals, magazines and radio broadcasts.[9] The visual and performing arts and literature, the Native Title Act and amendments to that Act (in 1993 and 1998) and Prime Minister Rudd's official apology to the Stolen Generations in 2008 have continually drawn public attention to the injustice of British colonisation and its enduring ramifications.

This multitude of available information has caused Mitchell Rolls to understand the absence of Aboriginal people in Australians' consciousness as a 'confected ignorance', an 'averted gaze'.[10] But I argue that mid-northern settler descendants' lack of knowledge regarding the historical experiences of Aboriginal people is not confected. My interviewees are relatively well educated; they have completed their secondary schooling, listen to the national broadcasting corporation (the Australian Broadcasting Corporation) and possess detailed knowledge about the lives of their colonial forebears. As freehold title holders, they, like urban dwellers, are under no threat from Native Title. They were sincere when they asked if Aboriginal people had ever lived in the local district or, more poignantly, on their property—they genuinely wanted to know. They were not hostile or defensive when I told them I was speaking with Aboriginal descendants or when I asked them what they thought about the fact that, while they continue to live on land occupied by their forebears, this was not the case for Aboriginal descendants. As such, why— despite the current preoccupation of government and community leaders and scholars and despite publicly available information and if they are not denying or repressing pre-existing knowledge—why are Aboriginal

98   S. KRICHAUFF

people's colonial experiences not known and why is Aboriginal history perceived as separate from or irrelevant to settler descendants' family histories and the history of the local district?

CONCRETE WORKINGS OF MEMORY
AND THE SIGNIFICANCE OF EXPERIENCE

Numerous historians from a variety of fields—including settler-colonial studies, the memory of frontier violence, cross-cultural history and the social memory of Australian colonialism—are interested in understanding non-Aboriginal Australians' consciousness of Aboriginal–settler relations and the colonial past. Nevertheless, there is a seemingly widespread lack of contemplation regarding the different ways information about the past is known and made sense of and the different degrees to which knowledge of the past is incorporated into an individual's and a collective's consciousness.

In deepening understandings of a society's historical consciousness, Pierre Nora's distinction between the past known through abstract means (such as through 'history') and the past known through lived experience and everyday life (through 'memory) is useful.[11] Nora separates *milieux de mémoire* ('settings in which memory is a real part of experience') and the past learned through history—through *lieux de mémoire* (sites consecrated to preserving and embodying our memories).[12] He describes 'true memory' as memory experienced from within, which is social, collective, all-embracing and exists in gestures, habits, intimate physical knowledge, ingrained reminiscences and spontaneous reflexes.[13] On the other hand, 'historicized memory'—'memory grasped by history'—is experienced from without; it is individual and subjective, wilful and deliberate.[14]

Other memory scholars similarly stress the important link between experience and memory and clearly state that neither collective nor individual memory is 'a terrain where anything goes'.[15] As Geoffrey Cubitt points out, nothing will be transmitted 'unless someone or other has at some time remembered it on the basis of personal experience and communicated this memory to others'.[16] At the individual level, Michel de Certeau and Luce Giard draw on studies of cognitive processes to affirm that people draw on their own experiences when making sense of the past (or indeed any new information):

New information is received and assimilated, that is, becomes appropriable and memorizable, only when the person acquiring it succeeds in putting it into *his or her own form*, in making it his or her own by inserting it ... into the coherencies that structure his or her previous knowledge. Failing to pass through this stage, new information will remain fragile and at any moment likely to be forgotten, distorted or contradicted.[17]

At the collective level, Iwona Irwin-Zarecka argues for the need to keep in view the 'experiential bases on which collective memory rests'.[18] Klaus Neumann has found the histories told in specific places are 'closely related to very specific experiences'.[19] More broadly, in *Gunfighter Nation*, Richard Slotkin demonstrates how myths arise in the course of human experience and how they have human/historical sources and are created and recreated in the midst of historical contingency.[20]

It is the *connection with experience* that is crucial in understanding the extent to which 'external' knowledge is absorbed and remembered. I found that, with regard to settler descendants who have grown up on land occupied by their forebears in the nineteenth century, their understandings of the colonial past are based on their own lived experiences and aspects of reality experienced by their forebears. In short, different experiences generate different consciousness. As such, in order to gain a deep and comprehensive understanding of the presence or absence of Aboriginal people in my interviewees' historical consciousness, a detailed awareness of historical events—in this case the extent and nature of their forebears' relations with Aboriginal people—is imperative. In the following section, I demonstrate how details such as a colonist's place of origin, social class, previous experience and individual personality are significant.

THE LIVED EXPERIENCES OF NINETEENTH-CENTURY COLONISTS: DIFFERENCES BETWEEN SQUATTERS-CUM-PASTORALISTS

A brief outline of the history of European occupation of the mid-north of South Australia demonstrates significant differences between the experiences of colonists who arrived in the early colonial period (the early 1840s to the 1860s) and those who arrived in the later colonial period (from the 1870s). After South Australia was officially proclaimed a British colony in December 1836, land surveys did not keep up with immigrants' demands for land. In the mid-north, squatters began spreading to unsurveyed districts by the early 1840s. Seeking well-watered, richly pastured land, they legitimised their right to graze stock through the purchase of occupation licences. Regardless of the size of the run, squatters paid £5 for a licence with an additional sixpence per head of cattle and penny per head of sheep.[21] Although the cost of a licence was low, the requirement that the licence holder adequately stock their run meant that those who could not afford to purchase ample sheep or cattle were restricted in the amount of land they could lay claim to. In the early years of the colony, it was those who had the funds to adequately stock their runs in accordance with the requirements of the licence who were able to secure vast tracts of rich land with permanent water sources. This country was of great spiritual, economic, social and political significance to its Aboriginal owners.

The Crown could resume or annul occupation licences with little notice, and squatters sought a more secure arrangement. From 1851, pastoral leases of fourteen-year duration replaced occupation licences. Pastoral leases provided greater revenue for the financially struggling colonial government. Land was classed according to its rainfall and stock carrying capacity; pastoralists paid £1 per square mile for first-class land, 15 shillings for second class land and 10 shillings for third class. In 1861, sixpence per head of stock was added to the fee. However, the Crown retained the right to resume land on 'adequate notice' albeit with compensation for any 'improvements' made (such as fences, wells, sheds). At the earliest opportunity, those who could afford it purchased the freehold of the prime land on which they had built their homesteads and significant improvements.

Occupation licence holders generally retained the best country on their existing runs when pastoral leases were introduced. Boundaries between leases became more clearly defined, and the area of land occupied more accurately recorded. These squatters-cum-pastoralists occupied huge tracts of land which was measured in square miles rather than acres during a period when Aboriginal people were ever present. For all—the overwhelming majority of whom were men—the potential for enormous profits outweighed the risks involved in 'opening up' a new district. Nevertheless, some broad distinctions can be made between these invaders in regard to their connection with the country they occupied and their relations with Aboriginal people, and even this broad categorisation of pastoral experience can reveal the differential impact of such experience upon memory.

I suggest there were three types of squatter-cum-pastoralist although distinctions between the three are by no means clear cut. First, there were those who had ready access to substantial amounts of capital. Men such as the Browne and Hallett brothers, Joseph Gilbert and Price Maurice who leased much of the country in or near the North-East Highland district (about 200 km north of Adelaide) are typical of this type of pastoralist. William and John Browne originated from Wiltshire. Both had medical degrees from Edinburgh University. They arrived in Adelaide aged in their early twenties in 1839 and 1840, respectively. The Brownes leased 160 square miles of country known as the Booborowie/Canowie run in the early 1840s.[22] They purchased the freehold of 46,978 acres of the Booborowie run in 1863.[23] John Hallett (aged in his early thirties) and his younger brother Alfred arrived from England in 1836 and 1838, respectively. In the early 1840s, the Hallett brothers were granted 'Lease no. 10'—'Willogoleche'—which consisted of about 200 square miles and included the mountain Mt Bryan (named by Governor Gawler), the Razorback Range and the areas on which the future townships of Hallett and Mt Bryan were built.[24] The southern part of the Willogoleche run was known as Wandillah. The Hallett brothers sold the northern half of the run (Willogoleche) to the Brownes' brother-in-law, Joseph Gilbert.[25] Gilbert originated from Wiltshire and was 39 years when he arrived in South Australia in 1839. In 1851, an occupation licence containing 156 square miles was issued to Gilbert for a run (which became known as Mt Bryan station) between the Halletts' and the Brownes' runs.[26] He purchased the freehold of 10 square miles of the Mt Bryan run in 1881. Price Maurice originated from Wrexham, England, and arrived in South Australia in 1840 aged 22 years. In the mid-1840s, he acquired pastoral leases for the Pekina and Oladdie runs, totalling 617 square miles.[27]

These well-educated and entrepreneurial men had access to significant sums of money which enabled them to weather the financial risks involved in opening up 'new' country (i.e. land previously unoccupied by Europeans). They could afford to stock their enormous leases, erect substantial stone dwellings (homesteads and wool sheds) and employ overseers to manage their runs while they resided in Adelaide or on country estates closer to Adelaide (whose freehold titles they had purchased). They controlled enormous landholdings across the colony—for example, the Brownes had licences and freehold title to land in the south-east near Mt Gambier, on Eyre Peninsula and the Flinders Ranges and at Buckland

Park nearer to Adelaide. These squatters-cum-pastoralists did not put down roots on their mid-northern pastoral stations and I suggest they are best understood as absentee pastoralists rather than settlers.

A second type of pastoralist was those like the Hawker brothers who occupied Bungaree (approximately 100 square miles) in December 1841, the Hughes brothers who leased Bundaleer (312 square miles) and Booyoolee (194 square miles) in 1842 and the White brothers who occupied land in the southern Flinders in 1843 (by 1853, the Whites had leased an area totalling 269 square miles).[28] Bungaree, Booyoolee and Bundaleer are in the central hill country of the mid-north. These men had access to moderate amounts of capital provided by their families in England which they used to purchase flocks, employ a few servants and erect basic but comparatively comfortable slab dwellings in which they resided.[29] Initially, the brothers worked as partners, pooling their resources while building up their flocks and stations. When they had established their runs and, more significantly, when the danger of cross-cultural violence had diminished, they married, bringing their brides to their leases and raising their children on them. These pastoralists played an active role in building up their properties albeit with the assistance of servants who worked as shepherds, stock-keepers and hut-keepers.

In South Australia's mid-north, both the first and second type of pastoralists were primarily middle to upper class, educated men who had not previously laboured as farmers or graziers. They were well off and not used to roughing it. Unlike their wealthier, absentee counterparts however, members of second group appear to have felt great satisfaction in physically participating in developing their pastoral properties. Although at the earliest opportunity all purchased freehold title to the land on which they had built their homesteads, shearing sheds and men's quarters, members of the second group were emotionally attached to their properties and, after the resumption of their leases, tended to retain their freehold sections for subsequent generations.

The third type of pastoralist initially had no capital to adequately stock large areas of land, employ others or erect comfortable dwellings. They included the likes of Billy Dare—a Cockney who arrived in South Australia parentless and penniless aged fourteen in 1838—and families like the Marchants who initially worked for the Browne brothers on their Booborowie/Canowie run and whose numerous children were put to work as shepherds and hut-keepers.[30] Dare gradually increased his flocks by shepherding for others. By pooling resources with friends, he eventually managed to scrape together enough money to jointly take out an occupation licence. This third type of pastoralist generally occupied drier and less sought after runs; Dare squatted on and then leased low rainfall, saltbush country (Piltimiltiappa) east of Burra while the Marchants occupied the Mannanarie run (north of Jamestown). They had no or few servants, lived in crudely constructed, basic huts and suffered the privations of squatting life while building up their flocks and fortunes.

In the mid-north, although there were a few Scots and Irish, the squatters-cum-pastoralists who occupied and leased land in the early pastoral years were predominantly English. This contrasts with the Port Phillip district during the same period where many squatters were Scottish.[31] The majority of mid-northern squatters who resided on their leases were young men in their twenties and thirties who, before arriving in South Australia, had little or no previous experience of life in the Australian colonies. This too contrasts with the Port Phillip district where experienced squatters oozed over the porous New South Wales border or crossed Bass Strait from Van Diemen's Land. While the bulk of the Port Phillip squatters' labour force was assigned servants, ticket-of-leave men or absconded convicts, South Australia's mid-northern squatters generally employed people with no previous colonial experience who, like themselves, arrived in the colony after it was officially established in 1836. There are, of course, exceptions to these broad generalisations. For example, Irishman EB Gleeson arrived in the Clare district in 1840. He came from India and brought 'coolies' (Indian servants) with him who worked as shepherds. Gleeson did not initially reside on his run, but employed a Scottish overseer, MacDonald, to manage it for him.[32]

So, is it possible to distinguish between the relations these different types of squatter-cum-pastoralist had with Aboriginal people?

SQUATTER-CUM-PASTORALISTS' RELATIONS WITH ABORIGINAL PEOPLE

During the early pastoral years, Aboriginal people outnumbered the Europeans and cross-cultural encounters were frequent. This was a frontier—a place of cross-cultural fusion, accommodation and friendship, but also of uncertainty and tension, violence and brutality.[33] Interactions were generally characterised by an initial, short-lived period of wariness followed by a brief period of friendly relations in which the newcomers gave gifts of mutton and other foods and goods. The squatters' adoption (or appropriation) of Aboriginal place names for their leases is a powerful reminder of cross-cultural communication and interaction. However, Aboriginal confidence in the peaceful intentions of the newcomers was soon shattered when pastoralists and their employees reacted violently to Aboriginal people's taking of stock and when Aboriginal men reacted violently to the misuse of their women and/or the newcomers' failure to compensate them for sexual relations with Aboriginal women.

There are no hard and fast rules regarding the nature of each pastoralist's relations with Aboriginal people. Much depended on an individual's personality, previous experience and family background. And although all arrived with a perception that Aboriginal people were primitive and uncivilised—the Europeans' social and cultural inferiors—some were more influenced than others by the humanitarian lobbyists who occupied powerful positions in the Colonial Office at the time of South Australia's establishment.

The wealthier pastoralists did not reside on their runs and were not involved in the day-to-day running of their leases. It is reasonable to assume that they did not have strong connections with the local people. It is also fair to say that, for these entrepreneurial men, a fervent desire to increase their profits took priority over any concerns for those whose land they had invaded. Many (if not most) of these absentee pastoralists condoned and even encouraged the repression of Aboriginal people. They employed overseers to do the dirty work that inevitably accompanied what colonists euphemistically referred to as the 'opening up' of a new country. Overseers made sure the local people understood that the newcomers were here to stay and would not tolerate Aboriginal people taking stock. I suggest that pastoralists employed overseers whose morals aligned with their own. This is exemplified by John Hallett. In 1843, Hallett's overseer, William Moore Carter, was found responsible for the deaths of two Aboriginal people near Mount Bryan. During police investigations, Hallett evaded answering questions in order to protect Carter. The Attorney General considered Hallett's conduct questionable, particularly as he was 'a gentleman who is himself in the commission of police'.[34] Further north, Price Maurice employed JF Hayward as overseer of his Pekina run from 1847 to 1850. Hayward's diary is filled with descriptions of persecuting 'thieving' and 'troublesome' Aboriginal people for taking stock. Hayward states that the natives 'had to be terrified before their depredations ceased, and that pretty well lasted my sojourn, say three and a half years' and that 'these campaigns against the niggers gave a zest to the wild life I led'.[35]

Magistrates on the frontiers of European settlement were comprised of members of the landed classes, and, as Amanda Nettelbeck and Robert Foster point out, a culture of solidarity and self-interest influenced officials acting as magistrates.[36] For example, when George Hawker acted as a magistrate, he altered Carter's original deposition to prevent Carter's judicial prosecution. However, the actions of Henry Price, the manager of the Brownes' Booborowie and Canowie stations in 1843, demonstrate the danger in homogenising pastoralists' and their employees' complicity and solidarity. Appointed a Justice of the Peace, Price took Carter's initial deposition. Appalled at Carter's brutal actions, he attempted to assure Carter's prosecution. On learning that Carter, through Hawker, had altered his statement, Price and the Attorney General questioned Hawker's actions. Carter escaped prosecution and fled to the north where he was involved in another violent incident (in which no lives were lost). On learning of this, Price wrote to Carter's new employers, the White brothers, informing them 'how improper a person Carter was'.[37] The Whites immediately dismissed Carter.

In contrast with the absentee pastoralists, the second and third types of pastoralist were in much closer and more frequent contact with local Aboriginal people. Initial relations were often friendly, but, within a short time, showdowns over stock, Aboriginal women and resources occurred. Reading through the diaries of George Hawker, Herbert Bristow Hughes and other early pastoralists, there is no doubt that many of those who were present in the 1840s were personally involved in physical conflict with Aboriginal people during their initial occupation of Aboriginal land.[38] For example, within days of their arrival at Bungaree in December 1841 and lasting until the second half of 1842, George Hawker's diary entries show his own and his employees' initial nervousness and tendency to react violently in tense situations. In general, most newcomers attempted to assert their power and authority physically. Some 'affrays' were reported—particularly if they involved shepherds or hut-keepers firing on Aboriginal people in alleged self-defence or to repossess stock. In reporting such cases, pastoralists and their staff sought to draw the government's attention to the lack of police presence in the newly settled districts—they understood they would be unlikely to suffer any judicial punishment but might, at worst, receive a caution from the Protector of Aborigines, Matthew Moorhouse.

However, within a reasonably short time, the second and third group of pastoralists appear to have come to some sort of understanding with the local people. For Billy Dare, this began immediately—he arrived in the district in which he was to settle in the company of Aboriginal people and a group of thirty or more lived with him for the next few decades.[39] For the Hawker brothers, amicable relations were seemingly established within twelve months of their arrival; by 26 August 1842, Hawker writes that he 'fenced in part of the wheat [with] the blacks helping. Made an arrangement with them'.[40] In December 1843, when Protector Moorhouse visited the Hawkers' station, he found '37 natives there', 'more than the average number as they had assembled for circumcising two boys'.[41] Moorhouse subsequently suggested the government distribute flour at Bungaree. By June 1845, George Hawker was annoyed that no blankets were sent to 'his blacks' for the annual Queens Birthday distribution.[42] In 1850, a census recorded 70 Aboriginal people at Bungaree.[43]

Some squatters-cum-pastoralists who resided on their runs developed long-term relations with local Aboriginal people. They became paternalistic protectors of 'their blacks' who were named in official documents according to the station on which they resided (e.g. 'Bungaree blacks'). The mass exodus of workmen who left the colony to try their luck at the Victorian gold diggings facilitated more reciprocal and accommodating relations. From 1851, Aboriginal people in the mid-north were, in general, suitably rewarded and respected for their work as shepherds, shearers and general station hands. For example, the Hughes' two stations Booyoolee and Bundaleer became places Aboriginal people felt it was safe to reside and were adequately compensated for their labour. By the 1850s, numerous Indian, Chinese and Aboriginal people were employed as shepherds and hut-keepers on these stations.[44]

The Arrival of Freeholders

After the Waste Lands Amendment Act (also known as the Strangways Act) was passed in South Australia in 1869, the colonial government gradually resumed, surveyed and subdivided the enormous mid-northern pastoral leases. From this time, settlers were able to purchase 80-acre freehold blocks and began arriving in large numbers. Towns began to form and, with them, the so-called signs of civilisation—churches, schools, shops and sporting clubs.

Although it was not uncommon for pastoralists to purchase land that had originally been part of their pastoral lease, very few pastoralist descendants remained in the mid-north. The entrepreneurial absentee pastoralists tended to be transient men primarily interested in making a quick fortune. On the resumption of their leases, they leased land in more distant districts with a substantial number returning to England to live. By 1861, the Whites had sold their leases and freehold sections and moved back to England.[45] The Brownes dissolved their partnership in 1866 and returned to England, after which their estate was controlled by trustees (Booborowie station was sold and subdivided in 1897, three years after William Browne's death).[46] Joseph Gilbert sold the freehold of 10 square miles of the Mt Bryan run in 1883. The Hallett brothers retained 14,000 acres of their southern section which was sold at public auction in 1877 after Alfred's death.[47] By the latter twentieth century, only the descendants of Billy Dare and the Hawker brothers continued to live on land occupied by their pastoralist forebears.

The limited number of descendants of early pastoralists who remained in districts occupied by their forebears is in stark contrast to the large number of freeholder descendants who continue to live on land occupied by their nineteenth-century forebears. Regarding the freeholders' relations with Aboriginal people, historical records and the oral narratives of both settler and Aboriginal descendants show that, by the time freeholders arrived, few Aboriginal people were living in the mid-north.[48] Although frontier violence and the psychological and physical trauma of restricted or denied access to ones' own country undoubtedly played a role, the majority of mid-northern Aboriginal people died of introduced diseases. Smallpox, tuberculosis, measles, whooping cough and typhus affected people of all ages while venereal diseases greatly reduced the birth rate and left females infertile.[49] In 1851, reporting on his tour of neighbouring Yorke Peninsula (less than five years after the peninsula was first invaded by Europeans and their stock), the Protector of Aborigines stated 'the native women were in a fearful state of disease' and 'three fourths of both men and women have become affected by it'.[50] A census taken in April 1871 records that groups of Aboriginal people living in the vast mid-north had populations in their tens or less.[51] In the North-Eastern Highlands, only one man and one woman were recorded as living near Mt Bryan in 1871. By the time the 1891 census was collected, no Aboriginal people were recorded as living in the Burra County, a large area which included Mt Bryan, Hallett and Booborowie.[52] Tragically (and preventably), within three decades of European occupation, Aboriginal populations which numbered in their hundreds in 1836 were reduced to twenty or less. As such, opportunities for interaction between the newly arrived freeholders and the traditional owners were limited.

THE LIVED EXPERIENCES OF CURRENT GENERATIONS

As previously stated, current generations' consciousness of the colonial past is based on aspects of reality actually experienced by previous generations of their family and their own lived experiences. As such, to comprehensively understand members of a particular group's consciousness of Aboriginal–settler relations and the colonial past, ethnographic studies that recognise an informant's lifestyle, education, gender, socio-economic group, occupation and place(s) of habitation are necessary. Mid-northern settler descendants who remain connected to land occupied by members of their family since the nineteenth century spent their formative years residing in houses built by their forebears and in landscapes scattered with tangible reminders of the lives of previous generations (including sheds, troughs, stone tanks, chimneys and trees). During interviews and site visits, these settler descendants demonstrated their knowledge of the history of their family. It was clear that, whether of pastoralist or freeholder descent, mid-northern settler descendants' consciousness of the colonial past is orientated around their first forebear (generally a male) to arrive in the district and occupy land that became the family property. Although their sense of history predates their forebear's arrival in the district (e.g. settler descendants know their forebear's place of origin, reasons for leaving, who accompanied him on his voyage out, experiences in the colony before arriving in the district in which he was to settle), because orientated around their 'foundation' forebear, their sense of the history *of the district* begins with their forebear's arrival.[53] They live in close geographical proximity with other settler descendants who are part of their social community and with whom they share histories of generational presence in place. Mid-northern settler descendants' knowledge of the past does not primarily or most powerfully come through history books, political statements or commemorative plaques (Nora's *lieux de mémoire*—sites consecrated to preserving and embodying our memories) but through 'settings in which memory is a real part of experience' (Nora's *milieux de mémoire*).

For this reason, the physical presence or absence of traditional owners—both historically and currently—is a significant factor which requires consideration when seeking to understand the presence or absence of Aboriginal people in settler descendants' historical consciousness. Like many non-Aboriginal Australians, my interviewees grew up in an era and a place where no traditional owners were present, when the historical experiences of Aboriginal people were not part of the school curriculum and the injustice of colonialism was not part of general knowledge or discussion. Those who now identify as Ngadjuri learned of their Ngadjuri heritage in the 1990s and are currently in the process of establishing a presence in the mid-north and reconnecting with the land of their ancestors. While no Ngadjuri descendants live in the communities or districts that were the focus of my research, a small group of Nukunu descendants have continuously remained on portions of their ancestral land—at Port Germein, Baroota Reserve and Port Augusta. However, no Nukunu have lived on the eastern side of the southern Flinders Ranges (the Wirrabara district) since the 1920s. In addition, the repressive and racist political and social atmosphere which predominated throughout the first three quarters of the twentieth century limited the extent to which Aboriginal people outwardly voiced their Aboriginality. For these reasons, Aboriginal people were not—either physically or intellectually—part of my non-Aboriginal interviewees' everyday lives or lived world during my interviewees' formative years.

Individual and Collective Memory of the Early Pastoral Years

The importance of recognising the significance of the lived experiences of both my interviewees and their forebears when analysing the absence of Aboriginal people in settler descendants' narratives became clear to me when I examined how the *pastoral era* and the *squatters-cum-pastoralists* feature in local residents' historical consciousness. During interviews and site visits, I learned that knowledge of the early pastoralists is not part of mid-northerners' collective memory. For local residents, the history of the district is understood as beginning with arrival of freeholders and the founding of the local town or district. In the public spaces of the towns I surveyed, there are virtually no references to the pastoralists or the pastoral era with a few informative exceptions, namely the townships of Hallett, Laura and Crystal Brook. Hallett was named after the Hallett brothers, and Laura was the first name of early pastoralist Edwin White's wife. This information is mentioned on the relevant towns' information boards. Descendants of the Hughes brothers still own (but do not reside on) Booyoolie which lies directly adjacent to the town of Crystal Brook, and the property and Hughes brothers are mentioned on Crystal Brook's information board. However, as is tangibly demonstrated by the centenary plaques which feature in the public spaces of every town I surveyed, it is not the pastoralists but the people who arrived *after* the land was subdivided who are recognised as pioneers and who are commemorated (Figs. 5.1, 5.2, and 5.3).

In their conversations with me, freeholder descendants did not mention the pastoral era. When I raised the topic, I soon learned that very little was known about the early pastoralists. In stark contrast, descendants of early pastoralists were knowledgeable about the pastoral era and had stories about Aboriginal people. However, mid-northern residents who have forebears who arrived in the 1840s and 1850s are well and truly in the minority, and people compose their memories and narratives in accord with the norms of the society in which they are ensconced.[54] Prevailing understandings of Aboriginal absence have influenced the remembrance and articulation of pastoralist descendants' scant stories of Aboriginal presence.[55] Among the few mid-northerners who *did* have stories of Aboriginal presence in the colonial era, Aboriginal people were not conceptualised as actively communicating with or establishing relations with their forebears or other Europeans, or as participating in the pastoral industry or contributing to the 'progress' and 'development' of the district. Instead, a settler-colonial narrative in which Aboriginal people's experiences and histories are perceived as separate from the Europeans framed their understandings.

5 SQUATTER-CUM-PASTORALIST OR FREEHOLDER? ... 111

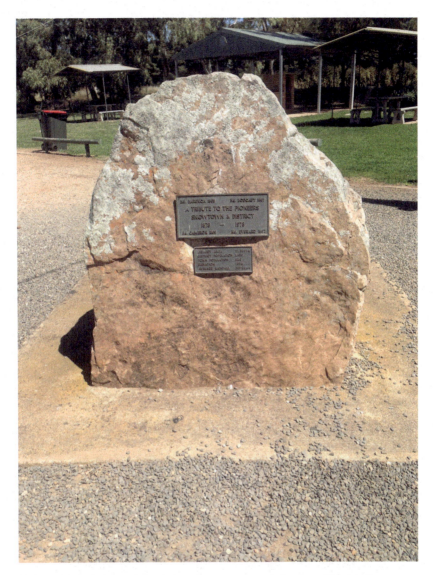

Fig. 5.1 A tribute to the pioneers, Snowtown and district 1878–1978

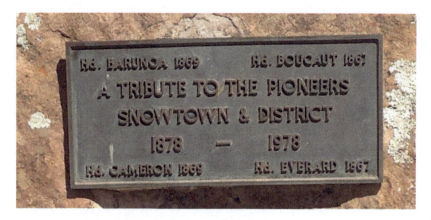

Fig. 5.2 Detail of the Snowtown centenary plaque

Fig. 5.3 Dedicated to the pioneers of Redhill, on the occasion of the centenary celebrations 1969

Conclusion

My finding that both Aboriginal people *and* pastoralists are absent in the overwhelming majority of mid-northern settler descendants' historical consciousness is significant. It led me to question whether the collective absence of knowledge about the pastoral years and the lack of reference to the pastoralists and their employees can be interpreted as a silencing or forgetting—as symptomatic of settler denial, disavowal or repression. In answering this question, it seemed to me that alternative explanations were required and that these explanations can be usefully applied to deepen our understanding of the absence of Aboriginal people in other non-Aboriginal Australians' consciousness.

I reiterate that, taking into account the concrete workings of settler descendants' memories, it is clear that, at the individual and family level, mid-northerners' consciousness of the colonial past begins with the first forebear of that family to arrive in the district in which he was to settle. I have remarked that, although my interviewees may have had access to wider information about Aboriginal history, this information hasn't resonated or connected with them. When seeking to understand this sense of distance, it is important to take into account the concrete workings of memory. It is the *connection with experience* that is crucial in understanding the extent to which 'external' knowledge is absorbed and remembered. The physical and social experience of face-to-face interaction, first-hand observation and everyday life differs fundamentally from 'an awareness' of an issue gained through external sources such as the media, literature or creative arts. Thus, when scholars such as Mitchell Rolls ask 'How does one reconcile experience – an awareness of Aboriginal deprivation and dispossession' that comes from the availability of an extensive range of literature, creative work and media coverage with Australians' 'systematic refusal to seek or trace the causal trajectory?', I argue for the value in distinguishing between different types of experience.[56] For settler descended Australians with social and geographical connections to place which extend back to the nineteenth century, the colonial past is not best known or made sense of through abstract means, through reading about it in books or newspapers, through history lessons or documentaries. Instead, the past most powerfully known and related to has been learned through everyday life and made sense of through lived experience. This is a key reason why, rather than incorporating externally acquired knowledge about Aboriginal people into their consciousness of the colonial past, mid-northern settler descendants see it as distant, as not relevant to themselves, their family's history or the history of the district in which they live.

My argument regarding the need to recognise the concrete workings of memory and, relatedly, to draw on the lived experiences of both current and previous generations when making sense of non-Aboriginal Australian's inability to connect their family's histories with the histories of Aboriginal people is applicable to other geographical areas and other groups. This chapter has aimed to demonstrate the value of nuanced histories that recognise the specificity and diversity of nineteenth-century colonists' experiences. The experiences of squatters-cum-pastoralists should not be conflated with the experiences of nineteenth-century freeholders, and historical contingencies must be genuinely taken into account. Aboriginal people outnumbered the newcomers during the early pastoral years when cross-cultural interactions were unpredictable and frequent, but, by the 1870s, there was little opportunity for cross-cultural interaction. This reality is reflected in the historical consciousness of the overwhelming majority of my interviewees' whose forebears arrived as freeholders from the early 1870s. By recognising differences in the nature, duration and extent of squatters', pastoralists' and freeholders' relations with local Aboriginal people, a deeper and more comprehensive analysis of current generations' knowledge and representation of Aboriginal dispossession and the injustice of colonialism is enabled.

NOTES

1. See, for example, Ann Curthoys, 'Expulsion, Exodus and Exile in White Australian Historical Mythology', *Imaginary Homelands, Journal of Australian Studies* 23, no. 61 (1999): 1–18; Robert Foster and Amanda Nettelbeck, *Out of the Silence* (Adelaide: Wakefield Press, 2012); Elizabeth Furniss, 'Timeline History and the Anzac Myth: Settler Narratives of History in a Northern Australian Town', *Oceania* 71 (2001): 279–297; Chris Healy, *From the Ruins of Colonialism: History as Social Memory* (Cambridge and Melbourne: Cambridge University Press, 1997); Chris Healy, *Forgetting Aborigines* (Sydney: UNSW Press, 2008); Andrew Lattas, 'Aborigines and Contemporary Australian Nationalism', in *Race Matters: Indigenous Australians and 'Our' Society*, eds. Gillian Cowlishaw and Barry Morris (Canberra: Aboriginal Studies Press, 1997), 223–255; Anthony Moran, 'What

Settler Australians Talk About When They Talk About Aborigines: Reflections of an In-Depth Interview Study', *Ethnic and Racial Studies* 32, no. 5 (2009): 781–801; Peter Read, *Belonging: Australians, Place and Aboriginal Ownership* (Cambridge and Melbourne: Cambridge University Press, 2000); Deborah Bird Rose, 'Rupture and the Ethics of Care in Colonized Space', in *Prehistory to Politics: John Mulvaney, the Humanities and the Public Intellectual*, eds. Tim Bonyhady and Tom Griffiths (Carlton South: Melbourne University Press, 1997), 190–216; Mitchell Rolls, 'Why Didn't You Listen: White Noise and Black History', *Aboriginal History* 34 (2010): 11–33; and Katrina Schlunke, *Bluff Rock: Autobiography of a Massacre* (Fremantle: Fremantle Arts Centre Press, 2005).

2. See, for example, respectively, Lorenzo Veracini, *Settler Colonialism: A Theoretical Overview* (Basingstoke: Palgrave Macmillan, 2010), 89–90; Curthoys, 'Expulsion, Exodus and Exile', 15–16; Mark McKenna, *Looking for Blackfella's Point* (Sydney: UNSW Press, 2002), 205; and Moran, 'What Settler Australians Talk About', 789.

3. Theresa Donnellan, *Home of the East Wind* (Jamestown: D. Meaney, 1995); Theresa Donnellan, *Tarcowie: Place of the Washaway Water* (Tarcowie: Tarcowie Progress Association Book Committee, 1998); JA Ellis, *Hard Yacka: The Story of a Mid-North Town in South Australia* (Yacka: Yacka Historical Group, 1995).

4. William [Bill] Murray, interview with Skye Krichauff, North Adelaide, 14 May 2010.

5. Kay Hannaford, interview with Skye Krichauff, Kings Beach, 16 May 2010.

6. See, for example, Healy, *Forgetting Aborigines*; Veracini, *Settler Colonialism*, 75–94.

7. These people are represented by a group of young women whom Read refers to as the 'Orley School Girls'. Read, *Belonging*, 77, emphasis added.

8. Moran, 'What Settler Australians Talk About', 789.

9. Ann Curthoys, 'WEH Stanner and the Historians', in *An Appreciation of Difference: WEH Stanner and Aboriginal Australia*, eds. Melinda Hinkson and Jeremy Beckett (Canberra: Aboriginal Studies Press, 2008), 246–247; Rolls, 'Why Didn't You Listen'.

10. Rolls, 'Why Didn't You Listen', 26.

11. For a more detailed account, see Skye Krichauff, *Memory, Place and Aboriginal–Settler History: Understanding Australians' Consciousness of the Colonial Past* (London: Anthem Press, 2017).

12. Pierra Nora, 'General Introduction: Between Memory and History', in *Realms of Memory Vol. 1 Conflicts and Divisions*, ed. Lawrence

D Kritzman, trans. Arthur Goldhammer (New York: Columbia University Press, 1996), 1–2.

13. Ibid., 8.

14. Ibid.

15. Iwona Irwin-Zarecka, *Frames of Remembrance* (New Brunswick: Transaction Publishers, 2009), 18.

16. Geoffrey Cubitt, *History and Memory* (Manchester: Manchester University Press, 2007), 121.

17. Michel de Certeau and Luce Giard, 'A Practical Science of the Singular', in Michel de Certeau, Luce Giard, Pierre Mayol, trans. Timothy J Tomasik, *The Practice of Everyday Life* (Minneapolis and London: University of Minnesota Press, 1998), 53, original emphasis.

18. Irwin-Zarecka, *Frames of Remembrance*, 17.

19. Klaus Neumann, 'Haunted Lands', *University of Technology Sydney* [*UTS*] *Review* 6, no. 1 (2000): 77.

20. Richard Slotkin, *Gunfighter Nation* (New York: Antheneum, 1992), 6–8, 25.

21. Much of the information about occupation licences and pastoral leases comes from Nancy Robinson, *Change on Change* (Leabrook, SA: Investigator Press, 1973).

22. The Brownes purchased the freehold of 46,978 acres of the Booborowie run in 1863. The exact date the Browne brothers began squatting on this lease is uncertain. See Rodney Cockburn, *Pastoral Pioneers of South Australia Vol. 1* (Blackwood: Lynton Publications, 1974 [1925]), 30.

23. The exact date the Browne brothers began squatting on this lease is uncertain. According to Cockburn, they 'acquired' this lease in 1843, i.e. by 1843, they had applied for and been granted an occupation licence for the Booborowie and Canowie runs. Rodney Cockburn, *Pastoral Pioneers of South Australia Vol. 1* (Blackwood: Lynton Publications, 1974 [1925]), 30. See also www.burrahistory.info/BOOBOROWIEHISTORYWALK accessed 3 April 2014 and www.goyder.sa.gov.au/page.aspx?u=108 accessed 3 April 2014.

24. Cockburn, 53; Marlene Richards, *Hallett: A History of Town and District* (Hallett: The Author, 1977), 17.

25. Gilbert married the Browne brothers' sister, Anna, in 1847.

26. Mt Bryan Branch of the Country Women's Association, *Mt Bryan: An Informal History* (Mt Bryan, SA: Mt Bryan Branch of the Country Women's Association, 1951), 6–7.

27. Cockburn, 54; Robinson, *Change on Change*, 38.

28. Frankie Hawker and Rob Linn, *Bungareee: Land, Stock and People* (Adelaide: Turnbull Fox Phillips, 1992), 41–43; Maurice Keain, *From*

Where the Broughton Flows (Spalding and Norton Summit, SA: Keain Publications, 1976), 24; Nancy Robinson, *Change on Change* (Adelaide: Investigator Press, 1971), 61, 69; and Heather Sizer, *Yet Still They Live*, 18.

29. Keain, 21.
30. Cockburn, *Pastoral Pioneers Vol. 1*, 58; Richards, 20; and Robinson, 37.
31. See 'Reminiscence of Pioneer Days', *Weekly Times (Melbourne)*, 13 August 1892: 2; Victoria's Chief Protector of Aborigines, George Augustus Robinson, provides a list of names of squatters he encountered in his travels around the colony from 1839 to 1845, in D. Clark (ed.), 'The Journals of George Augustus Robinson, Chief Protector, Port Phillip Aboriginal Protectorate', Vols. 1–4 (Melbourne: Heritage Matters, 1998).
32. See Robert Noye, *Clare: A District History* (Coromandel Valley, SA: Lynton Publications, 1976), 9, 12–14.
33. For a detailed study of cross-cultural relations on neighbouring Yorke Peninsula during the early colonial years, see Skye Krichauff, *Narungga Wargunni Bugi-Buggillu: A Journey Through Narungga History* (Adelaide: Wakefield Press, 2011).
34. See, for example, Colonial Office Correspondence held in the State Records of South Australia, GRG 24/6/1844/1248, GRG 24/6/1844/1293, GRG 24/6/1845/143.
35. JF Hayward, 'Reminiscences of Johnson Frederick Hayward', *Proceedings of the Royal Geographical Society of Australasia South Australian Branch*, Session 1927–1928, Vol. XXIX (1929): 89.
36. Amanda Nettelbeck and Robert Foster, 'Colonial Judiciaries, Aboriginal Protection and South Australia's Policy of Punishing "with Exemplary Severity"', *Australian Historical Studies* 41, 3 (2010): 324–334; Amanda Nettelbeck, '"Equals of the White Man": Prosecution of Settlers for Violence Against Aboriginal Subjects of the Crown, Colonial Western Australia', *Law and History Review* 31, no. 2 (2013): 378–379, 379, 388.
37. H Price to the Colonial Secretary, 19 November 1844, GRG 24/6/1844/1388.
38. George Hawker's Diary, PRG 847/Series 1-5, State Library of South Australia [hereafter SLSA], extracts from Herbert Bristow Hughes' diary microfiche D7469 (L) SLSA, and Celia Temple, manuscript, 'An account of [John Horrocks'] life by his sister Celia Temple, with a copy of his diary', John Ainsworth Horrocks, PRG 966/5, SLSA.
39. See Richards, 18, 20, 201; Cockburn, 58–59.
40. George Hawker's Diary, PRG 847/Series 1-5, SLSA.

41. Moorhouse to the Colonial Secretary, 7 February 1843, Protector's Letter Book, Aborigines Office, Adelaide, Vol. 1, May 1840–January 1857, State Records of South Australia, GRG 52/7.
42. See Moorhouse to Colonial Secretary, 9 June 1845, Protectors Letter book.
43. *Government Gazette*, 10 January 1850, 34.
44. See, for example, Robinson, *Reluctant Harbour*, 37–38.
45. Sizer, *Yet Still They Live*, 26, 31, 33, 35.
46. Prior to 1869, Canowie was sold to the Brownes' manager and close friend Henry Price, who subsequently sold it to R.B. James, J.F. Hayward and A. Scott; Cockburn, *Pastoral Pioneers Vol. 2*, 40. After 1866 (the date is not specified) 'Dutton and Melrose' purchased the North Booborowie run which was subsequently purchased by the government and subdivided in 1911. Richards, *Hallett*, 18.
47. See Richards, *Hallett*, 17–18; Cockburn, *Pastoral Pioneers Vol. 1*, 36–37, 52–53.
48. For Aboriginal accounts of this population decline, see Fred Warrior, Fran Knight, Sue Anderson, and Adele Pring, *Ngadjuri: Aboriginal People of the Mid North Region of South Australia* (Adelaide: SASOSE Council Inc., 2005), particularly 91,129. This was reiterated during interviews with Ngadjuri descendants: Pat Waria-Read, interview with Skye Krichauff, Port Adelaide, 26 November 2010; Vincent Branson, interview with Skye Krichauff, Elizabeth Grove, 1 June 2012.
49. See, for example, Noel Butlin, *Our Original Aggression* (Sydney: Allen & Unwin, 1983); Deborah Bird Rose, *Reports from a Wild Country* (Sydney: UNSW Press, 2004), 110–112.
50. *South Australian Government Gazette*, 17 April 1851, 264–265.
51. GRG 52/1/1871/168. The total number includes 'heathy' and 'sick and infirm' adults as well as children.
52. Warrior et al., *Ngadjuri*, 91.
53. See Krichauff, *Memory, Place and Aboriginal–Settler History*, in particular 121–122, 193.
54. See Skye Krichauff, 'A Boomerang, Porridge in the Pocket and other Stories of "The Blacks' Camp": An Analysis of an Australian Settler-Colonial Historical Epistemology', *Journal of Australian Studies* (accepted, forthcoming).
55. See Krichauff, 'Chapter 4: The Cultural Circuit: Making Sense of Lived History', in *Memory, Place and Aboriginal–Settler History*, 111–146.
56. Rolls, 26.

CHAPTER 6

Distress in Ireland 1879–1880: The Activation of the South Australian Community

Stephanie James

Crop failure and famine represented recurring crises in Ireland. But before the 1840s there was no imperial response template for such situations. This chapter looks at two instances of Irish famine or distress—1847–1848 and 1879–1880—and demonstrates the emergence of imperial humanitarian relief. Following a brief focus on South Australia's relief campaign of 1847, that colony's responses to Irish Distress of 1879–1880 attracts greater attention showing what both reveal about the colonial Irish and their place in the community. Finally, it evaluates the role played by Adelaide's principal activist—Irishman Michael Thomas Montgomery—both during the fund-raising months of late 1879 to mid-1880, and subsequently when the strength of his campaign reputation was seriously undermined.

S. James (✉)
Flinders University, Adelaide, SA, Australia

© The Author(s) 2019
P. Payton and A. Varnava (eds.),
Australia, Migration and Empire, Britain and the World,
https://doi.org/10.1007/978-3-030-22389-2_6

119

120   S. JAMES

In December 1879, an Adelaide meeting heralded a most unusual train of events in Australia's least Irish colony. In response to mounting stories of crop failure and famine distress in Ireland, a number of Irish-born residents, prevailed on the newly elected Lord Mayor, Edwin Thomas Smith, to call a public meeting to discuss the situation. In the context of colonial attitudes towards Ireland and the Irish, his positive response was not necessarily predictable.[1] Despite Smith's attempts to clarify the necessity for such action with his Dublin counterpart, he had not received confirmation before he convened the requested meeting on 19 December. Following advertisements for the gathering at White's Rooms, two hundred and fifty people attended, and so local fund-raising to relieve Irish Distress was underway.[2]

This was not Ireland's first experience of threatened famine but before the mid-nineteenth century, international assistance was not sought to ameliorate Irish food shortages, or their human consequences. One crisis in particular, 'the Forgotten Famine' of 1740–1741, resulted in mortality rates of 13%, a figure close to the 12% associated with the Irish Potato Famine of the 1840s.[3] Both also resulted in significant population outflows with similar migration ratios. But the mid-nineteenth-century famine attracted intense publicity, and international community response. In Adelaide, a British Destitution Relief Fund was established in the latter half of 1847; responding to the humanitarian appeal, funds and some foodstuff were sent. But there was limited local Irish involvement. However, following that famine many Irish emigrants arrived in South Australia. They brought searing first-hand accounts of the 1840s; their knowledge and experience became important elements in 1879–1780. By then, there had been a number of campaigns to collect for various imperial humanitarian crises, thus colonists had some familiarity with the various stages of subscription-raising. The first phase involved newspaper items generally describing the situation, the next would now probably be described as 'consciousness-raising', when informed experts provided harrowing details about death and disease resulting from the famine, and the third focussed on an organised colonial response (typically a large committee) to both activate the community and oversee fund-raising. In 1847, the colonial impetus did not emanate from the Irish-born, and aspects of the campaign to raise funds highlighted very negative attitudes towards Irish-South Australians; this provides an important backdrop and a significant contrast with the 1879–1880 appeal process.

Irish-South Australia 1836–1878

Described by Eric Richards as 'the least Irish part' of colonial Australia, and with the Irish 'late in the rush' to reach its shores in 'significant numbers', the relationship between South Australia and its Irish immigrants reflected some ambivalence.[4] Despite subsequent claims by Protestant Irishmen about the anti-Irishness of 'early colonial planners ... [wanting] to restrict their numbers to less than 5 percent of the ... population', colonists needed their labour.[5] By 1840, the Irish might have constituted only 7% of the population total, but Richards suggests that official assistance between then and 1866 'offered little evidence of under-representation' from Catholic Ireland.[6] That the colony's first forty years were threaded with overtly anti-Irish episodes seems unsurprising in view of its 'relentless ... [promotion] as a haven for Protestant Dissenters'.[7] Some historians have judged high covert levels of prejudice, only revealed at times of crisis.[8] Despite the positive, acknowledged contribution of a series of early Protestant Irishmen—George Strickland Kingston, Robert Richard Torrens and Edward Burton Gleeson, to name a few[9]—the majority of Irish immigrants were Catholic and unskilled. The first quality rendered them unwanted in an avowedly non-conformist community. The second trait, however, while not cancelling the unsavoury religious factor, certainly determined their necessity in the young colony. Migration/employment discontinuities led to an oversupply of female Irish domestics in 1855, a situation not only creating significant short-term community unhappiness, but contributing to lasting memories of unskilled, problematic immigrants.[10] In addition, Irish South Australians proved adept at negotiating ways and means of nominating family and friends as immigrants, leading to articulated mainstream concerns about the planned nature of the new society being undermined.[11]

The colony's early decades also reflected examples of unity between Protestant and Catholic Irishmen, in some Irish-focussed organisations, and particularly around the celebration of St Patrick's Day.[12] This was also true in the composition of the relief committees of both 1847 when Fr Michael Ryan was possibly the lone Catholic Irish member, and of 1879–1880 when Irish Catholics dominated. Historian Fidelma Breen argues, however, that ultimately in South Australia the smaller Irish population, and its geographical dispersion, contributed to different, less combative 'Irishness' than existed in other colonies.[13] Perhaps this trait helps explain the ground-breaking response in 1879–1880, when the colony's fund-raising actions precipitated a nation-wide campaign.

The Background of Imperial Fund-Raising

By the 1870s when Australia had a population of around two million, relief committees had been successful in generating colonial responses to various overseas crises. In their study of how Australians reacted to the photographic portrayal of India's famine victims between 1876 and 1878, historians Christina Twomey and Andrew J May commented that 'late nineteenth-century humanitarianism ... has a less well-developed historiography than either its antecedents ... or its successors ...'.[14] Their specific focus on Victoria's Indian Famine Relief Fund was facilitated by 'the richness of the archival record of its work'.[15] Australia's eventual donation of £52,000 to the imperial total of £689,000,[16] vastly exceeded contributions both to the Persian Famine of 1871—£1087.14.11—and the Chinese famine of 1878 in which 10 million died. Twomey and May acknowledge the sabotaging role of colonial anti-Chinese sentiment in the 'meagre funds' collected.[17] In their study, discussion of fund-raising efforts centred mostly on Victoria, so it is unclear whether the £3600 sent to China by November 1878 included funds from other colonies.[18] The authors also refer briefly to previous colonial campaigns beginning with the Irish Famine during the 1840s, the Crimean War sick and wounded, British victims of India's 'Mutiny', and those in Lancashire affected by the collapse of the cotton industry in the early 1860s. One significant aspect of earlier campaigns was that all those affected by these crises were 'fellow Europeans'.[19] While the plight of India's imperial citizens represented a potential challenge in terms of race, by the late 1870s colonists were able to link their generosity to a more complex articulation of imperial responsibilities. Thus establishing Indian Famine Relief Funds across the colonies enabled demonstration both of Empire loyalty, and Christian principles, as well as the more subtle 'desire to differentiate Australian colonists from other subjects of empire'.[20] Some of these motivations can be discerned in South Australian responses to both Irish crises of the nineteenth century.

The South Australian British Destitution Relief Fund 1847–1849

However, perceptions of the Irish both in Britain and in the Australian colonies, reflected ambivalence, often tinged with negativity and prejudice. Before examining South Australian responses in the late 1870s, this chapter will discuss that colony's reactions to the Irish Famine from June 1847. The colonial census of 1846 showed a total population of 22,390. But without place of birth being a census question, the only method of gauging insight into the Irish percentage was in Catholic numbers. In 1846, there were only 1846 Catholics, 7.4% of the population. So, the minority status of Irish-Australians in a small colonial population was clear. Looking briefly at the campaign of the late 1840s before a more detailed exploration of the later effort, not only provides a useful background for glimpses of attitudes towards Irish-South Australians, but also a context for comparing the two campaigns.

In June 1847, editor of Adelaide's *Register* newspaper, George Stevenson, took the lead in the second phase of the colonial response. Stevenson was always prominent in the colony and often divisive.[21] Many published newspaper items had highlighted growing problems in Ireland,[22] but the editor challenged the apathy of his fellow British-born colonists in terms of their response to 'the harrowing details of destitution, famine, disease and death prevalent ... in Ireland'. But, he was far more dismissive of 'Irish-born South Australians' designating them as those within whom 'the glow of charity is ... extinct'.[23] Moving to the third phase of the colonial response, a public meeting of 26 June established a Relief Fund Committee.[24] Then, over some days, the *Register* published lists of those who affirmed the details contained in the 'Address to the Starving and Suffering Millions of Great Britain and Ireland' published by the paper on 30 June.[25] In a clear demonstration of imperial loyalty, an announcement of 3 July explained that 'a general appeal is about to be made ... on behalf of our distressed fellow subjects'—South Australia's British Destitution Fund.[26] On 7 July, the *Register* included both the first subscription list (this included amounts between one guinea and £25) and the names of 42 committee members. Of these, at least seven were Irish-born.[27] Recognising the emigration opportunity represented by the situation, the committee soon agreed

124 S. JAMES

that subscribers could designate their funds towards equipping and transporting destitute families 'eligible for a free passage' to embarkation ports.[28] Publication of names confirming the individual concerns continued in July. And in August, a large meeting of subscribers, plus the South Australian British Destitution Relief Fund Committee, debated whether sending the whole remittance in wheat was feasible, whether there should be a mixture of wheat and funds, or whether the funds should have conditions attached. Ultimately, it was decided that half the money raised should be for 'unconditional relief' and the remainder dedicated to those destitute but eligible to emigrate.[29] On 28 August 1847, £1000 was dispatched to the London Committee with the promise of a similar amount in corn. The letter which accompanied the draft was only published in mid-October. A final statement echoed pride in colonial achievement, as well as an implicit sense of imperial obligation:

> [W]e may be permitted to observe that it is as remarkable as delightful, that a place that ten years ago was not, is now able to send as large an offering to our Father Land as that we now have the honour of sending.[30]

The debate about where the additional money was to be applied continued to bubble into 1848. In May, a subscriber meeting voted to specify that rather than travel to *any* colony as formerly agreed, the supported destitute emigrants should *only* travel to South Australia 'where their labour is wanted and their wages will be good ...'.[31] In September, when the Adelaide fund 'having at length closed their labours', the balance sheet details revealed that £2189.10.4 had been received locally, £95.15.1 spent on printing circulars, advertising, wheat cartage, and printing the 'final account and balance sheet in the four Adelaide papers'. The already mentioned sum of £1000 to the British Association, and another £1084.15.4 to 'her Majesty's Land and Emigration Commissioners in aid of Emigration to South Australia', apparently completed the accounts.[32]

In 1847, Irish-Australians had no role in initiating subscription collection for the Irish famine. In fact, as already indicated, the generosity of Irish-South Australians was questioned early. That perspective was evident at other points in the newspaper coverage of this fund-raising initiative. For example, in an exchange of letters in February 1849, 'Eclectic' responding to challenges from 'Observer' was sufficiently provoked to tell him 'painful facts ... about the Irish in South Australia'. In the writer's collection of 'about thirty pounds' for the Irish famine:

> Not a sixpence of this came from the Irish. They were some of them applied to, and made the following excuses: 1st. They did not believe that such distress as was stated in the Adelaide Committee's printed document, for they had not seen it, and recent arrivals had not told them of it. 2nd They were glad they were out of it, i.e. Ireland or the famine. 3rdly. They should, if it was true be applied to by their priests.[33]

The letter went on to state firmly that, were another Irish famine to occur, some in his area would not 'again take the lead in the proper work of Irish patriots', and, he predicted like 'a great part of this colony', these men would declare:

> WE SET YOU THE EXAMPLE ONCE, NOW SET US THE EXAMPLE.[34]

The demonstration of Christian principles was more implicit than explicit in the Famine Relief,[35] but the desire to demonstrate imperial loyalty was clear. Whether the abiding religious and national prejudices against the Irish Catholics limited the generosity remains a question.[36] Certainly, in 1847 the size and nature of the Irish Catholic community, and the economic state of the majority of Irish colonists, located them outside of a potentially influential role in South Australia. The situation faced two decades later, when another famine situation evolved, differed in almost every way from that of the late 1840s.

THE IRISH DISTRESS FUND OF 1879–1880

Without the pressure from Irish-born Adelaide residents, the meeting of 19 December 1879 was unlikely to have happened. As indicated, the gathering initiated an extraordinary few months in the colony. The previous census (1876) had revealed that 14,053 or 6.6% of the population of 213,271 were Irish-born. Many had emigrated after the Famine, greatly enlarging the colony's Irish population; by the 1870s, the successes of some of the Irish-born were visible and recognised.[37] A Catholic arrival of 1836, businessman and pastoralist, Patrick Boyce Coglin for example,

126   S. JAMES

had been in parliament since 1860.[38] Without threatening the community in any overt manner, it was evident that at least some Irish-born colonists had acquired social capital.[39]

An unwieldy committee of forty-two (one immediately comparable to 1847 in size) was formed on the night of the December meeting[40]; it included three MPs and five prominent Protestants, however, Irish Catholics predominated. Importantly, there were no priests.[41] Mayor ET Smith (English-born, an arrival of 1853, a Congregationalist and Freemason) became Honorary President,[42] Sir George Kingston (Irish-born, a pioneer of 1836, Anglican and also a Freemason) was Honorary Treasurer.[43] Both men were also MPs. The joint honorary secretaries were Irishmen, Patrick Healy (a Catholic arrival of 1864, someone dedicated to Irish affairs in SA until his death in 1920),[44] and Michael Thomas Montgomery, someone about whom little was known until recently.[45] Distress Fund coverage reveals both his Cork origins and his Catholicism.[46] Montgomery played a strident role in responding to the general items in the first phase of fund-raising, and displaying detailed knowledge of Ireland in the second, the pre-meeting newspaper discussion. He addressed the December meeting (the third phase), emphasising the extent of Ireland's alarming realities. Being appointed to the subcommittee at the committee meeting of 22 December guaranteed his subsequent identification with the cause of Irish Distress. An *Evening Journal* editorial of 31 December linked Irish 'cries for aid' to those heard previously from Lancashire, Cornwall,[47] India and China, mentioning that the earlier Indian Famine Fund had requested 'the cooperation of all the Municipal Corporations and District Councils'.[48] According to the editor, this system had worked well

> and all the bodies appealed to took the utmost interest in the movement, and did their best to further it. We believe they would do the same in the present case. The distress in Ireland appeals strongly, not only to Irishmen, but to colonists of all kinds ...[49]

In his role, Montgomery communicated with every local council about meetings, and spoke at many; he proved to be the pivotal link. The published lists demonstrate the effectiveness of his energetic template, within three months over £8000 was raised. The action in Adelaide precipitated an Australia-wide response which reportedly resulted in £100,000 being sent to Ireland.[50]

In 1989, Laurence Geary's article 'The Australasian Response to the Irish [Famine] Crisis, 1879–80' provided a 'big picture' analysis of Antipodean reaction to the crisis. Geary's astonishing use of extensive newspaper sources in that pre-Trove era established a significant platform for the now more accessible forensic use of the press. His discussion confirms Adelaide as the site of the first Australian response to the worsening famine situation.[51] Unlike Geary, this chapter will look only at South Australia, focussing particularly on the role played by MT Montgomery. His singular prominence in, and the overall success of the Irish Distress campaign, ensured his move into a number of public roles in South Australia where he continued to promote himself to the community.

MICHAEL THOMAS MONTGOMERY—KNOWN BACKGROUND AND ENTRÉE INTO IRISH DISTRESS CAMPAIGN

Intriguingly, Montgomery had played a minor role in November's lord mayoral election campaign in Adelaide. Seconding motions in support of Smith's suitability for election at three different city meetings raises questions about whether Montgomery and Smith were acquainted before the Irish Distress campaign.[52] Montgomery's history eluded Geary in the 1980s, much still remains hidden, notably his arrival in Australia, and his date and place of death.[53] But the 1899 Brisbane Electoral Roll, which listed him as a journalist, gave his age as 45, suggesting he was born in 1854. Thus, he may only have been 22, when he donated one guinea to Melbourne's St Patrick's Cathedral Daniel O'Connell statue fund in October 1876; this was his first colonial mention.[54] Resident in Victoria through 1878, he briefly contemplated standing for parliament.[55] From 1879 (when he was possibly only 25) until at least early 1884, he was in Adelaide.[56]

Montgomery's role in all phases of South Australian fund-raising was crucial. He had first entered the newspaper arena in mid-December 1879, when he challenged two senior local Irish priests. Their letters had advised caution about immediate responses to published requests for 'donations [to Ireland] as soon as possible' from a nun in County Kerry.[57] Her appeal precipitated a local editorial which, while acknowledging there was a humanitarian problem, also accused Irish leader CS Parnell of exaggerating Irish difficulties and suggested that diverting donations locally would allow better training of 'girls who emigrate here

128   S. JAMES

as servants'.[58] Such responses encapsulated the layered prejudice towards Ireland so often evident in South Australia. Montgomery, however, questioned the clerics' stance, suggesting they had not read

> the files of papers … [and] letters and leading articles describing the melancholy scenes of privation and want which are visible especially in the south and west of Ireland.

He provided details from recent editions of Sydney's *Freeman's Journal* (6th and the *Tablet* of 11th). One priest, Fr Prendergast, was derided for his 'unpatriotic expressions, incoherent sentences, bad grammar, and unintelligent English', evidence causing all colonial Irishmen to 'blush with shame'. Montgomery closed his letter by asserting that as 'one Irishman … glorying in the name [he] intend[ed] on the independent platform of the public press to protect the honour of his countrymen from insult …', he was ready.[59] This letter points to Montgomery's operational style: his preparedness for public attack on those with whom he disagreed or who questioned him, his willingness to use the press as a platform, and as became apparent, his readiness to use legal action. Such characteristics suggest not only the arrogant certainty of a young man, but also someone with whom it might have been very difficult to work.

THE EARLY MONTHS OF THE CAMPAIGN

Montgomery's impressive organisational skills were quickly evident. Following a telegram from Dublin's Lord Mayor-elect, 'Distress severe; assistance urgent', the large committee met. After Montgomery explained that 200 subscription books and 2000 subscription lists had been generated, the group decided

> to leave the details of the canvassing scheme [both in the city and country] to the sub-committee, members of the General Committee being urgently requested to communicate as frequently as possible with the sub-committee.[60]

With the backing of the subcommittee, Montgomery then authored the 'Public Appeal',[61] published 'in every paper in the colony'[62] from 1 January 1880.[63] Press articles were both favourable about the Appeal and optimistic about its outcome.[64] The *Advertiser* editorial of early January was positive about the campaign, articulating the humanitarian demand:

> The appeal to aid the distressed in Ireland is likely to be very generally and generously responded to. ... It is a duty of our common brotherhood and common citizenship to help each other in times of distress.[65]

In response, public meetings were quickly held—for example, Nairne on the 3rd, Kapunda on the 5th, and on the 8th at Wallaroo.[66] Detailed reporting from Kapunda's meeting revealed four speakers who shared memories of the Irish famine of 1847–1848.[67] Some attendees wanted the town to work independently of the Adelaide committee, anticipating that 'too much money [would] be spent on expenses'. At the meeting, Montgomery was diplomatic about the town going it alone, merely emphasising that such decisions would lead to greater transmitting costs.[68] Meetings were also advertised for both city and country centres: Kensington/Norwood,[69] Willunga,[70] Macclesfield,[71] Port Adelaide,[72] Tea Tree Gully,[73] Woodville,[74] Gilbert District Council (Riverton),[75] Prospect,[76] Gawler, North Adelaide, Burra and Jamestown.[77]

At the mid-January Central Committee meeting, Montgomery summarised progress. Government provision of £25 worth of stamps and free colonial railway passes for committee members, and some large donations were reported. He detailed district meetings,[78] a successful performance at the Theatre Royal, and future events such as a public lecture,[79] and a Grand Town Hall concert. Montgomery announced he had sent out 1747 subscription lists, including 427 to Postmasters, 206 to pastoral stations, 109 to banks, 18 to corporations, 101 to district councils (these had both received 'printed abstracts bearing on the distress in Ireland'), 25 to newspapers, 138 to unspecified establishments, 90 to institutions and 633 to hotels; another 120 'collecting books [were] in private circulation'.[80] The first thousand pounds was cabled to Dublin on 17 January,[81] and some days later, the honorary secretary was anticipating a further £3000 within two weeks.[82]

Days later, following a resolution about free rail transport of donated grain at an 'influential and well attended meeting at Yarcowie',[83] the Commissioner of Public Works announced free passage of 'Wheat and other Produce' on all colonial railways.[84] In farming communities like Melrose and Port Augusta, firms offered to transport Fund wheat

130 S. JAMES

without charge from the port.[85] But at Glenelg, where 'only half a dozen gentlemen' attended, another meeting needed to be scheduled, the mayor stating the need to first 'communicate with several influential gentlemen'.[86] Numbers were also disappointing at Gawler, where a mere 50 attended the meeting; much emphasis was put on previously successful local contributions for distress in China and India.[87] The mayor's tone subtly integrated nationalism, appreciation of Ireland, acceptance of the Irish as 'kin', as well as recognition of their value to Britain.

> [A]nd if we did that for foreigners how much more ought we to contribute for people of our own nationality. Whatever factions existed elsewhere we were Australians, and can claim many distinguished colonists as Irishmen, and out of our bountiful harvest we ought to give generously. Everyone must admit that Irishmen had made the Britisher what he is, and it was not asking too much for our own flesh and blood that we should aid in this famine.

Montgomery recounted Central Committee achievements to the Gawler audience and underlined the importance of press support, particularly from the *Advertiser* in facilitating his advocacy role. Explaining that farmers could donate wheat, he hoped to avoid 'the expense of a personal canvass' by the 'liberal scatter[ing]' of 2600 collecting lists and 400 books for wheat donations'. A 19 member committee was appointed, and at its first meeting on 22 January, 28 district collectors were named for the planned house-to-house canvass.[88]

EARLY SIGNS OF PUBLIC DISAGREEMENT

Cracks, however, soon appeared. By 20 January, Montgomery's first disputatious letter was published. His quarry was a Mr AH Mumme of Yankalilla whose letter had queried the non-receipt of subscription books.[89] Montgomery evidenced his double-edged style, thanking the writer for sympathy but 'regret[ting] his imprudence in writing to [the newspaper] before he communicated with me'.[90] From Kapunda came the claim that collection was 'not seemingly being so vigorously carried out as it might be'. And despite the numerous collecting books and subscription lists, 'notwithstanding so small was the amount received until a few days ago, that the committee were unwilling to advertise'. The writer insisted 'a house to house canvass is absolutely necessary'.[91]

A North Adelaide meeting several days later had 'very few present'. The chairman mentioned that 'the committee had not got so much as they had wished ... [but] it was the beginning of a good end'. Then, Montgomery spoke about Ireland, listed town donations and numbers of circulating books and lists. He stated that thirty public meetings had been held. He also anticipated that, owing to South Australia's colonial population density differing from interstate patterns of concentration in large centres ('scattered villages ... [without] rapid and regular communication with the metropolis'), 'the [colony's fund-raising] movement would last longer'.[92] From Mt Gambier, where Adelaide delegates did not attend the initial meeting, the mayor regretted that 'attendance [was] not larger'.[93] That there were also concerns about private lists in case 'these sums would not be included in the [town's] total', reveal early signs of the competitive element within the campaign.[94] The moderately attended Glenelg meeting of 27 January also exhibited evidence of this competition-oriented approach. Addressing the meeting, committee member, Rev. Thos Field MA, 'felt sure that the people of Glenelg would occupy a very fair position in the list of subscriptions'.[95]

ADDITIONAL FUND-RAISING STRATEGIES

As well as small attendances, newspaper coverage reported both continuing signs of optimism and disappointments. Using an idea gleaned from Mark Twain's *Innocents at Home*, Port Augusta supporters developed the magic bag of flour concept—'a bag of flour ... [was] sold and resold till it had realised over £80'. It was then sent to Adelaide.[96] And Montgomery's skill at drip-feeding information and contributing to potential rural competition was revealed from the regular, brief newspaper items from late January announcing, for example, receipt of £400,[97] £220,[98] and £370.[99] This also ensured the 'Irish Distress Fund' was kept in front of readers. However, the public seemed less interested in either the 30 January 'Grand Concert' despite the advertised presence of the Governor—'the attendance not large' and 'We fear the proceeds will not be nearly so large as anticipated'[100]—or the Theatre Royal Performance a week later. In both cases, summer heat became a possible explanation, but theatregoers were 'far from numerous' on 6 February, perhaps because it was an amateur performance 'somewhat drearily produced', 'or the fact that money has been raised in various other ways'.[101] The subtext here does suggest symptoms of compassion fatigue.

132   S. JAMES

February press coverage presented further bulletins about donation figures.[102] And, it was announced that subscription lists would be closed at the end of the month.[103] Progressive subscription lists were published, on 27 February there were figures of £810.5.1, with £3627.6.1 previously acknowledged.[104] Another £828.89 on 5 March brought the total to £5259.19.11,[105] with further updates on 12 March,[106] 19 March[107] and 9 April.[108] Montgomery cleverly utilised St Patrick's Day to announce that the colonial total had reached £8000.[109]

Factors Undermining the Unqualified Success of the Irish Distress Campaign

The somewhat startling success of the 1880 South Australian campaign to raise funds for a deeply distressed Ireland had many contrasts with the fund-raising efforts of the late 1840s. The latter colonial initiative led to an Australia-wide commitment which produced almost £100,000. But within both campaigns personality issues were a marring feature. This was a much larger factor in 1880. And on 8 March, the Central Committee proposed singled out one honorary secretary. Their plan put forward

> That a testimonial be raised for presentation to Mr MT Montgomery ... who declines accepting any remuneration for his services, and who has during the past ten weeks devoted his entire time with indefatigable zeal and disinterested earnestness to bring the movement to such a glorious success.

As treasurer and honorary secretary, Mayor ET Smith, and Irish businessman, J J Laffan,[110] thought 'there ought to be no difficulty in raising a handsome sum'.[111] Given the honorary secretary's 'highly appreciated' 'arduous labors' (sic) for Ireland, the outcome was considered assured. However, such was not the case despite Laffan replicating Montgomery's council contact template.[112] When the Lord Mayor and MP WK Sims each promised five guineas,[113] their generosity provoked 'An Irishman' to pick up his pen and query whether he would also be called upon 'to make a further donation to a Laffan-like object ... [and when] our liberality [is] likely to obtain a little rest?'[114] Several days later, there were responses, one headed 'A Snake in the Grass' which insisted those interested in the Irish cause would feel 'disgust' about that letter, and that 'three out of four readers will be able to guess who this *soi distant*

Irishman is …'.[115] Laffan's letter clarified his interest in doing 'a kindness to a personal friend – a friend to the national cause', his personal disinterest in remuneration, his speculative thinking about whether the writer had contributed, and his view that the letter 'savor[ed] strongly of a concoction of law and beer'. His final sally referred to it being 'well-known' that 'a representative of each' had displayed 'venomous jealousy at the popularity' acquired by Montgomery.[116]

But there was other evidence that Montgomery's style was less than universally well received. In Port Augusta, the local Irish Fund committee, noting that the £8 spent getting Mr Plummer and the 'magic bag of flour to Adelaide', was not reimbursed by the Central Committee, declined to assist the testimonial. '[T]hey are by no means satisfied with Mr Montgomery's treatment of Mr Plummer, and the way in which he acted generally on the matter of the … flour when it was sent down to Adelaide'.[117] In Georgetown too, the council declined to contribute.[118] The issue resurfaced in mid-June when the final closure of subscriptions and the presentation of £100 to Montgomery were announced in the press. 'A Subscriber to Both' 'question[ed] his taste in accepting' money, especially from the fund, queried what had become of Laffan's testimonial funds, challenged Montgomery's receipt of anything as 'Honorary Secretary', with 'An Old Irishman' asserting that had he known this would occur, he would have sent his money directly to Ireland.[119] From Mt Gambier came comment that the Relief Fund was '[s]omething like a sham'—the 'Honorary' secretary issue part of this, but 'the worst of it … [was] travelling expenses … [of] £110, and clerical assistance £54'. The item continued by describing fund collection as 'a very costly affair' with £580 spent of the £8335 raised; in comparison, the Indian Fund netted £11,448 with only £300 outlaid.[120] These comments confirmed the earlier hesitation about campaign costs expressed at the Kapunda meeting of early January.[121]

Further Public Disputation

In the background, both Montgomery's vindictive behaviour when challenged, and criticisms of his operational style, continued. Another offensive letter from him appeared in early March.[122] But the most revealing episode involved problems with a Catholic colleague on the subcommittee, Malcolm Hy Davis.[123] In early February, according to later court papers, Mr Davis said to several persons:

> If the Committee knew as much as I do concerning Mr Montgomery they would be placed in a position of painful anxiety, and I now state that Mr Montgomery is living on the money of the Irish Relief Fund, for I know he has no private income.[124]

Davis was also reported as saying that Montgomery 'expects to be and will be handsomely remunerated for his "honorary" services'.[125] Subsequently, after Kapunda's paper referred to his insinuations against Montgomery and the funds, and the possibility of a case for libel,[126] Davis's immediate response was that he had stated facts 'from which an inference can be drawn that ... [Montgomery] was not an "honorary secretary"'.[127] Requested by Montgomery's solicitor to withdraw the statements, Davis refused, so a slander case went to court.[128] But at the point of the hearing, Mr Davis apologised, and the matter was dropped.[129] Three months later when Davis refused to pay the costs (£30) as agreed because they were 'excessive', a breach of agreement case was listed. Mr Davis's case was judged as lacking 'a substantial defence'; eventually, the matter was settled out of court.[130]

That there was additional ill-feeling on the committee was suggested in July when, the other honorary secretary, Patrick Healy reacted to advertisements about the non-return of Montgomery's lists; he wrote of receiving one from a hotel proprietor and forwarding it to the committee. The fact that Healy did not communicate this matter directly to the Chairman or Montgomery (as the editor suggested) does indicate communication problems.[131] Clearly incensed, Montgomery hit back. Agreeing Healy had left a list of names on 5 February, he claimed there was no mention of the particular hotel, informed the public who 'may not be aware that this Mr P Healy was my supposed colleague', but added 'that he never attended one of our committee meetings' and only (to Montgomery's knowledge) visited the Fund office once. Worse, he

> adopted a mode of dealing with these collections by placing them to the credit of the fund in the Bank, and did not think it worth his while to inform me of the fact until it suited his own convenience, sometimes several weeks after.

And these actions were 'against ... [Montgomery's] expressed desire'.[132] The public airing of these difficulties in the working relationship of the two honorary secretaries does lend weight to the suggestion that Montgomery was a challenging colleague.

The Audited Report

The auditor's report of July revealed all costs had been subject to 'exhaustive examination' and commented that the account keeping had been complicated by Montgomery's 'necessary frequent absences from town'. In addition, the issue of the 'large number of non-returned Subscription Books and Lists' was noted, with the suggestion that the committee needed to decide whether to publish the outstanding details.[133] It seems the committee thought this useful because the information appeared that week.[134] The following table documents the material originally dispatched alongside the numbers returned and is broken down into the categories Montgomery supplied both to initially promote his efforts and then to show the non-returns.

Irish Fund Subscription List Details[135]

Where sent	No. sent	No. not returned
Postmasters	437	358
Editors	25	13
Establishments	140	43
Banks	101	51
Mayors	120	8
Clerks DC	*	46
Institutes	90	68
Hotel landlords	612	312
Schools	319	130
Police stations	89	36
Managers of stations	190	**
Lighthouses	16	**
Various committees	302	**
Distribution/return totals	2427	1008

*The final report did not differentiate between Mayors and District Clerks
**These places were not mentioned in the details provided on 17 July

According to the report, 628 books were returned with cash while 737 were sent back blank. While the total sum raised was very significant for a colony whose Irish population was small, the final reckoning suggested limited interest. Looking at the difference between returns and non-returns, in almost all categories this was around 50%. There cannot be certainty about the reasons for this discrepancy, but some factors can be suggested. One was certainly Montgomery's personal style. The number of deprecatory comments located in a Trove search (which although not cursory, was certainly not exhaustive) was significant. The nature of his public correspondence relating to opposition or challenge, and the unseemly issue of his testimonial, all combined to create some colonial distaste for the secretary. It seemed that the articulation of criticism increased in proportion to the fund's life. There were occasional glimpses too of what seemed to be local Irish resistance to the appeal. For example, the hamlet of Farrell Flat (adjacent to the Clare Valley) with a high percentage of Irish and their descendants, contributed twenty-six bags of wheat and £8, with the *Observer* commenting that 'there was not that interest taken in the affair apparently that there should have been by the residents who hail from the Green Isle'.[136] Of even more interest was the 'Irishman' whose letter of late March claimed that 'there are at this moment plenty of people in Adelaide in the same predicament as their fellow-sufferers in Ireland'. There were, in his 'personal experience', five hundred unemployed city men, and he predicted the government would need to start relief works or open the 'Adelaide Distress Fund'.[137] Although the final campaign accounting reinforced its ultimate financial success, it also highlighted that the total did not represent the full fund-raising potential.

Montgomery in South Australia After the Irish Distress Fund

Research into Montgomery's life following his prominence, if not notoriety, in the Distress Fund, revealed a pattern of legal and financial issues, a series of intercolonial moves, and elements of what seemed to be a downward spiral. But any signals of this were muted during the era of his significance in Adelaide's Irish community, an era in which he utilised prominence in the Irish Distress campaign to both promote his identification with Ireland, and his particular skills. Closely involved with the early development of the Irish Land League in Adelaide in July 1882, Montgomery was nominated as a member of its first committee.[138] His public statements and a subsequent letter to the *Advertiser* challenging the paper's statements about Ireland earned him editorial coverage, the tone of which was far from complimentary.[139] A further pro-Parnell letter appeared the following February just before the visit of the Irish delegates, John and William Redmond.[140] Then Montgomery, described as a 'member of the executive committee' of the Irish National Land League, was one of 300 on board the SS *Adelaide* welcoming the Redmond brothers to Port Adelaide on 4 February. His position led to an address to the younger brother, William; this was in lieu of a formal presentation because William's arrival was unexpected.[141] In early March in a move suggesting foolishness and unrestrained ego, he was reported as describing Charles Cameron Kingston, a well-known locally born MP of Irish descent, as 'a foreign element with alien sympathies' after he had refused the presidency of the newly established colonial branch of the Irish National Land League'.[142] From that time, Montgomery's name did not grace reports of any local Irish community events, but it certainly seemed his business dealings and his political ambitions had been enhanced by his fund-raising role for Ireland.

Alongside his labours for Ireland, Montgomery was also conducting a property business from at least late February 1880.[143] By mid-year, he was also a licensed country auctioneer.[144] After promoting Sunday trading he became the 'Acting Agent of the Licensed Victuallers Association' in July 1880.[145] But, months later, to avoid the opprobrium of insolvency, he assigned his debts.[146] Without any seeming embarrassment, in 1881 he stood for the South Australian parliamentary seat of Stanley.[147] In the 1860s and 1870s, the county of Stanley in which Clare was located was the colony's most Irish and most Catholic region. Given the Irish and Catholic demographic, Montgomery, and probably others, anticipated he would capture this vote. Certainly, his election speech was self-promoting, unashamedly using his Distress Fund role. He stated:

> A certain amount of intelligence and qualities were essential in a member of Parliament, and he hoped he would not be considered egotistical in saying that he had given the colony a proof of his ability, for he aroused the sympathies of the whole colony as to the state of Irish distress.[148]

Unfortunately, despite the potential voting pool, and Montgomery's confidence about his skills, he was third in the voting tally of six candidates.[149] After some months advertising as a 'Land, Estate and Insurance Agent' in 1881,[150] Montgomery attempted to scale new heights the next year when the already mentioned PB Coglin 'secured ... [his] able services ... as electioneering agent' in his fifth (and doomed), attempt to move from the House of Assembly to the Legislative Council.[151] Thus, Montgomery's early attempts to reinvent himself in association with the local Irish community met with no success.

138 S. JAMES

In August 1882 and May 1883, Montgomery was involved in court cases, losing the first and winning £16 from a potential landlord in the second.[152] However, financial issues resulted in renewed insolvency proceedings the following month.[153] The final hearing revealed liabilities of £148.19.2, and nil assets; it also became clear that MH Davis, a creditor and former Distress Fund Committee member and involved in earlier court proceedings, had sued him for a debt of £58. The court heard details of Montgomery's income and expenditure which were intriguing given his history, and the earlier claims from Davis about his income and expectations of gain from the Irish Distress campaign. Employment issues and creditor pressure were cited as the causes of insolvency. The case was coloured by claims and counterclaims about Montgomery's non-disclosure of bank accounts (something argued by Davis's Irish-born lawyer Patrick McMahon Glynn), about Davis 'acting against him for malicious purposes' and without the agreement of other creditors.[154] By the end of July, when Irishman Patrick McMahon Glynn was appearing for Davis, Montgomery accused Davis of 'acting against him for malicious purposes'. Despite Glynn's insistence that Montgomery had not fully disclosed his estate, the judge disagreed, and the insolvent was awarded second-class certificate because 'he had not kept books'.[155] There were further claims against him in March 1884, smaller amounts that time and he received a second-class certificate, suspended for two years 'on the grounds of previous insolvency'.[156] The extent of his public financial embarrassment was total. Montgomery's colonial history beyond 1882 belies the success of his fund-generating activities in 1880 over relatively few months. Intercolonial separation and distance worked for Montgomery because his Adelaide financial record after the Irish Distress Fund was unlikely to have recommended him as a secure business or employment risk.[157]

CONCLUSION

In South Australia, the differences between the responses to the two Irish famine funds were striking. In a large measure, these differences were determined by the size and nature of the Irish population—in 1847, small, often struggling, and generally insignificant, but by 1879, numerically more significant, and more visible and increasingly more comfortable. In contrast to 1847 where the fund-raising impetus came from the non-Irish, the 1879 momentum was located within the Irish community. Whereas the earlier campaign relied on individuals galvanising their various communities for contributions, in the latter campaign, the colony-wide money raising template was borrowed from an earlier humanitarian endeavour. Individuals, backed by enormous, if not unwieldy committees, were identified as the face of the campaign, and in both, there was unseemly public controversy. Egos, it seems, were major players in both colonial fund-raising ventures.

In 1847, the campaign organisers portrayed themselves in a somewhat superior manner, a semi-elite response to problems in Ireland. Those hundreds of individuals whose names were published in Adelaide newspapers during July 1847 as acknowledging the importance of responding to the confirmed newspaper details of Ireland's situation were successful citizens. And their level of attack against the contributions of the local, Catholic, Irish population reflected inherited and transported (from Britain) negative attitudes towards the Irish in South Australia.

The largely seamless (at least superficially) 1879–1880 venture vividly demonstrated a more unified colonial response to imperial loyalty. The emphasised references to the unparalleled distress in Ireland were framed in terms of the colonists' joint responsibility to other imperial subjects, the Irish suffering from the impact of crop failure and distress. And the funds came in; the process revealed that activation of the community for an Irish cause rose above inherited and/or transplanted attitudes and issues. Indeed, the likelihood of such successful activation was directly related to the role of the colonial Irish in initiating, and then supporting, the fund. And while the audited figures showed clearly that there was some colonial resistance to the campaign—the average non-return figure of 50% was definitive—the overall level of donation meant any opposition could be bypassed. But barely behind the scenes, there was dissatisfaction, enmity, some short-sighted decisions and mismanagement, legal cases and overt personality issues.

Critical to this apparently seething fund-raising environment was Irishman MT Montgomery. It was probably his finest brief hour in the colonies, and worth speculating whether without him, much less money would have been raised in South Australia. His public utterances revealed great knowledge about the extent of Irish problems. His systematic approach to the tasks associated with fund-raising certainly produced a large sum of money, an extraordinarily high figure considering the colonial context. His capacity to frame the famine situation in such a way that it largely bypassed pre-existing prejudice against Ireland and the Irish

140   S. JAMES

was striking. But there were also patterns of public disagreement with associates. An increasingly chameleon-like figure about whom much still remains unknown, he possessed some ruthless traits which he exercised against those colleagues prepared to challenge him. Very much in the foreground of this unique financial campaign in the 'least Irish part of Australia', Montgomery emerges as an intriguing, if somewhat controversial and enigmatic figure.

NOTES

1. For a detailed account of Smith's life, especially the levels of engagement with the colony epitomised by his role in promoting and fostering Adelaide's 1887–1888 Exhibition, see Peter Moore, 'Edwin Thomas Smith "in Reality the Author of the Exhibition Scheme"', in Christine Garnaut, Julie Collins, and Bridget Jolly (eds.), *Adelaide's Jubilee International Exhibition 1887–1888*, Crossing Press, NSW, 2016, pp. 48–63.
2. *South Australian Register* (*SAR*), 17 December 1879, p. 2.
3. See P Gray, *The Irish Famine*, Thames and Hudson, London, 1995; S Engler, F Mauelshagen, J Werner, and J Luterbacher, 'The Irish Famine of 1740–1741: Famine Vulnerability and "Climate Migration"', *Climate of the Past*, Vol. 9, 2013, pp. 1161–1179, https://doi. org/10.5194/cp-9-1161-2013.
4. Eric Richards, 'The Importance of Being Irish in Colonial South Australia', in John O'Brien and Pauric Travers (eds.), *The Irish Emigrant Experience in Australia*, Poolbeg Press, Dublin, 1991, p. 62.
5. *Adelaide Observer* (*AO*) (Supplement), 14 July 1849, p. 1. The St Patrick's Society of South Australia, largely composed of Protestant Irishmen, sought an increase in Irish immigration.
6. Richards, 'The Importance', p. 68. See Stephanie James, *"Deep Green Loathing"? Shifting Irish-Australian Loyalties in the Victorian and South Australian Irish-Catholic Press 1868–1923*, PhD thesis, Flinders University, 2013, p. 79 for South Australian Census Data from 1844 to 1921, showing Irish-born numbers.
7. Richards, 'The Importance', p. 63.
8. Susan (Pruul) Woodburn, *The Irish in New South Wales, Victoria and South Australia 1788–1880*, MA thesis, University of Adelaide, 1974, p. 381.
9. See Wilfrid Prest (ed.), *The Wakefield Companion to South Australian History*, Wakefield Press, Adelaide, 2001, pp. 295, 543–544; Dymphna Lonergan, 'G. S. Kingston and other Pioneer Irish in South Australia',

in *Irish South Australia: New Histories and Insights* (due for publication by Wakefield Press on 1 February 2019).

10. See Stephanie James, 'Irish South Australians in 1914: Unconditional Imperial Loyalty?' in Melanie Oppenheimer, Margaret Anderson, and Mandy Paul (eds.), *South Australia on the Eve of War*, Wakefield Press, Adelaide, 2017, pp. 179–182.

11. Ibid., pp. 182–190; Fidelma M Breen, '"Yet We Are Told That Australians Do Not Sympathise with Ireland": A Study of South Australian Support for Irish Home Rule, 1883 to 1912', MPhil, University of Adelaide, 2013, p. 46.

12. James, 'Irish South Australians in 1914', p. 181.

13. Breen, 'And Yet We Are Told', pp. 172–173.

14. Christina Twomey and Andrew J May, 'Australian Responses to the Indian Famine, 1876–78: Sympathy, Photography and the British Empire', *Australian Historical Studies*, Vol. 43, 2012, pp. 233–252.

15. Ibid., 234.

16. See Melbourne *Age* of 10 January 1880, p. 6 for statement by former premier, Irish-born Sir John O'Shanassy, that Victorians had subscribed £28,000.

17. Twomey and May, 'Australian Responses', pp. 248–250.

18. Ibid., p. 250.

19. Ibid.

20. Ibid., p. 234.

21. Prest, *The Wakefield Companion*, p. 517.

22. See, for example, *South Australian Gazette and Register* of 22 May 1847, mp. 4; the *SAR* of 16 June 1847, p. 4; and the *South Australian* of 29 June 1847, p. 3.

23. *SAR*, 16 June 1847, p. 2.

24. *SAR*, 26 June 1847, p. 2.

25. See *SAR*, 3 July 1847, p. 2 for an example. Among those 36 prominent citizens who responded early were Irish-born citizens including Thomas Young Cotter (the initial Colonial Surgeon), RR Torrens, Fr Michael Ryan and CB Newenham, the Sherriff.

26. *Adelaide Observer*, 3 July 1847, p. 2.

27. *SAR*, 7 July 1847, p. 1. Members were Wm Giles (Chairman), John Baker, Wm Hartley, Lewis Bryant, John Brown, Capt Bagot MLC*, Judge Cooper, Rev JW Coombes, WRS Cooke, Rev JD Draper, GF Dashwood, BM Dacosta, Fred H Dutton, Fras S Dutton, Rev R Drummond, AL Elder, Rev Jas Farrell*, Capt Frome, Anthony Forster, Thomas Gilbert, Jacob Hagen MLC, Rev R Haining, Alfred Hardy, John Hart, Rev R Kavel, Rev John Long, AM Mundy, JB Montefiore, Barnett Nathan, CB Newenham*, JB Neales, Major O'Halloran MLC*,

142 S. JAMES

Rev John Playford, CS Penny, JB Penfold, Rev Michael Ryan*, William Randall, Rev TQ Stow, Messrs Stanfords & Burley, Rev J Titherington, RR Torrens*, Rev Jas Watkins and Rev WJ Woodcock. The * denotes known Irish-born.

28. *SAR*, 10 July 1847, p. 1.
29. *SAR*, 21 August 1847, p. 2.
30. *SAR*, 13 October 1847, p. 2.
31. *South Australian*, 26 May 1848, p. 2. See *SAR* of 12 August 1848, p. 1 for London Committee's receipt of £1000 in March 1848.
32. *AO*, 9 September 1848, p. 1.
33. The writer, although 'silenced ... for the time' about the priestly role, continued here by referring to a 'certain mystery' about 'what *did* they contribute through their priests?'.
34. *SAR*, 28 February 1849, p. 3.
35. See *SAR* of 7 July 1847, p. 2 for comment about 'the generous sympathies' on display in the first day's subscriptions which showed that South Australians have not forfeited their claim to be generous Britons, – a humane and Christian people'.
36. See *Adelaide Times* of 2 October 1851, p. 2 for an excerpt from Hansard involving a question to the Colonial Secretary which queried the fate of funds raised in SA. Mr GM Waterhouse, Cornish-born and a SA arrival of 1843, was told the money, and interest, had been remitted in June 1849. The MP was concerned that contemporary accounts suggested the money was still held locally, and he wanted if it was not too late, 'I would propose to apply it to the relief of those subjects of Great Britain, who were at present in a destitute state on the Western Islands and Highlands of Scotland', in other words, the Irish were no longer deserving.
37. See Eric Richards, 'The Importance', pp. 62–102.
38. By 1878, there had been another 3 Irish-born Catholic MPs, HC Gleeson (1868–1871), W Lennon (1860–1861) and E McEllister (1858–1866), and a further 11 Protestant Irish MPs.
39. See Breen, 'Yet We Are Told That Australians Do Not Sympathise with Ireland', pp. 170–174.
40. See *South Australian Advertiser* (*SAA*) of 27 December 1879, p. 13. Committee members included JC Bray MP, WK Simms MP, E Ward MP, T Cowan, GWD Beresford, WJ Crawford, HD O'Halloran,* Professor Kelly,* AG Beresford, EW O'Halloran,* CC Kingston,* U Bagot,* LM Cullen,* C James, TD D'Arcy Burke, JT Reilly,* JT Landvogt, CE Mumme, D McNamara,* L Shinners,* FF Wholahan,* P Whelan,* JB Broderick,* John Young, Cunningham, Walsh, Conroy, P Hoban, JB Siebert, M McMullen,* Jerger, F Lyons,

JH Fitzgerald, John Keane, Isaac Smith, Thos Fitzgerald, Mathew Ford, Gubbins, Denis Cahill, Denis Conroy and L Quin. (The * denotes known Irish-born or of Irish descent.) See *Chronicle and Weekly Mail* of 27 December 1879, p. 7 for account of the first committee meeting at which a subcommittee including ET Smith, Messrs Bray, Simms, Kingston, Montgomery, Healy and Wholahan 'was appointed to take immediate action to obtain subscriptions'. See *Evening Journal* of 31 December 1879, p. 4 for report of the large committee meeting on 30 December at which Messrs Fraser MP, Buik and JD Woods were also appointed to the subcommittee, and JT Syme and M Ryan to the larger group.

41. *SAA*, 27 December 1879, p. 13. Vicar General F Byrne, Archdeacon Russell and Fr Prendergast were on the platform. See *Observer* of 17 January 1880, p. 26 for report of January 13 meeting at Norwood where the Vicar General claimed ideas that the Catholic clergy were not in support were 'most erroneous'. In fact, he argued they had 'changed the movement from a very circumscribed area into a general one. The clergy had been considered to be unfavourable ... because their names had not been placed on the committee list. The gentleman who drew up the names of the committee was very well known to him, and he was sure he was a person who would not offend anyone. He had either acted in ignorance or had sufficient reason for omitting their names.'

42. Howard Coxon, John Playford, and Robert Reid, *Biographical Register of the South Australian Parliament 1857–1957*, Wakefield Press, Adelaide, 1985, p. 207. Smith was twice mayor of Kensington and Norwood from 1867 to 1873, was a MHA from 1871 to 1877, and from 1878 to 1893, he was then a MLC from 1894 to 1902. He served as Lord Mayor from 1879 to 1882 and 1886 to 1888. He died in 1919

43. Kingston, described as an architect and surveyor, was born in County Cork in 1807 and arrived in SA in 1836. From 1837 to 1838, he was deputy surveyor-general and held various related positions till 1841. He was an elected Member of the Legislative Council between 1851 and 1857, then a Member of the House of Assembly till 1880.

44. Born in Co Clare in 1846, Healy came first to SA but spent some time on the Victorian goldfields before settling permanently in Adelaide. He had a large boot making business in the city. He was on the executive of every Irish Nationalist organisation in SA, the last United Irish League president, retiring just before his death in 1920.

45. See Laurence Geary, 'The Australasian Response to the Irish Crisis of 1879–80', in Oliver MacDonagh and WF Mandle (eds.), *Irish Australian Studies*, ANU Press, Canberra, 1989, p. 122, fn. 25.

46. *Express and Telegraph*, 15 December 1879, p. 3.

47. See *Kapunda Herald* of 9 January 1880, p. 3 for statement that Kapunda had provided 'the keynote to ... [the Cornish Relief Fund] and started it ...'.
48. See Twomey and May, 'Australian Responses', pp. 233–252.
49. *Evening Journal*, 31 December 1879, p. 4.
50. FB Keogh, 'The Irish in South Australia. What They Have Done for Ireland. Interesting Reminiscences', *Southern Cross*, 21 December 1900, p. 16.
51. Laurence Geary, 'The Australasian Response to the Irish Crisis, 1879–80', in Oliver MacDonagh and WF Mandle (eds.), *Irish Australian Studies* (Fifth Conference), ANU Press, Canberra, 1989, p. 101.
52. See *SAR* of 20, 22 and 25 November 1879, pp. 5, 6–7 and 6. The meetings were held at North Adelaide, Adelaide and the German Club.
53. Geary, 'The Australasian Response', p. 122, fn. 25. In Victoria, a Michael Montgomery died in 1911, and another in 1915, but neither death can be verified as the right one.
54. Melbourne *Advocate*, 21 October 1876, p. 1.
55. See Geelong *Advertiser* of 16 February 1878, p. 2; Bendigo *Advertiser*, 9 May 1878, p. 3; and Melbourne *Age*, 1 July 1978, p. 1.
56. See *SAR* of 1 July 1882, p. 4 for report of an Adelaide meeting of the Irish National Land League at which Montgomery proposed a motion and made a lengthy speech about the situation in Ireland and the importance of support from Adelaide's Irishmen. The meeting was also reported in the *Advocate* of 8 July 1882, p. 8.
57. See *Express and Telegraph* of 9 December 1879, p. 3 for the letter from Sister Mary Francis Clare, or the Nun of Kenmare, which was also published in other daily papers. See *Express and Telegraph* of 13 December 1879, p. 3 for letters from Monsignor Byrne and Fr W Prendergast.
58. Ibid., p. 2.
59. *Express and Telegraph*, 15 December 1879, p. 3.
60. *Evening Journal*, 31 December 1879, p. 4.
61. See *SAA* of 1 January 1880, p. 4.
62. *SAA*, 16 January 1880, p. 4. This was stated in the report of 15 January central committee meeting.
63. See *SAA* of 1 January, p. 2; *Register*, 1 and 2 January, p. 2; *Express and Telegraph*, 2 January, 1880, p. 2. See also *Southern Argus* (Port Elliot), 8 January, p. 2.
64. See *SAA* of 1 January, p. 4; *SAR*, 1 January, p. 4, *Express and Telegraph*, 2 January, p. 2; and *Adelaide Observer*, 3 January 1880, p. 27. The Appeal was also published on 9 January in the *Christian Colonist*, Gawler *Bunyip*, *Northern Argus* (Clare), *Yorke's Peninsula Advertiser* and *Narracoorte Herald*, in the *Border Watch* (Mt Gambier), *Wallaroo*

6 DISTRESS IN IRELAND 1879–1880 ... 145

Times and Mining Journal, the Areas Express (Booyoolee), *Port Adelaide News* and the local German language newspaper, *Australische Zeitung* on 10 January.

65. *SAA*, 9 January 1880, p. 4.
66. See *SAA* of 5 January, p. 4; *Wallaroo Times and Mining Journal*, 7 January, p. 2; and *Kapunda Herald*, 9 January 1880, p. 3. See *Evening Journal* of 14 January 1880, p. 2 for report of Nairne gathering.
67. James White was born in County Meath, Dr Blood in Clare and W Oldham in Dublin. Wm Redden's birthplace is unknown.
68. *Kapunda Herald*, 9 January 1880, p. 3.
69. *Express and Telegraph*, 10 January 1880, p. 1. This was called by the Town Clerk, see *Advertiser* of 14 January 1880, p. 6 for report of meeting, Fr Byrne; the Vicar General again challenged any lack of Catholic clerical support, focussing on their exclusion from the original committee list, and the subsequent refusal of some to have their names added because they 'felt slighted'. Two Jesuits, Frs Tappeiner and Peters joined the local committee.
70. *AO*, 10 January, 1880, p. 19. Six ratepayers were named as calling the meeting on 15 January.
71. Ibid.
72. *SAR*, 14 January 1880, p. 2. 25 signatures were cited as calling for the meeting, see *Express and Telegraph* of 15 January 1880, p. 2 for meeting report, Fr Ryan was on the platform and joined the committee. At the meeting, Montgomery said 'he intended to send subscription-lists to every public teacher and clergyman in the colony'.
73. Ibid. See *Evening Journal* of 19 January, p. 2 for report of this meeting; Montgomery and JC Bray had written to say they would attend but 'they did not put in an appearance'. Eight collectors were named.
74. *Express and Telegraph*, 15 January 1880, p. 1. Four ratepayers were named.
75. *Kapunda Herald*, 13 January 1880, p. 2.
76. *Express and Telegraph*, 17 January 1880, p. 1.
77. See *Evening Journal* of 20 January, p. 3 for an advertisement from Montgomery advertising the four last listed meetings. See *Evening Journal* of 19 January p. 2 for Burra meeting report. Canvassers were appointed for the various wards, 4 of the 8 were women. See Gawler *Bunyip* of 23 January 1880, p. 1, for Gawler report.
78. *SAA* of 16 January, p. 4, meetings at Saddleworth, Gumeracha and Little Adelaide were also listed.
79. See *Express and Telegraph* of 23 February 1880, p. 1 for notice that the lecture which was to have been held that evening at St Francis Xavier's

Hall had been indefinitely postponed, and that money would be refunded.

80. Ibid.
81. *Evening Journal*, 19 January, p. 2.
82. *Evening Journal*, 23 January 1880, p. 3.
83. See *Chronicle and Weekly Mail* of 24 January 1880, p. 8. The resolution asked the Central Committee to send a deputation on this matter to the government. See *Register* of 28 January, p. 1 for account of Yarcowie entertainment for the Distress Fund on 26 January, Montgomery was there.
84. *SAR*, 22 January 1880, p. 2.
85. *SAR*, 23 January 1880, p. 6.
86. Ibid.
87. The Gawler *Bunyip* of 22 January 1880, p. 1 included 4 mentions of previous Gawler generosity to India, the 'heathen Chinese', India and China, the Indian Famine Fund, and China and India.
88. Ibid.
89. *SAR*, 17 January 1880, p. 6. Mumme ('Manager', probably Albert Henry, a Presbyterian) wrote that no lists had been received in his part of the colony 'where there are a number of persons who would most gladly contribute their mite to the ... fund'.
90. *SAR*, 20 January 1880, p. 6. Montgomery's rebuttal included sending lists to the postmaster, DC clerk and local hotel landlord 10 days earlier; he assumed they had been delivered. In the previous week, he had posted collecting books to each clergyman, and one that day to Mr Mumme.
91. *Kapunda Herald*, 20 January 1880, p. 3.
92. *Evening Journal*, 23 January 1880, p. 3. Archdeacon Russell was prominent at this North Adelaide meeting, his name headed a committee of 12; the towns listed by Montgomery were: Willunga £46, Morphett Vale £37 and Saddleworth £37. See *Chronicle and Weekly Mail* of 24 January 1880, p. 8 for comment that attendance at Morphett Vale was 'representative', David McNamara from the Central Committee was there, and a local group of 10 was named. The item also reported on a well-attended committee meeting at Kensington & Norwood and enthusiasm at Willunga where 11 were named on the committee.
93. *Border Watch*, 24 January 1880, p. 3. A committee of 34 was named.
94. *Border Watch*, 24 January 1880, p. 2.
95. *Express and Telegraph*, 28 January 1880, p. 2. Timothy Lonergan moved for a committee to be established. It included the town councillors, the mayor and 13 others; one of these was Fr Prendergast, the cleric involved in early newspaper focus on Irish Distress. There was then

'brisk bidding' for 'the most wonderful bag of flour in the world', and later 'it was found that the sale had realised £20, making in all £100.' See *Border Watch* of 11 February 1880, p. 2 for report of the local committee meeting where Montgomery's letter about their first £150 was read amidst discussion about hopes for a second sum of the same amount. He was pleased to see the community 'coming out so nobly. I had a special notice put in each of the daily papers about it'.

96. *Chronicle and Weekly Telegraph*, 24 January 1880, p. 8.

97. *Evening Journal*, 30 January 1880, p. 2. The sum included £150 from Mt Gambier, £100 from Port Augusta and £40 from Clare.

98. *Express and Telegraph*, 4 February 1880, p. 2. The largest sums were £73.10 from Georgetown and £35 from Mintaro.

99. *Express and Telegraph*, 9 February 1880, p. 2. This amount included £185 from Burra.

100. See *Express and Telegraph* of 26 January 1880, p. 1 for advertisement, and *Register* of 31 January 1880, p. 4 for an account of the event. The Governor was Sir WFD Jervois.

101. See *Express and Telegraph* of 5 February 1880, p. 1 for advertisement, and *Evening Journal* of 7 February 1880, p. 2 for what amounted to a review. Publicity had promised.

102. *Express and Telegraph*, 18 February 1880, p. 2. Montgomery announced receipt of £62.13.3 from Melrose, £38.17.6 from Wallaroo and £28.14.3 from Tea Tree Gully.

103. *SAR*, 28 February 1880, p. 1.

104. *SAR*, 27 February 1880, p. 2.

105. *SAR*, 5 March 1880, p. 2.

106. *SAR*, 12 March 1880, p. 2.

107. *SAR*, 19 March 1880, p. 2.

108. *SAA*, 9 April 1880, p. 2.

109. *SAR*, 18 March 1880, p. 1; *Kapunda Herald*, 19 March 1880, p. 3.

110. John James Laffan was born in Templemore, Tipperary in 1837, he arrived in SA during 1864 and was a respected businessman, an early member of the Adelaide Stock Exchange. He died in July 1892. See *Southern Cross* of 29 July 1892, p. 6.

111. *SAA*, 16 March 1880, p. 4.

112. See *AO* of 27 March 1880, p. 12 for Laffan's circular to the Burnside, Angaston, Brighton and Moonta councils, and *Northern Argus* of 9 April, p. 3 for the Clare Council.

113. *Express and Telegraph*, 19 March 1880, p. 3.

114. *Express and Telegraph*, 19 March 1880, p. 3. See also *Bunyip* of 26 March, p. 2 with the comment that 'The rebuke ... is so well deserved and the *naivete* so charming, that we cannot refrain from reproducing it'.

115. *SAA*, 22 March 1880, p. 7. The writer was EW Lloyd.
116. *Express and Telegraph*, 22 March 1880, p. 3. The letter was followed by Lloyd's letter. It was common for correspondents to send letters to numerous daily papers.
117. *Port Augusta Dispatch*, 26 March 1880, p. 8.
118. *Chronicle and Weekly Mail*, 10 April 1880, p. 11.
119. *Evening Journal*, 24 June 1880, p. 4. See also *Register* of 22 June 1880, p. 6 for 'Subscriber's' letter.
120. *Border Watch*, 26 June 1880, p. 4.
121. See fn. 68.
122. *Evening Journal*, 1 March 1880, p. 3. In this, Montgomery attacked Mr W Little over his letter assuming a cask containing salted beef left outside at Port Adelaide bearing the name of Woodcock was connected with the Irish Fund. Having discounted the truth of the allegation, he concluded: 'Mr Little, by his letter, shows, after all, that there is something in a name'.
123. See *Kapunda Herald* of 2 March 1880, p. 3 for the 'City Letter'. This represents the only confirmation that Montgomery was a Catholic; many articles read as if this was the case but do not include any certainty.
124. *Evening Journal*, 8 April 1880, p. 2.
125. See *Kapunda Herald* of 5 March 1880, p. 3.
126. *Kapunda Herald*, 2 March 1880, p. 3.
127. *Kapunda Herald*, 5 March 1880, p. 3.
128. Montgomery claimed damages of £100.
129. *Evening Journal*, 8 April 1880, p. 2.
130. *AO*, 10 July 1880, p. 25.
131. *Evening Journal*, 22 July 1880, p. 2.
132. *SAR*, 23 July 1880, p. 6.
133. *SAA*, 10 July 1880, p. 3.
134. *AO*, 17 July 1880, p. 16.
135. It will be noted that many of the figures relating to the number of sent subscription books were inconsistent with those mentioned above which were drawn from the mid-January Central Committee meeting; presumably, the discrepancies related either to additional books being sent or to mis-directed ones when the audit figure was less than the one mentioned earlier.
136. *AO*, 6 March, p. 12.
137. *SAR*, 24 March 1880, p. 6.
138. *SAR*, 1 July 1882, p. 6. True to form, he proposed a motion endorsing the Irish programme and supporting Parnell before attacking the local press for the 'various infamous and venomous comments', singling

out the *Advertiser*, 'of which he had previously had a high opinion'. See also Melbourne *Advocate* of 8 July 1882, p. 8 for another report of this meeting, and *Kapunda Herald* of 11 July 1882, p. 3 for its description of Montgomery's 'cool impudence' in his attack at a subsequent Norwood meeting. (At the time, Adelaide did not have a Catholic newspaper.)

139. *SAA*, 23 August 1882, pp. 6 and 4. His letter was described as 'long and laboured', his style as 'highly inflated', and the letter 'if [it] be weighed – well, we do not wish to wound Mr Montgomery's susceptibilities by stating the result'.

140. *Chronicle*, 10 February 1883, p. 21. See *Evening Journal* of 2 November 1882, p. 3 for what seems his last advertisement for the sale of 'a first-class suburban hotel'.

141. *SAA*, 17 February 1883, p. 1.

142. *Mount Barker Courier*, 2 March 1883, p. 2.

143. See *Express and Telegraph* of 23 February, 20 March and 22 July 1880, pp. 4, 1 and 4.

144. *Chronicle*, 24 July 1880, p. 11.

145. See *Chronicle* of 30 July, p. 3, and *Express and Telegraph* of 9 August 1880, p. 1. By the second date, he was requesting that petitions be returned to him.

146. *AO*, 18 September 1880, p. 32.

147. The seat was left vacant by the November 1881 death of Irishman Sir George Kingston (father of Charles Cameron) mentioned above. The seat was centred on Clare in the colony's mid-North, the most Irish region of SA in the 1860s and 1870s. See M Stephanie James, *Becoming South Australians? The Impact of the Irish on the County of Stanley, 1841–1871*, MA thesis, Flinders University, 2009, pp. 247, 211, for percentages of 14.7% and 11.2% in 1861 and 1871.

148. *Northern Argus*, 4 March 1881, p. 2.

149. *Areas Express* of 30 April, p. 2. See *SAR* of 5 July 1881, p. 2; for Montgomery's brief time as Candidate for the seat of Yatala.

150. *Northern Argus*, 19 July 1881, p. 1.

151. *Yorkes Peninsula Advertiser*, 5 May 1882, p. 3. Coglin was born in County Sligo and had reached the colony in 1836. First opening a timber yard, then owning a hotel and becoming a city land owner, he moved to the pastoral industry; he represented Port Adelaide in parliament from 1860 but held many other seats both city and rural before his death in 1892. See *Register* of 26 April and 27 May 1882, pp. 2 and 2.

152. *AO*, 5 August 1882, p. 30; *AO*, 12 May 1883, p. 38. The first involved a 'breach of agreement' over a mining lease. In the second case, the

opposing lawyer was Malcolm Hy Davis; Montgomery was described as 'a large, heavy man' providing the only sense of his size or physical features.

153. *SAR*, 6 June 1883, p. 3. As the insolvent, he was allowed to keep his earnings of £8 per week.

154. *AO*, 7 July 1883, p. 32. Montgomery's earnings after he assigned his debts: commission from Australian Widows Fund Assurance Co. to April 1881, £147; unemployed for 4 months; commission from August 1881 to August 1882, £375; August 1882 till insolvency, sundry commissions, £70; verdict for damages from W Wheate £16; expenditure: Wheate £5; Davis £10; re insolvency £6.15; living expenses, about £5 per week, £6889.19.2. Excess of expenditure over income since September 1880 was £90.19.2

155. *Express and Telegraph*, 31 July 1883, p. 2.

156. *AO*, 22 March 1884, p. 30.

157. Montgomery was in Sydney by September 1886 and by February 1888 was on the committee of the Shamrock Club, but over the next 3 years was involved in a series of court appearances. Moving to Brisbane by 1899 where there were further legal issues, he was apparently in WA in 1904, but in Melbourne by mid-1906. He married a widow (of Irish background) in Sydney in January 1897, but after August 1898, there was no mention of his wife. Their deaths have not been located.

CHAPTER 7

'Yet We Are Told That Australians Do Not Sympathise with Ireland': South Australian Support for Irish Home Rule

Fidelma Breen

This chapter considers support for Irish nationalism in South Australia during the years of the Irish Home Rule movement which commenced in the 1870s and lasted for four decades. The movement grew from the desire to solve Ireland's social, political and economic woes—the Irish Question, as it was commonly known. Ireland's history was peppered with rebellions and uprisings, but the growth of a popular constitutional alternative to insurrection quelled that revolutionary spirit for more than forty years. The rise of the Irish Parliamentary Party (IPP) coincided with the enlargement of the franchise and the politicisation of the lower classes. The success of the movement saw a shift in favour of constitutional reform, but its ultimate failure was to prompt Ireland's greatest show of force, the Easter Rising of April 1916.

F. Breen (✉)
The University of Adelaide, Adelaide, SA, Australia
e-mail: fidelma.breen@adelaide.edu.au

© The Author(s) 2019   151
P. Payton and A. Varnava (eds.),
Australia, Migration and Empire, Britain and the World,
https://doi.org/10.1007/978-3-030-22389-2_7

South Australia was the least Irish colony of Australia, so it may seem an odd place to choose to research monetary and moral support for Irish Nationalism. However, despite the size of the Irish community there, two factors pointed to a significance which outweighed its relative smallness. In 1879, Adelaide established the first Irish Famine Relief Fund outside Ireland[1] and between 1883 and 1912, each of the five Irish nationalist delegations to Australia toured throughout the colony.[2] Given South Australia's essentially British character, the involvement of high-profile non-Irish and non-Catholic men in this movement was a curiosity, especially since the Irish there faced the 'unquestionable primacy of Anglo-Scottish colonisation'.[3]

A study of the existing literature revealed the absence of investigation into the effect of a late-arriving cohort of Irish immigrants, the differences between the Irish in South Australia and other colonies and the changing nature and acceptance of Irish political ambition. One of the earliest studies of the Irish in South Australia was Woodburn's 1974 thesis, 'The Irish in New South Wales, Victoria and South Australia, 1788-1880'.[4] Its outstanding feature is that it was the first study to include South Australia in comparison with other colonies, but while it illuminated some of the experience of the Irish in the colony up to 1880 it did little to contest the image of the community as anything other than smaller and rather insignificant in relation to its neighbours and made few references to the differences which existed between the Irish in South Australia and the other two colonies even before the Home Rule period. In its defence, the years immediately following 1880, the most energetic, both politically and socially, for the Irish cohort in South Australia, are clearly outside its timeframe. The numerical inferiority of the colony's Irish population cannot be disputed, but size appears to have determined importance for the remaining works in this area. The development of the various nationalist organisations and the widespread support of the Home Rule movement in the colony combined with the dense social web of interaction between the Irish and the wider society that the present study revealed would suggest that as a community the Irish were more highly organised, connected and more complex than has been considered previously.

In scholarly literature, the history of the Irish Home Rule movement in the colony does not exist outside fleeting mention in Greg Tobin's 'The Sea-Divided Gael: The Irish Home Rule Movement in Victoria and New South Wales 1880-1916'. Completed in 1969, this was the first study to look at Home Rule across two states and is considered by many to be a pioneering work. Tobin's introductory claim that the Irish have escaped the serious attention of historians was indisputable at the time of publication, but since then a considerable body of research has emerged to illuminate some of the Irish experience. However, it might be said that elements of the Irish as 'a group of secondary importance' remain.[5] Although South Australia is not its prime focus, the study provides some salient points for those considering the South Australian aspects of this subject. The dynamic of high levels of late assisted immigration amongst the Irish to South Australia gains significance with Tobin's statement that 'well back in the eighties observers had noted the gradual disappearance of the Irish-born element' in the eastern states. The Irish-born declined in the southern-most colony too, but this appears to have been offset by both the arrival of new Irish and the support of the non-Irish which are considered here as contributing factors to the longevity of the Adelaide branches of Irish nationalist support organisations that Tobin noted.[6]

Louise Mazzaroli's 1979 PhD thesis, 'The Irish in New South Wales, 1884 to 1914; Some Aspects of the Irish Sub-Culture', encompasses the important years of the movement in Australia and provides a picture of its support in the first colony.[7] A student of O'Farrell's, Mazzaroli, investigated the Irish in eastern Australia and echoed her mentor's conclusion that 'Ireland was too far away and too remote from their daily lives and activities' for the majority of them to maintain interest in Irish affairs.[8] She argued that Irish organisations attracted little support and that membership was riven by divisions of class, politics and issues of identity and claims that the 'establishment' Irish had little to do with the various clubs, were more interested in assimilation than participation in Irish affairs and did not want to foster a specifically Irish identity because of the aspersions of character that inculcated.[9] She concluded that membership of the clubs, depending on the subscription rate, was generally working class, but made no mention of committee composition or the patronage or involvement of leading business or political figures in the organisations. Of the Home Rule movement she claimed support came from two sections of society and for two different reasons: the 'establishment' Irish supported Home Rule because of its broadly appealing constitutional nature, i.e. theirs was a rational decision; the working class, however, frustrated by their economic and social position within colonial society, responded on a purely 'emotional and nationalistic' basis.[10] Mazzaroli attributed the success of the Home Rule movement in New

South Wales to the support of the non-Irish in the colony, but stated that when 'this support diminished, as it did after 1887, the Home Rule movement virtually collapsed'.[11] This stands in sharp relief to the 1892 statement by a visiting Irish delegate that the non-Irish support evident in South Australia was such as they had never before seen.[12] Such contrasts in the support for and lifespan of the movement in the two colonies naturally invite comparison.

It should be noted that both Tobin's work and Mazzaroli's work pre-date the revisionism that struck Irish historiography during the 1980s when many of the previously accepted interpretations of groups such as Irish immigrants were reconsidered and reconfigured in the light of new methodologies. These studies also preceded the international debate about the question of Irish identity in the diaspora, and so, they are limited to the aspects of the relationship between imperialism, colonialism and nationalism, that is, they are missing the internationalism of Irish identity. What is sought now is a perspective on how colonial engagement with essentially Irish issues can help us understand the nature and strength of Irish identity in a global setting.

Patrick O'Farrell's *The Irish in Australia* provides the foil for the South Australian experience. Although purporting to represent the Irish experience on the continent as a whole, South Australia received little space in this publication and, again, there is no recognition of the differences between it and other colonies with regard to the reception and support of the Home Rule movement and its delegates. This chapter provides an in-depth study of Home Rule support in South Australia which is currently missing from the literature, and in its consideration of the representative, cross-party support given there, it exemplifies a reversal of the 'contribution' history phenomenon. Rather than looking at Irish contributions to South Australian society, it seeks to understand colonial interest in Irish affairs.

The infamous 'Irish Question', which moved through the issues of famine, poverty, landlordism and self-government, occupied a significant amount of column space in the dailies and weeklies that brought South Australians their news of the world. Both the famine and the burgeoning constitutional Home Rule movement were quite literally a world away, and the compatriots of those suffering were a small and apparently insignificant portion of the South Australian population. How and why did the Irish nationalist movement spread throughout South Australia?

Sir Thomas Esmonde, one member of the 1889 delegation, wrote an account of the tour that recounts particularly harrowing trips through South Australia's interior in flood season. This demonstrates just what an effort touring regional Australia was at this time but of greatest interest to this research were his thoughts about the delegation's experience in South Australia. He wrote,

> And, in concluding this chapter upon South Australia, it may, perhaps, be worth the placing of this fact upon the record – viz. that at every one of the nine or ten meetings I addressed in the country districts of the Colony the chair was taken by the Mayor or leading magistrate, who in no instance was an Irishman. Yet we are told that the Australians, other than of Irish blood, do not sympathise with Ireland.[13]

So why would ordinary and not so ordinary South Australians care about Irish Home Rule?

What exactly was Home Rule? Essentially, it was a constitutional agitation for the return of the Irish Parliament which had been removed by the 1800 Act of Union. The movement successfully blended the republican tradition of the United Irishmen, Young Irelanders and the Fenians with the demands of the Irish National Land League—the 3 F's: fixity of tenure, fair rent and free sale. Several Home Rule Bills were formulated which, if passed into legislation, would have reinstated the Dublin Parliament with limited devolved powers over purely Irish matters. Imperial concerns such as defence were to remain the jurisdiction of Westminster. The first Home Rule Bill was introduced in 1886, the second in 1893 and the third in 1912. After the removal of the House of Lords veto the third bill would have been enacted as the Government of Ireland Act 1914 but for the outbreak of the Great War which caused its suspension.

In South Australia, the success of the touring Home Rule delegates was pre-empted by the organisation of the Irish Famine Relief Fund late in 1879 and the establishment of a network of Irish Land League branches between 1880 and 1882.

Ireland, which was still largely an agrarian-based economy with pockets of industrialisation in Dublin and Belfast, suffered recurring famine, and the last years of the 1870s raised the spectre of An Gorta Mór—the Great Famine/Hunger—of the mid-1840s. The fund proved to be a blueprint for the Home Rule movement as it provided a basis for public support and the involvement of leading figures in Adelaide society in one aspect of the Irish Question. The subsistence crisis was used as an example of England's mismanagement of Irish affairs. The genuine need of the starving in Ireland was given great exposure in the colonial press and colonists rallied to the cause. South Australia came second only to Queensland raising over £8500 by the time the fund closed in 1882. Branches of the Irish National League were set up throughout South Australia and indeed throughout the country. Despite reports of the ravages of the Irish Land War—boycotting, murder, intimidation—the Adelaide Press tracked Pierce Healey as he travelled the colony establishing the branches—the first indication that the SA press could be impartial in regard to Ireland and her politics.

While the fund was initiated by local Irishmen, it very quickly attracted the active support of Adelaide's philanthropists and politicians. Mayor Edwin (E. T.) Smith was lauded as the 'heart and soul' of the movement in the city. William Knox Simms, still on Australia's rich list, was noted as having actively canvassed for subscriptions to the fund. George Kingston was its treasurer. One of the most novel fundraising methods was that devised by Mr Plummer who brought to life Mark Twain's idea of a magic barrel of flour (from the novel *The Innocents at Home*). In South Australia, Plummer's Magic Bag of Flour was carted through the streets of the city and the towns—it was sold and resold to raise money for the starving Irish. This idea was later used by the many Indian Famine Relief Funds established in the colony. As well as the large sum of money mentioned previously, shiploads of grain were sent to Ireland from Australia.

The fund was the first significant public expression of concern for the Irish amongst South Australians—it introduced colonists to the agrarian and governmental problems of Ireland and made common knowledge the language of Irish political discontent. The Adelaide Press filtered and, through editorial comment, often neutralised reports from Britain, albeit unintentionally, thereby providing the public with a matter-of-fact perspective on what were deeply complicated and highly contentious issues. The fund was a precursor to the visits of the Irish envoys through the years 1883 to 1912 which raised the equivalent of millions of dollars for the Irish cause. At times during the fundraising campaigns, the colonists themselves were the victims of economic depression, but time and again the antipodean Irish were handed the begging bowl and they repeatedly filled it.

In the early 1880s, the IPP began to attract a different sort of elected member. No longer just landed gentry, the new members were working men who could not maintain a livelihood and be present at Westminster at the same time. Money was also needed to maintain the structure of the Irish National Land League, and funds were required to help farmers who were evicted from their small holdings—the Evicted Tenants Fund. The IPP reached out to the Irish diaspora in America and Australasia and it was not disappointed. Irish parliamentarians and associated nationalist activists visited the colonies on several occasions—brothers John & William (Willie) Redmond came in 1883 and John Redmond, in his first speech on Australian soil, remarked on the kindness the Australians had shown to Ireland in her hour of need. Scholars disagree on the exact amount raised, but the trip gathered some £15,000 at the very least (equivalent to almost $1.3 million dollars today). Patrick O'Farrell states £25,000 was raised and Thomas O'Riordan says it was closer to £30,000 (or $2.6m).[14]

The brothers were followed by John Dillon, John Deasy and Sir Thomas Esmonde in 1889. By this time, the first Home Rule Bill had been introduced and defeated in the House of Commons at Westminster.

In 1895, two years after the rejection of the second Home Rule Bill by the House of Lords, the colonies received the renowned 'Father of the Land League', Michael Davitt. Davitt's visit differed from the others on a number of levels. Firstly, Davitt himself was an amalgam of republican gunrunner, parliamentarian, journalist, social activist and a renowned labour identity. Secondly, his tour did not commence in aid of the Party but was conducted for personal income after suffering bankruptcy but, mid-tour, the money raised went into the campaign funds upon the announcement of a general election in Britain. In 1906, the MP for West Belfast, Joseph Devlin (or Wee Joe as he was better known), accompanied by nationalist lawyer J. T. Donovan, visited Australia. Five years later, Donovan made a return visit, this time accompanying William Redmond Jr. and Richard Hazleton. Between these official delegations, there were brief visits by other Irish nationalists, some of whom toured and collected funds (JR Cox in 1890 and 1891) and others who came on recuperative or leisure trips.[15]

The significance of the visits lay in the effect they had on the community in Australia: the evolution of a strong communal ethnic identity appears as the Irish become a 'public' group in South Australia during this period. The politics of Ireland could be seen as the definition of the Irish abroad. Without the public conversation surrounding Irish issues, the Irish in South Australia, because of a lack of critical mass, were just another migrant group. Home Rule provided an overarching and unifying umbrella of identity and meaning.

The sea-change from militancy to constitutional political participation evident in the rise of the IPP aided the acceptance of the Irish cause in South Australia as did the gentlemanly dispositions and oratory skills of some of the Party's delegates, particularly John Redmond. Investigation of the visits shows the increasing involvement of Adelaide's politicians and prominent citizens. The first visitors were welcomed with a public reception, and the second delegation had two receptions—one at Port Adelaide and another in Adelaide itself. Michael Davitt's arrival prompted some members of the legislature to travel out to greet his ship and he was invited to dine at Parliament House. The last delegation was offered the loan of a government car for the length of the visit. While this may appear unremarkable, the South Australian experience was at times much more positive than that met with interstate. The descriptions of the arrivals—streets lined with crowds, thousands waiting at Semaphore for the ship—are interesting. The delegates themselves said it may well have been an Irish crowd in an Irish town such was the enthusiasm that greeted them.

The effect of the patronage of leading public figures did not go unnoticed. One writer to the *Chronicle* feared that 'the eloquence of the Irish visitors may lead some of our quiet and thriving fellow colonists of Irish nationality into recklessness, especially when the Redmonds are patronised by Dr Reynolds, the Catholic bishop, members of Parliament, and prominent citizens'.[16]

IRISH SOUTH AUSTRALIA: SIZE AND PLACE

So what did the Irish in SA look like? Just prior to the first visit from the Irish envoys in the early 1880s, the Irish-born in South Australia represented 6.5% of the colony's population compared with an average of 9.5% across Australasia.[17] They resided alongside the Scots at 3.8%, the English who represented 21% of the total, Germans and Austrians at 3.2%, the remainder being mostly Australian-born (59.83%) with small numbers of Chinese and French.[18] Thus, as a group the Irish were almost twice as big as the next two most sizeable ethnicities in the colony. But there is absolutely no argument to be offered against the fact that the Irish were a small group in the colony. Size, however, should not always be equated with significance. The Irish were a much-talked about people—few other groups were a constant feature of the daily press. Famine Relief and then Home Rule support provided a focal point for activity.

The Irish did not cluster in particular areas of the colony to any great extent. Though there were recognisably Irish areas such as Clare and the Burra, there were few places which did not have an Irish-born component as illustrated in Table 7.1. The figures given also show the decline, particularly between 1891 and 1901, of the Irish-born in the colony. Some areas maintained their levels of Irish-born inhabitants through this decade, e.g. North Adelaide and East Torrens, and some, like Yatala and Onkaparinga, even increased. The Yatala district encompassed the town of Auburn where a strong Orange Lodge emerged from around 1874. Like this area, Wallaroo also had a noticeably smaller Catholic population and it too was an active Orange area suggesting that a good proportion of the Irish community here might have been Protestant. Between 1891 and 1901, areas such as Sturt and Gladstone saw a slight increase in their Irish-born populations, but the majority demonstrated a steep decline as the colonial-born ratio, not surprisingly, began to exceed all foreign-born figures. Of course, the nationalist movement also depended on the next generation of Irish-Australians. In 1895, Davitt referred to his 30,000 fellow countrymen in South Australia including in this the offspring of Irish immigrants.[19]

This time period sees a change in the class of the visible Irishmen in the colony. No longer represented by a Protestant Anglo-Irish elite, Adelaide's Irish nationalist community by the 1880s, increasingly like Ireland itself, had ordinary working men as its most prominent members and political and social leaders. Men of the stature of Torrens, Major O'Halloran and Kingston, were not of the same class as the study's subjects—had the Irish instigators of Home Rule support in Adelaide been men of their ilk, there would be less curiosity regarding their ability to attract wealthy, non-Irish support to the cause.

The Irish Question, based as it was on the issues of land control and self-government, found an audience in South Australia in part because of the close understanding the colonists had of those two issues, but the characteristics of the Irish in the colony played a role too. The size of the community itself is where its significant features lie—its smallness made for unity and control, especially during the various crises the movement

Table 7.1 Catholic and Irish percentages of population of each electoral district in 1881 and 1901. The Irish-born numbers for 1891 are also given to aid comparison[a]

Electoral district	Irish-born in 1881	Catholics as % of total pop of electoral district	Irish-born as % of total of electoral district	Irish-born in 1891	Electoral district	Irish-born in 1901	Catholics as % of total pop of electoral district	Irish-born as % of total of electoral district
East Adelaide	1260	14.94	8.38	1033	East Adelaide	847	18.72	5.31
West Adelaide	1814	25.44	11.74	1294	West Adelaide	959	29.47	6.55
North Adelaide	730	15.49	9.12	728	North Adelaide	566	11.7	3.4
Wallaroo	860	9.71	3.7	350	Wallaroo	253	8.38	1.53
Port Adelaide	768	13.09	4.93	637	Port Adelaide	563	13.8	2.54
West Torrens	839	14.38	6.2	743	West Torrens	618	14.39	2.86
Yatala	283	10.49	4.83	338	Yatala	214	12.7	2.8
Gumeracha	257	7.56	3.5	197	Gumeracha	149	5.7	1.5
East Torrens	1182	11.56	5.82	1173	East Torrens	993	11.5	3.1
Sturt	926	11.46	6.64	769	Sturt	771	10.3	2.6
Noarlunga	305	11.8	5.31	202	Noarlunga	140	7.7	2.25
Mount Barker	408	14.8	5.93	356	Mount Barker	288	10.4	3
Onkaparinga	194	6.64	2.61	206	Onkaparinga	153	6.5	1.5
Encounter Bay	190	9.11	3.62	135	Encounter Bay	90	6.3	1.6
Barossa	322	7.63	3.07	253	Barossa	210	7.9	1.6
Light	969	20.83	7.86	565	Light	399	13.99	3.3
				291	Yorke Peninsula	214	12.4	2.7
Victoria	748	21.04	7.23	540	Victoria	399	19.7	3.2
Albert	396	12.21	5.96	212	Albert	188	10.4	2.1
Burra	1915	22.32	9.14	538	Burra	367	15.9	3.4
Stanley	1269	21.45	7.22	422	Stanley	312	20.1	3.5

(continued)

Table 7.1 (continued)

Electoral district	Irish-born in 1881	Catholics as % of total pop of electoral district	Irish-born as % of total of electoral district	Irish-born in 1891	Irish-born in 1901	Catholics as % of total pop of electoral district	Irish-born as % of total of electoral district
Wooroora	624	16.6	6.16	374	267	14.7	3.3
Gladstone				553	593	22	3.7
Frome				835	585	22.9	4
Newcastle				802	507	26.8	4.3
Flinders	1730	19.78	8.29	463	369	17.7	3.6
NT	85	5.61	1.22	85	49	7.3	1.2
Shipping	172		2.46	272	180	14	4
	18,246			14,366	11243		

[a] Yorke Peninsula, Gladstone, Frome and Newcastle did not exist as electoral districts in 1881

suffered, which, in turn, supported an image of respectability and cohesiveness not always evident in other antipodean Irish communities. These characteristics combined with the lack of threat usually associated with the Irish element to allow support for the Irish Home Rule movement from the wider South Australian public.

LEADING IRISH NATIONALIST FIGURES

There were several individuals prominent in Irish and other societies and associations in Adelaide and South Australia generally. James Vincent O'Loghlin was the co-founder of the *Southern Cross* newspaper, a respected politician and eventual Senator. He was President of the United Irish League—one of the later manifestations of the South Australian Irish Land League. Patrick McMahon Glynn was a similarly respected politician, lawyer and journalist who was also renowned for his prowess at the hunt. His entry in the ADB states that 'his reputation as a sportsman contributed to his political success'.[20] Francis Keogh was heavily involved in civic life. From at least 1879 until his death in 1927, he was listed as a committee member, usually secretary, and sometimes auditor of various associations. Born in West Adelaide in 1861, he was a steady and consistent office-bearer in many of Adelaide's social, political, literary and business organisations. More than one report attests to his energy and likeability—no doubt strong factors in his success as a recruiter for groups like the Hibernians, the Irish Rifle Corps and the United Irish League. In these, he worked alongside men like William Joseph Denny, Pierce Healey and Patrick Whelan. Recruitment success continued in later years in organisations such as the Licensed Victuallers Association and the Adelaide Racing Club, both of which had Keogh as their secretary. In addition to these, he was an executive committee member of the St Patrick's Literary and Dramatic Society, the Broken Hill South Central Mining Company, the South Australian Building Society, Adelaide Handball Club and the Adelaide Catholic Club. He was a member for West Adelaide in the House of Assembly prior to the reduction of members, and from 1900 to 1902, he represented Grey Ward in the City Council. In the Assembly election, he polled more votes than all the other candidates together and this elevation in public life served to strengthen his position as a prominent member of both the Irish community and wider Adelaide society. His obituary reported that he was well known in other states as well. In his long career as a committee member and officer, Keogh traversed business, religious, sporting, economic, literary and political networks.

Patrick Whelan was similarly active and well known throughout the colony. A draper from Co Clare who arrived in 1876, Whelan, became involved with the Irish nationalist organisation and remained so until his death. When he tendered his resignation from the secretaryship of the Irish National Federation in June 1895 because he was moving to Western Australia, the members decided to vote him six months leave of absence instead in the hope that he would return. He had served the organisation in South Australia for fourteen years and his involvement continued in WA.

Like Keogh, James Bernard Broderick first participated in Adelaide's Irish national life as a teenager and remained active until his death at the age of 50 in 1900. He was involved with Catholic and Irish organisations from the age of 19 being listed as a ticket seller for the Catholic Young Men's Society Annual Picnic in 1869.[21] He was programme organiser of the picnic in 1875 and Chairman of the first St Patrick's Day celebration committee in 1878.[22] While the national festival had been celebrated for many years, a musical tribute in St Xavier's Hall being the usual celebration, 1878 was the first year St Patrick's Day was marked by a procession and it was hailed a great success there being from five to six thousand people in attendance.[23] By 1881, Broderick was President of the Hibernians Society and was listed as an officer of the Emerald Cricket Club.[24] He was an executive member of the Irish National League formed by John Redmond in Adelaide in 1883 and he became a Justice of the Peace in January 1894.[25]

Steady and consistent men like these were to leave an imprint on Adelaide's Irish organisations in their restrained and conservative manner. It is likely that these traits were attractive to the non-Irish businessmen and political leaders of the colony. Quietly working against the Irish stereotype, the cluster of long-serving men emerging in the 1880s kept a steady hand on the public image of the Irish National League and its successor organisations. The sober demeanour of these known Irishmen was a far cry from the archetypal 'fightin' Irish' persona which even the upper-class St Patrick's Society of the mid-century had failed to escape.[26]

A web of interaction between the Irish and some of the colony's elite was uncovered by looking at these relatively unknown Irish individuals. ET Smith and WK Simms jointly owned the SA Brewery Co. and Keogh was involved in the Licensed Victuallers Association. Simms and

Rounsevell were also connected in business as they owned a wool and produce brokerage called Bean Brothers Ltd. Broderick's livelihood was earned as a decorator and illuminator of the city's charity fetes and other events which were often held in the grounds of the homes of the colony's wealthiest men—his obituary stated that his business concerns made him a well-known personality around town. He was also instrumental in having Federal Hall in Grote St—part of the Central Market built. He represented Torrens Ward in the Thebarton Corporation for two years. Sports connections are evident in cricket, dog racing and horse racing. Glynn's aforementioned success at the hunt echoed the long relationship between the Irish and equine activity in Adelaide given Patrick Coglin's early involvement in the Adelaide Racing Club where Simms and Rounsevell were active members and Keogh was secretary. While these links may be considered tenuous, it is reasonable to attach a small measure of significance to this personal interaction between Adelaide's elite and the colony's Home Rulers. It might also be of some significance that there is an absence of Protestant/Orange figures in these circles.

The Irish community in South Australia was never large enough to sustain more than one nationalist body at a time. While an organisation called the United Irish Association appeared in 1882 and survived briefly until the following year, the group formed around the nationalist cause and modelled on and connected to the Irish parent organisation was the one which prospered. The United Irish Association was formed to facilitate political and literary discussion but not with a direct political purpose. It would not gain the respect or unity it sought, primarily because of the personality of its chairman, James Clements. It became clear that the organisation was incompatible with the general temperament of South Australia's Irish nationalists and their supporters. Clements, at least, was more extreme and vocal in his views than the wider body of South Australian Irish nationalists. He gained a reputation for extremism after publicly going head to head with both the leadership of the South Australian Land League and the *Advertiser*, at a meeting in 1883. The *Advertiser* subsequently admitted that it would 'not be fair to hold either the chairman or the audience on Friday evening responsible for the buffoonery of Mr J. Clements, who gave an exhibition at once of uncontrolled excitement and crass stupidity not often equalled'.[27] Clements appeared to be an embarrassment to Adelaide's Irish leaders, and the United Irish Association seems to have floundered because of this, there being no further reports of activity from mid-1883.

Aside from the fact that the 'leadership' of the South Australian Irish nationalist community and the most public of Irishmen appeared to be sensible, moderate, conservative men, what other factors contributed to South Australian support of the Home Rule movement? South Australia's early reputation for generosity may have been reason enough for the Irish fundraisers to visit the small Irish community, but the principles of the foundation of the colony, its demography and social structure and lack of Orange anti-Home Rule activity all played a part in the success of the Home Rule movement there. Although size, or lack of, has been part of the reason the community has received little academic attention, this factor played some part in the success of the Irish cause there. The Irish were to be found in almost all areas of the colony. Unlike in other parts of Australia, there was no large Irish community to isolate the ethnic group or insulate newcomers from the wider society in South Australia.

The small Irish community was also the reason for the movement's cohesion in South Australia when it was falling apart elsewhere (particularly in Melbourne). There was usually one Catholic/Irish newspaper and one nationalist organisation in existence compared with Sydney and Melbourne where competing personalities left the movement divided and sometimes fallen. The local experience of Irish people, especially during the 1870s, proved that Irish immigrants were neither indolent nor ignorant. This went some way towards lending the speeches of Irish visitors credence—the famine wasn't the result of idiocy or laziness. The local example was far removed from the picture painted by London reports and Punch cartoons of the Irish oaf.

Whatever the situation in other parts of Australia, the view of the Irish as talented and industrious had been long-standing in SA. As early as 1866, a tongue-in-cheek article had appeared in the *Register* alluding to the capability of Irishmen in colonial administration:

> The talk is that some such rule as that which regulates the admission of immigrants according to nationality might with advantage be adopted with reference to the occupants of public offices; that in the House of Assembly the Speaker and the two Clerks all hail from the Green Isle; ... that Irish gentlemen have a wonderful faculty for 'edging themselves into some canny post,' as Burns sings, and may be found in all the Australian Colonies enjoying pleasant billets. The further talk is that if they occupy these positions it is because their talents and education fit them for public offices.[28]

By the end of the nineteenth century, the Irish, though with a dwindling Irish-born element, were making progress in local and state government and, as an ethnic group, were looked to as a good example of national spirit in South Australia. There was little of the antipathy shown to them in other colonies, and a quiet respect for their unassuming and non-aggressive ambition was evident. In 1890, Sir William Robinson, a former Governor of South Australia (1883–1887), said of the Irish element in Australia: 'whatever they might be in their own country no one denies that they make excellent citizens in the colonies. They are steady, thrifty, contented, and intelligently interested in public affairs'.[29] Thus, without making too sweeping a generalisation, the good nature and temperament of the colonial Irish and their aptitude for civic duty may well have been a factor in their ability to attract non-Irish and non-Catholic support to their cause.

Whilst it is easy to say that the liberalism of South Australia complimented the notion of support for Home Rule, that support was not limitless. Even Rounsevell, one of those involved from the time of the Famine Relief Fund, qualified the idea of equity when he said that he did not wish South Australia to be 'entirely democratic', and so, the limited demands of Irish Home Rule as a dominion within the Empire may have appealed to his sense of social justice without endangering class-bound ideals of power and control.[30]

Writers like Williams and Shanahan have highlighted the fact that the rigid class structure evident in SA society appeared to go relatively unnoticed in the colony, but the land issue raised its head from time to time. A writer to the 'Chronicle' in 1883, 'Jones', claimed it was difficult to understand how an Irishman in Ireland could be as fiendish as he was reported (by English papers) when his compatriots residing in the colony were 'trustworthy, both in business and as friends'. Jones also said that Redmond's speech in the Adelaide Town Hall found him 'wavering, and has decided me in favor of Ireland, so that I shall be ready when the time comes with my subscription, or even to go further and enrol myself as a member of the league'.[31] One fault of the reporting of Irish events was raised in his letter: the papers had not made widely known 'the different relations here and in Ireland existing between landlords and tenants' which needed to be explained in 'plain, and forcible language'. Redmond's speech did that for the 'nation of freeholders, who have got into the way of thinking that a man may do what he likes with his freehold, without question from anybody...and when the terms of the lease he has granted expires take all improvements as his own'.[32] While the land problem was greatly improved by the time of their visits, when the Irish delegates lectured the colony's inhabitants, this example of misgovernment was used to reinforce the validity of the movement—it was a basis for seeking self-government as a means of restoring a modicum of self-determination to an oppressed and dispossessed nation.

The Land Question engendered fraternal feeling. The monopoly and sale of Crown lands and landlordism were similar local concerns. Non-Irish support was found amongst other locals like Louis Berens who became a supporter of the INL in Adelaide not because he was a socialist but because 'the cause of the people was the same in Ireland, England and Australia' and 'the monopoly of land by one class was the root cause of poverty and misery'.[33]

Non-Irish Support

In 1883, a Presbyterian minister and Scottish Highlander, the Rev A. C. Sutherland was appointed to Clare in South Australia from a post in Gibraltar. Due to his failing health, he moved to North Carlton in Victoria before returning to South Australia in 1891. During his fourteen-year ministry in Port Adelaide, he gained a reputation as 'one of the best known and most scholarly ministers of the South Australian Presbyterian Church'.[34] Sutherland emerged as a great Protestant friend of the South Australian Irish Home Rule movement. Recognised as one of the finest classical scholars in Australia, he was appointed as an examiner and was a member of the senate of the University of Adelaide in 1893. In July 1902, he wrote to Senator J. V. O'Loghlin claiming that 'if Irishmen be true to the best traditions of their race their demands for power to express their national peculiarities – their national genius – in their own way without harm to others, will as justice is only sleeping not dead, be granted. Then England will not be wedded to Ireland by force, but will have won the fair bride, to the infinite benefit and happiness of both'.[35] He signed the letter 'Slàn leat, Do Charaid', Scots Gaelic for 'Goodbye my friend' indicating both a personal closeness and a shared Celtic/Gaelic identity. In 1906, the *Register* stated that 'No Irish national gathering in Adelaide would be complete without the presence of the Rev. A.C. Sutherland'. Fellow Protestant C. T. Hargraves was a supporter of the Irish nationalist cause in Adelaide too. Present at meetings from about 1882, the high-ranking civil servant, a member of the Anglican Church, was also an enthusiastic student of Gaelic.[36]

Thomas Esmonde notes the cosmopolitan nature of the colonial representatives at the first Dillon lecture and states that the audience was of differing nationalities and religions: as well as the Archbishop of Adelaide, members of both houses of the legislature graced the stage. In addition, there were 'judges, magistrates, leading citizens of every nationality and of every religion', The audience was largely composed of the visitors' kinsfolk and had 'in it all that is truest and most sterling and most devoted of Irish blood in South Australia'. People travelled hundreds of miles, 'utterly regardless of distance, of discomfort, and of sacrifice to see John Dillon, and to show their loyalty to the old land and to the old cause'. The press concurred with this description of the meeting at the Town Hall where 'a more representative gathering had never assembled' and the scene 'was the most enthusiastic ever witnessed in Adelaide'.[37]

THE ORANGE ORDER

The movement's strongest opponent everywhere was the Orange Order, a Protestant defence organisation founded in Co Armagh in 1795. Yet the Loyal Orange Institution of South Australia offered little resistance either to local Irish nationalist organisations or the visiting Irish politicians. There is some disagreement about when the first lodge formed in Adelaide. It is generally accepted that it was established around 1870, but there are reports in Queensland and Tasmanian newspapers of a lodge and Orange activity in Adelaide from as early as 1847.[38] It is possible an early lodge was formed but faltered and that the movement received a renewed impetus from the Fenian scare of 1868 when James O'Farrell attempted to assassinate the Duke of Edinburgh.[39] There was a large influx of immigrants from Ulster from the mid-1870s onwards— between 1876 and 1880 some 4000 new Irish arrived and most of them came from the northern province—the hotbed of unionism. But this research revealed that the movement didn't really gain any traction in the state until around 1903. In 1877, the Grand Lodge had seven private lodges under its auspice. These were spread far and wide as demonstrated by the location of lodges 3, 4 and 6: Drumcalpin, Auburn was 120 km north of Adelaide, Lodge 4 Diamond Lake was at Honiton 240 km south-west and Royal Bismarck No. 6 was in Mount Gambier 435 km from Adelaide.

In 1903, Grand Master James Johns revealed that the Loyal Orange Institution of South Australia was organising a number of new lodges: he said,

> The order is progressing by leaps and bounds. When I took office four years ago the membership totalled 379; today we muster about 2,000 active members, and many new lodges have been opened.[40]

The Orange Order was a secretive organisation so it is hardly surprising that little public record of it remains. The only real public demonstration of the Order in Adelaide apart from the annual July parade and picnic was their supposed involvement in policing the anti-Catholic Slattery Lectures of June 1900 which occasioned a riot in Gawler Place when 3000 people crammed into that narrow city thoroughfare.

The only significant Adelaide protest against Home Rule was actually organised by Victorian Orangemen. In fact, the meeting did not even protest against Irish Home Rule; rather, it met to voice its objection to the resolution of support for Home Rule which had been manoeuvred in the federal parliament by Henry Bourne Higgins in 1906. There is no evidence of opposition to either local Irish nationalist organisations or the Irish visitors. In contrast to the large sums of money raised to support the IPP, the only record of money donated to Home Rule's nemesis, the Ulster Defence Fund, is the sum of 4d which was donated from Lodge funds to make up to £2.2.0 the members' voluntary donation to the anti-Home Rule forces in July 1914.[41]

Few political figures are recognisable as supporters or members of the Loyal Orange Order. At a meeting in 1906, the Grand Master himself admitted that few public men would stand on an Orange platform:

> The Orange Institution was not so fortunate in South Australia as in some of the States of getting public men to be present on the platform at its gatherings, the reason being that public men were afraid of the influence of the Roman Catholic vote. There were ministers of the Gospel in South Australia who feared to be seen on the platform.[42]

Adelaide, then, sits in striking contrast with the position of the Orange Order in Canada for example, where, 'by the 1880s, over a fifth of state parliamentarians were brethren of the Orange Order'.

In fact, the loudest and most persistent anti-Irish voice was that of the Honourable Samuel Tomkinson, a Welsh Protestant who was manager of the Adelaide branch of the Bank of Australasia for almost thirty years, yet there is no evidence that he was an Orangeman. He retired from the Bank in 1879 and in 1881 became the Member for Gumeracha, a constituency which contained one of the colony's lowest Catholic (7.5%) and Irish (3.5%) groupings. He was largely ridiculed whenever he voiced an opinion about the Irish. As late as 1895, his candidacy meetings were peppered with snide remarks about his anti-Irishism. The editor of the Register placed this addendum at the end of one of Tomkinson's submissions to the paper:

> (People…should also know that Mr Tomkinson is not accepted by South Australians as their spokesman, although he delights to arrogate to himself that position. He is noted for his resistance to reforms, for his incapacity to perceive the direction and gauge the feeling of public opinion, and for his prejudiced views on all public questions.—Ed.[43]

RAISING MONEY

The IPP tours had two purposes: to raise awareness of Ireland's dire political and social situation and to raise money. A definite sum of the money raised by Australians during the Redmond mission and the SA proportion of it is difficult to define: at its worst, the colony's contribution was at least equal to the meeting average of the tour and at best, this small population contributed almost a fifth of the funds raised. Whelan claimed that 'the Irishmen raised £24,000. South Australia, with its few scattered Irishmen and limited population, collected £3800' or almost 16% of the colonial total for this mission.[44] The 1889 delegation would not fare quite as well. This was not due to any discernible disinterest in the Irish cause nor an increase in opposition. The economic fortune of the colony had taken a downturn and it showed in the amount collected. The final reported total of South Australian contributions was only £1500, but the smaller amount subscribed to this mission should not be taken at face value nor imply that South Australian support for Home Rule was weaker than on previous occasions or than that in the other colonies. As Table 7.2 shows, the per capita wealth in New South Wales at this time was double that of South Australia and the fundraising clearly reflects this. What was received was all that could be expected.

Table 7.2 Comparative wealth of the colonies, 1889[a]

Private wealth—total and per inhabitant in each colony of Australasia for 1889

Colony	Private wealth	
	Total (million £)	Per inhabitant (£)
New South Wales	410	371
Victoria	386	350
Queensland	106	266
South Australia	57	182
Tasmania	26	180
New Zealand	145	235
West Australia	6	144
Total, Australasia	1136	300

[a]Edited table from Coghlan, p. 86

While the IPP at home was united and showing purpose, support amongst Irish-Australians was freely given and this appears to have been emulated by the non-Irish of the colony during this tour. Just as they felt close enough and informed enough to support Home Rule, Parnell's fall from grace and the ensuing Irish Parliamentary Party split had an effect on the diasporic Irish communities and some subsequent delegations would find events at home harmful to their efforts in Australia. The 'Parnell Split' appeared to hamper Davitt's 1895 visit, but John Richard Cox who visited Adelaide in 1890 and again in 1891 collecting money for evicted Irish tenants seemingly avoided the fallout from the Parnell affair attracting moderate success over his two visits. The overall total raised by Cox in Australia was far below the amount raised by the two previous missions, but despite recent recession, South Australian donations exceeded those made in all the other colonies.

Cox had addressed 20 meetings in New South Wales before arriving in Adelaide on 5 March 1890 and had collected £1200 for the Evicted Irish Tenants Fund by this time.[45] His Town Hall meeting raised £230 in subscriptions, a comparatively large donation given what was collected in the eastern states in the preceding weeks where the average was £120 per lecture.[46] At the Port Adelaide meeting, £32 was subscribed.[47] When Deasy and Cox spoke at Petersburg, they collected £159, Wilmington gave £50, Carrieton £40, Georgetown, Jamestown and Clare subscribed similar amounts.[48] Success attached itself to Cox's second tour of the colony in 1891. At the first meeting of the second campaign, £250 was collected.[49] In early May, Cox's appearance in Petersburg brought £80 to the fund. He left South Australia to tour the rest of Australasia and in New Zealand received the news of Parnell's death. He returned to Adelaide in November 1891 and his last appearance there was at a banquet held in his honour at the Selborne Hotel, Pirie St, on 16 November. He said the tour of New Zealand had been a successful one: 'in fact I was nearly as well received there as I was in South Australia, your colony responding to the appeals better than any of the others'.[50] While the visit procured only £3000—at least 20% of which was raised in South Australia—Cox noted the benefit attained in unifying and reorganising the supporters of Irish Home Rule in the colonies.[51]

Raising the credibility of the Irish cause in Australian eyes was as important a task as emptying Australian purses. Michael Davitt's tour of Australasia, almost four years after Cox's departure, was credited by Thomas Hunt, the representative of South Australia and Victoria at the 1896 Irish Convention in Dublin, as being worth more than money. He declared that the issue of Irish Home Rule was better thought of in Australia since the visits of the various delegations but that Davitt's visit 'had a distinctly beneficial effect in this connection'.[52]

On his arrival, Davitt had stated that the Irish party acknowledged the depressed Australian economy and money was not asked for. Though the object of his journey changed due to the resignation of Lord Rosebery and the possibility of a British general election, the greatest value of his visit was the renewal of interest in the Irish cause and the consolidation of labour support for the movement that it precipitated. As his was not specifically a political fundraising tour from the outset and also occurred at a period of economic depression, the amounts raised were small in comparison with previous tours. In September, he reported an amount of £2000 from the four colonies of Victoria, New South Wales, Queensland and South Australia although to this date the remittance from South Australia was only £75.[53] His personal qualities must have gone some way to swaying the opinion of those undecided about the worthiness of Ireland's claims for self-government to its favour. The one-armed, slight physical figure Davitt presented, the shrewd intelligence displayed and the reputation he enjoyed as a defender of workers and of human rights could not have been farther from the spectacle of a Fenian insurgent some may have expected. Davitt remained in the colonies for seven months before returning to Ireland. It would be more than a decade before another party of envoys would seek Australian assistance once more for the Irish Home Rule movement.

The next official delegation consisted of Joseph Devlin and J. T. Donovan who arrived in the colony in May 1906. The funds raised during their two-week tour amounted to £1000 averaging just over £100 per meeting. After speaking in Adelaide and Port Adelaide, the two delegates toured the regional towns of Port Pirie, Jamestown, Gawler, Seppeltsfield, Tanunda, Millicent and Mount Gambier between 23 and 29 May 1906. Jamestown and Millicent collected £80 and £100, respectively. Although the South Australian contributions seemed small in comparison with the donations made interstate, the delegates proclaimed their supporters in the colony generous, always careful to publicly declare their awareness of the size of the South Australian population. In addition to this, they made a point of declaring the second aim of the exercise—the raising of awareness of the Irish cause—a greater and more important success than the first. Money was not everything.

This standpoint continued to be evident in the final tour of country South Australia which commenced on 18 November 1911 when William Redmond Jr., Richard Hazleton and J. T. Donovan visited Jamestown and collected £150.[54] Further amounts were collected in Arthurton (£100) and Kapunda (£120), while the meeting at Hammond was the largest ever seen there.[55] After their tour of the north of the state, the delegation returned to Adelaide where a farewell social was held on 27 November. Here Hazleton reported that 'He could safely say that South Australia made fair to exceed its former support by over 100 per cent (Cheers, and a voice, "We'll give you more")'.[56] The tour lasted twenty months and raised a total of £30,000. William Redmond said that 'South Australia, in proportion to population, had almost topped the States in subscribing £2000: The success that had been achieved had been due not so much to the work of the envoys as to the noble and self-sacrificing efforts of the local secretaries and officers'.[57] Above all, he desired to place on record the great debt of gratitude they owed to the Home Rule Committee in Adelaide.

CONCLUSION

Based on figures alone, it sometimes appeared that the South Australian contribution to the Irish Home Rule movement paled in comparison with the funds raised in other parts of Australia, but proportionally, the money collected there usually matched and sometimes exceeded that obtained in the other states. Fundraising was only one of the two main aims of the tours. In South Australia, the influential coverage of the movement by the press, the patronage of the powerful and the warmth of the public combined to make the colony a fertile ground for the reception of the idea of Irish self-determination.

In attempting to define the nature and extent of the support for Irish Home Rule in South Australia, this investigation has shown that cross-party sympathy was largely engendered for the cause through the efforts of local Irish men, the nature of the colony and its press and the improving circumstances of the Irish Parliamentary Party. This sympathy manifested itself in physical, moral and financial support and ensured that the visiting Irish delegates were greeted with enthusiasm and openness in South Australia even when this was not the case in other Australian colonies.

The very nature of Irishness was different in South Australia. Antagonistic personalities comparable to Henry Parkes in New South Wales and formidable nationalist and Catholic names such as O'Donnell and Mannix did not exist there. Tomkinson was a consistent negative commentator, but neither the press nor the majority of Adelaide's inhabitants took a great deal of notice of his opinion nor let it colour their view of the Irish. On the whole, the Irish Home Rulers were moderate, conservative figures well connected in society though not generally wealthy. The lack of factionalism on the part of Adelaide's nationalist Irish groups helped support the image of a cohesive, sensible, non-inflammatory movement. Irish nationalism also lacked a specific opponent in the colony.

The appearance of the Orange Order in South Australia in the 1870s was not welcomed by most colonists. The Order, viewed as having introduced sectarianism into an argument widely considered in the colonies to be one about democracy and freedom of colonial attachment to the Empire, only became popular in South Australia in the early years of the twentieth century. By this time, it had shown itself either incapable or unwilling to engage in an anti-Home Rule movement and was largely seen to be a fraternal organisation with developing ladies lodges and juvenile branches. By the time the Loyal Orange Order had gained a credible membership in the state, support of Irish nationalism was well entrenched there.

The general amenability and sympathy of the South Australian press to Irish nationalist concerns did much to elicit the favourable opinion of the broader population towards the movement. There frequently appeared editorials in both the *Register* and the *Advertiser* supportive of the Home Rule movement and its local manifestations. These organs provided much of the background knowledge most South Australians held of Irish affairs. The *Advertiser* ran a serialised account of Irish history from the pen of Young Irelander, Charles Gavin Duffy, over many issues from 1880 through 1883. Opposition appeared infrequently and usually in the form of a letter to the editor from a member of the public. Overall, the conservative nature of Adelaide's Irish Home Rule movement made for its general acceptance amongst the wider colonial population.

Business, sporting, community and political links between the Irish and non-Irish are evident in South Australia. So was it familiarity and perhaps even friendship that involved the non-Irish in the Home Rule movement? Was it the 'just' nature of the plea that Ireland be given a chance to enjoy the self-government that most of the colonies had had since the 1850s that prompted Home Rule support? It took no great leap to imagine that if an Irish resident of South Australia could win an election to local council or parliament and participate in the administration of the country that those of his race could do the same under similar governmental conditions in Ireland. What is clear is that the cause of nationalist Ireland appealed to a majority of the South Australian population. Commencing with the humanitarian plea for famine aid in the late 1870s, Irish locals attracted high-profile South Australians to the cause and their support continued when the Irish Relief Fund became the organisational mechanism for the Home Rule movement there.

The social and political comfort of settled Irish colonists in the colony was a factor in the high rate of assisted nominated passage take-up amongst those still in Ireland. The Irish arrivals came to a new life in a foreign land, but cultural ease, in the form of Irish-led communities, smoothed the transition from the old world to the new. Michael Kenny's patronage of St Patrick's Day festivities in the Burra provided a demonstration of national identity on that one day every year, but the network of business contacts and migration worked ceaselessly throughout the year. Leadership of the Irish nationalist organisations was also particularly consistent with the same names reoccurring year after year. A fusion of older, successful, confident settlers with new Irish blood sustained both the Irish nationalist organisation and the fundraising efforts of the period. The geographical concentration of the Irish in South Australia may also have been a factor in this success. The other colonies were spatially larger. Therefore, while they had larger Irish communities, these were spread over a greater geographical expanse. It was the very 'smallness' of the South Australian Irish community, often cited by other scholars as a contributing factor in its relative unimportance in the bigger picture of the Irish in Australia, which concentrated the potency of Irish cultural capital and which facilitated the success of the Home Rule movement in a Protestant and British colony. The social capital of the ethno-religious community appeared all the more significant in this contained environment. Irish newcomers were not 'lost' as they may have been in the sprawling expanse of Sydney and Adelaide's position as a colonial metropole assisted this. Close connections between the Irish community leadership and the non-Irish representatives of the colony were evident in business, political and sporting links. These relationships flowed on through the wider Home Rule movement and high-profile support of each Irish delegation.

The ordinary Irishman was given an opportunity to simultaneously partake in a respectable local event patronised by many of the colony's dignitaries and parliamentarians and support his fellow countrymen in Ireland. The constancy of executive officers in the nationalist organisations and their individual character traits only enhanced their image as being the complete opposite of the characteristics usually associated with the Irish. The fortunes of the Irish Parliamentary Party and the personal attributes of the visiting delegates affected the reception of each group, but the background support of the local organisations maintained the momentum between tours.

In the last years of the movement, many ministerial posts were filled by Irish-Australians such as Bill Denny, Senator O'Loghlin and Laurence O'Loughlin, but non-Irish, non-Catholic support on the Home Rule platform continued with Protestant MPs such as Reginald Blundell, Harry Jackson and Senator Gregor McGregor, all of whom were also labour men. Working alone the movement could not have been sustained by the Irish of South Australia due to their size but their capacity to exert influence and attract the non-Irish and non-Catholic to support the Home Rule movement showed that Australians, other than those of Irish blood, did indeed sympathise with Ireland.

NOTES

1. *Advertiser*, 15 December 1879, p. 6.
2. Fidelma Breen, "'Yet We Are Told That Australians Do Not Sympathise with Ireland': A Study of South Australian Support for Irish Home Rule, 1883 to 1912," M.Phil thesis, University of Adelaide, 2013, p. 25.
3. Eric Richards, "Irish Life and Progress in Colonial South Australia," *Irish Historical Studies* 27, no. 107 (1991): 21.
4. Susan Woodburn (Pruul), "The Irish in New South Wales, Victoria and South Australia, 1788–1880," Masters thesis, University of Adelaide, 1974.
5. Gregory Tobin, "Sea-Divided Gael: The Irish Home Rule Movement in Victoria and New South Wales 1880–1916," Unpublished MA thesis, Australian National University, 1969, p. 1.
6. Ibid., p. 295.
7. Louise Ann Mazzaroli, "The Irish in New South Wales, 1884 to 1914; Some Aspects of the Irish Sub-Culture," University of New South Wales, 1979.
8. Ibid., p. 108.
9. Caricatures of the Irish as simian-featured, foolish, intemperate and disloyal were featured throughout the nineteenth and early twentieth centuries in both the British and Australian press. See L. P. Curtis, *Apes and Angels: The Irishman in Victorian Caricature*, Washington, DC: Smithsonian Institution Press, 1997.
10. Mazzaroli, p. 174.
11. Ibid., p. 175.
12. Sir Thomas Esmonde, *Round the World with the Irish Delegates*, Dublin: Sealy, Bryers and Walker, 1892, p. 82.
13. Thomas Esmonde, *Around the World with the Irish Delegates*, Dublin: Sealy, Briars and Walker, 1892, p. 82.
14. Today's equivalent of £15,000 is £724 650.00 (using Old Money to New calculator at http://www.nationalarchives.gov.uk/currency) which in turn equals AUD$1.3 million (using currency converter http://www.oanda.com/convert/classic, accessed 2 July 2010); O'Farrell, Patrick, *The Irish in Australia*, Kensington, NSW: New South Wales University Press, 1986, p. 229, claims £25,000 was donated. Thomás O'Riordan claims £30,000 was raised by the 1883 delegation: http://multitext.ucc.ie/d/John_Redmond, accessed 30 August 2010.
15. William O'Brien visited in 1901 but undertook no official engagements— *Clarence and Richmond Examiner*, 3 December 1901, p. 4; Willie Redmond toured with his Australian wife in 1904 and made several appearances which brought funds to the IPP but his was not an

official tour—*Advertiser*, 9 December 1904, p. 5; *Advertiser*, 12 April 1905, p. 4; *Register*, 21 April 1905, p. 3.

16. *Chronicle*, 17 February 1883, p. 12.
17. 1881 Census of Australia.
18. T. A. Coghlan and New South Wales Statistician's Office, *A Statistical Account of the Seven Colonies of Australasia*, Sydney: Charles Potter, Government Printer, Phillip St, 1890, p. 15.
19. *Register*, 15 May 1895, p. 7.
20. Gerald O'Collins, "Glynn, Patrick McMahon (Paddy) (1855–1931)," Australian Dictionary of Biography, National Centre of Biography, Australian National University, http://adb.anu.edu.au/biography/glynn-patrick-mcmahon-paddy-6405/text10949, accessed 6 February 2013.
21. *Advertiser*, 15 March 1869, p. 1. The CYMS commenced on 12 January 1860 at the Schoolroom in Franklin St with an attendance of over 100 brothers. *Register*, 13 January 1860, p. 3.
22. *Advertiser*, 13 March 1915, p. 7.
23. *Chronicle*, 23 March 1878, p. 1. The first celebration of St Patrick's Day was in 1840 when the Sons of Erin held a dinner at Fordham's. *Register*, 21 March 1840, p. 6. Later, more publicly inclusive events are advertised in the *Register*, 15 March 1845, p. 2; a supper hosted by Thomas McEllester at the Irish Harp in Rundle St and a programme of events hosted by Mrs Wilkins at the Market House, Thebarton.
24. *Advertiser*, 30 November 1878, p. 6.
25. *Advertiser*, 1 May 1899, p. 6; *Advertiser*, 15 February 1899, p. 6; *Register*, 18 March 1878, p. 5.
26. In May 1850 a St Patrick's Society dinner ended in a melee, the newly erected St Patrick's Hall in Leigh St being wrecked in the fighting. *South Australian*, 3 May 1850, p. 3.
27. *Advertiser*, 26 June 1882, p. 4.
28. *Register*, 5 March 1866, p. 2.
29. *Register*, 4 March 1890, p. 6.
30. G. L. Fischer, "Rounsevell, William Benjamin (1843–1923)," *Australian Dictionary of Biography*, National Centre of Biography, Australian National University, http://adb.anu.edu.au/biography/rounsevell-william-benjamin-8281/text14511, accessed 4 November 2012.
31. *Chronicle*, 17 February 1883, p. 12.
32. Ibid.
33. *Register*, 18 March 1889, p. 2.
34. *Register*, 17 October 1910, p. 8.
35. Rev A. C. Sutherland to J. V. O'Loghlin, 21 July 1902. O'Loghlin, ibid.
36. *Southern Argus*, 27 April 1882, p. 3.
37. *Chronicle*, 20 April 1889, p. 7.

38. "Orange Lodges," *Colonial Times*, 23 November 1847, p. 3. "Local Intelligence: Orange Lodge Formed in Adelaide," *Register*, 18 July 1849, p. 1.
39. See Richard Davis, "Orangeism in Tasmania, 1832–1967," *Papers and Proceedings: Tasmanian Historical Research Association* 55, no. 3 (December 2008): 145–159. Davis shows the formation of a lodge in Tasmania in August 1848 and he is able to follow newspaper reports of celebratory banquets until April 1851 when the movement appears to have petered out, not to be revived again until the Fenian Scare in 1868.
40. *Advertiser*, 1 May 1903, p. 3.
41. State Library of South Australia, Adelaide, SRG/293, Box 3, Loyal Orange Institution of South Australia, Minutes of LOL 7, Port Adelaide, 6 July 1914.
42. Patrick Ireland, *Only Distant Cousins: Irish Protestants and Politics in the U.S., Canada, and Australia*. Draft Paper for DIT, http://www.dit.ie/media/documents/psai/PatrickIrelandPSAIpaper82.pdf.
43. *Register*, 11 April 1889, p. 7.
44. *Register*, 5 June 1894, p. 7.
45. *Register*, 6 March 1890, p. 6.
46. *Register*, 17 March 1890, p. 1.
47. *Register*, 7 March 1890, p. 5.
48. *Register*, 17 March 1890, p. 5.
49. *Register*, 14 April 1891, p. 6.
50. *Register*, 16 November 1891, p. 6.
51. The Adelaide Irish National Federation received a letter from the Evicted Tenants Fund, Dublin, thanking them for a donation of £600. *Register*, 7 October 1891, p. 5.
52. *Kilmore Free Press*, 15 October 1896, p. 2.
53. *Burra Record*, 18 September 1895, p. 3.
54. *Register*, 21 November 1911, p. 6.
55. *Register*, 24 November 1911, p. 8.
56. *Advertiser*, 28 November 1911, p. 12.
57. *Advertiser*, 26 July 1912, p. 10.

CHAPTER 8

Cornish Miners in Western Australia 1850–1896

Anthony Nugent

As Dudley Baines, the demographer and emigration historian has noted, nineteenth-century 'Cornwall was probably an emigration region comparable with any in Europe.'[1] Although emigrants from Cornwall were drawn from a wide range of occupations, it was those from mining communities who remained distinctly visible overseas as a 'Cornish diaspora', such was the insatiable demand for Cornish labour on the rapidly expanding international mining frontier.[2]

WHEN CORNISH MINERS 'RULED' WESTERN AUSTRALIA

With the findings of Baines and Payton in mind, the first part of this chapter will discuss the insatiable demand for Cornish miners as it pertained to Western Australia, and in terms of the growing rivalry with mining interests in South Africa. In Western Australia, Cornish miners established the first lead mine on the Murchison River, some 55 kilometres Northeast of present-day Northampton, in 1849. The Geraldine Mine became the first of many metalliferous mines across Western Australia that

A. Nugent (✉)
Flinders University, Adelaide, SA, Australia
e-mail: nuge0008@uni.flinders.edu.au

© The Author(s) 2019
P. Payton and A. Varnava (eds.),
Australia, Migration and Empire, Britain and the World,
https://doi.org/10.1007/978-3-030-22389-2_8

181

owed its existence to the work of Cornish miners. Local folklore posits that a Cornish miner named Joe Jones was the first person to attempt to fix the flooding problem at the Geraldine Mine by making a 'lift' pump from hollowed out trees lined with sheets of lead.[3] Nevertheless, the first recorded Cornish mine captain, John James, arrived at the Geraldine Mine in August 1850, from South Australia.[4] John James had arrived in Adelaide from Cornwall in 1847, and soon earned a reputation as something of a mining authority through frequent letters to the press on South Australia's mining potential. His mining knowledge no doubt brought him to the attention of the discovers of Geraldine Mine (1848), Augustus and Charles Gregory who promptly engaged him; only to lose his services less than a year later after gold was discovered in Victoria. In November 1852, Captain John James sent a letter to a friend at the Swan River settlement. The letter described the chaotic scenes at Mount Alexander, in Victoria. 'At the diggings people from every part of the world are seen, in their different costumes, but not any so well fitted for the work as Cornish men'.[5] The high praise that Captain John James afforded his countryman at Mount Alexander did little to lessen the notion that Cornishmen were without peer as hard-rock miners. Indeed, this perception gained further currency when twenty-two Cornish miners dug up the 2217-ounce Welcome Nugget near Ballarat, in 1858. This was followed by the discovery of the largest alluvial gold nugget ever found, the 2284-ounce Welcome Stranger, at Mount Moliagul, Victoria, by two Cornishmen, John Deason and Richard Oats, in 1869.[6]

Before leaving Western Australia, Captain John James recommended another Cornishman, Martin Hosken as his replacement. The Gwennap born Martin Hosken (1814) was the eldest son of John Hosken and Mary (née Spargo), and brother of John (1816), Ann (1815), Charity (1822) and Elizabeth (1826).[7] Both Martin and John Hosken Jnr had started mining at the age of ten before leaving Cornwall in the late 1830s to work for the St. John d'el Rey Mining Company Ltd. at the Morro Velho gold mine in Nova Lima/Congonhas, Brazil. After briefly returning to Cornwall in 1851, Martin Hosken, along with Cornish miners Nancarrow, Tregoning, Hosken and Spargo, left for Western Australia and the Geraldine Mine, arriving in September 1852.[8] It would be another ten years before Martin Hosken was joined by his younger brother John Jnr and his wife Elizabeth (née Luke) and their five children, plus widowed daughter Mary Jane Paul, whose husband Joseph Paul had died in Brazil, of indeterminant causes, in February 1861.

The record indicates that Martin Hosken's tenure at the Geraldine Mine was beset by problems. In 1853, a fire destroyed the miners' cottage where Captain Hosken lived and he sustained serious burns when he attempted to save mine documents and other valuables.[9] On another occasion, he became hopelessly lost in the bush without water after being thrown from his pony. Fortuitously, Hosken was discovered some twenty-four hours later attempting to regain the road on foot.[10] Nevertheless, Martin Hosken's most pressing difficulties seem to have been a belligerent convict workforce and a personality clash with the man responsible for building and running the Warribanno smelter, Geordie and Francis Watson Pearson.[11] Arguably, the indifferent skills of the largely convict workforce and ongoing clashes with Pearson, prompted Martin Hosken leave the Geraldine Mine in late 1858, for an area called 'The Mines'.[12]

In 1867, Captain Sam Mitchell, and seven other Cornish miners, arrived at Geraldton aboard the 395-ton, *Zephyr*, which was then owned by the secretary to the WA Board of Immigration, Robert Mace Habgood, who was in turn, one of the Geraldine Mine's three mine owners.[13] Samuel Mitchell, for his part, had been born in Perranzabuloe, Cornwall, in 1839, while one of his two younger brothers, James, was born in 1847. Their parents were lead miner Samuel and his wife Mary Anne (née Saunders). By 1860, Sam Jnr had married Mary Jane (née Stephens) the daughter of Hugh Stephens a mine captain from Redruth.[14] After arriving in Western Australia and formally taking over at the Geraldine Mine, Mitchell opined that. 'The mine did not appear to have been wisely opened or worked'. However, in his reminiscences he further observed that 'there were innumerable drawbacks in those days that are not known now'.[15]

Captain Mitchell's first six months were highly productive until a flash flood inundated the mine and momentarily brought all mining work to a standstill. This prompted Mitchell and his Cornish miners to abandon the Murchison River shaft and move nearer to Northampton to mine for 'galena' (lead ore). At this new site, Mitchell proved that he was not averse to 'cutting corners' in his eagerness to ship the first lead ore out of Western Australia.[16] Despite abandoning sound mining practice in this instance, Mitchell was proud of his achievements and that of his band of Cousin Jacks. Indeed, Mitchell maintained that he was the first to demonstrate the commercial viability of mining carbonates of lead in Western Australia despite the oppressive heat and primitive working conditions.[17]

184 A. NUGENT

After completing his three-year stint as mine captain, which proved highly profitable for mine owners Joseph Lucas Horrocks, George Shenton and Robert Habgood, Mitchell was rewarded with a contract extension and free passage back to Cornwall on half pay, to procure mine equipment and additional Cornish miners.[18] Mitchell's second stint at the Geraldine Mine lasted until 1875 and was seemingly less successful due to factors beyond his control. These included labour shortages and the loss of a vessel containing nearly 60 tons of uninsured ore. Nevertheless, these setbacks were minor compared to the impact of plummeting lead prices.[19] Despite the bleak economic outlook, Mitchell, and his financial backer Charles Crowther, continued to open new mines, including the Wheal Ellen Mine, which Mitchell named after his eldest daughter. This was followed by the opening the Baddera lead mine in 1873. In due course the price of lead improved, and the Wheal Ellen Mine realised over 70,000 pounds and earned Mitchell the epithet 'model man' and the 'lead king'.[20] Samuel Mitchell's standing in mining circles was further enhanced in 1880, when he produced what was described as a 'voluminous and highly interesting paper entitled' *Mineral Wealth of Western Australia*, for the Melbourne Exhibition.[21] Of particular note was the addition of M.E. after his name on the paper. As Limbaugh has argued, M.E. (Mining Engineer) was often used interchangeably during this period to describe a 'Mining Expert', although there was little agreement in mining circles on whether 'book learning' was superior to practical experience.[22]

Meanwhile, another, recently arrived Cornishman, Frederic Charles Burleigh Vosper, who likewise lacked formal qualifications in mining, but who was evidently possessed of a quick and logical mind through exposure to his father's business interests.[23] Frederic Vosper, had been born in St. Dominic, Cornwall, in 1869, he was the son of Charles Walter Vosper a self-taught inventor of mining equipment. Nevertheless, in the 1881, UK census, Charles W. Vosper, is recorded as being a sewing machine manufacturer, moreover, when he died in 1922, aged 81, the *North Devon Journal* described him as an expert mechanical engineer and inventor of a 'pointing' machine that had revolutionised the silk glove trade.[24] At age 16, Frederic Vosper enlisted in the Royal Navy and was posted to the training ship *HMS Lion*, at nearby Torpoint. Details of his service record indicate that he added two years to his age when he enlisted in May 1885, moreover, the record also shows that Vosper was discharged on December 28, 1885.[25] Moreover, his brief Royal Navy service and his young age does little to advance the claim that Frederic Vosper had been to Bolivia and worked in that country's silver mines. Indeed, the dairy of Cornish miner James Bennetts Williams, who was working in Bolivia from December 1883 until September 1887, neglects to mention Vosper or, indeed, any boys from Cornwall.[26] On August 3, 1886, Vosper arrived at Maryborough, Queensland, aboard the *Scottish Hero*. There is anecdotal evidence that Vosper spent time engaged in a variety of occupations, including mining, before he embarked on a career in journalism, although there is little evidence to suggest he gained much practical mining experience during his seven years in Queensland.[27]

Although Vosper appears to have had little practical mining experience, his knowledge of geology was said to be extensive. It was while working as a journalist at Cue that Vosper indulged in his passion for geology, and he spent a great deal of his spare time prospecting in the bush. He eventually accumulated an extensive collection of minerals, which first went on display at Coolgardie, before he donated it to the Mineral Department, at the Perth Museum.[28] This and other evidence suggests that Vosper's interest in geology was largely academic, although he was committed to sharing his scientific knowledge more widely. In 1894, Vosper wrote and published *The Prospectors Companion: Guide to Simple Mineral Analysis with Tables, a Glossary and Appendix on Explosives*. The work was described as being 'so indispensable to mining men who have not had the privilege of a scientific training'.[29] *The Prospectors Companion* comprised eighty-eight pages and contained twenty chapters devoted to the description, appearance, characteristics and location of numerous minerals, and their behaviour under chemical treatment and smelting.[30] In the preface, Vosper described the books purpose thus.

> In the following treatise I have endeavoured to give, in a simple and comprehensive form, as much information concerning rudimentary mineralogy as the prospector or amateur interested in mining is likely to find it desirable to acquire without plunging deeply into the science...Every effort has been made to make the work thoroughly reliable, and it is my earnest hope that it may prove serviceable to the hosts of pioneers now engaged in opening up the vast and almost virgin mineral wealth of Western Australia.[31]

However, priced at two shillings and sixpence, the book barely recouped its production costs.[32] While the *Prospectors Companion* may not have been financially rewarding, professional recognition was soon forthcoming. In 1896, Vosper was accepted into the Australasian Institute of Mining Engineers, which allowed him to use the post-nominal title M.A.I.M.E.[33] Moreover, despite embarking on a political career in 1897, Vosper maintained an abiding interest in geology, becoming a founding member of the WA branch of the Geological Society of Australasia.

When former captain of Wheal Owles William Oats first arrived at Southern Cross on 18 November 1889 the settlement was—as Geoffrey Blainey points out—little more than a dead-end town, inhabited by absconders, debtors and murders.[34] Into this volatile mix Captain Oats recruited a contingent of Cousin Jacks from Sandhurst, present-day Bendigo. At Southern Cross, Captain Oats took charge of Fraser's Gold Mine until 1891, before moving to the adjacent Fraser's South GM and managing that until 1895. By 1892, the now 54 year-old Captain Oats, who hailed from the small village of Tregeseal, near St Just, had embarked on a career as a mining consultant organising prospecting tours to the north and east of Southern Cross. As is well attested, the next major gold discovery after Southern Cross was that made by Arthur Bayley and William Ford at Coolgardie in 1892. It was followed the next year (1893) by the discovery of gold at Kalgoorlie by Patrick Hannan, Tom Flanagan and Dan O'Shea.

After the discovery of gold at the Great Boulder, Captain Oats found himself in high demand and he became the consulting engineer at the Associated Gold Mines, Hannans' Proprietary Group, Brookman's Boulder, the Lake View and, at the Great Boulder, where he was employed as the first underground manager.[35] It was the discovery of gold at the Great Boulder that established his reputation and that of another Cornishman, the Camborne born, Captain George Prout. Both Oats and Prout were allegedly the only mining experts to report favourably on what would become the Great Boulder group of mines.[36] Admittedly, both were employed by Samuel W. Pearce at various stages and were in a position to claim some of the credit for the Great Boulder discovery. However, while the extent of their involvement is unclear, their association with the Great Boulder discovery proved a great boon to both their mining careers. After the Great Boulder discovery it was widely speculated that any prospectus that did not have the personal imprimatur of Captain Oats' stood little chance of attracting British capital.[37] Indeed, the following example taken from the *Kanowna Carbine Gold Mining Co.* prospectus, from 1896, and drawn up by Captain Oats, indicates that he was adept at 'talking up' his discoveries.

Taking into consideration the valuable prospects obtained from this reef at the various points opened up. There can be no doubt that when systematically developed to a greater depth this will prove one of the most valuable properties in the Kanowna district. I can highly recommend it to speculators as a sound mining investment.[38]

However, not everyone shared the view that 'of all West Australian mining engineers, Captain Oats is the mining engineer *par excellence*'.[39] The editor of the *Coolgardie Miner*, Alfred 'Alf' Chandler, was one who charged that previous forecasts attributed to Captain Oats had been 'wide of the mark', including some 'floats' that had failed to eventuate, and that Oats powers of prophecy were 'not worth a Niagara dam'.[40] Chandler's missive might have been a reference to Captain Oats' association with the American prospector Leslie Robert Menzies, after whom the Menzies goldfield was named. Captain Oats had accompanied Menzies to the Royal Phoenix Mine, in the Barossa Valley, South Australia, in June 1896. The latter had already visited the Royal Phoenix Mine on two previous occasions and the high value he placed on the opinion Captain Oats, was borne out when Menzies formed the Menzies Barossa Gold Mining Syndicate soon after. The syndicate attracted many of Western Australia's leading figures including Sir George Shenton, Alexander Matheson and the Mayor of Perth, Henry Saunders.[41] Unfortunately, for investors, the rechristened Menzies Barossa GM proved to be an unmitigated disaster. After considerable investment in plant, including the construction of the largest gold treatment plant in South Australia, which was designed to process 600 tons of ore per week, the mine was forced to close after operating for only a few months. The extensible reason for the mine's failure was that instead of producing 750 ounces of gold from the first 1500 ton crushing, only 30 ounces of gold was produced.[42] Despite further attempts at finding payable gold deposits, the poor return continued and the mill was closed for good in 1898. It appears that apart from recommending the mine to Leslie Menzies, and perhaps other investors, Oats ongoing involvement was minor. Indeed, by the time it became apparent the Menzies Barossa GM was a financial disaster. Oats had already returned to Western Australia, written a pamphlet entitled *The Immediate Future of West Australia and Our Mining Prospects*, and was elected, along with Frederic Vosper and Samuel Mitchell to the Legislative Assembly, in 1897.[43]

188   A. NUGENT

The highpoint of Cornish mining supremacy in Western Australia lasted until 1895. Indeed, the reputation of Cornish mine captains was such that by 1895, the Great Boulder, Lake View, Royal Mint, Australian, Ivanhoe, Maritana, Napier and Iron Duke Mines were all under Cornish management.[44] With so many Cousin Jacks working on the Eastern Goldfields in the 1890s, the Cornish had the capacity to 'hire and fire' as they saw fit. To understand the extent of Cornish domination prior to the arrival of Americans like Herbert Hoover, in 1897, the thoughts of the highly respected Warden of Kalgoorlie, John Michael Finnerty, are informative. During a speech in 1901, at the Mining Managers Association social, the Irish-born Finnerty reflected on what he found when he arrived in 1889.

> In the early days of the fields nearly every mining manager was a Cornishman, and a Cornish miner coming from anywhere was almost sure of getting a job on a mine that had a Cornish boss; for those who did not happen to be 'Cousin Jacks' had to make room for those who were.[45]

As Warden Finnerty's remarks clearly show the domination of the Eastern Goldfields by Cousin Jacks saw a procession of Cornish mine captains at most of the big mines. Indeed, the biggest, the Great Boulder, was no exception, and during its early development Cornish mine captains invariably held sway. Apart from William Oats, the other Cousin Jacks mentioned in connection with the Great Boulder Mine include, Bill Roberts, John (Jack) Warrick, William Beaglehole, John Dunstan and Edward Skewes.

In other Eastern Goldfield mines, Cousin Jacks were similarly represented. These included underground mine captains/managers, Jonathan Bray, Martin Carkeek, James 'Jim' Craze, William Henry East, Joseph James East, William Hambley, Alfred Henry Harvey, Tom Horton, Jos Liddicoat, Herbert Marshall Lowry, William Henry Mathews, William Nankivell, Alf Northey, Jack Pascoe, Thomas Pascoe, William Pollard, Frederick Rodda, William Henry Rodda, Charles Thomas Rowe, William Rowe, Merts Trebilcock, James Tregurtha, Charles Truscott and Tom Warren. While other mine captains/managers, including Thomas Gilbert Pearce at Richmond Gem, the Irish Lily, the Lady Loch and the Easter Gift, and John Treloar at Reefer's Eureka and Hannan's Brown Hill and, Charles Trevena, of Chas Trevena and Co. Coolgardie, promoter of McAuliffe's Reward and the Duke of Westminster Reef, made significant

8 CORNISH MINERS IN WESTERN AUSTRALIA 1850–1896 189

fortunes after transitioning into mine ownership.[46] However, for William Harris from Perranzabuloe and Robert Williams from St. Germans their discovery of a large 303 ounces gold nugget, which they named the Devon Consols Joker, found near Black Flag in 1895, gained both brief celebrity. After public interest in the find subsided William Harris returned to South Australia, while Robert Williams resumed work at his Gladstone Tin Mine lease at Dumpling Gully, Greenbushes, where a number of Cornish miners had already settled.[47]

In, *The Rush That Never Ended*, Geoffrey Blainey cites the intervention of British company, Bewick, Moreing & Co. and the arrival of American mining experts like Herbert Hoover, as the reason why Cornish miners lost their dominance.[48] However, this argument fails to consider other factors that were equally, if not more significant than the arrival of Herbert Hoover. In 1895, the same year as Harris and Williams discovered the Devon Consols Joker. Upwards of 2000 Cornish miners had left their homes in Cornwall and made their way to South Africa and the *Witwatersrand* in search of jobs and higher wages.[49] Moreover, South Africa not only offered a regular shipping service to and from Cape Town, it was, unlike Australia, relatively close to British ports and home.

By 1895, the Western Australian government had become aware that a sizeable Cornish exodus was heading to the mines of South Africa. Understandably, the government had begun to worry that their own mining industry might suffer from a lack of skilled miners. The government, therefore, sought the advice of their London-based Agent-General, Sir Malcolm Fraser, who was asked to provide a report on the availability of Cornish miners and whether they could still be enticed to Western Australia. The following year (1896) Fraser's report was tabled in parliament and he advised the government that with proper assistance and with very little encouragement, Cornish miners could still be enticed to Western Australia.[50]

Clearly, and in line with the argument presented by both Baines and Payton, the concern shown by the Western Australian government in 1895 reveals an insatiable demand for Cornish labour and, moreover, the growing rivalry between Western Australia and South Africa interests for Cornish mining expertise. Indeed, at the height of the competition a visiting British M.P. Henry Charles Richards, who had Cornish ancestry, decided to intervene on behalf of West Australian government. He advised his fellow Cornishmen 'to turn their attention to the Australian colonies, rather than Johannesburg, [where] they would find a healthy, settled form of government, perfect liberty, with bread one-third the price it is in the Transvaal'.[51]

While the Western Australian government was giving serious consideration to reversing the trend of Cornish miners going to South Africa, not everyone in South Africa was happy to see a large influx of Cornish miners. One individual who used the pen-name *Uitlander* wrote to the *Cornishman* to urge Cornish miners to stay at home. Part of *Uitlander's* concern was the clannish nature of the Cornish and their tendency to monopolise all of the mining work.[52] As to be expected, in tough economic times, *Uitlander's* plea fell on deaf ears and Cornish miners continued to leave for Johannesburg in ever increasing numbers.

Meanwhile, the necessity for Henry Charles Richards M.P. to intervene on behalf of Western Australia became nugatory as numerous mines began shutting down. Indeed, not long after receiving Sir Malcolm Fraser's positive report concerning the availability of Cornish miners, the economic situation on the Eastern Goldfields markedly deteriorated. The downturn was triggered by a tightening in British investment, which noticeably declined from the last quarter of 1896, until manifesting a slight improvement in 1903.[53] Asked about the prospects for Cornish miners in Western Australia, Zebina Lane of the British Westralia Syndicate, at a meeting of investors held at the Savoy Hotel in London, in April 1896, recommended that Cornish miners postpone coming to Western Australia because there were already a large number of miners without work.[54] Under the circumstances, the imperative to recruit Cornish miners was no longer necessary. Moreover, the economic downturn provides context for the words of Warden Finnerty in 1901, when he observed that Cornish miners where no longer the dominant force of just a decade earlier. Moreover, even after British investment returned after 1903, the decline in alluvial mining meant that Cornish miners had little prospect of reasserting their former dominance.

Faced with an unprecedented contraction in its once booming mining industry, the West Australian government turned its attention to opening up the colony to settlers by offering all-comers the chance to buy cheap land.[55] Indeed, at the same time as mining was in decline, wheat farming was experiencing unprecedented growth from 1905 to 1911, following a number of bumper harvests.[56] Accordingly, Cousin Jacks, who had joined the gold rush from eastern mining districts, were identified as being prime candidates to take up land for farming. To that end, the

Sunday Times observed that goldfield miners were being encouraged to pursue a life far removed from the 'hard yacker' and 'clogged lungs' of life underground. It further opined that a change in occupation could prove equally beneficial to the miners' wives and children who would be spared the blistering heat that accompanied living amongst the ore and mullock-dumps of Boulder and its surroundings.[57]

When the Second Boer War ended in 1902, South Africa resumed its position as the preferred destination for Cornish miners. As Payton has argued, there were an estimated seven thousand Cornish miners working on the Rand by 1905,[58] each earning in the vicinity of 300 pounds per annum, at a time when miners in Western Australia were earning about 208 pounds per annum.[59] Nevertheless, by 1906, many Cornish miners were returning home to Cornwall as improved tin prices had negated the need to work overseas.[60] Moreover, in something of ironic twist, the lack of work and inferior wages in Western Australia saw upwards of five thousand Australian born miners leave the Eastern Goldfields and decamp to Johannesburg during the early 1900s.[61] Indeed, once established, Australian miners began to supplant Cornish miners in skilled roles, while their aggressive attitude towards mine management, was in stark contrast to the more considered approach of Cornish miners.[62]

THE END OF CORNISH 'RULE' AND THE ARRIVAL OF THE 'AMERICANS'

Having spent the first part of this chapter examining the dominate role that Cornish miners played in establishing Western Australia's mining industry prior to 1895, and the economic factors that made South Africa a more appealing proposition to both Cornish and Australian miners after the Second Boer War. It is important in terms of context to consider the impact of American 'knowhow' on mining in Western Australia and whether this was a significant factor in ending Cornish domination. After being in the ascendancy for many decades, the practical approach of Cornish miners was increasingly being seen as 'old school'. Arguably, the first scientist to make this claim in Australia was Irish-born geologist, Edward Townley Hardman. Certainly, Hardman was eminently qualified to deliver such an assessment. He was, after all, not only an associate of the Royal College of Science in Dublin, but also a fellow of both the Royal Geological Society of Ireland and the Chemical Society of London.

In 1884, Hardman was forced to defend a geological report he had produced for the Western Australian government covering an area of 12,000 square miles (31,080 square kilometres) near the Fitzroy River. In his report, Hardman reasoned that there appeared to be little evidence of commercial quantities of ore in the areas he had surveyed. The report, which was later published in the *government gazette*, prompted criticism from an experienced miner named Thomas Lewis. In his letter to the editor of the *West Australian*, Lewis expressed concern that Hardman's findings might dissuade practical miners and prospectors from exploring the territory in question.[63] Suffice to say, the crux of the debate hinged on the merits of the scientific approach taken by Hardman against the practical approach championed by Lewis. It was in this exchange that Hardman observed that while Cornish miners were excellent practical miners when working under the direction of trained geologists. They were less successful when left to their own devices and invariably sank mine shafts anywhere their own sweet fancy impels them to work.[64]

Thirteen years after Edward Townley Hardman first highlighted the limitations of practical Cornish miners, the American geologist, and mining engineer, Herbert Hoover, arrived in Western Australia aged just twenty-two. It is clear from Hoover's memoir, published in 1951, that he (Hoover) shared similar views to Hardman concerning the scientific limitations of Cornish miners. In the first volume of his memoir covering the period 1870–1920, Hoover said in part, 'It was the American universities that took engineering away from rule-of-thumb surveyors, mechanics, and Cornish foreman and lifted it into the realm of application of science'.[65] It would not be an exaggeration to claim that Hoover's view was readily accepted by the Australian mining industry, who began recruiting university-trained geologists and engineers in preference to practical miners. Geoffrey Blainey, for one, describes the moment in 1886, when the board members of Broken Hill Proprietary Ltd. (B.H.P) made perhaps the most momentous decision in Australia's industrial history when they turned to America and not Cornwall for the best mining expertise that money could buy.[66] As for Cornwall, and its miners, Blainey opined that it had long since become the decaying home of Australia's mining skills.[67]

For his part, Herbert Hoover later claimed to have a great affection for Cornish miners as was evidenced by his attendance, as a former President, at a reunion of his mining colleagues at the Grass Valley in 1935. It was at the Grass Valley forty years earlier that Hoover first encountered Cornish miners as a two-dollar-a-day 'mucker' at the Reward Mine. He then went on to meet other Cornish miners at the Mayflower Mine, in the Nevada City district of California. In his memoir, Hoover mentions that it was two Cornishmen, Ed Gassaway, at the Reward Mine and Tommy Ninnis at the Mayflower Mine, who taught him the rudiments of hard-rock mining.[68] From reading his memoir one gets the real sense that Hoover was damming his teachers with faint praise when he said. 'The Cornish miners on my shift, while a little off-ish at first, warmed up to teaching the tricks of the trade to the anomaly of a college graduate working at common labor'.[69] Quite what the Cornish thought about their teaching skills being equated with trickery, and the work being described as common labour, is open to conjecture. Nevertheless, the following anecdote from Hoover's memoir is clearly at odds with what is known of the Cornish character. 'The Cornishmen on our level celebrated the advanced degree which came to me (Hoover) by bringing extra Cornish "pasties" for our midnight lunch'.

As many observers have noted, the Cornish cultivated an air of superiority and clannishness underground that many outsiders found irritating.[70] Indeed, Hoover's earlier observation that they exhibited a degree of scepticism towards the value of 'them college educated fellers' is probably closer to what they really thought of Hoover's mining ability and overly confident demeanour.[71] Moreover, one can argue that Hoover received more than just practical training from his Cornish teachers as he became aware of the overt favouritism directed to other Cousin Jacks.[72] Indeed, Captain Samuel Mitchell was typical in this regard, as were most Cornish mine captains, including Captain Richard Piper, who in 1883, recruited 408 men, women and children, from Cornwall, on behalf of the Wallaroo and Moonta mines in South Australia.[73] Mitchell, too, looked to his homeland for miners when he arranged for eight Cornish families comprising thirty-five individuals to come to Northampton, WA, in 1881, courtesy of the *Robert Morrison*.[74]

From what is known of the operations of Bewick, Moreing & Co. in Western Australia, the Cornish practice of privileging the employment of other Cousin Jacks was not continued after Herbert Hoover arrived. Indeed, Bewick, Moreing & Co. along with other large mine companies were in the process of creating a highly structured workforce that valued scientific training and remunerated accordingly.[75] With that in mind, there is a certain irony in the claim that Herbert Hoover recruited fifteen 'university' trained mine managers, metallurgists and mechanical engineers from the United States, to fill supervisory roles in Western Australia. At first glance, this seems to be an example of Hoover privileging scientific training over practical mining skills. However, recent research has shown that only seven of the fifteen miners that accompanied Hoover were 'university trained'. Indeed, of the four who attended Stanford University with Herbert Hoover, one, Frank Dennis, held a degree in history.[76] Another miner in this cohort, who Hoover curiously fails to mention in his memoir, was the Cornish born William Pollard. Pollard, who was no mere acolyte, became the chief underground manager at the White Feather Main Reefs, Lake View Consols, Great Boulder Perseverance G. M. and the Oroya Black Range Mine, at Sandstone, for Bewick, Moreing & Co.[77] Similarly, Hoover also neglects to mention Joseph M. Davy who had been mining in Arizona prior to coming to Australia with the other 15 'Americans'. Some accounts have described Davey as 'a square, level-headed Yankee'; however, it appears that Davey had at least a familial connection with Cornwall.[78] A newspaper report from the *Murchison Advocate*, in 1909, states that J. M. Davey, the late underground manager at the Great Fingall Mine, was in Cornwall where he is now convalescing due to 'miners' complaint', before, it was hoped, returning to Western Australia and resuming his mining career.[79] Regrettably, a year later another newspaper report noted that Mr J. Davey had recently died in London of 'miner's phthisis'.[80]

Many historians have characterised Hoover as being blunt and driven: and having a low regard for Australian mining expertise.[81] However, it was during his second stint in Western Australia that Hoover felt comfortable enough to publicly question government policy. It is noteworthy that the target of his disdain was the *Industrial Conciliation and Arbitration Act 1900*, an act that had been championed by George Foster Pearce, a former carpenter, and the son of Cornish immigrants. The State's arbitration law according to Hoover placed 'a weapon in the hands of workmen for injustice against the employer'.[82] Similarly, Hoover's answer to keeping 'the gold stealer and the demagogue' from gaining employment was equally draconian.[83] He therefore sought to introduce a 'ticket system' as a way of blacklisting undesirables and effectively driving such people out of the goldfields. Whether this included 'professional agitators' and socialists, the other undesirables in his crosshairs are open to conjecture. However, perhaps his most controversial decision was to introduce Italian miners to the goldfields in the expectation that they would provide competition for British and Australian miners, thereby stifling wage demands.[84] This brought Hoover into conflict with the implacable John 'Jack' Holman, who had established his reputation as a no-nonsense trade unionist and activist for miners' rights at Broken Hill.[85] Holman was the son of Cornish miner Edward Holman, who had been born in Gwinear, near Redruth, in 1841. The senior Holman later moved with his wife Mary Annie (née Barkell) to Clunes, in Victoria, where John Barkell Holman was born in 1872. In 1899, Jack Holman was an organiser with the Amalgamated Workers Union succeeded in maintaining the strike that forced Bewick, Moreing & Co., into abandoning the idea of reducing the wages of underground workers by 5 shillings per week.[86] This outcome did nothing to improve Hoover's demeanour towards the Labour Party and trade unions, and he was evidently overjoyed when the Labour Party was routed at the 1905 State election.

During the early part of his career in Western Australia, Herbert Hoover exhibited a clear distain for Australian miners and the State's labour laws. Meanwhile, his Cornish contemporaries in the political sphere like Samuel Mitchell, Frederic Vosper and William Oats were significantly more attuned to the plight of the average miner. As Payton has argued, the notion of workers being true to each, as exemplified by the Cornish motto 'One and All', was readily co-opted by the labour movement, and by those Cornish miners familiar with its significance.[87] Frederic Vosper, for one, referenced the Cornish motto on more than one occasion to encourage those on the goldfields to work cooperatively to achieve their political aims.[88] Although, ideologically, Vosper was perhaps closer to Marx than to the Cornish conception of 'One and All'. In an interview that was somewhat prophetic Vosper cautioned against giving a few wealthy capitalists control of mining leases, this he said, would lead to either a cut in wages or the importation of cheap foreign labour. His closing remarks also exhibit some understanding of the work of Karl Marx, when he conceded that Western Australia might soon have to address an impending struggle between labour and capital.[89] On that point, Vosper expressed the hope that an honourable statesman might emerge to avert such an outcome.[90] Whether he considered himself equipped for the role of statesman is open to conjecture. However, Vosper's premature death on 6 January 1901 as a result of erysipelas following an appendectomy, not only ended a promising political career, but also removed the most likely adversary to the *laissez-fair* doctrine of Bewick, Moreing & Co. and Herbert Hoover.

While Frederic Vosper invoked Marxist rhetoric to warn of an impending conflict between capital and labour, Captain Samuel Mitchell was, for his part, an admirer of British statesman and Liberal Party politician William Gladstone.[91] At heart Mitchell was no political ideologue, save for the occasional letter advocating the benefits of private ownership over public.[92] In his booklet *Looking Backward*, containing his reminisces, Mitchell makes the point that he only entered parliament after being overlooked for the position of Warden, after serving briefly as the acting Warden at Cue. Commenting on his parliamentary career, Mitchell later said, 'it was the worst, if not the very worst thing, I did in my entire life'.[93] Aside from regretting his parliamentary career, which he claimed drained his finances, Mitchell's booklet offers little clue as to his political views. That said, Mitchell did maintain an abiding interest in Cornish politics and had copies of the *West Britain* shipped to Australia so he could stay abreast of the fortunes of the Liberal Party.[94] His close friend, journalist, Roland Charles Howes, who wrote for a number of newspapers under the pen-name *Le Grondeur*, conceded that Mitchell was a comparative failure in the 'Gas House', but that he did achieve a lot for the district he represented.[95] Moreover, one of the few instances where Mitchell's political views were recorded in print occurred in 1880 when he was asked to say a few words during the laying of the foundation stone for the Northampton Working Men's Association Hall.

> To me there appears something sublime in the words 'Working Men's Association,' and wherefore, because in the first place, these words indicate in their widest meaning union. And secondly, union means strength, out of which arises power to the working class.[96]

It is probably true to say that Mitchell was closer to capturing the spirit of 'One and All' than Vosper when he urged the working class to stay united. Mitchell did, however, add the rider that he meant 'union' in the broadest sense of the word. Doubtless, Mitchell's experience as a mine owner prevented him from accepting the role of the union movement uncritically. This probably explains why he did not adopt the socialist values of his Cornish colleagues Captain Oats and Fredric Vosper and, instead, aligned himself with John Forrest.

Like Mitchell, Captain William Oats started his political career at the local level by becoming chairman of the Yilgarn Roads Board in early 1892.[97] In 1894, he was re-elected but was given the loftier title of the Mayor of Southern Cross. During the 1897 election campaign, Captain Oats, perhaps, aware that miners had a reputation for moving to greener pastures once the valuable ore had been mined out. Made the following public statement to allay any fears that he would likewise abandon Western Australia, once he had accumulated sufficient wealth.

> I am not that kind of man, W.A. is my adopted country, and in W.A. I'm going to live and die. Besides, look at the mines-the W.A. mining industry is only in its swaddling clothes.[98]

As was common, and before the advent of party discipline in politics, Oats tended to concentrate on issues that were important to his mining constituents. Indeed, this focus probably explains his own political longevity: he held the seat of Yilgarn for seven years. Moreover, in concert with the member for Northeast Coolgardie, Frederic Vosper, William Oats became a leading figure in the Coolgardie branch of the Anti-Asiatic League.[99] Again, like Vosper, Oats occasionally espoused Marxist sentiment, as in the example below.

> (T)hat his policy always had been, and would be, "That the people should rule the people" and he wanted no class distinctions. He loved the laboring class and would see their rights were respected.[100]

Although William Oats lacked the eloquence of Vosper, and the political pretensions of Mitchell, he considered himself a 'man of the people', a rough uncouth labourer with his heart in the right place.

Conclusion

The arrival of Captain Martin Hosken, along with Cornish miners Nancarrow, Tregoning, Hosken and Spargo at the Geraldine Mine in November 1852, arguably, heralded the beginning of period of significant wealth generation for the nascent colony of Western Australia. This was due, in no small measure, to the discrete skills of the Cornish miner. Indeed, following his arrival in 1867, Captain Samuel Mitchell imported a steady stream of Cornish miners and their families, brought in on the vessels of mine owner Robert Mace Habgood, over a twenty-year period, which not only helped establish both Geraldton and Northampton, but also provided the impetus for the first railway in the colony. When gold was discovered at Southern Cross in 1897, and then at Coolgardie (1892) and Kalgoorlie (1893), Cornish miners like William Oats and George Prout were in high demand as mining experts and prospectors. Moreover, the Western Australian gold rush witnessed an influx of Cousin Jacks from the Eastern colonies that was unprecedented in terms of its impact on Western Australia. Indeed, as Warden Finnerty observed when he arrived on the goldfields in 1889, every mine had a Cornish boss and if you did not happen to be a Cousin Jack, you had to make room for those that were. Nevertheless, my research suggests that Cornish miners had a clear preference for the gold mines of the *Witwatersrand*, which was both closer to home and offered more money than Western Australia. The prospect of losing its skilled Cornish workforce to South Africa in 1895, prompted the Western Australia government to contact its Agent General in London, to discern if Cornish miners could still be recruited. However, the loss of British investment and the closure of a number of mines led the Western Australian government to re-evaluate their commitment to mining, and henceforth the focus shifted to land settlement and farming.

There can be little doubt that the pull of South Africa and the West Australian mining downturn had a profound effect on the number of Cousin Jacks that remained in Western Australia after 1896. Indeed, as the second part of this chapter has argued the arrival of Herbert Hoover and his employer Bewick, Moreing & Co. in 1897, was not the most decisive factor in ending the Cornish presence, as some commentators have claimed. However, it was necessary in terms of context to examine the impact of the 'Americans' to determine if they played any role in ending the Cornish domination of metalliferous mining in Western Australia. The assumption that the university-trained 'Americans' were somehow superior to their Cornish counterparts in the late 1890s is not sustained by the evidence. Indeed, the mining careers of Samuel Mitchell, William Oats and Frederic Vosper, show that they all published papers and mining reports that were highly regarded by their peers. Moreover, recent research has shown that Hoover overstated the number of American university-trained mining engineers he brought to the Eastern Goldfields. Indeed, Cornishman, William Pollard became one of the leading underground managers for Bewick, Moreing & Co., a position he held until his sudden death in 1911. Likewise, another so-called university trained recruit, Joseph Davey, returned to Cornwall in 1909, to recover from 'miners' complaint' suggesting that he too, was a Cornish miner. However, in terms of labour relations Herbert Hoover introduced a number of changes that did have a profound effect on the West Australia mining industry. These changes included increasing the working hours of miners, reducing both the underground workforce and shift allowances, and recruiting Italian labour.[101]

Last, by briefly examining the political careers of Mitchell, Vosper and Oats, one can discern a strong sense of moral responsibility for the well-being of miners, a position absent from the alleged utterances of Herbert Hoover. This is clearly evident in the acceptance of the notion of 'One and All' as a guiding principal held by Mitchell, Vosper and Oats. Hoover, on the hand, had no time for such notions, observing in a letter to his friend, Deane P. Mitchell, '[t]wo months on the gold-fields [have] cured [me] of any sympathy for socialism'.[102] Indeed, one can argue that Hoover was probably aware that Cornish miners could be problematic if they were sufficiently united by unjust work practices. This view is entirely consistent with Hoover's remarks in his memoir in which he ascribed no special talent to Cornish miners other than they were good mining men who were very determined in their religious views.[103] However, in England, the 'principals' at Bewick, Moreing & Co. were less convinced by Hoover's tactics and cautioned that he act judiciously lest he supersede other labour completely and raise the ire of the labour unions and precipitate strike action.[104] With that said, there was a degree of inevitability in the Cornish losing their dominance once the gold rush had subsided. There is, however, considerable research that still needs to occur before a thorough understanding of the transition from Cornish to American mining practice in Australia is fully understood. This chapter, therefore, merely represents another opportunity to explore the range of factors behind what Geoffrey Blainey described as 'the most momentous decision in Australia's industrial history'.[105]

NOTES

1. Dudley Baines, *Migration in a Mature Economy: Emigration and Internal Migration in England and Wales, 1861–1900.* Cambridge Studies in Population, Economy, and Society in past Time; 3. Cambridge [Cambridgeshire]; New York: Cambridge University Press, 1985, 157–159.
2. Philip Payton, 'The Cornish Diaspora', in Donald M. MacRaild, Tanja Bueltmann, and J.C.D. Clark, editors, *British and Irish Diasporas: Societies, Cultures and Ideologies*, Manchester: Manchester University Press, 2019, 280–313.

3. *Geraldton Guardian Express,* 'Early Murchison Days', Saturday 20 November 1937, 6.
4. Ken Spillman, *A Rich Endowment: Government and Mining in Western Australia 1829–1994,* University of Western Australia Press, Nedlands, WA, 1993, 18.
5. *Inquirer,* 'Mining Journal', Wednesday 17 November 1852, 2.
6. Geoffrey Blainey, *The Rush That Never Ended: A History of Australian Mining,* Melbourne University Press, Carlton, VIC, 1969, 45.
7. Martha Jean Smallacombe, *The Hosken Odyssey,* Published by Author, Forrestfield, WA, 2005, 4–5.
8. *Inquirer,* 'Mining Journal', Wednesday 22 September 1852, 2.
9. *Inquirer,* 'Freemantle', Wednesday 9 November 1853, 2.
10. *Inquirer and Commercial News,* Wednesday 9 January 1856, 2.
11. Martin Gibbs, 'The Technology of Colonial Ore Processing in Western Australia: The Warribanno Lead Smelter', 62.
12. Martha Jean, Smallacombe, *The Hosken Odyssey,* 11.
13. *Herald,* 'Shipping Intelligence', Saturday 16 November 1867, 2.
14. *Cornubian and Redruth Times,* 10 August 1883, 2.
15. Samuel Mitchell, *Looking Backward, Reminiscences of 42 Years,* 4.
16. *Geraldton Guardian,* 'Memories of Samuel Mitchell', Saturday 23 September 1950, 2.
17. *Geraldton Guardian,* 'Memories of Samuel Mitchell', Saturday 23 September 1950, 2.
18. John Glover, 'Samuel Mitchell, a "Practical Mining Man"', *West Australian Geologist,* Available: http://www.wa.gsa.org.au/WAG/WAG_Apr_May_2010.pdf. Accessed 4 January 2017, 5.
19. John Glover, 'Samuel Mitchell, a "Practical Mining Man"', 6.
20. InHerit 'Wheal Ellen Mine Site' W.A. State Heritage, *Shire of Northampton,* Available: http://inherit.stateheritage.wa.gov.au/Public/Inventory/PrintSingleRecord/513d10bf-166c-451f-af01-895566d80e69 Accessed 4 January 2017. '"Model Man' Mitchell's Cognomen', *Inquirer and Commercial News,* Wednesday 2 August 1876, 3. *Victorian Express,* 'How I Defended the Camp', Saturday 20 December 1890, 2.
21. *Inquirer and Commercial News,* Wednesday 25 August 1880, 2.
22. Ron Limbaugh, 'Pragmatic Professional: Herbert Hoover's Formative Years as a Mining Engineer, 1895–1908', 45.
23. E. Jaggard, 'F. C. B. Vosper, the Agitator', in Lyall Hunt Editor, *Westralian Portraits,* University of Western Australia Press, Nedlands, WA, 1979, 104–110, 107.
24. *North Devon Journal,* 19 October 1922, 5. Note: Charles Vosper received a silver medal at the Royal Cornwall Show, as did Alexander

Graham Bell for his 'Telephone'. *Royal Cornwall Gazette*, 31 August 1877, 5.

25. E. Jaggard, 'F. C. B. Vosper, the Agitator', *Westralian Portraits*, Lyall Hunt Editor, 105. The author describes him as being 'much taller than average, he was very thin and his prominent, clean-shaven jaw set off his long, curling black hair'.

26. Alan Taylor, 'Daffodils Never Hear' the Life of a Cornish Family in the 1880s, Including Working in Bolivian Silver Mines. Available: http://at.orpheusweb.co.uk/Daffodil/index.htm. Accessed 22 January 2019.

27. Paul D. Twomey, 'The Sedition Trials of F. C. B. Vosper', *Journal of the Royal Society of Queensland* 12, No. 2 (1985): 203.

28. *Coolgardie Miner*, 'Local and General', Monday 23 December 1895, 2. See also: *Western Mail*, 'Perth Museum', Friday 5 November 1897, 7.

29. *The West Australian*, 'Mining Intelligence', 9 February 1894, 6.

30. *Victorian Express*, Friday 6 April 1894, 3.

31. Frederic Charles and Burleigh Vosper, *The Prospectors Companion: Guide to Simple Mineral Analysis with Tables, a Glossary and Appendix on Explosives*, City Press, Perth, 1894.

32. *Coolgardie Miner*, Saturday 26 January 1894, 4.

33. *W.A. Record*, 'The Coolgardie Goldfields', Saturday 25 January 1896, 11.

34. *West Australian*, 'Mining News', Wednesday 13 November 1889, 3. See also: Geoffrey Blainey, *The Rush That Never Ended*, 172.

35. *Southern Cross*, 'Captain William Oats, M.L.A.', Saturday 20 April 1901, 1.

36. J.J. Pascoe, *History of Adelaide and Vicinity*, 'Mr. George Prout', Hussey & Gillingham, Adelaide, SA, 1901, 511. Available: http://trove.nla.gov.au/work/2092654?selectedversion=NBD2076367. Accessed 16 October 2017.

37. *Coolgardie Miner*, 'Mining and Finance', Wednesday 17 June 1896, 3.

38. *Coolgardie Miner*, 'Advertising', Monday 3 August 1896, 7.

39. *Kalgoorlie Miner*, 'Captain Oats', Saturday 8 May 1897, 2.

40. *Coolgardie Miner*, 'A Respectable Place', Friday 1 October 1897, 4.

41. *South Australian Register*, 'Gold Mines in South Australia', Friday 26 June 1896, 6. Note: After significant investment including the construction of largest stamps in Australia the Menzies Barossa folded in 1901. After it failed to meet its over hyped expectations. In this instance, Oats was the earliest of a number of mining experts from W.A. to assert that the Menzies mine was rich in gold.

42. Brian R. Hill, 'The "Merican Expert" L. R. Menzies and His Role in a South Australian Mining Fiasco', *Journal of Australian Mining History* 9 (2011): 168. Available: http://www.mininghistory.asn.au/wp-content/uploads/11.Hill-FINAL.1.Vol_.9.compressed.pdf. Accessed 16 January 2019.

43. *Western Mail*, 'The Mining Bill', Friday 28 October 1898, 48.
44. Philip Payton, *The Cornish Overseas*, 319.
45. *Evening Star*, 'Mining Managers Association Social', Friday 8 March 1901, 3. Note: John Michael Finnerty married Captain Oats' daughter Bertha Mary Oats at Southern Cross in 1891.
46. Philip Payton, *The Cornish Overseas*, 319–320. See also: *Inquirer and Commercial News*, 'McAuliffe's Reward Mine', Friday 22 November 1895, 7. *Kalgoorlie Miner*, 'Items of News', Friday 6 March 1896, 2.
47. *West Australian*, 'Mining News', Saturday 18 January 1896, 6. See also: *Kalgoorlie Miner*, 'Personal', Thursday 25 June 1908, 4. And: *Western Mail*, 'Greenbushes', Friday 13 August 1915, 20. Note: Captains John Dunstan and John Treglown also spent sometime in Greenbushes. See: *Southern Times*, 'Bridgetown Notes', Tuesday 5 March 1889, 5.
48. Geoffrey Blainey, *The Rush That Never Ended*, 202.
49. Philip Payton, *The Making of Modern Cornwall: Historical Experience and the Persistence of 'Difference'*, Dyllansow Truran, Redruth, 111.
50. *The Inquirer and Commercial News*, 'General News', Friday 17 July 1896, 8.
51. *Coolgardie Miner*, 'An English M.P. on His Travels', Friday 17 September 1897, 3. Note: Henry Charles Richards was born in Sussex, although he professed to be of Cornish origin.
52. *Royal Cornwall Gazette*, 'Cornish Miners and the Rand', Tuesday 12 July 1900, 6. Note: First published in the *Natal Witness*, date unknown, and signed 'Anti-Cousin Jack'.
53. Geoffrey Blainey, *The Rush That Never Ended*, 206–207.
54. *Inquirer and Commercial News*, 'Mr Lane in London', Friday 15 May 1896, 7.
55. Martin Webb and Audrey Webb, *Golden Destiny*, 513.
56. Bruce Devenish, *Sir James Mitchell, Premier and Governor of Western Australia*, Hesperian Press, Carlisle, WA, 2014, 23.
57. *Sunday Times*, 'Peeps at People', Sunday 12 February 1911, 25.
58. Philip Payton, *Cornwall*, 245. Note: John Nauright claims, the number Cornish miners on the Rand in 1904, was between 17,500 and 18,000.
59. *West Australian*, 'Miners' Wages', Friday 3 April 1903, 5.
60. *Kalgoorlie Miner*, 'Notes from London', Saturday 30 June 1906, 2.
61. Jonathan Hyslop, '"The Imperial Working Class Makes Itself White": White Labourism in Britain, Australia, and South Africa Before the First World War', *Journal of Historical Sociology* 12, No. 4 (December 1999), 407.
62. John Nauright, 'Cornish Miners and the Witwatersrand Gold Mines in South Africa, c. 1890–1904', Published in *Cornish History*, 2005, 17–18. Available: https://www.academia.edu. Accessed 22 January 2019.
63. West Australian, 'A Practical Miner on the Discovery of Minerals', Saturday 26 January 1884, 3.

64. *West Australian*, 'A Practical Miner on the Discovery of Metals', Edward T. Hardman, W.A. Government Geologist, 2 February 1884, 3.
65. Herbert C. Hoover, *Memoirs, Years of Adventure 1874–1920*, Macmillan, New York, 1951, 131.
66. Geoffrey, Blainey, *The Rush That Never Ended: A History of Australian Mining*, Melbourne University Press, Carlton, VIC, 1969, 202.
67. Geoffrey Blainey, *The Rush That Never Ended*, 154.
68. George H. Nash, *The Life of Herbert Hoover: The Engineer, 1874–1914*, W. W. Norton, New York, 1983, 45.
69. Herbert C. Hoover, *Memoirs, Years of Adventure 1874–1920*, 26.
70. Philip Payton, *The Cornish Overseas*, 342.
71. Philip Payton, *The Cornish Overseas*, 143.
72. Philip Payton, *The Cornish Overseas*, 24–25.
73. Oswald Pryor, *Australia's Little Cornwall*, 50.
74. *Victorian Express*, 'Northampton Notes', Wednesday 13 July 1881, 3.
75. Charles Harvey and Jon Press, 'Overseas Investment and Professional Advance of British Mining Engineers, 1851–1914', 70.
76. Ron Limbaugh, 'Pragmatic Professional: Herbert Hoover's Formative Years as a Mining Engineer, 1895–1908', 53.
77. *Black Range Courier and Sandstone Observer*, 'Mr. William Pollard', Thursday 2 February 1911, 3. See also: *Kalgoorlie Western Argus*, 'Mining Notes', Tuesday 5 July 1904, 6.
78. Ron, Limbaugh, 'Pragmatic Professional: Herbert Hoover's Formative Years as a Mining Engineer, 1895–1908', 54.
79. *Murchison Advocate*, 'Day Dawn', Thursday 2 December 1909, 2.
80. *Black Range Courier and Sandstone Observer*, 'General News', Friday 17 June 1910, 2.
81. Ron, Limbaugh, 'Pragmatic Professional: Herbert Hoover's Formative Years as a Mining Engineer, 1895–1908', 54. See also: George H. Nash, *The Life of Herbert Hoover: The Engineer, 1874–191*, 59.
82. George H. Nash, *The Life of Herbert Hoover: The Engineer, 1874–1914*, 487.
83. Note: The word 'demagogue' was routinely used during this period to describe socialist politicians and unionists. See *Coolgardie Pioneer*, 'Gallery Notes', Saturday 10 September 1898, 19. Pastoralist and businessman Frederick Monger M.L.A., describes Labor M.L.A. Frederic Vosper as a demagogue.
84. Richard, Hartley, 'Bewick Moreing in Western Australian Gold Mining 1897–1904: Management Polices & Goldfields Responses', *Labour History* 65 (November 1993): 4.
85. Lekkie Hopkins, *The Magnificent Life of Miss May Holman, Australia's First Female Labor Parliamentarian*, 79. See also: Geoffrey Blainey, *The Rush That Never Ended*, 303.

86. Richard Hartley, 'Bewick Moreing in Western Australian Gold Mining 1897–1904: Management Polices & Goldfields Responses', 4.
87. Philip Payton, *One and All, Labor and the Radical Tradition in South Australia*, 117.
88. *Coolgardie Miner*, 'Coolgardie Miner' 'Delegation at Esperance', Saturday 2 January 1897, 5.
89. *Southern Times*, 'Correspondence', Saturday 20 May 1899, 3. Note: The pamphlet, *Wages Labour and Capital*, by Karl Marx was freely available and often discussed at political gatherings, socialist meetings and in the Australian Press.
90. *W.A. Record*, 'The Coolgardie Goldfields', Saturday 25 January 1896, 11.
91. *Victorian Express*, 'Town Talk', Wednesday 3 September 1884, 2.
92. *Victorian Express*, 'Northern Railway', Saturday 28 February 1891, 3.
93. Samuel Mitchell, *Looking Backward, Reminiscences of 42 Years*, 4.
94. *Victorian Express*, 'Town Talk', Wednesday 3 September 1884, 2.
95. *Geraldton Express*, 'Capricious Carping's', Wednesday 17 July 1912, 3.
96. *Victorian Express*, 'Northampton', Wednesday 2 June 1880, 3.
97. *Eastern Districts Chronicle*, 'General News', Saturday 26 March 1892, 5.
98. *Kalgoorlie Western Argus*, 'Captain Oats', Thursday 6 May 1897, 3.
99. *Kalgoorlie Western Argus*, 'Captain Oats', Thursday 6 May 1897, 3.
100. *Western Mail*, 'The South Province', Saturday 30 April 1904, 12.
101. Jeremy Mouat and Ian Phimister, 'The Engineering of Herbert Hoover', *Pacific Historical Review* 77, No. 4: 558.
102. George H. Nash, *The Life of Herbert Hoover: The Engineer, 1874–1914*, 61.
103. Herbert C. Hoover, *Memoirs, Years of Adventure 1874–1920*, 25.
104. Jeremy Mouat and Ian Phimister, 'The Engineering of Herbert Hoover', 558.
105. Blainey Geoffrey, *The Rush That Never Ended: A History of Australian Mining*, 154.

Select Bibliography

Baines, Dudley, *Migration in a Mature Economy: Emigration and Internal Migration in England and Wales, 1861–1900*, Cambridge University Press, Cambridge, 1985.

Blainey, Geoffrey, *The Rush That Never Ended: A History of Australian Mining*, Melbourne University Press, Carlton, VIC, 1969.

Devenish, Bruce, *Sir James Mitchell, Premier and Governor of Western Australia*, Hesperian Press, Carlisle, WA, 2014.

Eakin, Marshall, C., *The St. John d'el Ray Mining Company and the Morro Velho Gold Mine, 1830–1960*, Duke University Press, Durham and London, 1989.

Gibbs, Martin, 'The Technology of Colonial Ore Processing in Western Australia: The Warribanno Lead Smelter', *Australasian Historical Archaeology* 15 (1997): 55–65.

Glover, John, 'Samuel Mitchell, a "Practical Mining Man"', *West Australian Geologist*, Available: http://www.wa.gsa.org.au/WAG/WAG_Apr_May_ 2010.pdf. Accessed 4 January 2017, 5–7.

Hartley, Richard, 'Bewick Moreing in Western Australian Gold Mining 1897– 1904: Management Polices & Goldfields Responses', *Labour History* 65 (November 1993): 1–18.

Harvey, Charles and Press, Jon, 'Overseas Investment and Professional Advance of British Mining Engineers, 1851–1914', *The Economic History Review, New Series* 42, No. 1 (February 1989): 64–86.

Hill, R. Brian, 'The "Merican Expert" L. R. Menzies and His Role in a South Australian Mining Fiasco', *Journal of Australian Mining History* 9 (2011): 166–182.

Hoover, C. Herbert, *Memoirs, Years of Adventure 1874–1920*, Macmillan, New York, 1951.

Hopkins, Lekkie, *The Magnificent Life of Miss May Holman, Australia's First Female Labor Parliamentarian*, Fremantle Press, Fremantle, WA, 2016.

InHerit 'Wheal Ellen Mine Site' W.A. State Heritage, *Shire of Northampton*, Available: http://inherit.stateheritage.wa.gov.au/Public/Inventory/Print SingleRecord/513d10bf-166c-451f-af01-895566d80e69.

Jaggard, Edwin, 'F. C. B. Vosper, the Agitator', in Lyall Hunt, Editor, *Westralian Portraits*, University of Western Australia Press, Nedlands, WA, 1979, 104–110.

Limbaugh, Ron, 'Pragmatic Professional, Herbert Hoover's Formative Years as a Mining Engineer, 1895–1908', *Mining History Journal* 11 (2004): 43–58.

Mouat, Jeremy and Phimister, Ian, 'The Engineering of Herbert Hoover', *Pacific Historical Review* 77, No. 4 (2008): 553–584.

Naomi, Segal, 'Anti-Union or Pro-Property? Worker Surveillance and Gold Theft in Western Australian Gold Mines, 1899–1920', *Labour History* 97 (November 2009): 37–52.

Nash, H. George, The *Life of Herbert Hoover: The Engineer, 1874–1914*, W. W. Norton, New York, 1983.

Nauright, John, 'Cornish Miners and the Witwatersrand Gold Mines in South Africa, c. 1890–1904', Published in *Cornish History*, 2005, 1–22.

Pascoe, J.J., *History of Adelaide and Vicinity*, 'Mr. George Prout', Hussey & Gillingham, Adelaide, SA, 1901.

Payton, Philip, 'The Cornish Diaspora', in Donald M. McRaild, Tanja Bueltmann, and J.C.D. Clark, Editors, *British and Irish Diasporas: Societies, Cultures and Ideologies*, University of Manchester Press, Manchester, 2019, 280–313.

Payton, Philip, *One and All: Labor and the Radical Tradition in South Australia*, Wakefield Press, Adelaide, 2016.

Payton, Philip, *The Cornish Overseas: A History of Cornwall's 'Great Emigration'*, University of Exeter Press, Exeter, 2015.

Payton, Philip, *The Making of Modern Cornwall: Historical Experience and the Persistence of 'Difference'*, Dyllansow Truran, Redruth, 1992.

Pryor, Oswald, *Australia's Little Cornwall*, Rigby Limited, Adelaide, 1962.

Smallacombe, Martha Jean, *The Hosken Odyssey*, Published by Author, Forrestfield, WA, 2005.

Spillman, Ken, *A Rich Endowment: Government and Mining in Western Australia 1829–1994*, University of Western Australia Press, Nedlands, WA, 1993.

Taylor, Alan, 'Daffodils Never Hear' the Life of a Cornish Family in the 1880s, Including Working in Bolivian Silver Mines. Available: http://at.orpheusweb.co.uk/Daffodil/index.htm.

Twomey, D. Paul, 'The Sedition Trials of F. C. B. Vosper', *Journal of the Royal Society of Queensland* 12, No. 2 (1985): 203–223.

Webb, Martin and Webb, Audrey, *Golden Destiny*, City of Kalgoorlie-Boulder, Kalgoorlie, WA, 1993.

Vosper, Frederic and Charles, Burleigh, *The Prospectors Companion: Guide to Simple Mineral Analysis with Tables, a Glossary and Appendix on Explosives*, City Press, Perth, 1894.

CHAPTER 9

Bal-Maidens and Cousin Jenny: The Paradox of Women in Australia's Historic Mining Communities

Philip Payton

During 1840, applications for free passage to the recently proclaimed colony of South Australia were received from Sukey and Jane Fletcher, two female mineworkers ('bal-maidens' in Cornish parlance) at Wheal Butson, a small copper mine and adjoining hamlet in the parish of St Agnes in Cornwall.[1] The mine had been lying idle since the late 1830s, and it was perhaps no surprise that the Fletcher sisters—both single—sought to join the forty-five male miners (often with their families) from St Agnes who in 1840 had also applied to emigrate to South Australia. Cornwall had already been identified as a likely source of suitable settlers for the embryonic colony, and reports of South Australia's supposed mineral wealth had by now created some considerable excitement in Cornish mining

---

P. Payton (✉)
College of Humanities, Arts and Social Science,
Flinders University, Adelaide, SA, Australia
e-mail: philip.payton@flinders.edu.au

Emeritus Professor of Cornish and Australian Studies,
University of Exeter, Exeter, UK

© The Author(s) 2019
P. Payton and A. Varnava (eds.),
Australia, Migration and Empire, Britain and the World,
https://doi.org/10.1007/978-3-030-22389-2_9

207

circles. Indeed, following the chance discovery of silver-lead deposits at Glen Osmond, in the Adelaide Hills, by two emigrant Cornish miners, Australia's very first metalliferous mine, Wheal Gawler, was in production by May 1841, to be joined by neighbouring Wheal Watkins during 1843.[2]

As their nomenclature suggested ('wheal' was a common mine-name prefix, meaning literally 'a working' in the Cornish language), the mines at Glen Osmond were worked according to Cornish practice, as indeed was the burgeoning South Australian mining industry throughout the subsequent decades and into the early twentieth century, the colony's mining communities becoming the fabled home of 'Cousin Jack' (a Cornish miner abroad) and 'Cousin Jenny' (an emigrant Cornishwoman).[3] It was hardly surprising, then, when a visitor to the Glen Osmond mines in February 1847 found bal-maidens hard at work, sorting and preparing the ore brought to surface from underground. They toiled alongside boys and young men, 'pickey boys' as they were known, who, as in Cornwall, also helped grade the ore, useful preparatory experience for their later employment as underground miners. As the visitor observed, at 'the foot of the hill, a number of boys and girls were busy washing and cleaning the ore, which was heaped up in large quantities, and of all weights, from that of five or six cwt (hundred-weights) to that of a grain'. As the visitor explained, this 'process of cleaning is a very important operation, as it saves paying freight on stones and sand, and makes the ore very much more valuable', a major consideration given that the ore had to be sent (initially, at least) to Britain for smelting.[4]

Pickey boys became an enduring part of the South Australian mining scene (John Verran, Premier of the State's first majority Labour government in 1910 had once worked as a pickey boy, sorting ore at the Kapunda copper mine).[5] Bal-maidens, however, soon disappeared from view, not only in South Australia but across the continent as their early role in the emerging mining industry came quietly to an end. Moreover, despite the large numbers of single young women clamouring to emigrate from Cornwall to South Australia in the late 1830s and early 1840s, Sukey and Jane Fletcher remained the only clearly identifiable female mineworkers, the vast majority of would-be emigrants self-identifying as domestic servants, dairymaids and farm servants, together with those in more skilled occupations such as sempstress or milliner. This was even true of mining parishes such as Redruth, Gwennap and St Austell, which had produced sizeable numbers of applicants, male and female.[6] Thereafter, despite the rapid growth of the mining industry across the colony, and by the 1850s in neighbouring Victoria too, bal-maidens were identified but rarely in emigration documentation. This did not mean that there were not bal-maidens, possibly a considerable number of them, among emigrants to Australia in this period; merely that they were invisible to official view. Many, of course, would have been enumerated only as the wives of emigrating male miners, of which there were a great many, but some may well have misrepresented their own occupations to emigration agents. As Patricia Lay noted in her study of the 4000 Cornish assisted emigrants arriving in New South Wales between 1837 and 1877, many (male and female) had lied about their occupational backgrounds, often with the connivance of officials, to secure assisted passages, attempting to align their skills with those actively sought in the colony.[7] Significantly, despite the rapid growth of the Australian mining industry from the early 1840s onwards, there were no calls for female mineworkers from any of the Australian colonies, and bal-maidens did not feature in the lists of preferred occupations. Why was this?

As this chapter will argue, despite the significant skill set possessed by female mineworkers, women who had worked at mines in Cornwall—or in other mining regions of the UK—were not deemed suitable for employment in the Australian mining industry. Women had been prevented from working underground in British mines since 1842, but continued to be employed at surface even until the 1920s in some places, as 'pit-brow lasses' in the coals mines of the Midlands and North of England, and as bal-maidens at the Cornish mines.[8] This continued employment was vociferously opposed by many, however, the mid-Victorian doctrine of 'separate spheres' insisting that a mine was no place for a woman, and the gradual replacement of women as surface workers in the mining industry was due at least as much to attempts to ease females out as to increased mechanisation which did away with manual labour. Observers in Australia looked askance at the inertia they detected in Cornish mines, adding their voices to those demanding the end of female mine labour in Cornwall and elsewhere, and congratulated themselves that women in the colonies were not subjected to such employment. Nonetheless, as we shall see, despite attempts to confine these women to the domestic sphere, a curious paradox (or at least double standard) emerged in which, however reluctantly, Australian (male-dominated) society recognised the practical value of the erstwhile female mineworker's skill set in the colonies, although only when it was useful to do so. Moreover, notwithstanding the attempted confinement to the domestic sphere, there is abundant evidence that female agency could on occasion play a decisive role in the community life of Australia's mining towns.

In Cornwall, bal-maidens were comparatively well paid and often single, and they exhibited an independence of spirit which (as well as increasingly discomforting those men who thought such women should be confined to home duties), cultivated an air of professional self-confidence. The bal-maiden's chant, first recorded in the copper-mining parish of Gwennap in 1837, boasted technical competence—an ability, for example, to 'buddy' (operate the buddles, where ore was washed) and to 'looby' (literally, to toss ore)—as well as asserting an equality with male mineworkers, plus the happy knack of humouring the surface or grass captain (manager), the 'old Jan':

> I can buddy; and I can rocky,
> And I can walk like a man,
> I can looby and shaky,
> And please the old Jan.[9]

Such boastful assertions of independence and gender equality were almost bound to provoke male criticism. Writing in the late 1850s, George Henwood, a frequent contributor on Cornish mining themes to the *Mining Journal*, objected that the 'indiscriminate association, in their [bal-maidens'] employment, of the sexes naturally begets a want of modesty and delicacy, so important in the formation of character'. Moreover, he added, 'the masculine labour which women are frequently compelled to undertake, together with being away from home for so long, render them wholly unfit to perform and attend to those domestic duties which should constitute the comfort and charm of every home'. Henwood had recently visited a mine where, he said, 'two Amazons', bal-maidens by the names of Mary and Nanny, were employed filling and emptying barrows of copper ore 'with the long-handled Cornish shovel', moving the ore from one pile to next and taking it to be weighed. These hand-barrows contained 3 cwts each, and 'these poor girls wrought most vigorously, being spurred on to the task by the challenges of the men; such as "Bravo, Mary!" and "Well done, Nanny!" amid course jokes and jeers that were not fit for ears polite, and certainly such as young girls should not have heard'. It was, said Henwood, a task 'quite improper to the female frame, and ought never to have been allowed'.[10]

There was more. According to Henwood, these bal-maidens, 'their being associated in such numbers, and before men, a spirit of rivalry in dress (perhaps inherent in all women) is soon engendered, and every attention – all their thoughts and earning – are devoted to this method of making themselves attractive'. Thus:

> To see the 'bal maidens' on a Sunday, when fully dressed, would astonish a stranger; whilst at their work the pendant earrings and showy bead necklaces excite the pity as well as the surprise of the thoughtful. All desire to save a few shillings for after-life is discarded, and nothing but display thought of. This is carried on to an incredible extent, and all the preaching in the world will never interfere with the wearing of a fine bonnet or shawl, or an attempt to imitate the fashions of their superiors.[11]

The bal-maidens, it seemed, could not win—despised for adopting masculine characteristics and condemned for displaying feminine finery and acting above their station. And, as Henwood had hinted, there were also the perceived moral dangers of corruption and degradation. In 1868, for example, Samuel Scaddon, a grass captain (who managed the surface workers) at Penhale Wheal Vor mine in Cornwall, was accused of raping Mary Harvey, a bal-maiden in his charge. When the case came to court, the judge remarked that the accusation was an easy one to make but far more difficult to refute. He observed that Captain Scaddon had taken liberties with Mary Harvey before, and that she had not objected, and he instructed the jury to take note of the 'demeanour' of the prosecutrix, adding that she should have made 'every resistance in her power' to deter Scaddon.[12] Mary Harvey was thus discredited, her case thrown out. Not only were bal-maidens subjected to the unwanted attentions of their superiors, but they were also considered 'fair game', with predators like Scaddon sure in the knowledge that complaints against them were unlikely to be taken seriously.

Such hostility was echoed in the Australian press. The *Mount Alexander Mail*, for example, published in the heart of the Victorian goldfields, in July 1858 carried an article 'Female Labourers in the Cornish Mines'. The newspaper's aim, in playing to its mining community readership, was to add its influential voice to those who had insisted that hard labouring work 'is, or ought to be, foreign to a woman's mind and temper. At any rate, heavy physical work is altogether unsuitable, and the worst social evils have arisen whenever this has been lost sight of'. At a time when Cornish mining practice was still recognised as world-leading, it was important that the continued employment of bal-maidens in Cornwall be confronted and shown to be anomalous, lest the unfortunate precedent set at Glen Osmond a decade earlier be resurrected anywhere in Australia. As the *Mount Alexander Mail* explained, in Cornwall girls aged as young as six or seven were sent to the mines, where they were taught initially to sort the ore and then to 'buck' and 'jig', breaking and separating the ore, partly by washing it and partly by striking it with heavy hammers. This, the newspaper opined, 'was unsuitable for women, and still less fitting for young girls. Their strength is overtasked by the severity of the work', it was alleged, to such a degree that 'a large proportion of these workers are carried off by consumption in the prime of life'.[13]

The physical depredations were one thing but perhaps even more insidious, thought the *Mount Alexander Mail*, were the 'other evils – moral and social' that followed in their wake. In a damning indictment of female mineworkers, the newspaper listed their failings as women:

> Ignorant of household work and household economy, inexperienced in the business of domestic life, they are unprepared to perform their duties as the wives of workmen and the mothers of children; and, when they are married, their homes are untidy, their habits thriftless, their children ill-managed and badly brought up. Associating, as they do, at work, and often at meal times also, with the roughest and rudest, their character as women degenerates.[14]

The logical conclusion, of course, was 'the speedy discontinuance of this kind of female employment in the Cornish mines'.[15] In fact, the practice lingered in Cornwall a good while longer. But in Australia, vigilance, such as that advocated by the *Mount Alexander Mail*, ensured that women were prevented from joining the formal waged mining economy, an exclusion made permanent by the mining trade unions as they emerged. Such was the success of this exclusion, that, almost a hundred years later, the idea of women working at the mines was a matter of historical curiosity, the 'Australiana' section of the *World's News* (published in Sydney) in July 1952 informing its no doubt intrigued readers that back in the 1840s at the Glen Osmond silver-lead mines in South Australia, 'girls washed and cleaned the ore. This was an old Cornish custom and [they] were given the name of Bal-maiden'.[16]

That is not to say that women did not work in the unwaged informal mining economy, especially on the gold-diggings as they emerged, first in New South Wales and Victoria in the 1850s and then across Australia. Small syndicates in the early days of the rushes were often family groups, where a helping hand from the female members was usually welcome. Although there were those who insisted that the goldfields were 'no fit place for any respectable woman',[17] there were women aplenty nonetheless, many engaged in small-claim extraction, such as streaming and panning or shallow pickings. Some women found the work exhilarating, for they were working for themselves or family syndicates. Mary Ann Tyler, a self-styled 'gold diggeress', worked in this way for over five years, and explained its attraction. 'You work from day to day with anticipation', she said, 'and soon the years pass ... You can work for very little, and all at once you drop across a fortune. That is why it is so enchanting. You live in expectation ... my soul was lit with delight that I should one day discover more gold'.[18] However, such informal self-employment could not survive the increasing capitalisation of deep mining, in Victoria or elsewhere, and as the big mining companies took charge, the small-claim syndicates gradually disappeared. And as they faded from the scene, so too did the women, for there was neither room nor welcome for them in the new era of industrial-scale mining.

However, in addition to the informal tapping of female labour on the goldfields, men were sometimes not above appealing to the technical knowledge of erstwhile female mine labourers, as in the intriguing example of Sidwell Woolcock, a former bal-maiden. Born in Illogan, Cornwall, Woolcock arrived in South Australia as a single woman in 1855, accompanied by other members of her family. In 1858, she married a Norwegian, one Henry Kruge, and by 1870, the couple were living at remote Priory Station, a pastoral property in outback New South Wales, some forty miles from what later became the mining town of Cobar. By now, Woolcock was well known in the district as a former mineworker, and when a party of well-sinkers discovered some 'coloured stones' in the locality, they were advised to seek her professional opinion. She immediately identified the samples as copper carbonates, such as she had dealt with in Cornwall, and, according to one contemporary report: 'She spoke so strongly as to the value of the find that the contractors returned to the place and took up a 40-acres lease'.[19] This became the site of the Great Cobar mine, soon to be one of Australia's leading and most famous copper producers.

There was no doubting Sidwell Woolcock's expertise, nor the seriousness with which the well-sinking party took her advice. However, it is telling that she was not invited to join the syndicate that so promptly acquired the lease (nor was the Aboriginal guide, Budgery Bill, who was also present at the find). A male 'Cousin Jack' (a Cornish miner), offering similar specialist identification (together with the prospect of further technical help), might well have been co-opted into the team, but Woolcock was merely a 'Cousin Jenny' (an emigrant Cornishwoman) and thus passed over. Her advice had proved invaluable, and yet she was so easily dispensed with afterwards. Likewise, despite the significance of the discovery, Woolcock received no particular recognition in her lifetime. In 1894, the *Sydney Mail* dismissed her somewhat pejoratively as 'an old Cornish jenny',[20] and later she earned a certain notoriety, partly as a result of her second and unhappy marriage (she was reported as having separated from her new husband), and partly due to her curmudgeonly nature as she descended into dementia and old age. After her death, the *Cobar Herald* noted merely that Woolcock had 'worked in the copper mines of Cornwall'. But the newspaper did recount her sorry decline, and how for the last eighteen months of her life she had been bed-ridden, almost blind, and suffering from 'senile decay'. She was reputedly 79 when she died but, as the *Cobar Herald* put it, 'there is reason to believe that the old lady had lost count, for many who knew her verily believe that she was at least ten years older than stated'.[21]

As in Cornwall, so in Australia there was sometimes the sense that women who had been female mine labourers nurtured ideas above their station. In the *Yorke's Peninsula Advertiser*, published in the copper coast district of South Australia, a humorous Cornish dialect story appeared in February 1871. Entitled 'A New Chum to his Friends in Cornwall, near England', the article was supposedly written by a recent (male) emigrant and was designed to enlighten readers back home as to the details of colonial life as experienced in the mining towns of Moonta, Wallaroo and Kadina. Commenting on the pretentious behaviour of two recent female emigrants, the author exclaimed: 'But I doant knaw, there was Sally Prout an' Mary Pryor an two or three ov they there maidens bout Camborne and Tuckingmill [in Cornwall], wat was so proud as enny lady in the land –an' they war nothing but bal maidens'.[22]

Sexual harassment was also a feature of life on the mines, as it had been in Cornwall. Sexual coercion resulted in youthful pregnancies, and John Reynolds in his *Men* [sic] *and Mines* illuminated the double standards that were the order of the day, retelling the (somewhat limp) Cousin Jack joke in which sexual indiscretion on the part of men (but not women) was relatively far down the list of social misdemeanours:

> Two miners, family men, are talking and Cousin John remarks to Cousin Thomas 'That boy of yours is a bad lad'. 'Yes', Thomas agrees, 'he is a bad lad'. John – 'he got my Jenny in the family way down in the costeen (deep trench)'. Thomas – 'Yes, he is a very bad lad: he broke the family axe twice last week, a very bad lad'.[23]

But such behaviour was no laughing matter for one critic who in March 1877 drew attention to 'the great immorality existing on the [Moonta] Mines'. He was ashamed to admit, he said, in an area 'renowned for its Christianity, you may see sights and hear sounds that would shock the modesty of any right-feeling human being'. As he explained, 'you may see crowds of young men (Sundays not excepted) standing at their rallying corners ... cursing and swearing in a manner that is disgraceful'. Moreover, 'respectable young ladies [are] halloed and hooted after. I have been informed by respectable young ladies that they are almost afraid to go to Chapel on Sunday evenings on account of this'. And, 'if they should pass these rowdies without speaking they are cursed and sworn at'.[24] Sometimes the harassment was explicit. In September 1888, for example, Richard Mayne, a miner, was forced to apologise publicly to Beatrice Williams for 'having on several occasions ... trespassed on the premises occupied by you at Wallaroo Mines, and solicited you to allow me to have sexual intercourse with you'. He regretted 'having been guilty of this conduct' and undertook 'not to anywise interfere with or molest you in the future'.[25]

At least Beatrice Williams had been able to deploy the law in her favour on this occasion, protecting her reputation and 'respectability' while exposing her unwanted pursuer to public gaze, and no doubt to ridicule from his male peers. Sometimes, however, women in mining communities found themselves the butt of an unpitying misogynist humour. Geoffrey Blainey has told the tragi-comic story of a man at Broken Hill charged with the melancholy duty of breaking the sad news to the wife of a miner who has just been killed in an underground accident. Arriving at the deceased miner's cottage, the man's insistent knocking brought the housewife hurrying to the door. Doffing his cap in a respectful if theatrical manner, he said: 'Good afternoon,

Widow Tregonning'. She instantly objected: 'I'm no widow. My husband's down there, working'. The man paused for just a moment: 'Would you like', he said, 'to take a bet on it'.[26]

It was an exceptionally cruel trick to play on the recently but unknowingly widowed Mrs Tregonning. Yet there was another way of reading story and with it the news-breaker's intention. Mrs Tregonning's subsequent actions are not recorded but the news-breaker, like the community as a whole, would have expected her to conduct herself with the quiet stoicism, fatalism and self-restraint becoming of a respectable woman suffering in adversity on the mining frontier. The Cornish miner was widely assumed to exhibit superior qualities, possessing an innate expertise in all matters mining, especially when compared to potentially competing ethnic groups on the international mining frontier. This was the 'myth of Cousin Jack', as it has been dubbed, a myth that the emigrant Cornish promoted with considerable success throughout the nineteenth century, across Australia, America, South Africa and elsewhere.[27] It was a decidedly masculine myth. But there was a parallel 'myth of Cousin Jenny', in which it was asserted that emigrant Cornishwomen—just like their menfolk—also exhibited superior qualities that enabled them to flourish on the harsh mining frontiers of the New World, establishing domesticity and order where others might fail. Co-opted into the stories the emigrant Cornish told about themselves, 'Cousin Jenny' lent a powerful feminine gender dimension to the narratives of mining communities in Australia and was one on which Mrs Tregonning could draw for comfort and for guidance.[28]

Despite having been comprehensively excluded from the formal waged mining economy, female agency asserted itself in new ways in Australia's mining communities, accepting confinement to the domestic sphere and yet finding avenues for women—especially former mineworkers—to adopt salient roles. In their supposed restriction to the domestic sphere, women in the mining towns, as elsewhere, were expected to fulfil their duties as mothers and housewives, bearing and rearing children, and performing the multiplicity of chores around the home. In 1873, a (male) visitor to Moonta Mines, the impromptu village of makeshift miners' cottages constructed on the mineral leases at Moonta in South Australia, pondered the bewildering industrial landscape, but paused to consider 'the cottages all round, with the trim housewife waiting for her husband to come home after morning core [shift], the glimpses of the snugness and comfort within'.[29] Oswald

Pryor, who had himself been a grass (surface) captain at Moonta, published his folksy local history *Australia's Little Cornwall* in 1962. He observed that the cottages on the mineral leases were 'whitewashed, inside and out, every Christmas', and explained that the 'inside of a cottage was spotless – Cousin Jenny never neglected the sweeping, cleaning and dusting'. Moreover, he insisted: 'No Cousin Jack miner's wife regarded her home as complete until the "best room" had a carpet on the floor, with a harmonium – a book of Wesley's hymns lying on its cover – a round table with the family album right in the centre, and half a dozen polished cedar chairs with crocheted antimacassars spread over the backs'.[30]

As Pryor implied, Cousin Jenny had managed to bring domestic order and comfort, even cosiness, to her modest home, despite being surrounded on every side by the noise and filth of deep mining, and despite the arid environment of extreme heat, water shortages, flies, dust, sand storms and much else. During the 1870s, when 'black measles' and 'colonial fever' decimated the infant population of the mineral-lease dwellers at Moonta Mines, the women bore the brunt, nursing their dying children and providing solace for the survivors, exhibiting the quiet stoicism and self-restraint that would be expected of widow Tregonning at Broken Hill. This, then, was the myth of Cousin Jenny in action—she had triumphed over adversity on the inhospitable mining frontier, where lesser women would have succumbed.[31]

As her myth had suggested, Cousin Jenny's role on the mining frontier in Australia was not only to provide domestic security in the midst of an unpromising industrial landscape and hostile physical environment. She was also required to show strength of character if she were to succeed in her task. And here, paradoxically, despite her apparent confinement to the domestic sphere, her erstwhile status as a self-reliant and physically strong bal-maiden (as many of them had been in Cornwall) meant that Cousin Jenny was well-equipped to play a wider role in achieving communal security. As Oswald Pryor conceded, when building cottages on the mineral leases, such as those at Moonta Mines and neighbouring Wallaroo Mines, 'Wives usually gave a hand, and some of them could use a shovel as skilfully as a man'. As he explained: 'Usually these were "bal-maidens", who had worked as ore-dressers at mines in Cornwall'.[32] Thus, the work experience and skill set of former bal-maidens did much to underwrite the myth of Cousin Jenny in Australia, providing practical evidence of the ways in which it could be deployed to advantage.

218   P. PAYTON

This practical, 'hands on' dimension of Cousin Jenny's myth was exemplified in the fictional Mary Elizabeth 'Polly' Thomas, the heroine of Phyllis Somerville's novel *Not Only in Stone*, published in 1942. Born, supposedly, in St Ives, Cornwall, in 1838, Polly had arrived in South Australia in the early days of the infant colony. She died in Adelaide in 1927, according to her creator, after a long and difficult but triumphant life in which she had stood firm against all the hardships fate had thrown at her. Her sister Ellen, we are told, died not long after Polly's arrival in the colony. Polly then lost her life's savings in a property swindle and was faced with the growing disability of her husband Nathan, a copper miner who was soon unable to work in his traditional occupation. Worst of all, were the premature deaths at Wallaroo Mines of two of her four children, her son Alan drowning in a 'leat' (drain) on the mine workings, and her daughter Annie succumbing to 'colonial fever'.

At Wallaroo Mines, Polly and Nathan had acquired one of the many mineral-lease cottages, thrown-up hastily by mining families with the tacit approval of the mine company. Improvements and expansions, usually to accommodate growing families, were allowed, normally following an approving nod from one of the mine captains. Polly, self-willed Cousin Jenny that she is, decides that she needs a garden and determines to move the fence surrounding her cottage to encompass some adjoining unoccupied land. Her bemused neighbours watch as she moves the fence outwards, 'sapling by sapling, and redriving each post firmly in the ground ... Nobody questioned her right to do this, but many stopped to remark on it'. When at last her husband Nathan comes home from the mine, he is amazed: '"Polly", he called, as he opened the door, "Polly, where 'ee to?"'.

> 'Well, said Polly, coming forward, 'what now, Nat'?
> ''Thees 'ave shifted the fence?'
> 'I 'ave!' This with a hint of pride.
> 'Land o' Goshen, oo gave un leave?'
> 'Nobody gave un, so I just took un'.
> 'What'll cap'n say?' said Nathan in a hushed voice.
> 'If cap'n da say aught I'll up an' tell un I 'ad to 'ave me garden an' 'twere easier to move fence than 'ouse, any day'.
>
> Nathan rubbed a calloused hand across his chin and looked at Polly, and there was awe as well as admiration in his eyes.[33]

This is Polly Thomas as archetypal Cousin Jenny. Later, when Nathan is unable to work, the family moves to nearby Moonta, where Polly becomes the breadwinner, opening a successful millinery shop. By now, she has acquired a reputation across the community for her tenacity and resourcefulness and is often called upon for assistance in desperate times: '"Go for Mrs Thomas!" came to be the cry for help that went out from many homes in Moonta; and Polly's stout little figure was often first to cross a troubled threshold, even before doctor or minister had been called'.[34] Although, of course, there had never been any question of Polly working as a bal-maiden in Australia, in establishing her own millinery business she had established independence of a kind beyond the domestic sphere. The cry 'Go for Mrs Thomas' also indicated her stature in the community beyond the domestic sphere—or at least in the collectivity of domestic spheres in which local women co-operated and supported one another—and established Polly Thomas as an exemplary Cousin Jenny, as no doubt Phyllis Somerville had intended.

Exemplary in a different way was Serena Thorne, the 'Girl Preacher of North Devon' as she was known. The offspring of Mary O'Bryan (daughter of William O'Bryan, the Cornish founder of the Bible Christian denomination) and the Rev. Samuel Thorne, one of the Thorne family of Shebbear, North Devon, the Bible Christian head-quarters, Serena Thorne was sent as a missionary to Queensland in 1865. The Bible Christians, alone of the Methodist denominations, used female local preachers in their evangelical work, and Serena Thorne proved especially effective, moving on from Queensland to Victoria, and from there to South Australia. It was in South Australia that she met her future husband, the Rev. Octavius Lake, whom she married in March 1871, a Bible Christian minister active among the miners at Moonta, Wallaroo and Kadina. Octavius Lake worked closely with the miners' trade union, joining their committee set up to tackle poverty and insisting that poor laws locally were 'receiving a most harsh and illiberal interpretation'.[35] Serena Thorne, meanwhile, was a powerful temperance advocate, warning against the dangers of strong drink. They made an impressive team.

As Edwin A. Curnow has observed, Serena Thorne—'Seductive Serena', as he has dubbed her—made quite a stir; the 'excitement, novelty and controversy surrounding the arrival of an attractive young woman preacher who drew hundreds to her meetings cannot be under-estimated'.[36] Here, then, was another kind of female impact beyond the domestic sphere in Australia's mining towns. Strength of character was again important, as was the bringing of civilisation—not least temperance and sobriety—to the mining frontier. But there were feminine traits that, in this strictly religious context, now seemed legitimate in their allure and entirely wholesome and 'respectable' in the way they captivated her male audiences. In marked contrast to the disdain in Cornwall for bal-maidens, with their corrupted sexuality and showy attempts at feminine display, here was a positive response that enthusiastically endorsed Serena Thorne's femininity and its deployment in the service of God. At the opening of the Bible Christian chapel at Clunes, on the Victorian goldfields, in 1868, for example, it was reported, in response to her energetic preaching, that the 'breathless attention, the sparkling eye, the heaving breast, and the silent tear declared that many felt it good to be there'.[37] On another occasion, in March 1869, it was reported that:

> Miss Thorne, as a public lecturer, considering that she is one of the weaker vessels, may be pronounced good, if not excellent. She is pleasing in manner, engaging in address, and in every way suited to the task … the fair lecturer (if the presence of a pair of large and expressive dark eyes, and brown hair, warrant the remark), succeeded admirably in engaging the attention of her hearers of both sexes for a solid hour, and, it may be surmised, with profit as well as pleasure to all present … bachelors included.[38]

Among Serena Thorne's acquaintances was John Prisk, a Bible Christian local preacher at Moonta and leading trade unionist (he sat on the poverty committee with Rev. Octavius Lake, Serena's husband). In April 1874, when Prisk was secretary of the Moonta Miners' Association, a strike broke out at the Moonta Mine and other mines in the neighbourhood. The industrial action appeared solid throughout the district, except for the pump-engine drivers who had been induced by the mining companies to keep the pumps going, the engine-men having been warned that if they abandoned their pumps the mines would be inundated and possibly ruined. John Prisk saw that the pumps were the key to bringing the strike to a swift and successful conclusion and decided that drastic action was needed.

'There is a rumour', John Prisk was reputed to have told a meeting of local women, 'that you're going to sweep all the nuisances out of their engine-houses'.[39] Suitably enthused, the women promised 'to do their best with their mallee poles'—brooms made from sticks of mallee scrub—and, as Prisk had urged, swept the blacklegs from the engine-houses, bringing the pump engines to an abrupt halt.[40] As the *Yorke's Peninsula Advertiser* explained, the 'women went vigorously to work with their brooms, charging in all directions':

> The females attached to the sweeping regiment numbered about a hundred strong ... carrying, many of them, their brooms, poles and pine branches. Never before, perhaps, was such an extraordinary spectacle witnessed as here presented itself. The space between Bower's and Ryan's [shafts, at Moonta], an area covering acres of ground, was alive with people of all classes, miners, mechanics, tradesmen and travellers, boys and girls, women (some with children in arms) excitedly talking, shouting, laughing and hurrying towards the engine house.[41]

At the Wallaroo Mine, the women acted likewise. Despite pleas from Captain Samuel Higgs that they should take no action 'for which they would suffer to their dying day', they set to with the same enthusiasm as their sisters at Moonta. They marched first to the Matta Matta mine, at Kadina, whose engine-house was closest to the 'meeting ring' at Matta Flat where they had gathered, ejecting the drivers, firemen and boiler-tenders and then proceeded to all the other pump engines in the locality. One engine-driver who resisted was threatened that he would have his 'brains knocked out' by the enraged women, and his hat was sent flying by a mallee broom. At another engine-house, a woman was reportedly wrestled to the floor by a cornered driver, despite earlier assumptions that no physical resistance would be offered to the 'fair sex'.[42]

Be that as it may, the women were spectacularly successful, forcing the cessation of pumping throughout the mines. It was an event that entered local folklore, an important part of collective memory on the Peninsula of the 'Great Strike', as the contest of 1874 was known, and a device that the women would not be frightened to threaten again in the future. As one versifier put it:

> Now Cousin Jenny is no fool
> She does not work by red-tape rule,
> But by the glorious rule of right –
> Not recognising wealth or might,
> God bless her! She's a little Queen
> For every one she swept out clean.[43]

Later, in March 1888, there was a further, brief strike at Moonta and Wallaroo, and a visiting journalist from the Adelaide *Advertiser* was sufficiently intrigued to note the continuing prominence of local women in its conduct and deliberations. 'It is astounding the amount of interest evinced by the female population in the matter', he reported: 'Members of the fair sex turn out at all meetings and discuss the question in a most animated manner. Several informed me today that rather than their husbands should give way they would start taking in washing themselves'.[44] Implementation of the payment system the companies had proposed would directly affect a family's weekly budget, often managed by women (as part of the domestic sphere), ensuring the 'female population's' close attention to developments. But the willingness to share the burdens of strike action, and to devise economic strategies (such as taking in laundry) to cope with potential loss of family income, was remarkable evidence of continuing cross-gender and community solidarity in the aftermath of the 'Great Strike' of 1874.

Similarly, when, in 1898, W.G. Spence, representative of the Amalgamated Miners Association (which the Moonta Miners' Association had recently joined) visited the Peninsula from union headquarters in Creswick, Victoria, to resolve a looming industrial dispute he was surprised to find that Cousin Jenny's exploits were still fresh in memory, some fifteen years after the 'Great Strike'. As Spence discovered, however, in the intervening period, as the episode was mythologised, so that memory had become blurred. For some, the events of 1874 and an earlier strike of 1864 had become conflated, a confusion in which women were reckoned to have also played a distinctive part in the action of 1864. Returning to his hotel at Kadina after a day of negotiations at the Moonta Mine, Spence met the landlord, who explained that local women were preparing to play a dramatic role again in any impending industrial unrest. He 'told us', Spence recorded, 'that a big Cornish-woman had just been there to borrow his stable broom because, she said, "it had plenty of wood in en" and she "might want to sweep Captain Hancock [manager of the Moonta mine] out"'.[45] Muddling the events of 1874 and 1864, the hotel landlord insisted that Captain Henry Hancock's predecessors had been swept out of town in like fashion by Cornish women.

Spence was able to diffuse the situation in 1889, averting a strike, so the brooms were not required. He had negotiated a compromise with the mine companies, which he presented to the workers. It was a tense moment when he put the outcome to the miners—and to the women, who were ready with their brooms, as Spence had already discovered in his discussion with the Kadina innkeeper. As he later explained:

> The delivery of our report and ultimatum to the miners was a scene never to be forgotten. Excitement ran high. The brooms were ready, and their plucky owners equally so. No sooner had the signal bell rung for knock-off work at 5 pm than the men assembled around the platform of the tramway, from which we were to speak. All hands came just as they were. The women stood generally in the outer circle of the crowd. They left the work of decision to the men, but were prepared to loyally carry it out, whatever it might be, even if it meant going hungry in order to secure justice.[46]

However, to Spence's evident relief, 'the meeting fully accepted our recommendation [not to strike] ... and later [the miners] were specially glad that no strike had eventuated, and that had been no need for that broom with "plenty of wood in 'en"'.[47] In November of the same year, however, a self-styled Women's Brigade, the 'daughters of the union', as its members were described in the *Barrier Miner* newspaper, was in action in the silver-lead mining district of Broken Hill in New South Wales, where many miners and their families from Moonta and Wallaroo had settled recently. The Brigade, said to be 400-strong, marched to the mines, armed with brooms and mops, Moonta-fashion and swept them clear of blacklegs, in some cases stripping recalcitrants down to their underwear.[48] Such was its success, that the strategy was employed again in July 1892, when blacklegs once more were driven from the mines by women brandishing brooms, mops and poles, an action 'now part of a [Broken Hill] tradition', as Brian Kennedy has described it.[49]

But if women were elevated to heroic status for their courageous—and gender-specific—role in the dramatic events of these great strikes, it did not prevent the trade union movement at Broken Hill from systematically excluding women from virtually all kinds of paid employment in the city and its environs. In 1909, during a lockout at the Broken Hill mines, women had formed a Relief Committee to assist those struggling to make ends meet. Women were similarly active during the eighteen-month strike in 1919–1920. One consequence of this lengthy and bruising industrial action, however, was the formation of the Barrier Industrial Council by the local trade unions, a means of coordinating policy and a forum for acting in unison. Women, as we have seen, had been systematically prevented from working in the formal waged mining economy in Australia. But at Broken Hill, the men went one step further. Having decided that a mine was no place for a woman, they then declared that a mining community was a place where the employment of women generally should be restricted. Informal social pressure was given a new legitimacy when it was decreed by the Barrier Industrial Council in 1930 that married women were now banned from working in Broken Hill. The rationale, advanced at the time, was that this would give single women more opportunity to fill the relatively few clerical, retail and other 'female' jobs available in the city. At the same time, it was argued, husbands in any event should earn enough so that their wives need not go out to work. The ban was not lifted until 1981.[50]

CONCLUSION

Despite their early visibility in the foundation of Australia's mining industry, female mineworkers—'bal-maidens' as they were known in Cornwall—soon found themselves excluded. As in Britain by the mid-nineteenth century, so in Australia men (and society in general) had decided that a mine was no place for a woman. But while ancient customary practice survived in Britain, albeit heavily criticised and increasingly under pressure, in Australia it proved easier to achieve exclusion from the mines and to restrict women to the domestic sphere. Yet the industrial experience and skill sets acquired by former female mineworkers could not be so easily dismissed, especially when they were needed for tasks ranging from the identification of newly discovered ores to the hurried erection of cottages on the mineral leases.

Moreover, female migrants from mining districts, not least Cornwall, were considered especially suited to the rigours of the mining frontier—'the myth of Cousin Jenny'—succeeding in their civilising mission to bring order and domesticity where lesser women might fail. Although they were excluded from employment in the mines, there was collusion of a sort—women in mining communities were allowed a supportive role that strayed beyond the strictly domestic sphere into direct action in support of male miners, female agency proving a powerful weapon within the trade union arsenal. Yet there were limits to this accommodation, the very trade unions that had benefitted from female action continuing to rigorously police the boundaries of female employment, not only in the mines themselves but in the mining communities beyond. This was most noticeable at Broken Hill. Paradoxically, it was in Broken Hill in March 2001 that a Women's Memorial was erected in Town Square, in the city's centre. Unveiled by Eddie Butcher, president of the Construction Forestry Mining Energy Union, the memorial was dedicated, Butcher explained, to the women of Broken Hill 'who over the years have not been recognised for what they have contributed to the community. They were the unsung heroes as they stood by their men, through the toughest and darkest hours of mining history. Women are the backbone of Broken Hill's society and they truly deserve the recognition that this monument will give them'.[51] Even at the turn of the Millennium, the women's principal raison d'etre, it seemed, was to stand by their men— this was again the myth of Cousin Jenny writ large.

NOTES

1. State Library of South Australia (SLSA), 1529, Alphabetical Index to Applications for Free Passage from the UK to South Australia 1836–1840. For the location of Wheal Butson, see M.H. Bizley, *Friendly Retreat: The Story of a Parish*, privately published 1955, republished, St Agnes Museum Trust, St Agnes, 1994, 80.
2. H.Y.L. Brown, *The Mines of South Australia*, Government of South Australia, Adelaide, fourth edition, 1908, 173–177.
3. Oswald Pryor, *Australia's Little Cornwall*, Rigby, Adelaide, 1962; Geoffrey Blainey, *The Rush That Never Ended: A History of Australian Mining*, Melbourne University Press, Melbourne, second edition, 1964, 105–116; Philip Payton, *The Cornish Overseas: A History of Cornwall's 'Great Emigration'*, University of Exeter Press, Exeter, second edition, 2015, 161–200 and 256–295.
4. *South Australian*, 23 February 1847.
5. Philip Payton, *One and All: Labor and the Radical Tradition in South Australia*, Wakefield, Adelaide, 2016, 13.
6. SLSA, 1529.
7. Patricia Lay, 'Not What They Seemed? Cornish Assisted Immigrants in New South Wales 1837–77', in Philip Payton (ed.), *Cornish Studies: Three*, University of Exeter Press, Exeter, 1995, 33–59.
8. A.R. Griffin, *The Collier*, Shire Publications, Aylesbury, 1982, 27.
9. C.C. James, *A History of the Parish of Gwennap in Cornwall*, privately published, Penzance, 1947, 242.
10. George Henwood in Roger Burt (ed.), *Cornwall's Mines and Miners*, D. Bradford Barton, Truro, 1972, 118–119.
11. Ibid., 120.

12. *Cornubian* (Redruth), 26 June 1868; *West Briton* (Truro), 6 August 1868; see Sharron Schwartz, 'In Defence of Customary Rights: Labouring Women's Experience of Industrialization in Cornwall, c1759–1870', in Philip Payton (ed.), *Cornish Studies: Seven*, University of Exeter Press, Exeter, 1999, 8–31.
13. *Mount Alexander Mail*, 23 July 1858.
14. Ibid.
15. Ibid.
16. *World's News* (Sydney), 12 July 1952.
17. Attributed to one Tom Lloyd in Clare Wright, *The Forgotten Rebels of Eureka*, Text Publishing, Melbourne, 2013, 129.
18. Mary Ann Tyler cited in Wright, *The Forgotten Rebels*, 138.
19. *Australian Town and Country Journal*, 2 June 1888.
20. *Sydney Mail*, 24 February 1894.
21. *Cobar Herald*, 18 April 1913.
22. *Yorke's Peninsula Advertiser*, 25 February 1871.
23. John Reynolds, *Men and Mines: A History of Australian Mining 1788–1971*, Sun Books, Melbourne, 1974, 17.
24. *Yorke's Peninsula Advertiser*, 21 February 1877.
25. *Kadina and Wallaroo Times*, 15 September 1888.
26. Geoffrey Blainey, *The Rise of Broken Hill*, Macmillan, Melbourne, 1968, 94.
27. Payton, *The Cornish Overseas*, 13.
28. Philip Payton, *Making Moonta: The Invention of Australia's Little Cornwall*, University of Exeter Press, Exeter, 2007, 28.
29. *South Australian Register*, 10 June 1873.
30. Pryor, *Little Cornwall*, 66.
31. Payton, *Making Moonta*, 28.
32. Pryor, *Little Cornwall*, 65.
33. Phyllis Somerville, *Not Only in Stone*, Sydney, 1942, republished, Rigby, Adelaide, 1973, 58–59.
34. Ibid., 199.
35. *Yorke's Peninsula Advertiser*, 18 May 1877.
36. Edwin A. Curnow, *Bible Christian Methodists in South Australia 1850–1900: A Biography of Chapels and Their People*, Uniting Church SA Historical Society, Adelaide, 2015, 311.
37. *Bible Christian Victorian Record*, April 1868.
38. Travis McHarg, *The Bible Christian Church in Victoria, 1850s–1902*, Mercia Press, Boronia (VIC), 2011, 50.
39. Pryor, 37.
40. *Yorke's Peninsula Advertiser*, 10 April 1874.

41. *Yorke's Peninsula Advertiser*, 10 April 1874; see also *South Australian Register*, 8 April 1874.
42. Keith Bailey, *James Boor's Bonanza: A History of Wallaroo Mines, South Australia*, privately published, Kadina, 2002, 31.
43. SLSA D4876 (Misc), The Great Strike, W. Shelley, c.1874.
44. *Advertiser* (Adelaide), 3 March 1888.
45. W.G. Spence, *Australia's Awakening: Thirty Years in the Life of an Australian Agitator*, Sydney, 1909, 29.
46. Spence, 1903, 30.
47. Ibid.
48. *Barrier Miner*, 12 November 1889; *Pictorial Australian*, November–December 1889.
49. Brian Kennedy, *Silver, Sin and Sixpenny Ale: A Social History of Broken Hill, 1883–1921*, Melbourne University Press, Melbourne, 1978, 70; *The Leader*, 3 September 1892.
50. http://www.womenaustralia.info/exhib/bh/intro.html, accessed 22 December 2018: Unbroken Spirit—Women in Broken Hill.
51. http://www.womenaustralia.info/biogs/AWE405b.htm, accessed 22 December 2018; The Australian Women's Register (an initiative of the National Foundation for Australian Women in conjunction with the University of Melbourne), Broken Hill Women's Memorial (2001). The inscription on the memorial reads: 'This memorial is dedicated to the women of Broken Hill who have stood by their men during troubled industrial times'.

SELECT BIBLIOGRAPHY

Bailey, Keith, *James Boor's Bonanza: A History of Wallaroo Mines, South Australia*, privately published, Kadina, 2002.

Bizley, M.H., *Friendly Retreat: The Story of a Parish*, privately published 1955, republished, St Agnes Museum Trust, St Agnes, 1994.

Blainey, Geoffrey, *The Rush That Never Ended: A History of Australian Mining*, Melbourne University Press, Melbourne, second edition, 1964.

Blainey, Geoffrey, *The Rise of Broken Hill*, Macmillan, Melbourne, 1968.

Brown, H.Y.L., *The Mines of South Australia*, Government of South Australia, Adelaide, fourth edition, 1908.

Burt, Roger (ed.), *Cornwall's Mines and Miners*, D. Bradford Barton, Truro, 1972.

Curnow, Edwin A., *Bible Christian Methodists in South Australia 1850–1900: A Biography of the Chapels and their People*, Uniting Church SA Historical Society, Adelaide, 2016.

Griffin, A.R., *The Collier*, Shire Books, Aylesbury, 1982.

James, C.C., *A History of the Parish of Gwennap in Cornwall*, privately published, Penzance, 1947.

Kennedy, Brian, *Silver, Sin and Sixpenny Ale: A Social History of Broken Hill, 1883–1921*, Melbourne University Press, Melbourne, 1978.

Lay, Patricia, 'Not What They Seemed? Cornish Assisted Immigrants in New South Wales 1837–77', in Payton, Philip (ed.), *Cornish Studies: Three*, University of Exeter Press, Exeter, 1995.

McHarg, Travis, *The Bible Christian Church in Victoria 1850s–1902*, Boronia (VIC), 2011.

Payton, Philip, *Making Moonta: The Invention of 'Australia's Little Cornwall'*, University of Exeter Press, Exeter, 2007.

Payton, Philip, *The Cornish Overseas: A History of Cornwall's 'Great Emigration'*, University of Exeter Press, Exeter, second edition, 2015.

Payton, Philip, *One and All: Labor and the Radical Tradition in South Australia*, Wakefield Press, Adelaide, 2016.

Pryor, Oswald, *Australia's Little Cornwall*, Rigby, Adelaide, 1962.

Reynolds, John, *Men and Mines: A History of Australian Mining 1788–1971*, Sun Books, Melbourne, 1975.

Schwartz, Sharron, 'In Defence of Customary Rights: Labouring Women's Experience of Industrialization in Cornwall c1759–1870', in Payton, Philip (ed.), *Cornish Studies: Seven*, University of Exeter Press, Exeter, 1999.

Somerville, Somerville, *Not Only in Stone*, Sydney, 1942, republished, Rigby, Adelaide, 1973.

Spence, W.G., *Australia's Awakening: Thirty Years in the Life of an Australian Agitator*, Sydney, 1909.

Wright, Clare, *The Forgotten Rebels of Eureka*, Text Publishing, Melbourne, 2012.

CHAPTER 10

Mary Booth and British Boy Immigration: From Progressivism to Imperial Nationalism

Bridget Brooklyn

The history of British migration in the first half of the twentieth century is one in which the imperial relationship has been intrinsic: this migration was in the service, or emphasised the strength, of ties between the metropole and periphery of the British Empire. In Australia generally at this time, adherence to 'imperial' values could take many forms and could be combined with strong nationalism, as was the case with Dr Mary Booth, a physician, feminist and social activist who was born in Sydney in 1869 and died there in 1956. Her early career in the field of child health and eugenics also shows the influence of Progressivism, the reform movement originating in the United States in the late nineteenth century. Always conservative, Booth appears to have been galvanised by the Great War into greater faith in both the British Empire and Australia, and after the war, she became active in support of British boy immigration. She maintained a strong commitment to British youth immigration

B. Brooklyn (✉)
School of Humanities and Communication Arts,
Western Sydney University, Sydney, NSW, Australia
e-mail: B.Brooklyn@westernsydney.edu.au

© The Author(s) 2019
P. Payton and A. Varnava (eds.),
Australia, Migration and Empire, Britain and the World,
https://doi.org/10.1007/978-3-030-22389-2_10

229

and an active involvement in aftercare, from its peak in the mid-to-late 1920s until the end of the 1930s. The following chapter analyses Booth's activities in support of British immigration in the interwar years. Putting them into the context of her intellectual and political outlook reveals her postwar imperial nationalism as growing out of, rather than departing from, her pre-war Progressivism.

Booth graduated in medicine from the University of Edinburgh in 1899 and returned to Australia in 1900.[1] She then worked for education departments in New South Wales and Victoria, where she specialised in child health and eugenics, and for which she became well known. Advocacy of eugenics was one of the hallmarks of Progressivism, the social reform programmes of which also emphasised the importance of the state and 'national efficiency'. This efficiency extended to a wide range of public health measures. The Progressive influence is particularly evident in Booth's use of anthropometry, a form of data collection, in her role as a School Medical Inspector in Victoria from 1910 to 1912.[2] Related to (but distinct from) Booth's eugenics was her Australian nationalism, which I describe as 'imperial nationalism'.

From the smorgasbord of nationalisms that existed in early twentieth-century Australia, choosing a name that best describes any nationalism of this time is an exacting task: descriptions that might fit include the Federation-era 'colonial nationalism' studied by Richard Jebb and discussed by Eddy and Schreuder; Curran and Ward's 'race nationalism'; Meaney's 'conservative imperialism'; and McGregor's 'British-Australian' nationalism and 'imperial loyalism'.[3] I have chosen the term 'imperial nationalism' as most closely reflecting Booth's membership of the professional, or upper, middle class and her imperially loyal sympathies, which she held in tandem with her nationalism. These sympathies bore some similarities to the conservative imperialism of the historian Ernest Scott (as described by Meaney),[4] but with a much stronger sense of Australian identity than Scott's. Booth shared the combination of strong national pride buttressed by strong race pride, as expressed by C. E. W. Bean, shaper of the Anzac legend. Bean and his wife Effie were supporters of Booth's interwar activities and organisations.

The outbreak of the First World War caused some important changes in Booth's life, notably, the cessation of professional work to embark on voluntary activities. The latter she did for the rest of her life, probably facilitated by an inheritance in 1913.[5] During and after the war, her values became more imperial nationalist in tone, but without completely negating her Progressivism. Booth saw the heroism of the First AIF as an example to be set for generations to come, an indication of the best of British Australia. The combination of British genes and a healthy Australian environment in which they could flourish would ensure that the British race would find new life. Neither Booth's imperial nationalism nor her political conservatism offered any quarrel with Progressivism and the eugenic principles that she drew from it. Progressivism could intersect and overlap quite happily with conservatism and radicalism alike, and with a nationalism that favoured Protestantism and whiteness.[6] It could overlap as well with the 'new social order' embraced by reformers such as J. D. Fitzgerald, Robert Irvine and Meredith Atkinson.[7]

Progressive eugenics could take several forms, where again modernity overlapped with conservatism. Belief in the importance of using eugenics to establish a healthy environment—preventative eugenics, or euthenics—had been popular among conservative thinkers since before the First World War.[8] Although Booth did not use the term 'euthenics', she was interested in town planning issues. She was a member of the Town Planning Association of New South Wales and gave evidence in support of flat-dwelling to the 1920 Royal Commission on the Basic Wage.[9] She remained an activist on behalf of environmental causes in the urban setting of Sydney until late in life.[10] The roots of her environmentalism in the early twentieth century correspond to the aims of Australian urban reformers of this time, who advocated the ruralisation of Australian cities through both the greening of the urban landscape and the encouragement of a sense of community and national identity. There is much in connection with her aims for her two clubs, the Soldiers' Club and the Empire Service Club, discussed below—the latter in particular—that speaks of the need to remove the vulnerable young man from the deleterious influences of city life.[11]

In the interwar years, Booth channelled her medical eugenic principles into goals that affirmed class and race loyalty. In doing so, she did not undergo any substantial shift in her outlook—compared, say, to social reformers such as Fitzgerald and George Taylor.[12] Rather, it was a recalibration that saw her make a transition from her wartime activities to her work in immigration aftercare in the 1920s and 1930s. Throughout the 1930s, when the numbers of immigrants were fewer, Booth continued to provide support to the boys who passed through her Empire Service Club, located successively in Sydney's inner districts, and through her magazine, *The Boy Settler*.

232   B. BROOKLYN

But before that, there was her pre-war career as a child health specialist practising anthropometry. A form of cerebral measurement designed as a means of connecting human capabilities and tendencies to physical characteristics, anthropometry was a strong component of Francis Galton's 'cerebral physiology', which led him to establish an 'anthropometric laboratory' in South Kensington, London.[13] In Australia, it became what Warwick Anderson has described as 'a national obsession', affecting a number of practitioners, including those who worked with Aboriginal people, such as Norman Tindale, who used the techniques in the 1930s.[14] Booth's anthropometric work in schools formed the basis of some of her published work on eugenics, in which she stressed the importance of both hereditary and environmental factors to the betterment of 'the race'.

Often dismissed by historians as a 'pseudo-science',[15] eugenics nevertheless attracted many scientific thinkers. Accompanied by what Levine and Bashford refer to as an 'evaluative logic',[16] eugenics harnessed the scientific tools afforded by the understanding of natural selection to a non-scientific aim to 'improve' human beings. This has led eugenics down the path of discrimination, segregation and even extermination, but it has also had a strong health dimension. Its evaluative logic continues to the present day, for example in the in utero monitoring of baby health for abnormalities and 'birth defects'.[17]

Given the breadth of meaning of eugenics, and given that its practice has become inextricably bound with its extreme end under the Third Reich, it is important to establish a working definition of eugenics in the early decades of the twentieth century. This definition, then, is of eugenics as a set of beliefs, based on prevailing scientific knowledge of heredity, which sought human perfectibility through a variety of measures. These measures could include hereditarian approaches, such as selective breeding, or environmental ones that were aimed at improving the conditions under which people lived, such as through public health policy. Booth's work in the field of improving child health through work in public schools made her principally an 'environmental' eugenicist. As will be discussed further below, she nevertheless believed that hereditary factors were very important.

Booth's medical education would have exposed her to all the latest eugenic thinking. She graduated from the University of Edinburgh, one of the world's leading medical schools, in 1899. This was a critical time, when eugenics was becoming entrenched as a solution for a multitude of social and health ills, and western countries were also gripped by anxiety about population numbers. The two—eugenics and population anxiety—are often regarded as kindred phenomena. Kindred, yes, but different: eugenics was concerned with the quality of the human population, pronatalism with boosting the quantity. Yet the two were closely linked by an essentially racial foundation: at the height of British Empire, whiteness was seen, paradoxically, as both superior and vulnerable to attack from inferior forces. Non-white populations were considered eugenically inferior but nevertheless capable of overrunning a white race that was not vigilant about its health and fitness, and which had large tracts of land that were sparsely populated by white people, as Australia did. Booth's publications on eugenics indicate that, as a specialist in this field, she was familiar with the latest scholarship on both 'hereditary' and 'environmental' eugenics and considered each to be significant. Booth was not a vocal pronatalist beyond seeing parenthood as a duty that some selfish people shirked by using 'patented facilities and perverted knowledge'.[18] But she was concerned about population numbers and shared with other advocates of British immigration the imperative to fill up Australia's less populated hinterland. As Michele Langfield points out, this motive was about more than just the 'yellow peril'; it was also about the perpetuation of Britishness.[19] Along with empire building generally, there was the eugenic motive of providing healthy, outdoor work for young Britons.[20] For Booth, all of these factors played a part, with the link between eugenic and imperial motives being the strongest.

Booth's interest in eugenics did not extend to some of the fears that other members of her class could hold. She did not, for instance, demonstrate one of the typical concerns that an overly fecund working class posed public health threats. Nor did she indicate any worry that a specifically working-class ignorance of the principles of household management would lead to either racial degeneration or a shortage of good servants. Rather, her focus was on the duty of the white Australian population in general to raise healthy families, and the duty of all citizens to practise healthy habits—habits that should be inculcated in the school system.[21]

In her published medical work, Booth emphasised race more than class. Accordingly, inherent racial characteristics were more important factors to be noted. Where, for instance, certain schools in poor neighbourhoods repeatedly recorded pupils' height, weight and chest measurements that were below expectations and therefore might reveal 'a poor-class Irish or Italian community',[22] the emphasis is on the racial repercussions of poverty generally. The idea of a racial hierarchy associated with class is suggested, as it was in so much Progressive (and other) thinking of the day, but Booth also placed considerable importance on environmental factors, such as housing. Booth strongly believed that many 'defects', denounced as hereditary by more hard-line eugenicists, could be redressed by public health interventions.[23]

Booth also demonstrated Progressive principles in a 1912 article on 'the feebleminded', arguing that, if the total of the Australian population that fit this category were indeed what was generally estimated as 1% of the population, this amounted to roughly 16,500 children in New South Wales alone who should be under the aegis of the State. Here, she invoked the influence of the noted psychiatric medical practitioner, John Fishbourne, who advocated the treatment of feeblemindedness as a disease like any other.[24] Success, counted in such measures as 'improved social hygiene encouraging the survival of the greater numbers of the unfit' and 'special education and care for the happiness of the feebleminded' emphasises a humane approach that puts Booth at odds with contemporaries who advocated sterilisation or segregation.[25] Her humanity is also reflected in her advocacy of education to raise awareness. This was, presumably, to inculcate a similarly humane approach in the general public so as to effectively manage the problem of feeblemindedness.[26] In matters of public health, eugenics and the management of the population's health, she was a Progressive through and through.

It is important to bear in mind the many different goals of eugenics, and the varying ways in which these goals were pursued, as a reminder of just how broad a church eugenics was. As mentioned above, it was also characteristically not value-free, and Booth's medical writing strayed into the realm of racial politics. Her work in school anthropometrics had as its ultimate goal to maximise human potential in terms of fitness, particularly the ability of white people to populate the north of the continent. Booth's environmental priorities as a medical practitioner did not preclude a belief in hereditary differences between the races in a way that echoed typical white Australian fears of the time of Asian invasion. More generally, Booth was interested, like many of her medical colleagues,[27] in determining the capacity of white people to survive in the tropics:

We are an old race in a new land, removed from the near neighbourhood of Teuton and Norman cousins to that of oriental races. We have acquired responsibility for a Northern Territory full of new and untried problems, upon the solution of which depends our power to keep our continent our own. We must use every method science puts into our hands, and guide the national destiny by counsels based on our investigations.[28]

Such plans made a priority of the increase in the Australian-British 'race'. Thus, eugenics was combined with concerns about the numbers of Australia's white population, addressing both the quality and the quantity of Australians. But her advocacy of greater numbers of the 'right' type did not veer into avid pronatalism; increase by immigration was by and large the method Booth considered most effective. Here, the sense of threat of other races seems largely to have come from the possibility of invasion by Asians. The 'new and untried problems' would seem, given Booth's medical interests, to refer to the challenge of peopling the North—the publication of this article coincided with the transfer of responsibility for the Territory from South Australia to the Commonwealth in 1911, under the *Northern Territory Acceptance Act 1910* (Cth). There is a possibility that it may also refer to what was regarded among urban white Australians as 'the Aboriginal problem'. This is unlikely; the rest of article does not refer to Aboriginal people at all.

One of Booth's medical publications from the pre-war years alludes to Australia's British legacy as something of a mixed blessing during the country's formative years. Writing in 1912, she considered Australia's convict origins to be a hereditary cause of feeblemindedness in New South Wales, and this offers a possible explanation for her wish to direct her energies towards the British immigrant, rather than the 'unclothed immigrant' (or newborn baby) favoured by the pronatalists.[29] On a more cheerful note, Australia's convict genes were counterbalanced by the other formative contribution to the gene pool, that of the hard-working free settler. In the following passage, Booth weighs up the components of white Australia's eugenic and environmental inheritance:

It is probable that the special hereditary and environmental factors of life in Australia may modify the figures in one or other direction; for instance, the early convict element, the adventurous and capable type of good immigrant settler, and the more varied mixture of family strains than obtains in older countries where population is less nomadic.[30]

In 1914, Booth began the phase of her life as a voluntary worker rather than a child health professional. Her eugenic thinking turned from its strictly medical focus towards some of the eugenic concerns shared by wartime volunteer agencies more generally: that of keeping uniformed men off the streets. In this capacity, the emphasis on prevention to protect racial health gave Booth's eugenic thinking a patriotic edge. In 1915, she formed the Soldiers' Club, a place in the centre of Sydney that aimed to get new recruits and returning servicemen out of the way of harm in the form of venereal disease and other threats to racial hygiene.[31] Her activities were not entirely eugenic in focus, however. In the same year, she formed the Centre for Soldiers' Wives and Mothers, a charitable organisation with many branches around the Sydney metropolitan area that helped the dependents of servicemen. The Centre also engaged in political activity, such as support for Prime Minister Hughes's 'Yes' campaign in the first conscription referendum.[32] Booth's wartime voluntary work marked the beginning of this second phase of her life as an activist and lobbyist.

After the war, Booth continued this combination of charitable work and activism, much of it directly related to the war and remembrance of it. In 1921, she successfully applied under the regulations of the *War Precautions Repeal Act 1920* (Cth) to use the word 'Anzac' in the name of her postwar organisation, the Anzac Fellowship of Women. The Fellowship became the umbrella organisation under which Booth's other activities were grouped. These activities included political lobbying on issues such as the Anzac Memorial in Sydney's Hyde Park and a campaign to prevent Anzac Day becoming a public holiday.[33]

The name of Booth's organisation provides indication of something of a shift from Progressivism to a form of activism that was more aligned with the imperial nationalism that was strengthened among Australian conservatives during the interwar period. Beginning with her volunteer activity in support of the war effort, almost everything she did from the end of the war until the end of her life was connected in some way to Anzac. It is noteworthy that the Fellowship—which comprised civilian women with no immediate connection with Anzac—thrived as a mainstream organisation and had strong connections with returned servicemen.[34] It was also the organisation under whose auspices Booth carried out her work in immigration aftercare, where a link to Anzac would seem tenuous at best. But the link was very real for Booth and emphasises both the 'imperial' and the 'nationalist' in 'imperial nationalist'.

The significance of the achievements of the First AIF, and particularly the Anzacs, was underlined in the name of Booth's Anzac Fellowship of Women. The organisation had a number of goals:

a. To provide the comradeship of women who were engaged in war work during the Great War.
b. To foster the spirit and traditions of Anzac Day.
c. To have regard for the welfare of soldiers and their bereaved.
d. To be helpful and friendly to newcomers from the Old Country.
e. To enlist the sympathy of others who are sympathetic with the above objects.[35]

Growing out of Booth's wartime Centre for Soldiers' Wives and Mothers, 'Fellowship' in the new organisation's name asserts the importance of women's networks in this aftermath of men's war-making. The organisation, like its predecessor, quickly developed a capacity for political action. Given Booth's eugenic motives, the work in immigration aftercare carried out under the Fellowship's oversight must also be seen as having a political character—as indeed did other charitable institutions that supported British immigration.

Booth's interest in the support of British boy immigration found expression in the early 1920s, at about the time of the closure of her Soldiers' Club in 1923, and in time to catch the biggest wave of British youth immigration. What is usually collectively known as empire migration began in the first decade of the twentieth century and continued until the outbreak of the Second World War. From the early 1920s, government funding was carried out under the British *Empire Settlement Act* of 1922. This legislation, later supported by Australia's *Development and Migration Act 1926* (Cth), enabled the British Government to enter into arrangements with government and/or private organisations in the dominions for the direct emigration of residents of the United Kingdom.[36] Migration programmes that targeted British youth flourished in the 1920s, with over 18,000 young farm workers arriving between 1922 and 1930, which constituted about 10% of all assisted migration in these years.[37] However, Australian Commonwealth funds were severely curtailed with the election of the Scullin Labour government in 1929, coinciding with the onset of the Great Depression. Figures for British immigration generally did not ever return to the numbers reached in the years immediately preceding the First World War,

238   B. BROOKLYN

when 393,048 migrants arrived between 1906 and 1914—all British, including some small pockets of 'exotic recruitments ... from within the older British diaspora'.[38] In the decade of the 1930s, despite some cautious increase in assisted immigration under the UAP government,[39] the era of targeting young Britons to work on farms was in decline.

To survey briefly the secondary literature on empire settlement during these years, Michael Roe's *Australia, Britain and Migration*, comparing official interests with those of the immigrants themselves, remains substantial, as does the work of James Jupp.[40] In his equally substantial *Destination Australia*, Eric Richards sets out the factors that drove empire settlement on each side of the globe: postwar economic imperatives in the imperial centre reasserted a balance between 'the industrial metropole and the agricultural periphery'.[41] Other studies have focussed on voluntary organisations. Michele Langfield, while observing that the aims of most charities were loosely 'imperial' in their interests, exempts the work of the Salvation Army from this purview, demonstrating ways in which its migration goals fit the organisation's general goal of helping people in need.[42] Also working on the Salvation Army, Esther Daniel has examined how the Army's youth migration programme, in sending young migrants to work on the land, pursued goals of moral uplift, which intersected with imperial goals.[43] Concentrating more specifically on dominion interests, Scott Johnston has also worked the eugenic/ imperial lode in exploring the Boy Scout movement's adherence to these imperatives in its support of British youth migration.[44] Grant and Sendziuk, writing about pre-war youth immigration to South Australia, similarly discuss how such schemes fit into a binary construction of urban decay and rural regeneration.[45]

The scholarship on these various British immigration schemes collectively acknowledges the motivations behind the immigration of British boys and youths to be, variously, strengthening racial purity, shoring up Australia's defence against Asian invasion and fostering values that saw rural life as both a physical and a moral antidote to the ills of city life.[46] One of the most prominent charitable programmes was the Dreadnought Scheme, which began operation in 1911, and was driven by conservative interests.[47] This Scheme was funded by money that had been raised to purchase a Dreadnought battleship for the British Navy; the instigation of a modest Australian Navy in 1909 obviated the need for this money. Consequently, some of the Dreadnought funds were returned, and the remainder was used to instigate another scheme believed to be vital for the defence of Australia: the immigration of British youths, with the aim of employing them on the land. The main periods of Dreadnought activity were 1912–1913 and 1921–1929, after which it ceased.[48]

Youth immigration schemes that targeted British boys and young men and, to a lesser extent, girls, began to proliferate in the years before the First World War. Why mainly boys? There were also schemes to bring in British girls, and the Australian demand generally always exceeded the British supply.[49] There were several reasons, however, why boys were preferred, particularly in the years after the First World War. To begin with, in the economic uncertainty of the 1920s, female labour was not as responsive to changing labour conditions as was male labour.[50] And in the aftermath of a war from which approximately 60,000 men, mostly of marriageable age, had not returned, the consequential sex imbalance was evident between 1919 and 1921.[51] This meant that, in postwar Australia at least, there was little need to increase Australia's 'surplus women', regardless of how much of this surplus also existed in the mother country.[52] In addition, in a country with a strongly protectionist labour movement, work for female immigrants was often thought to threaten male wage rates.[53] The philanthropic agencies, too, tended to prefer boys.[54]

While following the trend in the 1920s to favour boy over girl immigration, Booth did not neglect the needs of women. In fact, her postwar assistance to women preceded her involvement with Dreadnought Boys—specifically, imperial ex-service women, through her Ex-Service Women's Club, which appears to have been shortlived.[55] She also chaired the Women's Standing Committee of the biggest charity aiding immigrants, the New Settlers' League (although she fell out with them later in that decade), which was supported financially by the Commonwealth Government. In addition, she formed the Women's Migration Council of NSW.[56] The fact that her energies became more focussed on boys and young men is probably because of the comparatively large number of boys coming out to Australia, but also provides an echo of her wartime work with servicemen in the kind of assistance she offered, especially her very successful clubs, discussed below.

Given the ability of Progressive principles to appeal to both conservatives and radicals, Booth's medical Progressivism before the war evolved quite smoothly into her more vigorously imperial thinking after it. She began her work with immigrant youth in the early 1920s, continuing throughout the 1930s, against the general downward trend. While other

240   B. BROOKLYN

organisations of course continued to operate in the face of the 1930s decline, Booth reveals an enthusiasm for the enterprise that went beyond just the usual imperial motives, with her pre-war Progressive thinking still evident. Working in the field of immigration aftercare, as distinct from being involved in selecting immigrants to assist, Mary Booth did not limit her support to Dreadnought Boys, but much of her work involved them. She also had contacts with other empire migration societies such as the Big Brother Movement and the Millions Club. While Booth's involvement in the aftercare of boy immigrants shows similar preoccupations to those driving organisations such as the Big Brother Movement, there is also the possibility that she was attracted by the funding offered by the Dreadnought Trust.[57] If so, this motive alone would not be sufficient to explain the extent of Booth's involvement and her choice of this activity, and the goals of the Anzac Fellowship of Women offer further illustration of Booth's motives.

On 18 October 1923, under the auspices of the Anzac Fellowship of Women, Booth officially opened her Empire Service Club premises at 97 George Street North, near Sydney's Circular Quay, the headquarters of her immigration activities.[58] The reason for choosing this site was that the new Commonwealth Immigration Office, part of the Prime Minister's Department, was being built on the site opposite.[59] The transition from helping soldiers through her Soldiers' Club to helping immigrant boys through her Empire Service Club (whose name closely echoed the Imperial Service Club for returned officers which opened in Sydney in 1917) was almost seamless. Booth's wartime activities with the Soldiers' Club provided her with a template for her postwar Empire Service Club. During its lifetime from 1915 to 1923, the Soldiers' Club had been furnished in 'homely and comfortable fashion', with free admission to 'Rooms for Music, Writing, Games, Reading, Billiards, Newspapers and Light Refreshments'.[60] The postwar Empire Service Club cultivated a comparably 'homely' atmosphere. Empire Service Club volunteers, generally drawn from the Anzac Fellowship of Women, would meet boatloads of boys shortly after their arrival in Sydney, giving them a welcome party and free tickets to the zoo. The Empire Service Club was initially open in the evenings from 7 to 10 p.m.[61] By 1927, it was open on weekdays from 10 a.m. to 5 p.m. as well as Monday, Tuesday and Friday evenings and 'very often at other times'.[62] Here, boys could engage in singalongs, play games or write letters home with the writing materials the Club provided.[63] An executive meeting of the Anzac Fellowship of Women in 1933 recorded that there were at that time more than 3500 boys on its membership register.[64]

By the interwar period, Booth's medical and moral imperatives as a Progressive eugenicist had made a shift from the 'national efficiency' of Progressive rhetoric to 'national defence', expressing a different set of priorities. She saw 'safeguarding the Boy Settlers [as] thereby contributing also to the National Defence and Safety of our Country'.[65] Booth derived inspiration from the heroic feats of British Australians at Gallipoli and on the Western Front, echoing other imperial nationalists such as C. E. W. Bean, who took the mixture of bush legend and eugenics that proliferated in Australian writing of the 1890s and moulded it into the enduring 'Anzac legend'.[66] Similarly, Booth saw the soldier of the First AIF as representing the apogee of Britishness. The value of British stock was equal to the value of the bush as a place for this stock to reach its full potential in Australia's healthy and wholesome climate—both literal and figurative—with its sunshine and its cultivation of manly independence. The best way to perpetuate the achievements of the First AIF was to bring out more young men of British stock, free of any taint of the dubious convict legacy she had mentioned in her pre-war writing. If the example set by the First AIF was evidence of the taint being all but erased, Booth did not say so specifically. Rather, the postwar years saw a coming together of eugenic and imperial nationalist motives: if Britain provided the best stock in the world, Australia provided the best conditions under which to allow it to flourish.

As the umbrella organisation for Booth's immigration aftercare activities, the Anzac Fellowship of Women set out the principles upon which all of Booth's activities in the postwar years were based. Always reflecting Booth's view that Anzac and Britishness were linked, the first four of the Anzac Fellowship of Women's objectives, discussed above, nevertheless underwent some shifts in hierarchy during the interwar years, suggesting shifts in Booth's own priorities. The object of helping 'new comers from the Old Country'—fourth in line in 1921—rose up the scale of priorities as the 1920s wore on. By the time of the Fellowship's 1927 Annual Report, 'supporting newcomers from the Old Country' featured as one of two principal goals. The second was 'fostering the traditions of Anzac Day', as opposed to the actual 'spirit' of Anzac extolled in earlier versions of the Fellowship's goals. It is likely that this change of wording in the second goal had a political dimension, given that it appears at a time when the ratification of Anzac Day as a public holiday—something she vehemently opposed—was in the process of occurring in state legislatures around Australia.[67] Taken together, these goals were '[t]win objects which are essential to the security and well-being of our country'.[68] As well as echoing her other statement from around this time, mentioned above, asserting a link between 'boy settlers' and national security, Anzac and Britishness are united as priorities in a cultural sense—that of 'tradition'—as well.

Ten years later, an Anzac Fellowship circular of March 1937 indicates another recalibrating of the objectives, when Booth's presidential address reported on how much had been done to carry out the objects of the Fellowship, both as regards <u>fostering the tradition of ANZAC DAY</u> and its twin object, the <u>welfare of Overseas Boy Settlers</u>'.[69] The value of British immigration is now more specifically identified as boys, and although the 'Old Country' is no longer specified, boys from the UK remained the cohort with which she worked. Given that this was a time when boy immigration was in decline, it is possible that Booth broadened the terminology in order to accommodate any future boy immigrants from non-British countries whose racial qualities were congenial to her imperial vision. Nevertheless, she did continue to target British boys, despite the decline in British youth immigration generally, and the suspension of the Dreadnought scheme at the onset of the Depression. She provided a high level of long-term support in the 1930s for the boys, through the Empire Service Club, and through her magazine, the *Boy Settler*, which was published monthly from November 1925 until November 1937, after which it appeared irregularly until the final issue in February 1944.

The adaptability of Progressivism to a broad spectrum of political and social persuasions has already been noted. This protean characteristic is evident in attitudes to modernity among eugenicists that were multifarious to the point of being conflicting, particularly in the interwar years. Booth's Progressivism was on the conservative end of the continuum. The similarity between the Soldiers' Club and the Empire Service Club invites the conclusion that Booth saw young immigrant men, like soldiers, as similarly prey to the racial degeneration that might follow if they spent too much unsupervised time in the fleshpots of Sydney. Her formula for a 'homely' place appears to have been very popular with both the soldiers and the immigrant boys that she targeted and can be interpreted as eugenic in its implication that a wholesome environment kept young men out of the kind of trouble that might affect the health of the next generation. Her environmentalism and her nationalist emphasis on the bush as a palliative to the corrupting influence of the city was an Australian variant of the Country Life movement that was also a feature of interwar Australia and another remnant of Progressivism. Like other reformers, she adhered to Progressive principles, which in this respect could emphasise urban solutions to urban problems alongside sentimental longings for a rural idyll.[70] But it also reflects the conservatism of the postwar decade generally in all the combatant countries. The Progressive emphasis on mental hygiene could be combined with a strong sense of discomfort with modernity and was voiced by Booth's contemporaries in her former profession of public health, such as Dr Harvey Sutton and Dr John Dale.[71]

Booth pressed history into service to reinforce the eugenic aspect of her nationalism. In the interwar years, particularly in the 1930s, her celebration of the 'pioneer legend' increased steadily. By the time of the 1938 Sesquicentenary in New South Wales—a veritable pioneer-fest—her beliefs were thoroughly in tune with the Zeitgeist, when white Australia's convict origins were excised from the Sesquicentenary celebrations.[72] In her increasing confidence in this pioneer heritage and her avoidance of mentioning the eugenic stain of convictism, she departed from the empiricist foundations of her published medical work, where she had lauded the 'rigid statistical analysis' of the Eugenics Laboratory—instigated by Francis Galton and continued by Karl Pearson—whose work she so admired.[73]

Instead, the interwar years were marked by a greater appeal to tradition, evoking more of a nostalgic conservatism than is generally associated with Progressivism. Booth's wish to use her clubs to create communities seems to have arisen out of the belief that their effectiveness lay in their function as a home away from home. But for all the affirmation of cosy certainties, she was still not very far from principles that were perfectly consistent with Progressivism. There is always in the background the suggestion that her clubs, apart from providing a wholesome alternative to roaming the streets of the city, served a larger eugenic purpose. This purpose was interwoven with her imperial nationalism. Her aim was not just to remove the immediate threat of venereal disease, but to build up Australia as a great nation—a member of the British Empire but also an independent country. In 1928, she editorialised in *The Boy Settler*:

244   B. BROOKLYN

Australia has been founded and developed by the British. It is said to be the purest British stock in the Empire – a population with 98 per cent. British-born or of British descent. Australia sent over 300,000 volunteers (60,000 of whom made the supreme sacrifice) to fight for the Empire in the Great War. Hence ... it [is] the duty of every Australian to foster the tradition in one way or another[,] ... to do everything possible to ensure that British lads coming to settle and help develop this great country should have a good start and a fair chance to do the best for himself, and therefore for the country and the Empire.[74]

Here, Booth sets out very clearly her aims for Britain and for Australia as a member of its empire. The sacrifice of 60,000 of the First AIF to the cause of empire is evidence of the tradition of Britishness, of which Anzac was a part. Youth immigration offered the possibility of peopling the Australian hinterland with the right kind of immigrant, of the same stock from which Australia's fighting force was drawn, and who would remain untainted by urban decadence. Apart from being a view that could be found within the range of Progressive thinking, this retreat into a rural idyll was also consonant with the rise of Australian rural conservatism in the 1920s, evidenced in the formation of the Country Party in 1920 and 'countrymindedness'.[75]

A backward-looking frame of mind that suggests conservatism more than Progressivism is also evident in the suggestion that Booth's ideal boy settler was one who brought not only his genes but the right kind of values. Her enthusiasm for British migration had a class dimension to it, as Geoffrey Sherington has observed of the Big Brother Movement, quoting the aim of its founder, Richard Linton, to bring out 'boys of high standard, morally, physically, and of education in accordance with our schedule'.[76] Along similar lines, a pamphlet issued by Booth's Women's Migration Council in the mid-1920s contained the text of a speech given in 1925 by Rev. A. G. West, a visiting clergyman, formerly of Adelaide but now vicar of St Dunstan's, London. The speech expresses many of the sentiments Booth expressed herself: a belief in the superiority of British values—not just whiteness or ethnic similarity—but those of establishment conservatism. Booth's organisations sought young men whose stock was good, but also who were 'brought up in the fear of God, brought up in the old morals, with a good sense of honour towards women and justice'.[77]

Michael Roe's *Nine Australian Progressives* remains the only comprehensive analysis of Australian Progressive thought and policies, documenting through the lives of individual Progressives a movement that managed to contain within it a dizzying array of competing objectives and yet present a coherent map for social reform. Roe counts Booth as influenced by Progressivism.[78] In the period after the First World War, Mary Booth's activities incorporated both Progressivism and a more backward-looking imperial nationalism. Britishness was Australia's eugenic and cultural heritage, and its most perfect expression was, first, the sturdy qualities of the (non-convict) pioneers and, second, the heroism of the First AIF, where eugenic and population concerns were merged under the general rubric of 'Anzac'. Under the auspices of her Anzac Fellowship of Women, Booth combined her Progressive belief in eugenics with her imperial nationalism in a number of ways, including the nurturing of British boy immigrants.

NOTES

1. Jill Roe, 'Booth, Mary (1869–1956)', *Australian Dictionary of Biography*, National Centre of Biography, Australian National University, http://adb.anu.edu.au/biography/booth-mary-5291/text8927. Published first in hardcopy in Vol. 7 (1979). General Editors: Bede Nairn and Geoffrey Serle, accessed online 15 February 2019.
2. For a case study in the application of Progressive principles to State education, see Grant Rodwell, *With Zealous Efficiency: Progressivism and Tasmanian State Primary Education, 1900–20*. Darwin: William Michael Press, c1992.
3. J.J. Eddy and Deryck Schreuder, 'The Edwardian Empire', in *The Rise of Colonial Nationalism: Australia, New Zealand, Canada and South Africa First Assert Their Nationalities, 1880–1914*. Edited by John Eddy and Deryck Schreuder. Sydney: Allen & Unwin, 1988, 20; James Curran and Stuart Ward, *The Unknown Nation: Australia After Empire*. Carlton, VIC: Melbourne University Press, 2010, 12; Neville Meaney, '"In History's Page": Identity and Myth', in *Australia's Empire*. Edited by Deryck M. Schreuder and Stuart Ward. Oxford: Oxford University Press, 2008, 378; and Russell McGregor, 'The Necessity of Britishness: Ethno-Cultural Roots of Australian Nationalism', *Nations and Nationalism* 12, no. 3 (2006), 494–502.
4. Meaney, "In History's Page", 378.

5. W. S. Gray, Solicitor, to Booth, 6 December 1913. Mary Booth Papers, Mitchell Library, State Library of NSW (hereafter Mary Booth Papers, Mitchell Library), MSS2109, Box 4, Item 5.
6. Michael Roe, *Nine Australian Progressives: Vitalism in Australian Bourgeois Thought 1890–1960.* St Lucia: University of Queensland Press, 1984, 10–12.
7. Paul Ashton, '"This Villa Life": Town Planning, Suburbs and the "New Social Order" in Early Twentieth-Century Sydney,' *Planning Perspectives* 25, no. 4 (2010), 458.
8. Ashton, "This Villa Life", 457.
9. Jill Roe, 'Booth, Mary'.
10. Vertical file, 'Dr Mary Booth Lookout', Extracts from North Sydney Council Minutes, General Purpose Committee, 1947. Stanton Library Heritage Centre Archives, North Sydney.
11. Soldiers' Club: *The Camp and Gunroom*, 28 April 1915, 2. Mitchell Library, State Library of New South Wales; Empire Service Club: Mary Booth Papers, Mitchell Library, MLMSS 2109, Box 4, Item 10.
12. Ashton, "This Villa Life", 461.
13. Greta Jones, *Social Darwinism and English Thought: The Interaction Between Biological and Social Theory.* Sussex: Harvester, 1980, 103–106.
14. Warwick Anderson, *The Cultivation of Whiteness: Science, Health and Racial Destiny in Australia.* Carlton, VIC: Melbourne University, 2005, 235.
15. For example, Milton Lewis, *Managing Madness: Psychiatry and Society in Australia 1788–1980.* Canberra: Commonwealth of Australia, 1988, 23.
16. Philippa Levine and Alison Bashford, 'Introduction: Eugenics in the Modern World', in *The Oxford Handbook of the History of Eugenics.* Edited by Alison Bashford and Philippa Levine. New York: Oxford University, 2010, 4.
17. For a discussion of the evolution of genetic science after 1945, see, for example, Nils Roll-Hansen, 'Eugenics and the Science of Genetics', in *The Oxford Handbook of the History of Eugenics*, 80–97.
18. Mary Booth, 'The Development of a Public Health Conscience'. In Australasian Medical Congress, *Transactions of the Eighth Session,* Melbourne, October, 1908, vol. 2. Melbourne: Government Printer, 1909, 148.
19. Michele Langfield, 'Voluntarism, Salvation, and Rescue: British Juvenile Migration to Australia and Canada, 1890–1939', *The Journal of Imperial and Commonwealth History* 32, no. 2 (2004), 104.
20. Eric Richards, *Destination Australia: Migration to Australia Since 1901.* Sydney: University of New South Wales Press, 2008, 103.
21. Booth, 'The Development of a Public Health Conscience'.
22. Mary Booth, 'School Anthropometrics: The Importance of Australasian Measurements Conforming to the Schedule of the British

Anthropometric Committee, 1908.' In Australasian Association for the Advancement of Science, *Report of the Thirteenth Meeting.* Sydney, 1911. Sydney: WH Smith, 1912, 692.

23. Mary Booth, 'The Scope and Organisation of a School Medical Service'. In Australian Medical Congress, *Transactions,* 1911, 690.

24. Mary Booth, 'The Need for Educating Public Opinion on the Problem of the Feebleminded', *Australian Medical Gazette* 32 (12 October 1912), 378.

25. Roe, *Nine Australian Progressives,* 14; Wendy Michaels, 'When the Political Becomes Personal: Millicent Preston Stanley's Embrace of Eugenics, 1915–1927', *ISAA Review* 15, no. 2 (2016), 60–61.

26. Booth, 'The Need for Educating Public Opinion', 378–379.

27. Anderson, *The Cultivation of Whiteness,* 106–124.

28. Mary Booth, 'School Anthropometrics', 696.

29. Alison McKinnon, '"Bringing the Unclothed Immigrant into the World": Population Policies and Gender in Twentieth-Century Australia', *Journal of Population Research* 17, no. 2 (2000), 109.

30. Booth, 'The Need for Educating Public Opinion on the Problem of the Feebleminded', 377.

31. *Camp and Gunroom,* 28 April 1915, 2.

32. *Sydney Morning Herald,* 2 October 1916, 8; 7 October 1916, 17–18.

33. Bridget Brooklyn, 'Claiming Anzac: The Battle for the Hyde Park Memorial, Sydney', *Melbourne Historical Journal* 45, no. 1 (2017), 112–130; Mary Booth Papers, Mitchell Library, ML MSS2109, Box 4, Item 1.

34. Not that these connections were always harmonious: Brooklyn, 'Claiming Anzac'.

35. Constitution of Anzac Fellowship of Women, Mary Booth Papers, National Library of Australia (hereafter, Mary Booth Papers, NLA), MS2864, Box 14, Folder 7.

36. Michael Roe, *Australia, Britain, and Migration, 1915–1940: A Study of Desperate Hopes.* Cambridge: Cambridge University Press, 1995, 38–42.

37. Geoffrey Sherington, 'British Youth and Empire Settlement: The Dreadnought Boys in New South Wales', *Journal of the Royal Historical Society* 82, no. 1 (June 1996), 2–5; Roe, *Australia, Britain, and Migration.*

38. Richards, *Destination Australia,* 44–45.

39. Roe, *Australia, Britain, and Migration,* 166–176.

40. For example, *The English in Australia.* Cambridge: Cambridge University Press, 2004.

41. Richards, *Destination Australia,* 87–88.

42. Langfield, 'Voluntarism, Salvation, and Rescue', 88.

43. Esther Daniel, '"Solving an Empire Problem": The Salvation Army and British Juvenile Migration to Australia', *History of Education Review* 36, no. 1 (2007), 33–48.

44. Scott Johnston, '"Only Send Boys of the Good Type": Child Migration and the Boy Scout Movement, 1921–1959', *Journal of the History of Childhood and Youth* 73 (2014), 377–397.
45. Elspeth Grant and Paul Sendziuk, '"Urban Degeneration and Rural Revitalisation": The South Australian Government's Youth Migration Scheme, 1913–14', *Australian Historical Studies* 41, no. 1 (2010), 75–89.
46. Although Grant and Sendziuk observe that imperial motives less prominent is South Australia than elsewhere: "Urban Degeneration and Rural Revitalisation", 83, fn. 56.
47. Sherington, 'British Youth and Empire Settlement', 4.
48. Sherington, 'British Youth and Empire Settlement', 2.
49. Janine Gothard, '"The Healthy, Wholesome British Domestic Girl": Single Female Migration and the Empire Settlement Act, 1922–1930', in *Emigrants and Empire: British Settlement in the Dominions Between the Wars*. Edited by Stephen Constantine. Manchester: Manchester University Press, 1990, 86.
50. Gothard, "The Healthy, Wholesome British Domestic Girl", 86.
51. Eric Richards, *Destination Australia*, 77.
52. Stephen Constantine, 'Empire Migration and Social Reform 1880–1950', in *Migrants, Emigrants and Immigrants: A Social History of Migration*. Edited by Colin G. Pooley and Ian D. Whyte. Chapter 4. London: Routledge, 1991, 66.
53. Roe, *Australia, Britain, and Migration*, 27.
54. Langfield, 'Voluntarism, Salvation, and Rescue', 98.
55. Anzac Fellowship of Women, *Annual Report, 1927*, 5. National Library of Australia, http://nla.gov.au/nla.obj-281467557.
56. See, for example, *Boy Settler*, 25 February 1926, 6; Roe, *Australia, Britain, and Migration*, 248.
57. The Club received assistance of £25 per quarter from the Dreadnought Trust for its work in support of Dreadnought Boys, which continued at intervals through the 1930s. Annual Report, 30 June 1931; Financial Statements, 1932–1933, 1933–1934. Minutes for 5 May 1938 mention a final subsidy of £30 for 1937, bringing the amount for that year to £100: Minute Book, Empire Service Club/AnzacFellowship of Women, Mary Booth Papers, NLA, MS2864, Box 17.
58. Notice, 15 October 1923, Mary Booth Papers, NLA, MS2864, Box 3, Folder 3.
59. *Boy Settler*, 14 May 1928, 2.
60. *Men of the AIF*, advertising notice [n.d.], Mary Booth Papers, Mitchell Library, MSS2109, Box 4, Item 6.
61. Empire Service Club Rules [ca. 1923], Mary Booth Papers, NLA, MS2864, Box 3, Folder 3.
62. Anzac Fellowship of Women, *Annual Report, 1927*, 17.

63. Notice, 15 October 1923, Mary Booth Papers, NLA, MS2864, Box 3, Folder 3; 'Migrants. The Dreadnought Boys', *Sydney Morning Herald*, 12 September 1925, 11.
64. Minute Book, Empire Service Club/Anzac Fellowship of Women, Mary Booth Papers, NLA, MS2864, Box 17.
65. Anzac Fellowship of Women Newsletter, 19 July 1926, Mary Booth Papers, NLA, MS2864, Box 3, Folder 3
66. Douglas Cole, '"The Crimson Thread of Kinship": Ethnic Ideas in Australia, 1870–1914', *Australian Historical Studies* 14, no. 56 (1971), 519–520.
67. John Moses, 'The Struggle for Anzac Day 1916–1930 and the Role of the Brisbane Anzac Day Commemoration Committee', *Journal of the Royal Australian Historical Society* 88, no. 1, 68–71.
68. Anzac Fellowship of Women, *Annual Report*, 1927. National Library of Australia, http://nla.gov.au/nla.obj-36220128.
69. Anzac Fellowship of Women, Circular, March 1937 [Report of Special Meeting, 26 February 1937; emphasis in original], Mary Booth Papers, NLA, MS2864, Box 6, Folder 9.
70. Kate Murphy, '"The Modern Idea Is to Bring the Country into the City": Australian Urban Reformers and the Idea of Rurality, 1900–1918', *Rural History*, 20, no. 1 (2009), 122–123.
71. Kerreen Reiger, *The Disenchantment of the Home: Modernizing the Australian Family 1880–1940*. Melbourne: Oxford University Press, 1986, 108–109.
72. Julian Thomas, '1938: Past and Present in an Elaborate Anniversary', *Historical Studies* 23, no. 91 (1988), 82, 86–88. Indigenous recognition was the other area of contention, as seen in the National Day of Mourning protest: Jack Horner and Marcia Langton, 'The Day of Mourning', in *Australians: A Historical Library; Australians 1938*. Edited by Bill Gammage and Peter Spearritt. Sydney: Fairfax, Syme and Weldon, 1987, 29–35.
73. Booth, 'School Anthropometrics', 694.
74. *Boy Settler*, 14 May 1928, 2.
75. Don Aitken, '"Countrymindedness": The Spread of an Idea', *Australian Cultural History* 4 (1985), 34–41.
76. Geoffrey Sherington, '"A Better Class of Boy": The Big Brother Movement, Youth Migration and Citizenship of Empire', *Australian Historical Studies* 33, no. 120 (2002), 270.
77. 'British Migration. The Part of Australia in the Redistribution of British Population within the Empire'. Pamphlet Series no. 1. Issued by the Women's Migration Council of NSW, c/o Empire Service Club [ca.1925], Mary Booth Papers, NLA, MS2864, Box 5, Folder 6.
78. Roe, *Nine Australian Progressives*, 318.

SELECT BIBLIOGRAPHY

Aitken, Don, '"Countrymindedness": The Spread of an Idea', *Australian Cultural History* 4 (1985), 34–41.

Anderson, Warwick, *The Cultivation of Whiteness: Science, Health and Racial Destiny in Australia*. Carlton, VIC: Melbourne University, 2005.

Ashton, Paul, '"This Villa Life": Town Planning, Suburbs and the "New Social Order" in Early Twentieth-Century Sydney', *Planning Perspectives* 25, no. 4 (2010), 457–483.

Brooklyn, Bridget, 'Claiming Anzac: The Battle for the Hyde Park Memorial, Sydney', *Melbourne Historical Journal* 45, no. 1 (2017), 112–130.

Cole, Douglas, '"The Crimson Thread of Kinship": Ethnic Ideas in Australia, 1870–1914', *Australian Historical Studies* 14, no. 56 (1971), 511–525.

Constantine, Stephen, 'Empire Migration and Social Reform 1880–1950'. In *Migrants, Emigrants and Immigrants: A Social History of Migration*. Edited by Colin G. Pooley and Ian D. Whyte. London: Routledge, 1991.

Curran, James, and Stuart Ward, *The Unknown Nation: Australia After Empire*. Carlton, VIC: Melbourne University Press, 2010.

Daniel, Esther, '"Solving an Empire Problem": The Salvation Army and British Juvenile Migration to Australia', *History of Education Review* 36, no. 1 (2007), 33–48.

Eddy, J. J., and Deryck Schreuder, 'The Edwardian Empire', in *The Rise of Colonial Nationalism: Australia, New Zealand, Canada and South Africa First Assert their Nationalities, 1880–1914*. Edited by John Eddy and Deryck Schreuder. Sydney: Allen & Unwin, 1988.

Gothard, Janine, '"The Healthy, Wholesome British Domestic Girl": Single Female Migration and the Empire Settlement Act, 1922–1930'. In *Emigrants and Empire: British Settlement in the Dominions Between the Wars*. Edited by Stephen Constantine. Manchester: Manchester University Press, 1990.

Grant, Elspeth, and Paul Sendziuk, '"Urban Degeneration and Rural Revitalisation": The South Australian Government's Youth Migration Scheme, 1913–14', *Australian Historical Studies* 41, no. 1 (2010), 75–89.

Horner, Jack, and Marcia Langton, 'The Day of Mourning', in *Australians: A Historical Library; Australians 1938*. Edited by Bill Gammage and Peter Spearritt. Sydney: Fairfax, Syme and Weldon, 1987.

Johnston, Scott, '"Only Send Boys of the Good Type": Child Migration and the Boy Scout Movement, 1921–1959', *Journal of the History of Childhood and Youth* 73 (2014), 377–397.

Jones, Greta, *Social Darwinism and English Thought: The Interaction Between Biological and Social Theory*. Sussex: Harvester, 1980.

Jupp, James, *The English in Australia*. Cambridge: Cambridge University Press, 2004.

Langfield, Michele, 'Voluntarism, Salvation, and Rescue: British Juvenile Migration to Australia and Canada, 1890–1939', *The Journal of Imperial and Commonwealth History* 32, no. 2 (2004), 86–114.

Lewis, Milton, *Managing Madness: Psychiatry and Society in Australia 1788–1980*. Canberra: Commonwealth of Australia, 1988.

McGregor, Russell, 'The Necessity of Britishness: Ethno-Cultural Roots of Australian Nationalism', *Nations and Nationalism* 12, no. 3 (2006), 493–511.

McKinnon, Alison, '"Bringing the Unclothed Immigrant into the World": Population Policies and Gender in Twentieth-Century Australia', *Journal of Population Research* 17, no. 2 (2000), 109–123.

Meaney, Neville, '"In History's Page": Identity and Myth'. In *Australia's Empire*. Edited by Deryck M. Schreuder and Stuart Ward. Oxford: Oxford University Press, 2008.

Michaels, Wendy, 'When the Political Becomes Personal: Millicent Preston Stanley's Embrace of Eugenics, 1915–1927', *ISAA Review* 15, no. 2 (2016), 53–70.

Moses, John, 'The Struggle for Anzac Day 1916–1930 and the Role of the Brisbane Anzac Day Commemoration Committee', *Journal of the Royal Australian Historical Society* 88, no. 1, 54–74.

Murphy, Kate, '"The Modern Idea Is to Bring the Country into the City": Australian Urban Reformers and the Idea of Rurality, 1900–1918', *Rural History* 20, no. 1 (2009), 119–136.

Philippa Levine and Alison Bashford, 'Introduction: Eugenics in the Modern World', *The Oxford Handbook of the History of Eugenics*. Edited by Alison Bashford and Philippa Levine. New York: Oxford University, 2010.

Reiger, Kerreen, *The Disenchantment of the Home: Modernizing the Australian Family 1880–1940*. Melbourne: Oxford University Press, 1986.

Richards, Eric, *Destination Australia: Migration to Australia Since 1901*. Sydney: University of New South Wales Press, 2008.

Rodwell, Grant, *With Zealous Efficiency: Progressivism and Tasmanian State Primary Education, 1900–20*. Darwin: William Michael Press, c1992.

Roe, Jill, 'Booth, Mary (1869–1956)', *Australian Dictionary of Biography*, National Centre of Biography, Australian National University, http://adb.anu.edu.au/biography/booth-mary-5291/text8927, published first in hardcopy 1979. Edited by B. Nairn and G. Serle, vol. 7, Melbourne: Melbourne University, 1979, accessed online 17 February 2019.

Roe, Michael, *Australia, Britain, and Migration, 1915–1940: A Study of Desperate Hopes*. Cambridge: Cambridge University Press, 1995.

Roe, Michael, *Nine Australian Progressives: Vitalism in Australian Bourgeois Thought 1890–1960*. St Lucia: University of Queensland Press, 1984.

Sherington, Geoffrey, '"A Better Class of Boy": The Big Brother Movement, Youth Migration and Citizenship of Empire', *Australian Historical Studies* 33, no. 120 (2002), 267–285.

Sherington, Geoffrey, 'British Youth and Empire Settlement: The Dreadnought Boys in New South Wales', *Journal of the Royal Historical Society* 82, no. 1 (June 1996), 1–22.

Thomas, Julian, '1938: Past and Present in an Elaborate Anniversary', *Historical Studies* 23, no. 91 (1988), 77–89.

CHAPTER 11

The Memorialisation of Hector Vasyli: Civilisational Prestige, Imperial Association and Greek Migrant Performance

Andonis Piperoglou

'Tears Were Shed by White and Colored People'

On 9 June 1918, an eleven-year-old schoolboy of Ionian and Cypriot background, Hector Vasyli, walked along a road near the southern end of Victoria Bridge in Brisbane to join a group of children who were welcoming and cheering returning soldiers. The soldiers were travelling in a convoy of cars from the South Brisbane railway station to the Military Hospital at Kangaroo Point.[1] One of the leading cars had to slow down and, in an attempt to avoid a collision, a vehicle driven by W. J. Jackson suddenly veered to the side and struck Hector. The following day the *Brisbane Courier* noted that Jackson instantly stopped, picked up the boy and drove him to St. Hellens Hospital. As medical assistance was not immediate, he motored Hector to a nearby public hospital where it was pronounced that the young boy had already succumbed to his injuries. An examination of the body disclosed that his skull was fractured and there was a compound fracture on his right arm. 'The tragic occurrence

A. Piperoglou (✉)
Griffith University, Brisbane, QLD, Australia

© The Author(s) 2019
P. Payton and A. Varnava (eds.),
Australia, Migration and Empire, Britain and the World,
https://doi.org/10.1007/978-3-030-22389-2_11

253

was quite unavoidable', the *Brisbane Courier* reported, 'Mr Jackson from first to last did everything possible to avoid the fatal consequences of the mishap'.[2]

After Hector Vasyli's funeral at the Toowong Cemetery, which had two religious services—a Church of England service and a Greek Orthodox service—the attributes of the young boy were expressed in a letter to the editor in the *Daily Mail* by someone who went by the telling pseudonym of 'Veritas' (the name given to the Roman goddess of truth—and a word linked to Greco-Roman understandings of rightness, justice and a will to power).[3] 'In an interview with his people', Veritas professed it had become evident that:

> ... the little boy was an example of Christianity and self-denial, of love and obedience to his parents, of patriotism to his country and its brave soldiers ... He had friends amongst yellow, black, and brown people, and a little black boy was his most devoted and affectionate friend. At his coffin tears were shed by white and coloured people ...[4]

'Hector Vasyli has taught us all a lesson', Veritas concluded,

> Let everybody ask himself now: "What have I done for my country?" Little Hector did what he could. He did his bit for the Empire, and we should not forgot this little lad. We should honor his memory. I would like to see a bronze plate on the Victoria Bridge, on the very spot where he fell in doing his noble work ... mentioning his name and the tragic circumstances of his sudden death.[5]

Clearly, as Veritas' words demonstrate, the short-lived life of Hector Vasyli evoked a sense of great loss within the emotionally war-affected and culturally diverse city of Brisbane. In welcoming home Australian soldiers who had fought in the First World War, Veritas believed that Hector's 'noble work' revealed that a great amount of respectability and dignity was to be gained when one performed Christian notions of self-sacrifice and imperial loyalty.[6] What is more, acknowledgement of his friendships with 'coloured people' seemed to indicate that the Hector was able to seamlessly traverse the constructed boundaries of race in a settler-colonial society, as Eric Richards notes, where 'racism and liberalism coexisted'.[7] In having 'friends amongst yellow, black, and brown people' while also doing his 'bit for the empire', Hector Vasyli seemed to embody a model type of patriotic imperial youth.[8]

Yet the 'tears [that] were shed by white and coloured people' at his funeral would have been at odds with a prevailing national sentiment that wished to bar coloured people from full inclusion within the Australian polity.

Soon after Veritas' letter to the editor—and most probably to his great delight—it was decided by some citizens in Brisbane that the life and unfortunate death of Hector Vasyli would certainly not be forgotten. On 10 July, at a well-attended meeting at Brisbane's ANZAC club, a Hector Vasyli Memorial Committee was established and members of the Club, the Returned Soldiers' and Sailors' Imperial League, and a number of notable figures in the Greek-Brisbane populace agreed that Hector's memory would be preserved through the erection of a tablet.[9]

It is the unveiling ceremony of the Hector Vasyli Memorial, the memorial itself, along with some of the visual culture available in the archival residue of early Greek settlement in Queensland that this chapter will explore.[10] The memorialisation of Hector Vasyli, I will argue, reveals a not uncommon historical convergence between British imperialism, the making of a Greek-Australian identity, and, what Ann McGrath has recently termed, the importation of 'northern antiquity into a deeply storied southern continent'.[11]

GREEK MIGRATION TO SETTLER-COLONIAL AUSTRALIA

Hector Vasyli was the only child of a Cypriot-born father and Ionian-born mother.[12] His father Georgios Vasylios, who arrived to Brisbane in 1902, was, at the time of his son's death, the proprietor of an Oyster Saloon in South Brisbane and held close kinship relations with a prominent Greek settler in Queenslander, Christy Freeleagus, President of the Hellenic Association of Brisbane and owner of the lucrative Fresh Food and Ice Company.[13] Freeleagus' business operations specialised in wholesale and retail food provision to restaurants, many of which, as Charles Price's pioneering work *Southern Europeans in Australia* informs us, were predominantly owned by early Greek settlers in Australia.[14]

These restaurant proprietors were part of the global wave of European labour that migrated to the settler-colonial societies that bordered the Pacific in the late nineteenth and early twentieth centuries. From the moment of the Commonwealth's inception in 1901, as the work of Nicholas Doumanis notes, Greeks in Australia became a visible populace of shopkeepers in cities and towns across Australia; however, their ability

256   A. PIPEROGLOU

to do so was not straightforward in a country that was concerned with prohibiting and curtailing the arrival and settlement of people deemed to be vagrants, non-white, and non-British.[15] Similar to racialised labour controversies in the settler-colonial societies of Canada and the United States, the intersecting politics of immigration and labour became a key area for determining who could and could not participate in the Australian polity. For Greeks living in this settler-colonial Anglosphere, the immediate years prior to Hector's death coincided with a turbulent period of anti-Greek sentiment. From Kalgoorlie to Toronto, as the work of John Yiannakis and Thomas Gallant inform us, anti-Greek sentiment (sparked by the Greek nation's wartime neutrality and supposed sympathies towards Germany) resulted in violent hostilities.[16] To counter anti-Greek sentiment, as Joy Damousi discusses, Greeks in Australia were at pains to insist that they were loyal to Australia and the Allied cause.[17]

By focusing on the memorialisation of Hector Vasyli, while also taking seriously what historian Ioanna Laliotou terms 'migrant performances', this chapter hopes to broaden our understanding of the dynamics of Greek migration to the British world by unpacking a culturally specific moment where occidental imaginings of civilisational origins covered over stories embedded within the landscapes initially occupied by First Nations peoples.[18] I accordingly trace here a specifically localised period towards the end of the First World War, where the performative dynamics of Greek migrancy in Australia become intertwined with the exclusionary operations of Australian settler colonialism. By analysing the memorialisation of Hector Vasyli, this chapter will unpack how Greeks in Queensland positioned themselves as permanent and proud pro-British Australian settlers, while also exploring how the historical and cultural prestige of Greek antiquity—transmitted to Australia via a 'web' of British imperial philhellenism and Greek people themselves—played an active role in positioning settler-colonial Australia as a global example of superior civilisational advancement.[19] I am engaging with a developed scholarship in the United States which has traced how people from the Mediterranean world drew upon their civilisational heritage and, in turn, came to identify with the convoluted politics of whiteness. A scholarship which is curiously only in an embryonic stage in historical studies of migration to Australia and the British empire.[20]

This literature, as a distinct facet of the 'transnational turn' in historical inquiry, has recognised the importance of better understanding the construction of race and European civilisational discourse through the use of conceptual frameworks provided by historical whiteness studies, diaspora studies, and histories mobility more generally.[21] The works of Laliotou, Mai Ngai, Yiorgos Anagnostou, along with David Roediger and Sarah Gualtieri have all, for example, differentiated the processes of racialisation and its multifaceted relationship to the 'whitening' process of non-Anglo peoples in British—or in the case of the United States, formerly British—settler-colonial societies.[22]

Greeks, as Toula Nicolacopoulos and George Vassilacopoulos note, were ambiguously classified as 'white-but-not-white-enough' within the messy operations of racial exclusion that underpinned the power dynamics of settler-colonial 'white men's countries'.[23] At one level, non-English-speaking Greeks—peoples alien in language and culture—were positioned as racially inferior and unwelcome immigrants. At another level, Greeks—as the imagined inheritors of Greek antiquity—bestowed upon settler-colonial societies a civilisational exemplariness.[24] The prestige of their civilisational heritage contributed to the colonising authority's sense of superiority over previous inhabitants. To borrow a phrase from Mathew Fry Jacobson, Greeks, along with other people from the Mediterranean world, were seen as 'white' yet simultaneously positioned as 'racially distinct from other whites'.[25] They were, in other words, *outside-yet-firmly-within* the invasive structure of settler-colonialism colonialisation in Australia—an ongoing happening that, as Patrick Wolfe's influential work informs us, is much more than an historical event.[26]

Tied to this ambiguous experience of racial marking, as the parallel Greek immigration histories of Australia, Canada and the United States demonstrate, are experiences of work, ethnic community building and family life.[27] Through the processes of 'chain migration', a term coined by Australian demographer Charles Price, able-bodied 'pioneers' crossed the Atlantic and Indian Oceans and began to adapt to life in their host countries.[28] In mining hubs in Western Australia and Colorado, and across urban centres in Chicago, Toronto and Brisbane, labour was sold, businesses were established, properties were bought, churches were built, couples were betrothed, and remittances were sent back to homelands.[29] Over time, as celebratory immigration narratives inform us, Greeks—as hard-working miners, kitchenhands, bootblacks, fishermen, cane cutters, farmers and shopkeepers—came to acquire a sense of permanent belonging.

Through sacrifice, perseverance and hardship, Greeks across settler-colonial societies became integrated while maintaining Greek culture aboard. Such immigration narratives have become normalised in the established national historical imagination of Canada, the United States and Australia. As I have noted elsewhere, historical stories of 'struggle' and 'success' have become commonplace within the multicultural or 'melting-pot' ethos of contemporary settler-colonial nations.[30] By moving from ports of entry to suburban streets, Greeks ultimately obtained the privileges of national inclusion. Greek migrants, as immigration historiographies proclaim, became successful inclusions. They became acceptable and respectable hyphenated citizens. While such evaluations have significantly contributed to our understanding of the modern Greek migration experience, the predominant emphasis on successful assimilation has avoided discussing the historical implications that notions of Greekness—in particular notions of Greek civilisational prestige—had with the contested politics of race and migration in the British empire and elsewhere.

With the intention to reframe the history of modern Greek migration and diasporisation, this chapter reveals how Greeks in Australia constructed their own independent sense of the British world. It seeks to place Greek migration and settlement to, and across, the British world as an integral part of the story of British imperialism and colonialisation. It also seeks to re-position Greek mobilities (in their varied forms—bodies, texts, ideas and visual culture) as part of wider trans-imperial (Ottoman, British, French, Italian), intra-imperial (British protectorates in the Mediterranean, crown colonies in Africa, self-governing dominions in Australasia and North America), transnational (Greek, Egyptian, Turkish, Macedonian) or transoceanic (Mediterranean, Atlantic, Indian, Pacific) processes of movement and exchange. In short, by exploring the memorialisation of Hector Vasyli, this chapter hopes to situate the movement of ideas associated with Greece, along with the movement of Greek peoples themselves, as part of the complex global phenomena of migration, nation-building and empire-building.

Such an historical approach to Greek migration calls for a re-positioning of the over-celebratory stories of migrant contribution to settler-colonial nation states and pushes for a reframing of migrant crossings—say between the Port of Piraeus and Ellis Island or Port Said and Port Brisbane—as colonial crossings that were entangled within overlapping national and imperial spaces. They force us to consider how Greece, the British empire, and Australia discursively interrelated, while framing modern Greek mobilities as invasively moving onto deeply storied landscapes that have their own pre-colonial and enduring senses of history and belonging.[31]

Before we proceed to examine specificities of the Hector Vasyli memorial, it is important to note that during the nineteenth and early twentieth centuries, a commercial and sea-fearing identity constituted for Greeks a treasured self-representation that portrayed Greeks as superior to other peoples from the same geopolitical region and as foundational members of an imaginary Mediterranean space that was understood as the bedrock of 'European Christian civilization and progress'.[32] Such an image, as we shall see, transmitted itself to Australia via imperial routes and portrayed Greeks, in the words of Laliotou, as 'sharing a cultural proximity with the "civilized" nations of the time'.[33] As the Greek social commentator and jurist, Michalis Dendias wrote in his 1919 publication *The Greek Colonies Around the World,*

> like the English of today our ancestors sought to discover new lands to established themselves there in order to disseminate their civilization, to create commercial center for the trade and consumption of their goods to provide their native countries and their own hands with sources of wealth.[34]

Such stories of migration, as Dendias' words testify, linked Greek national history to the contemporary meta-narratives of historical and civilisational progress that were circulating across the British empire.[35] The phenomenon of Greek labour migration was situated within an ancient period of Greek expansion around the Mediterranean coasts, as well as the diasporisation of Greek merchants in the Levant from the early modern period to the nineteenth century. The supposed ancient and inherent desire of the Greek people to migrate was combined with the image of the seafaring Greek nation in a historical narrative that presented the Greek migration as a history of Greek colonialism.[36] In moving across spaces in Asia, Egypt, Russia, the Americas, or in the case of this chapter's focus, Australia and Greeks, it seemed not only desired to retain their own culture and identity but also wished to propagate Hellenic culture in the host countries that they had chosen to settle in. What is more, the role Britain played in the making of modern Greece

260   A. PIPEROGLOU

played a significant role in the way this propagation of Hellenic culture circulated. As we shall see, the edifying and civilising mission of Greek migration was particularly emphasised at the unveiling the Hector Vasyli memorial.

'The Subline Heritage of the Civilized World'

When the memorial to Hector Vasyli was unveiled on 8 December 1918, Freeleagus, in his role as President of the Hellenic Association of Brisbane, delivered a rousing speech. Speaking to a crowd of one thousand attendees, Freeleagus gave perhaps the first public speech given by a Greek in Queensland. Proudly representing his kinsfolk, he informed his audience of the assistance Britain had offered Greece in its struggles for independence. 'We Greeks', he said, 'fully and frankly admit our never-to-be cancelled debt of gratitude to Britain'.[37] In words that resonated with the premise of Greek racial continuity with the classical era, he also insinuated that Greek antiquity was the cultural, political, and even military, archetype of the Australian nation. 'I am sure your noble hearted nation', he professed,

> will not deny that you owe a laurel wreath to Ancient Greece as the common source of inspirational river, which, flowing out the dead centuries, brought the blessings of civilisation and of civilised law to mankind. Why, even to-day, when the greatest pages of the world's history are being written, you still use the names of the old Grecian warriors and sages as symbols and criteria, as we moderns see in the great men of our own age embodiments of Aristotle, or Lycurgus, or Alcibiades, or Miltiades, of Xenophon, of Leonidas, of Themistocles and of Alexander, and when I read that the gallant men from Australia showed "Spartan courage" in the most Homeric fighting, I, as a Greek, proudly feel that the passage of the centuries had not dimmed the prestige of my ancestors, who impressed their names and deeds as an imperishable remembrance. This remembrance is the sublime heritage of the civilized world, and it will be honoured and cherished as long as mankind endures upon the earth.[38]

By informing his audience of his people's civilisational heritage and racial trajectory, modern Greeks, so thought Freeleagus, were endowed with a cultural prestige that should be recognised and honoured. In positioning Greece, in the words of historical anthropologist Michael Herzfeld, as the 'cultural exemplar of Europe', Freeleagus was keen to remind his audience that no other country was permitted such a generative role in relation to the rest of European, and by settler-colonial extension, Australian culture.[39]

Such a strong articulation of diasporic national consciousness—a consciousness that we could view as devoted to the Greek cultural principles 'courage', 'greatness', 'honour' and 'prestige'—seemed to reinforce a fundamental element of Greek nationhood: that Hellenism was of treasured global merit. His loaded description of Australian soldiers as courageous Spartan warriors, however, revealed that his commitment to the principals of Greek civilisational progress was also defined by contemporary Western European culture and politics.[40] In this respect, Freeleagus positioned Greece and Australia as culturally and historically connected via British involvement in the making of modern Greece. His use of language, in particular the use of the phrase 'civilised world', implied that some portions of the world were uncivilised and backward while others were not.[41] Indeed, via a hegemonic rhetoric that placed Greek antiquity as unquestionably 'sublime' within European civilisational discourse, Freeleagus appeared to be engaging with a well-established British philhellenic representation of Greece. A representation of Greece that was taking place during a period when global 'geographies of civilisation' were being crystallised in tandem with the making of the British world.[42] Indeed, Freeleagus' articulations seemed to place Greek migrants in Australia as the embodied champions of modern civilisational advancement across the British world.[43]

Amongst the crowd who attended the memorial ceremony were boy scouts, Hector's fellow pupils, and returned soldiers. Addresses were given by the Mayor of South Brisbane, Alderman Peter Forrest, Lieutenant Grant Hanlon of the Returned Sailors' and Soldiers' Imperial League, and a representative from the Church of England, W. P. B. Miles.[44] The memorial was attached to one of the southern pylons of Victoria Bridge, comprised of a white marble tablet (see Fig. 11.1). Greek and Australian flags adorned both sides of the tablet, before it was officially unveiled by the Mayor. Supported by two Corinthian columns on a background of grey slate, a bronze medallion of Hector Vasyli stood as a symbolic reminder of the untimely death.

On the tablet a translated Greek inscription, 'EVERY LAND IS HIS NATIVE LAND TO A BRAVE MAN' seemed to affirm the cross-cultural and settler-colonial ties that Greeks in Australia had acquired.[45] 'In his veins', the caption on the tablet read, 'ran the heroic blood of

Fig. 11.1 Hector Vasyli Memorial, 1918, Brisbane (*Source* John Oxley Library, State Library of Queensland)

Greece, and in the breast of a child he carried the heart of a man'.[46] The tablet—its design and inscriptions—seemed to suggest that the patriotic work of the deceased youth should not merely be remembered as a symbolic example of Greek settler loyalty but also as an embodied example of patriotic wartime masculinity. Hector Vasyli's death thus represented a particularly Greek male exemplification of performative imperial loyalty that, through the principals of civilisational prestige, connected the sombre occasion to an ancestral nobility that bound Greece, and therefore Greek people, to Australia.

'A Knowledge of the Fundamentals of History'

Amply prepared to take full advantage of the public occasion, Freeleagus prophesised that the memorial would be a permanent 'symbol ... of the good feeling existing between my countrymen and people of British blood'.[47] After thanking those present for their attendance and stating the importance of the memorial for future generations, he informed the large crowd that those of his countrymen,

> who have a knowledge of the fundamentals of history, cherish the belief that modern Greece partly owes its independence to the sword and to the pen of Britain, and perhaps to the poets of Byron and Keats who sang the song that inspired your countrymen to aid us in our bitter struggle for liberty.[48]

The structure of Freeleagus' speech mirrored the language employed by many of his kinsfolk throughout the war. Language, as Damousi informs us, which insisted that Greeks in Australia were proud pro-British imperial loyalists.[49] For Freeleagus, however, the unexpected death of Hector Vasyli seemed to act as personified proof of Greek settler loyalty to their adopted homeland. While the political, civilisational, and, perhaps even racial affiliations between Britain and Greece was articulated, the death of the boy appeared to reconfigure Greek ties with Australia along an actual historical line of cross-cultural interaction. The memorialisation thus stood as a sombre moment of public recognition that tied British philhellenic sympathies—realised both intellectually and militaristically—to the founding of the modern Greek nation.[50] In recognising this 'fundamental' of modern Greek history, Greeks it seemed should not only be accepted within the host settler society but were active contributors to its making.[51]

In addition to Freeleagus, the Queensland Governor, Hamilton Goold-Adams, who had previously served as High Commissioner in the British colonial possession of Cyprus, spoke at the memorial.[52] In inviting the Governor to speak, Freeleagus reemphasised the premise of Greek civilisational prestige. He noted, for example, that the imperial representative could 'claim a pro-consular association' which, 'bridging thirty centuries, connected him with the days when Homer was a Governor of the Grecian Islands and spent his leisure in recording the glorious deeds of Agamemnon and of Hector and of Achilles'.[53] By mentioning the doyen figure of ancient Greek literature, Freeleagus' analogy imaginatively tied the memorial ceremony to a trans-historical imperial association that connected ancient Greece to the British empire. As David Lambert and Alan Lester have noted, British imperial careerists, like Goold-Adams, facilitated 'the continual reformulation of imperial discourses, practises and culture'.[54] As Freeleagus' comments suggest, however, the imperial appointments of Goold-Adams in Cyprus and Queensland allowed for imperial philhellenic sympathies to be reformulated within a specific settler-colonial space. The Greek leader's acknowledgement of the Queensland Governor's service in Cyprus therefore testified to the power of philhellenic connections across the British imperial world, while his articulations also insinuated that such connections were critical in formulating a Greek-Australian settler-colonial consciousness.

The means of representation adopted by Freeleagus and displayed for all to see in the memorial was, indeed, spectacular. The representation of historical events and peoples not only evoked the civilisational grandeur of Greek antiquity, but also served as a strong credential of the cultural capital that was bestowed to people who had Greek descent. In this context, we can view the memorialisation of Hector Vasyli as denationalising Greek history and ethnicising Greeks abroad. As Laliotou notes, historical representations in the emerging Greek diaspora of the English-speaking world—unlike national celebrations that took place in Greece—'did not operate as symbolic representation of national existence and sovereignty', but rather served as symbolic representations of high cultural and ideological traits that were supposedly inherently embodied by Greek migrants, and their children like Hector Vasyli.[55] This particular representation was based on the assumption that the British empire did not just accommodate its colonial possessions and dominions, but in fact occupied civilisational title the world over. Greek settler investments in the British dominion of Australia was then based on the condition that the settler-colonial society could accommodate transnational forms of identification, and thus, Greek migrant-cum-settler identifications often collided with notions of cross-cultural interaction.

CONCLUSION: GREEK MIGRATION AND BRITISH COLONIALISM

By way of conclusion, let us consider a peace celebration photograph, that was printed in supplement of the *Queenslander Pictorial* in early January 1919, only a few months after the unveiling of the Hector Vasyli memorial (see Fig. 11.2).[56] Posing for the camera are Greek migrants in Childers, Queensland. The man in the centre of the image is Paul Cominos, who was a close confidant of Christy Freeleagus, and, like Freeleagus, born on the Ionian island of Kythira: an island that was for a large portion of the nineteenth-century part of a British Mediterranean empire that include other island such as Sicily, Malta and Cyprus, as well as places like Palestine and Egypt.[57] In other words, the fathers and grandfathers of Freeleagus, Cominos, and young Hector Vasyli, would have lived within a British imperial domain that was connected, via the routes of empire, to southern Queensland cane hub that was Childers.

Gazing firmly at the camera, the men conspicuously flaunt their presence on the landscape. At first glance, the photograph exemplifies a specific kind of performance. The men are partaking in a provincial peace celebration. The experience of arduous, dirty and physically taxing labour usually associated with seasonal cane-cutting and shopkeeping is rendered invisible. The men are sporting togas, and the women above acts as a personified representation of the goddess Athena—the goddess of wisdom, courage, inspiration, civilisation, law and justice.[58] She stands on top of a makeshift chariot holding a large Greek flag and a tableau with depictions of the ancient Olympic Games. From an initial viewing, we may be inclined, if not encouraged, to see this moment as a story of Greeks negotiating an embryonic Australianness. We may see it as an example of Greeks acculturating in a new land in the British world.

But if we consider the image through the lens of British settler-colonialism our interpretation quickly changes. At a second glance, we may be inclined to consider the land under the horse's hoofs. Land that would have sustained the palm branches that border the front and back of the makeshift chariot. In the Marble Café that Paul Cominos

Fig. 11.2 'Mr Paul Cominos Ancient Greek Display', *The Queenslander Pictorial*, supplement to *The Queenslander*, 4 January 1919, 25 (*Source* John Oxley Library, State Library)

ran in Childers, he would have serviced hundreds of transient seasonal cane-cutters, many of whom were Greek.[59] Before he purchased his café, Cominos was himself a cane-cutter, and he, along with other Greek cane gangs, would have cleared and worked the land behind them—land inhabited by the Dundaburra peoples who are part of Gabi Gabi tribes of the region. The Dundaburra, as historian Raymond Evans informs us, would have spoken one of at least ninety indigenous languages and dialects that were in use across the landmass that we now call Queensland.[60] A landmass that, as Emma Christopher notes, was dreamt as having the potential to act as a new plantation society after the abolition of slavery.[61] First Nations peoples, like the Dundaburra, were moved off their lands and a profit-driven economy was created. Unskilled South Sea Islander labourers, along with other non-white indentured labourers, were—through violent means—recruited on and then deported off the land.[62]

The land and its resources—upon which material wealth was based—had been taken. Invasive laws, lives and labour that Greek migrants in Australia negotiated and identified with radically reconstructed the environment in image.

In this sense, after a second viewing, we can view the Greek-Australian peace celebration in Queensland as posturing in an environment that is scarred by the colonial intrusion of their presence. They are migrants that have served, and are serving, settler-colonial interests. They are participating, in the words of Tracey Banivanua Mar, in the 'violence of forgetting' that had been experienced by First Nation and South Sea Islander peoples in the region.[63] Through deeper historical observation, we can view this image of Ionian migrants dressed as Olympian deities on Dundaburra land as a particular representation of civilisational intrusion and an example of settler colonialism via the culturally specific dynamics of Greek diasporisation in the British world.

With this in mind, our understanding of Hector Vasyli memorial shifts. The memorialisation becomes a culturally distinct facet of settler-colonialism. The supposed affectionate friendship shared between the pre-adolescent sons of a Greek migrant with a 'little black boy', as the commentator "Veritas" informed the readers of the *Daily Mail*, is noticeably absent.[64] In its place is the imposed, planned and ordered representation of civilisational prestigiousness that tied Greece and the British empire with an urbanising—and emotionally war-affected—settler-colonial Brisbane.

Seeing the memorial, and other migrant-specific sites, as part of series of institutional, cultural and historical webs has the potential to enhance how we understand movements across porous imperial borders and through malleable cultural landscapes. It allows us for a more enhanced interpretation of how non-Anglo migrants came to self-identify as permanent and proud British imperialists, while also acknowledging culturally specific roles that Greeks played, and perhaps continue to play, in operations of colonialism in Australia.

I finish here by reiterating the importance of viewing British philhellenism (love of Greece), the global phenomena of modern Greek migrancy across English-speaking countries, and the intrusive operations of settler-colonial nationalism as deeply related historical processes. Indeed, as the memorialisation of Hector Vasyli illuminates, how Hellenism could be transmitted and mobilised in the British empire—be it colonialist romanisations of Greek civilisational prestige or articulations of Greek diasporic nationalism—reveals the intersection of migration, nation and empire. In other words, ideas associated with Greece—in particular imaginings of Greek antiquity as the civilisational bedrock of British imperial expansion—functioned as a cultural axial point around which binary distinctions that were central to occidental fantasies of superiority were staged. By critically historicising the performative modes of Greek diasporisation in Australia, like the unveiling and design of the Hector Vasyli memorial, we are perhaps better placed to unpack how authoritative articulations of European civilisational superiority came to be reworked across the settler-colonial Anglosphere.

In sum, after its unveiling, the Hector Vasyli memorial became an important instrument for the forging of closer links between Greek settlers in Australia and the wider settler populace in Brisbane. Each Anzac Day until the Second World War, a brief ceremony was held at the memorial.[65] These commemorative occasions—where entangled expressions of Greek and Australian patriotic sentiment were on public display—were powerful performative signifiers of Greek settlers' civilisational connection to their adoptive country. Because Greek settlers, as Freeleagus' words suggested, were the alleged modern exponents of the classical era, the 'noble hearted nation' of Australia was to honour and cherish the cultural inheritance and wartime loyalty that Greeks had offered.[66] By eagerly capitalising on the memorialisation of Hector Vasyli, we can interpret Freeleagus' actions and the visual and textual messages in the memorial itself as permanently performing Greek settler loyalties to Australia and the British empire. Yet, by viewing the memorialisation of Hector Vasyli as an ethnically specific site of settler-colonial civilisational dominance, perhaps a fuller and more historically grounded interpretation of the making of British imperialist and Australian nationalist notions of civilisational superiority can be advanced.

NOTES

1. Hector Vasyli was the son of George Vasyli, an owner of a cafe in Melbourne Street, South Brisbane. See Denis A. Conomos, *The Greeks in Queensland*, Brisbane: CopyRight Publishing, 2002, 183.
2. *Brisbane Courier*, 10 June 1918, 8.
3. *Daily Mail*, 21 June 1918, 7.
4. *Daily Mail*, 21 June 1918, 7.

5. *Daily Mail*, 21 June 1918, 7.
6. *Daily Mail*, 21 June 1918, 7.
7. See, for example, Eric Richards, *Destination Australia: Migration to Australia Since 1901*, Sydney: University of New South Wales Press, 2008, 19.
8. *Daily Mail*, 21 June 1918, 7.
9. *Telegraph*, 12 July 1918, 2. It should be noted that a fig tree was planted in memory of Hector Vasyli on the grounds of the South Brisbane Boys State School. See, *Telegraph*, 11 July 1918, 6.
10. It should be noted that the memorial to Hector Vasyli still stands. The one-hundred-year anniversary of his death and the erection of the memorial were recently recognised in a feature piece by the Australian Broadcasting Commission. See, Hailey Renault, 'Patriotic Spirit of Greek-Australian Boy Hector Vasyli Endures 100 Years After Tragic Death', *ABC*, 9 June 2018, https://www.abc.net.au/news/2018-06-09/greek-australian-boy-hector-vasyli-100-years-since-death/9845100. Accessed online 23 November 2018.
11. Ann McGrath, 'The Visit of Hope to Sydney Cove and Botany Bay, 1788 and 1901', Paper delivered to the School of History at the Australian National University, 9 May 2018.
12. As I have noted elsewhere, between 1815 and 1864, the Ionian Islands were a British colonial protectorate called the United States of the Ionian Islands. The Islands acted as a strategic location for the British in the Mediterranean, ensuring a safe passage to the ports of the Ottoman Empire, and onwards to the imperial centres of India, Ceylon, and the Australasian and Pacific colonies. The British introduced a bicameral legislature and in 1864 the British ceded the Islands to Greece, expanding the territorial domain of the modern Greek nation state. See Andonis Piperoglou, '"Border Barbarisms", Albury 1902: Greeks and the Ambiguity of Whiteness', *Australian Journal of Politics and History*, Vol. 64, No. 4, 2018, 529–543.
13. For a detailed biographical account of Christy Freeleagus see, Alex Freeleagus, 'Christy Freeleagus 1887–1957', in Maximilian Brandle (ed.), *The Queensland Experience: The Life and Work of 14 Remarkable Migrants*, Brisbane: Phoenix Publications, 1991.
14. Charles Price, *Southern Europeans in Australia*, Melbourne: Oxford University Press, 1963, 159–163.
15. Nicholas Doumanis, 'The Greeks in Australia', in Richard Clogg (ed.), *The Greek Diaspora in the Twentieth Century*, St Anthony's College: Palgrave Macmillan, 1999, 58–86; Andonis Piperoglou, 'Vagrant "Gypsies" and Respectable Greeks: A Defining Moment in Early Greek-Melbourne, 1897–1900', in M. Tsianikas, G. Couvalis, and M.

Palaktsoglou (eds.), *Reading, Interpreting, Experiencing: An Inter-cultural Journey into Greek Letters*, Adelaide: Modern Greek Studies Association of Australia and New Zealand, 2015, 140–151.

16. On anti-Greek sentiment in Kalgoorlie and Toronto see, John Yiannakis, "Kalgoorlie Alchemy: Xenophobia, Patriotism and the 1916 Anti-Greek Riots", *Early Days: Journal of the Royal Western Australian Historical Society*, Vol. 11, No. 2, 1996, 199–211; Thomas Gallant (eds.), *The 1918 Anti-Greek Riot in Toronto*, Toronto: Thessalonikeans Society of Metro Toronto, 2005. On Greece involvement in the First World War see, George Leontaritis, *Greece and the First World: From Neutrality to Intervention, 1917–1918*, New York: Columbia University Press, 1990.

17. Joy Damousi, *Memory and Migration in the Shadow of War: Australia's Greek Immigrants After World War II and the Greek Civil War*, Cambridge: Cambridge University Press, 2015. See also, Joy Damousi, '"This Is Against All the British Traditions of Fair Play": Violence Against Greeks on the Australian Home-Front During the First World War', in Michael Walsh and Andrekos Varvana (eds.), *Australia and the Great War: Identity, Memory and Mythology*, Melbourne: Melbourne University Press, 2016, 128–145.

18. Ioanna Laliotou, *Transatlantic Subjects: Acts of Migration and Cultures of Transnationalism Between Greece and America*, Chicago: Chicago University Press, 2004, 123–126.

19. Here I am drawing off Tony Ballantyne's notion of the weblike spatiality of British imperial networks. See, Tony Ballantyne, *Webs of Empires: Locating New Zealand's Colonial Past*, Vancouver: University of British Columbia Press, 2012, 17–18. See also, Tony Ballantyne, *Between Colonialism and Diaspora: Sikh Cultural Formations in an Imperial World*, Durham: Duke University Press, 2006.

20. Exceptions include; Ann Monsour, *Not Quite White: Lebanese and the White Australia Policy, 1880 to 1947*, Brisbane: Post Press, 2010; Andonis Piperoglou, 'Greeks or Turks, "White" or "Asiatic": Historicising Castellorizian Racial Consciousness, 1916–1920', *Journal of Australian Studies*, Vol. 40, No. 4, 2016, 387–402.

21. See Maurizio Isabella and Konstantin Zanou, *Mediterranean Diasporas: Politics and Ideas in the Long 19th Century*, New York: Bloomsbury, 2016, 8–10.

22. Mai Ngai, *Impossible Subjects: Illegal Aliens and the Making of Modern America*, Princeton: Princeton University Press, 2014; Yiorgos Anagnostou, *Contours of White Ethnicity: Popular Ethnography and the Making of Usable Pasts in Greek America*, Athens, OH; Ohio University Press, 2009; David Roediger, *Working Towards Whiteness: How America's Immigrants Became White: The Strange Journey from Ellis Island to the*

Suburbs, New York: Basic Book, 2006; and Sarah Gualtieri, *Between Arab and White: Race and Ethnicity in the Early Syrian American Diaspora,* Berkley: University of California Press, 2009.

23. Toula Nicolacopoulos and George Vassilacopoulos, *Indigenous Sovereignty and the Being of the Occupier: Manifesto for a White Australian Philosophy of Origins,* Melbourne : Repress, 2014, 102; Marilyn Lake, "White Man's Country: The Transnational History of a National Project", *Australian Historical Studies,* Vol. 34, No. 122, 2003, 346–363.

24. Andonis Piperoglou, "'Border Barbarisms'", Albury 1902: Greeks and the Ambiguity of Whiteness', *Australian Journal of Politics and History,* Vol. 64, No. 4, 2018, 529–543.

25. Matthew Frye Jacobson, *Whiteness of a Different Color: European Immigrants and the Alchemy of Race,* Cambridge, MA: Harvard University Press, 1999, 6.

26. Patrick Wolfe, "Settler Colonialism and the Elimination of the Native," *Journal of Genocide Research,* Vol. 8, No. 4, 2006, 388.

27. See for example, Anastasios Tamis, *The Greeks in Australia,* Melbourne: Cambridge University Press, 2005); Charles Moskos, *Greek Americans: Struggle and Success,* New Brunswick; Transaction Publishers, 2009.

28. Charles Price, *Southern Europeans in Australia,* Oxford: Oxford University Press, 1963, 108–110.

29. On Western Australia see John Yiannakis, *Megisti in the Antipodes: Castellorizian Migration and Settlement to WA, 1890–1990,* Sydney: Hesperian Press, 1996); On Colorado see, Mark Walker, 'The Ludlow Massacre: Class, Warfare, and Historical Memory in Southern Colorado', *Historical Archeology,* Vol. 37, No. 3, 2003, 66–80; and Dan Georgakas, 'Greek-American Radicalism: The Twentieth Century', *Journal of the Hellenic Diaspora,* Vol. 20, No. 1, 1994, 7–33.

30. Andonis Piperoglou, 'Rethinking Greek Migration as Settler Colonialism', *Ergon: Greek/American Arts and Letters,* October 2018. http://ergon. scienzine.com/article/essays/rethinking-greek-migration-as-settler-colonialism. Accessed online 25 November 2018; Bárbara Cruz and Michael Berson, 'The American Melting Pot? Miscegenation Laws in the United States', *Organization of American History, Magazine of History,* Vol. 15, No. 4, 2001, 80–84.

31. On Aboriginal senses of the past see, Ann McGrath and Mary Anne Jebb (eds.), *Long History, Deep Time: Deepening Histories of Place,* Canberra: ANU Press, 2015.

32. Maurizio Isabella and Konstantin Zanou, *Mediterranean Diasporas: Politics and Ideas in the Long 19th Century,* New York: Bloomsbury, 2016, 9.

33. Ioanna Laliotou, *Transatlantic Subjects*, 66.
34. Michale Dendias, *Greek Colonies Around the World*, Athens: Privately printed, 1919, cited in Laliotou, *Transatlantic Subjects*, 66.
35. On British imperial endeavour and Greek antiquity see, Phiroze Vasunia, 'Hellenism and Empire: Reading Edward Said', *Parallax*, Vol. 9, No. 4, 88–97; See also, Catharine Hall, *Macaulay and Son: Architects of Imperial Britain*, New Haven: Yale University Press, 2012, 227.
36. On Greek merchant mariners in the early-modern age see, Molly Green, *Catholic Pirates and Greek Merchants: A Maritime History of the Early Modern Mediterranean*, Princeton: Princeton University Press, 2013.
37. 'Souvenir and Address Mr. Christy Freeleagus', *Protestants' Sentinel*, 13 December 1918, John Oxley Library.
38. 'Souvenir and Address Mr. Christy Freeleagus', *Protestants' Sentinel*, 13 December 1918, John Oxley Library.
39. Michael Herzfeld, *Ours Once More: Folklore, Ideology, and the making of Modern Greece*, New York: Pella, 1986, 10.
40. 'Souvenir and Address Mr. Christy Freeleagus', *Protestants' Sentinel*, 13 December 1918, John Oxley Library.
41. 'Souvenir and Address Mr. Christy Freeleagus', *Protestants' Sentinel*, 13 December 1918, John Oxley Library.
42. Maurizio Isabella and Konstantina Zanou, 'Introduction: The Sea, Its People and Their Ideas in the Long Nineteenth Century', in Maurizio Isabella and Konstantina Zanou (eds.), *Mediterranean Diasporas: Politics and Ideas in the Long 19th Century*, New York: Bloomsbury, 2015, 12.
43. Maurizio Isabella and Konstantin Zanou, *Mediterranean Diasporas: Politics and Ideas in the Long 19th Century*, New York: Bloomsbury, 2016, 9.
44. 'Hector Vasyli Memorial', *Brisbane Courier*, 3 December 1918, 6.
45. Unidentified, Memorial to Hector Vasyli, John Oxley Library, State Library of Queensland. Accessed online 23 November 2018. http://rosettadel.slq.qld.gov.au/delivery/DeliveryManagerServlet?change_lng=en&dps_pid=IE276978.
46. Unidentified, Memorial to Hector Vasyli, John Oxley Library, State Library of Queensland. Accessed online 23 November 2018. http://rosettadel.slq.qld.gov.au/delivery/DeliveryManagerServlet?change_lng=en&dps_pid=IE276978.
47. 'Souvenir and Address Mr. Christy Freeleagus', *Protestants' Sentinel*, 13 December 1918, John Oxley Library.
48. 'Souvenir and Address Mr. Christy Freeleagus', *Protestants' Sentinel*, 13 December 1918.
49. Joy Damousi, '"This Is Against All the British Traditions of Fair Play": Violence Against Greeks on the Australian Home-Front During the First

World War', in Michael Walsh and Andrekos Varvana (eds.), *Australia and the Great War: Identity, Memory and Mythology*, Melbourne: Melbourne University Press, 2016, 131–133.

50. On British philhellenism and the making of modern Greece see, Margarita Miliori, 'Europe, the Classical *polis*, and the Greek Nation: Philhellenism and Hellenism in Nineteenth Century Britain', in Roderick Beaton and David Ricks (eds.), *The Making of Modern Greece: Nationalism, Romanticism, & the Uses of the Past (1797–1896)*, Farnham: Ashgate Publishing, 2009, 65–79.

51. Souvenir and Address Mr. Christy Freeleagus', *Protestants' Sentinel*, 13 December 1918, John Oxley Library.

52. See Andrekos Varnava, *British Imperialism in Cyprus, 1878–1915: The Inconsequential Possession*, Manchester: Manchester University Press, 2012.

53. Souvenir and Address Mr. Christy Freeleagus', *Protestants' Sentinel*, 13 December 1918, John Oxley Library.

54. David Lambert and Alan Lester (eds.), *Colonial Lives Across the British Empire: Imperial Careering in the Long Nineteenth Century*, Cambridge: Cambridge University Press, 2006, 2.

55. Ioanna Laliotou, *Transatlantic Subjects: Acts of Migration and Cultures of Transnationalism Between Greece and America*, 124.

56. *The Queenslander Pictorial*, supplement to *The Queenslander*, 4 January 1919, 25.

57. On British colonialism on the Ionian Island see, Thomas Gallant, *Experiencing Dominion: Culture, Identity, and Power in the British Mediterranean*, Notre Dame: University of Notre Dame Press, 2002); Sakis Gekas, *Xenocracy: State, Class, and Colonialism in the Ionian Islands, 1815–1864*, New York: Berghahn, 2017.

58. *The Queenslander Pictorial*, supplement to *The Queenslander*, 4 January 1919, 25.

59. Denis A. Conomos, *The Greeks in Queensland*, Brisbane: CopyRight Publishing, 2002.

60. Raymond Evans, *A History of Queensland*, Melbourne: Cambridge University Press, 2007, 3.

61. Emma Christopher, 'Dreams of a New Plantation Society: Legacies of British Slavery in Queensland, Australia', Blog Entry for 'Legacies of British Slave-Ownership', University College London, 2018. https://lbsatucl.wordpress.com/2018/07/25/dreams-of-a-new-plantation-society-legacies-of-british-slavery-in-queensland-australia/. Accessed online 25 November 2018.

62. On Australian-Pacific Indentured Labour trade see, Tracey Banivanua-Mar, *Violence and Colonial Dialogue: The Australian-Pacific Indentured Labor Trade*, Honolulu: University of Hawaii Press, 2007.

274   A. PIPEROGLOU

63. Tracey Banivanua-Mar, *Violence and Colonial Dialogue: The Australian-Pacific Indentured Labor Trade*, 175.
64. *Daily Mail*, 21 June 1918, 7.
65. 'A Patriotic Greek Boy: To the Editor', *Brisbane Courier*, 28 April 1927, 9; 'Greek Service', *Brisbane Courier*, 25 April 1929, 19; 'Youthful Patriot Honoured', *Brisbane Courier*, 26 April 1929, 17; 'Boy Who Died Welcoming Digger Home', *Courier Mail*, 26 April 1939, 8; 'Greeks Place Wreaths', *Courier Mail*, 26 April 1940, 6.
66. *The Queenslander Pictorial*, supplement to *The Queenslander*, 4 January 1919, 25.

SELECT BIBLIOGRAPHY

Anagnostou, Y., *Contours of White Ethnicity: Popular Ethnography and the Making of Usable Pasts in Greek America*, Athens, OH: Ohio University Press, 2009.

Ballantyne, T., *Between Colonialism and Diaspora: Sikh Cultural Formations in an Imperial World*, Durham: Duke University Press, 2006.

Ballantyne, T., *Webs of Empires: Locating New Zealand's Colonial Past*, Vancouver: University of British Columbia Press, 2012.

Banivanua-Mar, T., *Violence and Colonial Dialogue: The Australian-Pacific Indentured Labor Trade*, Honolulu: University of Hawaii Press, 2007.

Beaton, R., and Ricks D. (eds.), *The Making of Modern Greece: Nationalism, Romanticism, & the Uses of the Past (1797–1896)*, Farnham: Ashgate Publishing, 2009.

Brandle, M. (ed.), *The Queensland Experience: The Life and Work of 14 Remarkable Migrants*, Brisbane: Phoenix Publications, 1991.

Clogg, R. (ed.), *The Greek Diaspora in the Twentieth Century*, St Anthony's College: Palgrave Macmillan, 1999.

Conomos, D. A., *The Greeks in Queensland*, Brisbane: CopyRight Publishing, 2002.

Cruz, B., and Berson, M., 'The American Melting Pot? Miscegenation Laws in the United States', *Organization of American History, Magazine of History*, 15(4), 2001, 80–84.

Damousi, J., *Memory and Migration in the Shadow of War: Australia's Greek Immigrants After World War II and the Greek Civil War*, Cambridge: Cambridge University Press, 2015.

Evans, R., *A History of Queensland*, Melbourne: Cambridge University Press, 2007.

Gallant, T. (eds.), *The 1918 Anti-Greek Riot in Toronto*, Toronto: Thessalonikeans Society of Metro Toronto, 2005.

Georgakas, D., 'Greek-American Radicalism: The Twentieth Century', *Journal of the Hellenic Diaspora*, 20(1), 1994, 7–33.

Green, M., *Catholic Pirates and Greek Merchants: A Maritime History of the Early Modern Mediterranean*, Princeton: Princeton University Press, 2013.

Gualtieri, S., *Between Arab and White: Race and Ethnicity in the Early Syrian American Diaspora*, Berkley: University of California Press, 2009.

Hall, C., *Macaulay and Son: Architects of Imperial Britain*, New Haven: Yale University Press, 2012.

Herzfeld, M., *Ours Once More: Folklore, Ideology, and the Making of Modern Greece*, New York: Pella, 1986.

Isabella, M., and Zanou, K. (eds.), *Mediterranean Diasporas: Politics and Ideas in the Long 19th Century*, New York: Bloomsbury, 2016.

Jacobson, M. F., *Whiteness of a Different Color: European Immigrants and the Alchemy of Race*, Cambridge, MA: Harvard University Press, 1999.

Lake, M., "White Man's Country: The Trans-national History of a National Project", *Australian Historical Studies*, 34(122), 2003, 346–363.

Laliotou, I., *Transatlantic Subjects: Acts of Migration and Cultures of Transnationalism Between Greece and America*, Chicago: Chicago University Press, 2004.

Lambert, D., and Lester, A. (eds.), *Colonial Lives Across the British Empire: Imperial Careering in the Long Nineteenth Century*, Cambridge: Cambridge University Press, 2006.

Leontaritis, G., *Greece and the First World: From Neutrality to Intervention, 1917–1918*, New York: Columbia University Press, 1990.

McGrath, A., and Jebb, M. (eds.), *Long History, Deep Time: Deepening Histories of Place*, Canberra: ANU Press, 2015.

Monsour, A., *Not Quite White: Lebanese and the White Australia Policy, 1880 to 1947*, Brisbane: Post Press, 2010.

Moskos, C., *Greek Americans: Struggle and Success*, New Brunswick: Transaction Publishers, 2009.

Ngai, M., *Impossible Subjects: Illegal Aliens and the Making of Modern America*, Princeton: Princeton University Press, 2014.

Nicolacopoulos, T., and Vassilacopoulos, G., *Indigenous Sovereignty and the Being of the Occupier: Manifesto for a White Australian Philosophy of Origins*, Melbourne: Repress, 2014.

Piperoglou, A., 'Vagrant "Gypsies" and Respectable Greeks: A Defining Moment in Early Greek-Melbourne, 1897–1900', in M. Tsianikas, G. Couvalis, and M. Palaktsoglou (eds.), *Reading, Interpreting, Experiencing: An Inter-cultural Journey into Greek Letters*, Adelaide: Modern Greek Studies Association of Australia and New Zealand, 2015.

Piperoglou, 'Greeks or Turks, "White" or "Asiatic": Historicising Castellorizian Racial Consciousness, 1916–1920', *Journal of Australian Studies*, 40(4), 2016, 387–402.

Piperoglou, A., "'Border Barbarisms", Albury 1902: Greeks and the Ambiguity of Whiteness', *Australian Journal of Politics and History*, 64(4), 2018, 529–543.

Price, C., *Southern Europeans in Australia*, Melbourne: Oxford University Press, 1963.

Richards, E., *Destination Australia: Migration to Australia Since 1901*, Sydney: University of New South Wales Press, 2008.

Roediger, D., *Working Towards Whiteness: How America's Immigrants Became White: The Strange Journey from Ellis Island to the Suburbs*, New York: Basic Book, 2006.

Tamis, A., *The Greeks in Australia*, Melbourne: Cambridge University Press, 2005.

Varnava, A., *British Imperialism in Cyprus, 1878–1915: The Inconsequential Possession*, Manchester: Manchester University Press, 2012.

Vasunia, P., 'Hellenism and Empire: Reading Edward Said', *Parallax*, 9(4), 88–97.

Walker, M., 'The Ludlow Massacre: Class, Warfare, and Historical Memory in Southern Colorado', *Historical Archeology*, 37(3), 2003, 66–80.

Walsh, M., and Varvana, A. (eds.), *Australia and the Great War: Identity, Memory and Mythology*, Melbourne: Melbourne University Press, 2016), 128–145.

Wolfe, P., "Settler Colonialism and the Elimination of the Native," *Journal of Genocide Research*, 8(4), 2006, 387–409.

Yiannakis, J., *Megisti in the Antipodes: Castellorizian Migration and Settlement to WA, 1890–1990*, Sydney: Hesperian Press, 1996.

Yiannakis, J., "Kalgoorlie Alchemy: Xenophobia, Patriotism and the 1916 Anti-Greek Riots", *Early Days: Journal of the Royal Western Australian Historical Society*, 11(2), 1996, 199–211.

CHAPTER 12

Dealing with Destitute Cypriots in the UK and Australia, 1914–1931

Andrekos Varnava and Evan Smith

Introduction[1]

In 1927 and 1928, the Australian authorities debated whether to discourage Cypriot emigration. Australia House in London informed the British government that no facilities could be provided for Cypriots to immigrate to Australia because the Australian authorities did not consider them as a class of migrant who could readily find employment in Australia and because there had been cases of destitution. On 30 August 1928, Leo Amery, the Secretary of State for the Colonies, informed the Governor of Cyprus, Sir Ronald Storrs, who had wanted to encourage the settlement of Cypriot agriculturalists in Australia, that Cypriots should not proceed to Australia unless they had friends or relatives there to look after them or

A. Varnava (✉) · E. Smith
College of Humanities, Arts and Social Science, Flinders University, Adelaide, SA, Australia
e-mail: andrekos.varnava@flinders.edu.au

E. Smith
e-mail: evan.smith@flinders.edu.au

A. Varnava
Honorary Professor of History, De Montfort University, Leicester, UK

© The Author(s) 2019
P. Payton and A. Varnava (eds.),
Australia, Migration and Empire, Britain and the World,
https://doi.org/10.1007/978-3-030-22389-2_12

277

adequate means to support themselves for a few months after their arrival.[2] The Australian authorities had already considered the question of Cypriot immigrants to Australia, and in October 1927, the Governor General, Lord Stonehaven, informed the British government that with the exception of Cypriots who had a British national status, all others would be obliged to possess £40 in landing money in cases where landing permits were not held to avoid the growing problem of destitution.[3] Furthermore, the Australian authorities confirmed that the 'granting of assistance' under the migration agreement, 'either in the way of reduced passages to, or assisted settlement in, Australia is confined to British subjects resident in the United Kingdom', and therefore not available to Greek Cypriots in Cyprus.[4] Arthur Dawe in the Colonial Office appreciated that the Australians only wanted the best agriculturalists, but expressed 'a great deal of sympathy for the Governor's point of view [because] if foreigners are allowed to settle in Australia – why not Cypriots who after all are British subjects?'[5]

Much of the literature on Cypriot emigration has been on the post-Second World War period, whether it be migration to the UK or to Australia, the two main destinations of Cypriots.[6] There are three exceptions: an article on Cypriot migration to the USA, covering the period from 1910 to 1930[7]; various works from 1987 to 2000 on the Cypriots in the UK during the interwar years[8]; and, most recently, an article on how the Cypriot community in London during the 1930s was stigmatised as deviant for its perceived criminality and communism, and others restricted from migrating to the UK from 1935.[9] In more general accounts, Cypriots have generally been excluded, not considered as significant to Jewish, Italian or even Greek stories of migration.

This chapter focusses on destitute Cypriots after the Great War until 1931 in the UK and Australia (and to a lesser extent the USA), framing the problem in a more global sense, by showing that it was not unusual to Australia and that it was a wider phenomenon. Cypriot emigration in the aftermath of the British occupation continued to nearby destinations which had linguistic, religious and other cultural similarities, namely in various parts of the Ottoman Empire and in Egypt, but this began to change in the years before the Great War. The new destinations became the USA, Latin America, France and the UK, along with Australia and Canada. The increase in emigration saw a corresponding increase in destitution and repatriation from host countries. Although discussing the problem of destitute Cypriots more broadly, the chapter focusses on how the British and Australian authorities handled, what was often, a complex issue, bound up in questions of citizenship, race and border control policy and practise.

BRITISH AND AUSTRALIAN IMMIGRATION CONTROL IN THE INTERWAR PERIOD

Both Britain and Australia placed restrictions on European migrants in the first half of the twentieth century. Concerns about migrants from Central and Eastern Europe in the late nineteenth century, especially poor Jewish migrants, led the British Tory government (on its last legs) to introduce the Aliens Act in 1905. This Act, influenced by anti-Asian legislation in the USA, Australia, South Africa and New Zealand,[10] was crafted into legislation that could bar any 'undesirable' migrants from entering the country. 'Undesirable' was a broad category that included 'the poor, the mentally ill, the infirm, [and] non-political criminals', amongst others, and being potentially barred from entry to Britain was also subject to detention and removal.[11] British colonial subjects were still, for the most part, free to enter, work and reside in Britain at this stage, and except for the large number of Irish migrants, Panayi has stated that relatively few non-European migrants from British colonies came to the country prior to the late 1940s, compared with the number of Germans, French and Italians.[12] The First World War saw the Aliens Restriction Act 1914 introduced to deal with potential German and Austro-Hungarian 'enemies' in Britain,[13] while the end of the War saw further amendments in 1919, which carried over wartime restrictions into peacetime. Both Taylor and Tabili have shown that the 1919 Act created the framework for greater restrictions on migrants on medical and health grounds and the exclusion of African and Asian seamen under the Coloured Alien Seamen Order in 1925.[14] Except for Cypriots and Maltese migrants (who were considered British subjects), most European migration to Britain was restricted by the 1919 Act until the introduction of the Immigration Act 1971, which collapsed the distinction between alien and Commonwealth migration.[15] Cypriots were restricted at the port of departure in the 1930s.[16]

The 'White Australia Policy' was introduced with the Immigration Restrictions Act 1901 shortly after Federation, which controlled all non-European migration to Australia, primarily aimed at preventing migrants from Asia and was part of a push across the settler colonies to restrict Asian immigration.[17] For the Australian government, the desire was for British, Irish and northern European migrants, with quotas placed upon migrants from southern and eastern Europe (except for Italy, which had a special arrangement between the Italian and British governments made in 1883).[18] Like Britain, the First World War had a profound impact on the migration flows of European migrants to Australia, with the preference for Germans, one of the largest migrant groups prior to 1914, being 'ended abruptly' once the War began.[19] Austrians, Hungarians, Bulgarians and Turks were also barred entry to Australia from 1920 (initially for five years).[20] Even migrants from southern European nations that eventually fought on the allied side were considered 'suspect' and treated with varying degrees of hostility by the Australian authorities and public.[21] The introduction of quotas on southern Europeans migrating to the USA in the early 1920s had repercussions on Australia, with an increase in southern (and eastern) European migration by the late 1920s and into the 1930s, leading to Australian restrictions. Quotas and landing fees, as well as the use of the dictation test, were used to manage these migrants and to keep out 'undesirables'.[22]

POLICING DESTITUTE MIGRANTS

British and Australian authorities were concerned about destitute migrants and took measures to prevent their entry. A royal commission into alien immigration to the UK reported in 1903 on 'the extent to which pauperism exists amongst Alien Immigrants', stating that 3234 alien migrants in London (from a total population of over 135,000 counted as living in London in the 1901 census) had received some Poor Law Relief in 1903, up from 2766 in 1902.[23] The Aliens Act 1905 addressed this concern by stating an immigrant would be considered 'undesirable' if they could 'not show that he has in his possession or is in a position to obtain the means of decently supporting himself and his dependents (if any)'.[24] There were also concerns about destitute people from the British colonies, especially from India, but also seamen from Africa, the West Indies and other parts of Asia. As many of these destitute people were ex-seamen, there was little intervention by the authorities in Britain or in the colonies to prevent more from arriving, but there was interdepartmental wrangling over how to send them back to the colonies.

Destitute Indians in the UK was a problem. Saini has shown that because they were British subjects (granted by the Queen's Proclamation of 1858), some destitute Indians in Britain tried to obtain assistance via the Poor Law Unions but were often denied access and often had to rely on the help of the 'Strangers' Home for Asiatics, Africans and South Sea Islanders'.[25] The 'Strangers' Home' had existed since the late 1850s and was used as a temporary home for foreign workers in London (primarily seamen), as well as 'a repatriation centre, providing employment on ships returning to the East for any wandering Asian sailor'.[26] The newly established India Office was supposedly charged with helping to repatriate destitute Indians in Britain, but this became 'a constant source of tension and debate among the India Office, the Strangers' Home and the Poor Law authorities largely because the law itself was unclear', exacerbated by reluctance from the India Office to pay for the repatriation of Indians.[27] In the early 1900s, the India Office became 'more willing to repatriate Indians stranded in other countries' (including the UK), partly due to the pressure placed upon them by organisations concerned about the plight of destitute Indians in Britain and India.[28] In 1909, a Committee on Distressed Colonial and Indian Subjects was formed, but its overall recommendation was to 'not depart' from the India Office's 1887 policy of not using the revenues of India to provide relief to destitute Indians.[29] By the early 1910s, the India Office was considering a repatriation agreement and a bond, but was unable to transform this into practice before the outbreak of the Great War and the introduction of the British Nationality and Status of Aliens Act in 1914.[30]

Other colonial subjects who were destitute and required repatriation came to the attention of the British authorities too. In the Edwardian era, the Colonial Office knew of several cases of West Indians becoming stranded in London and Liverpool, who required repatriation. For example, the Select Vestry of the Parish of Liverpool informed the Local Government Board (who told Downing Street and the Colonial Office) in December 1904 of the numerous cases of West Indians 'at present chargeable to the poor rates of the Parish as inmates of the Belmont Road Workhouse'.[31] Downing Street informed the Local Government Board that:

> In general the West Indian Colonial Governments refused to meet the cost of repatriation in such cases, an exception being made in the case of seamen distressed by shipwreck in this country.[32]

However, on this occasion, the Local Government Board paid the Select Vestry £60 to pay to send these men back to the British West Indies.[33]

On another occasion, after the report of the Committee on Distressed Colonial and Indian Subjects was released, the colonial administration in Bermuda wrote to the Colonial Secretary to stress that circumstances under which the colonial government would pay for the repatriation of Bermudan seamen were rare. The Colonial Treasury in Bermuda clarified:

> There is an Act on our Statute Book (Act No. 5, 1880) which makes provision for the repatriation of distressed Bermudan seamen falling into distress abroad, but the operation of this Act is limited to the cases of seamen serving in a Bermuda vessel (i.e. registered in this Colony) employed in the service of the Colony,...[34]

Consular circulars show that in many cases the Colonial and Foreign Offices left it to colonial administrations to determine whether to fund repatriation of destitute colonial subjects in the UK or elsewhere within the Empire. A 1905 communication stated:

> As a general rule no payments are made by Consular officers on account of British Colonial subjects except under authority from the Governor of the Colony to which such persons belong, and the officer must therefore apply to the Colonial authorities before giving relief.
> Exceptions to this rule exist as regards certain British Colonies, where the local Governments have accepted the responsibility of repaying the expenses incurred on behalf of distressed natives...[35]

This meant that some colonial governments, such as the Maltese, were willing to pay for the repatriation of destitute Maltese within the British Empire,[36] but others, such as the Cypriot, were more reluctant to do so.

Between 1911 and 1914, there were discussions about whether the Board of Guardians of the Poor Law Union, the Local Government Board and the Charity Organisation Society should take responsibility for the costs of the repatriation of distressed and destitute colonial subjects in Britain, but these discussions were rebuffed at different times by both the Colonial Office and Treasury.[37] The Treasury told the Colonial Office in 1911 that while there were 'undoubtedly many cases of distress' regarding colonial and Indian subjects in Britain, 'they [were] not so numerous or so persistent as to render inoperative the existing channels of relief through Charitable and other agencies'.[38] It was concerned that if the British government did pay for the repatriation of colonial subjects it 'would encourage undesirable immigrants'.

The cases of natives of the Crown Colonies and Protectorates...present a problem of greater complexity as many of the distressed persons coming therefrom are coloured and there is therefore great difficulty...in employment being secured for them in Great Britain. At the same time it is this very class which should be most strongly discouraged from entering this country, and, as My Lords have stated, they fear facilities for repatriation would have exactly the opposite effect.[39]

In the post-war period, seamen from the British colonies were also subject to deportation if found destitute in Britain. Tabili and Prais have shown that the Coloured Alien Seamen's Order of 1926 was used to refuse entry to 'undesirable' seamen, particularly from West Africa, and an informal arrangement was made with shipping companies to repatriate the unemployed seamen.[40] Sherwood has shown that the 1926 Order was used arbitrarily by the British authorities and many British colonial subjects (including Canadians, South Africans, Australians, Indians, Ceylonese and Africans) were registered as 'aliens' incorrectly,[41] and thus liable to deportation. Byrne has also detailed the stories of Arab seamen (including Yemenite British subjects) being subject to deportation orders under the 1920 Aliens Order (a result of the 1919 amendments to the Aliens Restriction Act 1914) for being unemployed in South Shields, a dockside area of Tyneside.[42] On the other hand, Dunlop and Miles have described how after a riot by white workers in Glasgow in 1919 attacked colonial seamen, the government withdrew an offer to repatriate unemployed colonial seamen and '100 seamen were left destitute in Glasgow' with 'several being taken to a city poorhouse in Barnhill suffering from the cold and hunger'.[43] The introduction of the 1926 Order made it easier for colonial seamen to be refused entry into the country if the authorities believed that they would not return to their port of origin after disembarkment.[44]

In Australia, the Immigration Restriction Act 1901 specifically allowed the refusal of migrants that were 'likely in the opinion of the Minister or of an officer to become a charge upon the public or upon any public or charitable institution'.[45] While the number of refusals on these grounds is difficult to discern, the archival documents reveal that from the beginning of the Commonwealth, bonds were used by the Australian authorities as sureties against destitution for both British colonial subjects and aliens (this can be seen in the correspondence with the Colonial Office later in this paper). A case from 1907, when several 'coloured' seamen were hospitalised in Australia, also showed that crew from British ships did not need to pay this deposit 'as the responsibility in such cases is already secured by the Merchant Shipping Act', and furthermore, 'nor in the case of foreign ships where it appears that the Consul or Agents are prepared to assume the responsibility for expenses'.[46]

With the possibility of deporting any migrant who might have required state assistance, Vickers, citing Craig, has argued that this 'demonstrat[ed] the historical relationship between welfare by the (capitalist) British state and exclusionary forms of citizenship in relation to immigrants',[47] with similar processes occurring in Australia. This is a demonstration of both countries using their border control systems as a form of what Garland has described as 'social control'.[48] As Smith and Marmo have argued, the border was used as a filter, allowing migrants to enter the country according to the needs of the host society, but also allowing the nation-state to reject these migrants if deemed 'undesirable' or surplus to requirement.[49] This notion of 'un/desirability' has often been racialised and expressed through a 'desire to maintain an unequal balance between the "white" host society and the non-white migrant minority', meaning potential migrants were viewed via a 'lens of worthiness to the host nation' if they were able to fit into this majority/minority paradigm.[50]

CYPRIOT EMIGRATION AND DESTITUTION IN UK AND USA

Historically, Cypriots, no less or more than other Mediterranean peoples, migrated to nearby places or made use of their island lifestyle to travel abroad for seasonal work. The most popular destinations were within the Ottoman Empire and particularly in Egypt, namely Alexandria and Cairo, where there existed a modest yet significant Cypriot community.[51] But in the years before the war Cypriots became more adventurous. When Cyprus finally became a Crown Colony in 1925 hundreds of people began to take out British Cypriot nationality over the next 20 years. Migrants before the British annexation of November 1914 and their children born abroad were evident in traditional migrant places such as Cairo, Mersin, Adana and Symi (Dodecanese),[52] but also more unusual places, such as Trieste, Italy, Port Sudan, Sudan, Khartoum, Sudan, Dire Dawa, Abyssinia, Tanga, Tanganyika and Chunking, China.[53]

When the war broke out, Egypt remained a popular choice of Cypriot emigrants, with Sir Henry McMahon, high commissioner of Egypt, reporting to Sir John Clauson, the high commissioner of Cyprus, that because the refugee problem in Egypt was difficult and expensive, a large number of Cypriots arriving since July 1915 were causing problems, and would be 'be grateful for any steps you may be able to take to check further similar arrivals [otherwise] the Egyptian authorities may be obliged to forbid their entry'.[54] Information to Clauson showed that because harvest had finished early in Cyprus people in Paphos were going to Alexandria, 300 had left in September alone.[55] Clauson believed that the migration was therefore partly seasonal, but because entire families were also leaving, he was prepared to act under martial law, suggesting similar provisions as Law 1 of 1882 or the Proclamation of 27 July 1898.[56] But he told McMahon that the emigration was normal, worse in 1915 only because of the economic situation, and was instructing his district commissioners to prevent departures of those who did not have means of subsistence, clarified as £5.[57]

As mentioned, during the three or four years prior to the outbreak of the Great War, Cypriots, especially Cypriot Orthodox Christians, started migrating to non-traditional places, to the UK (helped by the annexation of November 1914 upon the Ottoman entry into the German side), Western Europe and North and South America. This became a major problem when in summer 1916 Clauson was asked to establish the Cypriot Mule Corps for service on the Macedonian Front[58] and he was confronted with competing with the emigration of men to the USA, their engagement as seasonal workers in Egypt and for the French armed forces, as well as efforts to induce them (from Anthony William Caruana, a Maltese who was reinventing himself as a migration agent after serving five years in gaol for frauds committed in the Larnaca Post Office) to migrate to Australia, New Zealand, Canada and South Africa.[59] Between 1 January and 21 October 1916, 940 passports had been issued to Cypriots for the USA. The average Cypriot immigrant commanded two or three dollars a day and could live on half a dollar, while those knowing some English could earn up to five dollars a day. Clauson was equally worried about Cypriot labourers being offered work in France for an incredible 6–£8 a day. Both options were 'adversely affecting the recruitment of transport drivers'.[60] Consequently, on 19 October 1916 Clauson passed a law forbidding the emigration of males of military age, which he published five days later in the *Cyprus Gazette*:

> From the 19 October 1916, and until further order, no person deemed fit for Military Service will be allowed to leave Cyprus without special permission.[61]

This may have stopped the problem of destitute Cypriots for the duration of the war, except that there were already Cypriots who had left Cyprus for the UK, since the British consul in Paris had to repatriate 20 of them in May 1917 before they even made it to the UK.[62]

The restrictions on migrating were lifted in 1919 and Cypriots started to emigrate again,[63] although women were still restricted to those who could prove that they had adequate means, relatives or a definite offer of employment.[64] Stevenson made enquiries about how Cypriots could enter German East Africa but was told that nobody could enter without permission from that government, and applicants needed to state their purpose for visiting and their capital.[65] The USA was the preferred destination although there were barriers. Cypriots had to obtain visas in person from the American diplomatic agency at Cairo and visas would not be issued to men who were not physically capable or could not read a European language.[66] Then in October 1920 visas for the USA were refused to Cypriots unless they were travelling to meet relatives, study or on business, and then twelve months later Cypriots were included in the 'Asian' category in the quota system, which meant 78 from Asia per year, a tiny number, which led to the refusal to allow Alphonse Romani to land in February 1922.[67] The US quota system, something that the Australian authorities were also prepared to introduce, annoyed the British authorities and in 1924 Cypriots were included in the 'all others' quota of 1900.[68]

Once the US quota began to take effect and the Australian authorities became less welcoming to the Cypriots (and themselves considered placing a quota on them), the UK became the main option. In 1921, the British census showed that there were only 316 Cypriots in England and Wales (105 in London), but by 1931, there were 1059 (734 in London).[69] Additionally, between 1923 and 1931 the Cypriot government issued 10,000 passports to Cypriots declaring an interest to migrate to the UK, indicating that most did not, that there was some travel back and forth from the UK and Cyprus, and a third destination via the UK.[70]

Cypriots emigrated because, with a rise in population since the British arrival in 1878, rural poverty manifested given the lack of agricultural development and employment in towns, and Cypriots, especially men, took-up the emigration possibilities presented after the Great War.[71] Amongst the earlier migrants in the interwar period were sailors working in the East End docks,[72] students and lace merchants, but as time went on more and more unskilled labourers emigrated, and, as Oakley and Panayi have established, they ended up in the food and hotel service industry in London, mostly working in establishments owned by the Cypriot community in London's West End.[73] Some of these Cypriots found themselves in trouble when they fell on hard times or became involved in crime.[74] This seems to have been the case in Australia, although on a smaller, though no less insignificant, scale, since the Australian Census of 1933 recorded 500 Cyprus-born people.[75]

When Cyprus was annexed in November 1914, the British government decided that all residents would become British subjects if they were residing in the island at the time. This left those living abroad in limbo. In early 1917, the Foreign Office urged the Colonial Office to act and informed the consular authorities in San Francisco that the nationality registration claim of Neoclis Coumides, who had been born in Cyprus in 1882, resided there until 1912 before moving to South America, Johannesburg and finally San Francisco in 1916, was rejected until a policy could be determined.[76] It took most of 1917 before a final decision and Order in Council was announced in November, which stipulated that Cypriots residing abroad at the time of the annexation had to prove that they had been born in Cyprus and then had to reside in Cyprus for a year or in a British Dominion for five out of the last eight years to apply for a certificate of British Cypriot nationality.[77] The problems were that many passports were issued giving Cypriots various statuses and therefore protection, often incorrectly.[78] Cases were reported in both the UK and the USA. In December 1919, the British embassy in Washington revealed that it had received many applications for passports from Cypriot natives mostly wanting to return to Cyprus, and they had issued them passports describing them as 'a native of Cyprus'. But this practice was stopped when the Colonial Office objected and since a Cypriot who does not have status as a British subject by annexation can only obtain such a status in the island, the embassy wanted to know how such people in the USA wanting to return to Cyprus should be described on passports.[79]

As far as the UK was concerned, Malcolm Stevenson, the high commissioner of Cyprus, referred to numerous cases in a memorandum in February 1920.[80] These were of Cypriots destitute in England and seeking to return to Cyprus. The passports of G. Peperides and J.M. Christodoulides, who had served in the Canadian Forces during the war, wrongly described them as 'British subjects', the passport of Miss August Loizides describing her as a 'British subject by annexation' was also 'an error on the part of the examiner', S. Papadopoulos applied for passport to return to Cyprus and declared that he was 'a naturalised British subject', which proved incorrect, while H.M. Michaelides was issued a passport describing him a 'native of Cyprus', so that he did not have protection elsewhere. The Foreign Office recommended that since in each of these cases the passports were only granted to enable the bearers to return to Cyprus, the passports should all be impounded and cancelled, which was so ordered.[81]

One such case dragged on. M.S. Theodossiades had obtained a British passport to return to Cyprus and resided in Nicosia, but the Cypriot authorities had withheld the passport and refused to recognise him as a 'British protected person'. He wanted to return to London, but the Cypriot authorities would only give him an 'emergency pass', which he did 'not consider would give him the protection which he is entitled to as a British protected person' and he had sought intervention by the Foreign Office.[82] In August 1919, the Colonial Office had informed his lawyers in London that he had to reside 12 months in Cyprus before becoming eligible for a certificate of British nationality and the Foreign Office had agreed with the actions of the Colonial Office and the Cypriot government.[83] The Colonial office added that 'it is just these unattached people that we don't want as Br. Migrants'.[84]

As these cases were appearing in both the UK and USA, the Foreign Office had to intervene. In June 1920, Lord Curzon, the Foreign Secretary, decided that such persons,

> if enquiries are satisfactory, may be given passports as "British Protected Persons" provided that they are required for the purpose of a journey to Cyprus with a view of obtaining such a certificate but that it would be well to make passports in these cases valid only for the single journey. If the journey is to some other destination passports should be issued only after reference to the officer administering the Government of Cyprus and then only describing the holders as "Natives of Cyprus".[85]

Curzon later clarified that Cypriots going to other parts of the British Empire could also be described as 'British protected persons' and could there obtain a certificate of British nationality under the Cyprus (Annexation) Amendment order in Council of 1917.[86] So the regulations stipulated three criteria governing the issue of the certificates of British Nationality under the said Order:

a. The applicant shall apply to the High Commissioner before the expiration of two years from the termination of the war, and
b. he shall have resided in Cyprus for not less than one year immediately preceding such application, and
c. shall have resided in Cyprus or some other part of His majesty's dominions [sic] for a further period, making a total period of residence in Cyprus or some other part of His majesty's dominions [sic], as the case may be, of five years within the last eight...

The last regulation, noted the British embassy in Washington, would 'debar from qualification for this Certificate any person who was absent from Cyprus or some other part of His majesty's dominions [sic] during the war'.[87] It was ultimately decided to not apply the third regulation.

The problem of destitute Cypriots in the USA was somewhat resolved by this action and by the quota imposed in 1921 and 1924,[88] but in the UK the matter grew. In June 1920, L.P. Michaelides, an unmarried British subject unable to find work and staying at the Catholic Seamen's Home and Institute, Lambeth, wanted his passage paid to Alexandria where he had relatives and had previously worked as a mechanic or to Cyprus.[89] In the following year, Ioannis Gavril Haji Ttofi and Andreas Ioannou Kertepene, two Cypriots in London, applied for repatriation to Cyprus and Stevenson agreed that Cypriot funds could cover the costs because he anticipated recovering the costs from Ttofi's father.[90]

Before the war, the Cypriot authorities and the Colonial Office had implemented a plan to restrict passports to the UK to those who could guarantee their repatriation costs (i.e. via a guarantor in Cyprus). But this was not always easy to implement, even when the person was willing to be repatriated. John Christopher (also known as Christophatis) was born in England to Cypriot parents, lived on legacies from his parents (since 1907) and royalties from books published (he had a PhD). He had served in the British army in the Great War, injured, he fell on hard times when in 1923 his brothers in Cyprus cut off his legacy from their parents and urged him to return to Cyprus. Funds sent by his brother to cover his trip to Cyprus never arrived and he then lost his passage orders, which he received from the Colonial Office, which had agreed to pay for them because £50 had been deposited on his behalf before a previous passage from Cyprus to England. He now objected to the Colonial Office 'arranging to send me _like a Coolie_, as a deck passenger without food'. He claimed that his treatment would ruin his reputation and would be offensive to Cypriots:

> One of my brothers is the Chief Clerk to the British Government in Cyprus, and apart from my personal feelings, the method of practical deportation _or repatriation_ arranged by your Office would be so offensive to him, and to all of the Cypriots, in addition to...ruining my reputation, any career, by being deported...in the eyes of the Cyprian population, like a Criminal![91]

He now wanted the £50 to settle debts in the UK (including to land-lady) and to be repatriated according to his status, because 'this is to any man, practically unbearable; and to an ex-service and wounded soldier, and scholar is _becoming a despair, beyond human endurance_'.[92] The Colonial Office reported that

> The [usual] agreement is that a guarantee of £50 has to be given in Cyprus before any Cypriot is allowed to leave the island; if he becomes destitute in a foreign country, this £50 is drawn upon in order to provide him with a return passage to Cyprus and any incidental expenses. In other words, it is a safeguard against these people becoming destitute abroad and so causing expense to the Government of the Island. It is not possible to draw upon this £50 except for the purpose of repatriation.[93]

At this moment the Colonial Office was not yet concerned about des-titute Cypriots, but to ensure that the £50 was only used to repatriate them, like Christopher, although it did offer to 'square the landlady by promising to pay on condition that he embarks'.[94]

LOOKING TO AUSTRALIA

As the situation seemed at hand in the UK, the issue of destitute Cypriots appeared in Australia, where the authorities were concerned about 'certain alleged abuses in connection with the issue of passports to Cypriots to enable them to proceed to Australia', whereupon some became destitute. According to the 1911 census, there were 26 Cyprus-born people in Australia, then at least five Cypriot-born men served in the Australian Imperial Force during the Great War, and in the 1933 census, there were 502 Cypriot-born people in Australia.[95] Although Cyprus as a birthplace was not listed in the 1921 census, the two categories the Cypriots could have been counted under, 'Other British Possessions in Europe' and 'Other British Possessions in Asia' contained 192 and 145 respectively, indicating that either way there were less than 200 Cyprus-born in Australia in 1921 and therefore the population more than doubled from a maximum of 192 in 1921 to 502 in 1933 during that period.[96] While in the Australian Imperial Force the records show five men who were born in Cyprus. The matter of destitute Cypriots came to a head in March 1925, when Sir Joseph Cook, the Australian High Commissioner in London, detailed the history of the problem to Amery at the Colonial Office.

> The occurrence of cases of exploitation in Egypt of Cypriot emigrants at the hands of persons passing themselves off as bona fide agents was first reported to this Government in 1922 by His majesty's Consul, Port Said. The Consul represented that his chief difficulty in counteracting the evil was the passivity with which victims allowed themselves to be deceived and cheated and he suggested that before they left Cyprus emigrants might be suitably warned of the dangers that they were likely to encounter.

A notice was posted in all the villages of the Island and shown to those applying for passports, but this action had failed. In October 1924, the British High Commissioner in Egypt reported to Cook on the continued occurrence of such cases and full particulars of instances of fraud were obtained and confirmed from a private source. A fraudulent concern in Egypt known as the 'Atlas Company' had attracted a custom from Cypriots by advertising in Cypriot newspapers and working in concert with Cypriot passenger agents. Action was again taken locally. The facts were made public and government notices issued and

> the Police have thoroughly investigated the scope of the activities of the passenger agents in Cyprus and steps have been taken to impress on these persons that they work under close vigilance...I trust that this course will prove efficacious as it is difficult to see what additional measures would be feasible locally.[97]

The Colonial Office did not believe that any further action was necessary and all it could do was hope for the best.[98]

The problem of destitute Cypriots in Australia was serious enough to warrant further complaint and action by the Australian authorities, even the consideration of imposing a quota. This time the Governor General, Lord Stonehaven (John Baird, previously a Tory member of the House of Commons), complained, in October 1927, to Whitehall that Canberra wanted to oblige Cypriot arrivals to carry £40 in landing money in cases where landing permits were not held to avoid the growing problem of destitution.[99] He claimed that

> As opportunities for obtaining employment are strictly limited in this country, particularly in the case of persons who are not of British European race and who are unable to speak English fluently, it is in the interests of the migrants that they should have sufficient capital to maintain them for a few months after arrival if they have no one here to look after them until they can establish themselves.

Immigration officers were advised to not enforce the requirement of landing money if the Cypriot possessed a passport of British Cypriot nationality and if the officer believed that they would not become a charge upon the public. But Stonehaven asked that passports not be granted to Cypriots for travel to Australia unless they had £40 landing money.[100]

Clearly, the Australian authorities thought the problem of destitute Cypriots sufficient enough to restrict them from coming to Australia, yet Sir Ronald Storrs, the Governor of Cyprus at the time, after seeing an article in *The Times*, believed that the Australian authorities might consider it 'feasible and desirable to provide facilities for the settlement in Australia of selected parties of agriculturalists from Cyprus'.[101] Arthur Dawe, who was responsible for Cyprus in the Colonial Office, sympathised with Storrs because foreigners were allowed to settle in Australia, so 'why not Cypriots who after all are British subjects?' But thinking more broadly, Dawe, also an expert on Malta, believed that the two cases were different, since Malta was 'populated down to the bedrock', Cyprus was not, and 'if a rare effort at development were made, the Island (Cyprus) could support much more than its present population'. Aside from the interesting admission that the British were not doing all that they could for the development of Cyprus, he was sure that the Australian's only wanted 'the best agriculturalists' anyway.[102]

Before giving Storrs the bad news, the Colonial Office investigated the matter further. It found that Cypriot Muslims were 'absolutely barred' from admission to Australia, because, although Cypriot Muslims were part of the British Empire and served in the Cypriot Mule Corps,[103] 'Turks are prohibited under the provision excluding late enemy aliens'. As for Cypriot Orthodox Christians Stonehaven's information was used, adding that speaking colloquial English and complying with the usual health regulations was also required, adding that if there was 'any indication that Greek Cypriots desire to enter Australia in any numbers, a quota would doubtless be fixed as has been done in the case of Maltese', set at 20 Maltese at any one port per month, while there was a quota of no more than 100 all-up per month for Albanians, Yugoslavs and Greeks.[104] Dawe, following information from Australia House, told Storrs that

> The granting of assistance by the Commonwealth Govt under the migration agreement, either in the way of reduced passages to, or assisted settlement in, Australia is confined to British subject's resident in the United Kingdom.[105]

Yet Storrs would not give up. After receiving an even more forthright response from the Australian authorities against Cypriot immigrants, the Colonial Office believed that it might be a mistake to encourage migration from Cyprus to Australia since Australia wanted agriculturalists, who were 'just the people who ought to be kept in the Island' and the Dominions Office would be 'embarrassed if it were proposed to press Australia to grant facilities to Cypriots', especially because Australia had 'not hitherto obtained many agriculturalists' from Cyprus.[106] The Colonial Office then wrote to Storrs more directly:

> A communication has been received from the Government of Australia, in which it is stated that it is regretted that no facilities for natives of Cyprus to migrate to Australia can be granted. The communication adds that as natives of Cyprus are not a class of migrant who can readily find employment in Australia, and as some cases of destitution have recently brought under notice, it is advisable in their own interests that they should not proceed to Australia unless they have friends or relatives there to look after them on arrival or adequate means to support themselves for a few months after their arrival in the country.[107]

The Great Depression and the Society of the Friends of Foreigners in Distress in London

While the American and Australian authorities had placed restrictions on Cypriots immigrating to their countries, the British authorities were yet to act. It was obvious by 1924 that few repatriated Cypriots were reimbursing the government for their repatriation and by 1928 the government had a list of 60 repatriated Cypriots from across the island (excepting Kyrenia) of which few were repaying these costs, some of which had amounted to over £20 and £30, since most were casual labourers living in poverty.[108] The problem only became worse in 1930 as the Great Depression was hitting the UK and numerous people, not only Cypriots, were living rough. The payment of funds to cover repatriation in the event of destitution was done away with and the Cypriot government appealed to the Colonial Office to request that the Crown Agents for the Colonies obtain, in each case, and forward to Cyprus a formal understanding to repay any sum expended in connection with the repatriation of destitute Cypriots so that it could, whenever possible, recover such sums from the persons concerned.[109] This policy was difficult to enforce from both ends: it would be hard to recover the funds expended in Cyprus given the limited work opportunities, while it would also be difficult to have these men fill in and sign the forms in London, since the Crown Agents revealed that

> 90% of the destitute men with whom we have to deal will be unable to read [the form of agreement], or to sign it, and of the other 10%, the majority will sign in Arabic; the genuineness of such signatures being a matter on which we shall be unable to judge.

A form was devised but the Crown Agents wondered if another procedure could be adopted.[110]

Indeed, Storrs informed Passfield, the Colonial Secretary, that the form of the Crown Agents to repatriate destitute Cypriots was 'somewhat complex'. Storrs wanted it simplified because most of the applicants were illiterate, so he suggested that the form be verbally explained to them and a mark made if they could not sign their name and checked against the signature on their certificate of British nationality or passport.[111] The Crown Agents was unconvinced, rejecting the simplified form and claiming that it would have difficulty comparing signatures in

Arabic, and in explaining the terms of the undertaking to someone with no knowledge of English.[112] The Colonial Office was impressed: 'They stick to their guns!'[113] At the same time, they were confused about the Arabic, asking for clarification.[114] The Crown Agents replied that they had kept no statistical records, 'but our opinion is that of the repatriated distressed Cypriots who have been able to sign their names, more than half have done so in Arabic characters'. This meant that more Cypriot Muslims had settled in the UK in the 1920s than first thought and that they no less than their Christian brothers, were prone to destitution in hard times.[115]

As the Great Depression hit even harder, destitute Cypriots were seeking the support of the Society of the Friends of Foreigners in Distress, one of England's oldest charities (established in 1806).[116] The Society seemed rather distressed itself, when it asked the Cypriot government to compel destitute Cypriots in London to be repatriated because many were refusing in fear of their guarantors back in Cyprus. Storrs rejected intervening, claiming that as far as his government was concerned

> The system of security bonds...has now been in operation for eight years and has proved most satisfactory. During the last five years over 10,000 British passports have been issued in Cyprus, mostly to persons of small means. Repatriation has never been refused to the holders of such passports except when the applicant has been of unsound mind and the total cost of repatriation during the same period to this Government has been under £500. The arrangement by which a Cypriot British Subject can apply to any of His Majesty's Consuls throughout the world and obtain a passage to Cyprus without delay is one of the valued privileges of British Nationality in this Colony.

He was clear that his government was not concerned about the relations between emigrants and their guarantors, both were aware of the risks and no stories of hardship and breakdown in relations between the parties had been bought to his attention. Storrs suspected that the real reluctance of Cypriots in England to be repatriated was their fear that 'at the expense of their surety they will have difficulty in obtaining a fresh guarantee if they wish to proceed abroad again', so that was why they preferred to remain in England for as long as they could.[117]

The Colonial Office backed their man, wanting to say as little as possible to the Society. It reiterated the letter by Storrs and argued that the system, whereby Cypriots leaving the Island are required to enter into a surety bond indemnifying the Government against any cost (up to £50), which it may be called upon to pay within two years...has proved most satisfactory.[118]

There was no better alternative being considered and there were 'considerable advantages in this system' because it 'prevent[s] Cypriots coming to this country unless there is some reasonable prospect of support', thus reducing 'the numbers who might otherwise become destitute in this country'.[119] The Colonial Office did not want to concern itself with 'overcoming the objections of distressed Cypriots in this country to returning to Cyprus and facing their guarantors'.[120]

The Society was not satisfied. Its information was that 'the Cypriots rapidly succumb to the climatic conditions here', and that there were at least five cases known to Archimandrite Michael Constantinides of the Greek Orthodox Church of St Sophia, in Bayswater, of inmates in various institutions suffering from advanced tuberculosis and much more suffering from venereal disease.[121] As the majority of Cypriots worked in catering as scullery-men or kitchen hands, it raised a serious problem, affecting the health of the community generally. The Society argued that the risks may be known by both guarantor and emigrant,

> but in view of the undoubted fear which Cypriots have of returning at the guarantor's cost, it seems a fairly safe risk for the guarantor, and that the hardships resulting therefrom are upon those who feel themselves obliged to remain here rather than run the risk of the guarantor being called upon to refund the cost of repatriation.[122]

It claimed that most of the applicants before the Committee of the Hellenic Benevolent Society were Cypriots and all offers 'to repatriate them are unavailing unless the passage can be arranged at the costs of the Hellenic Benevolent Society'. The Society proposed the abolishment of the system of guarantors and for the Cypriot government to take responsibility for repatriation of destitute Cypriots. Storrs was merely moving destitute Cypriots in Cyprus to the UK,

> ...which suggests that England is being made a dumping-ground for the unfit or unemployable Cypriots; as these men arrive here without any knowledge of the language or any useful trade in their hands, which, as we have before pointed out, tends to drift them into a class already too

numerous in England, and become a burden either upon the rates or Charitable Institutions.[123]

The Colonial Office rejected the idea that the Cypriot government should pay for repatriation. It believed that that the cost of maintaining any destitute person in the UK was a responsibility resting upon the poor law authorities and the cost of repatriation of any such person would have to be met by the same authorities, as was the long-held policy in relation to Indians.[124]

The Society would not let up, presenting evidence from Archimandrite Constantinides on the extent of the problem. He claimed to have visited 19 Cypriots in hospital in 1931, with eight still in hospital, 10 had died in the last four years, the youngest being 19 and the oldest being 27. Crime was also a problem. Two were in East Acton Prison for minor offences, while one was on death row in Pentonville. Constantinides believed that venereal disease was rife and contracted in London

> ...generally the conditions under which they live are awful. I heard from many of them that three quarters of the young Cypriots in London are suffering from venereal diseases. This is the new generation of Cyprus! If the Colonial Office takes drastic measures to stop the growing wave of Cypriot immigration, it will undoubtedly be the greatest favour for the welfare of Cyprus.[125]

The figures mentioned by Constantinides were those the Hellenic Benevolent Society was willing to assist, the most serious cases, and did not reflect the number of applicants for assistance.

> Up to about eighteen months ago it was by no means uncommon for the Committee to find five or six or even more Cypriots in the waiting room on Committee mornings. Some of these men were so insistent and trucurlent that they had to be forcibly ejected, and only threats of handing them over to the police had any deterrent effect.[126]

The Colonial Office remained unperturbed. It did not think the number of destitute Cypriots considerable.[127] It believed that the idea to make the Cypriot government guarantee the emigrant was ludicrous, since more Cypriots would emigrate because they would have nothing to lose by being repatriated at government cost, while the government would be liable to considerable expense. The best policy was to have the Hellenic Benevolent Society urge those people to go back to Cyprus and face their guarantors, which would warn others against emigrating without adequate prospects of making a living.[128]

The Society now agreed that their idea of a Cypriot government guarantee would worsen matters and that most of the Cypriots could not be persuaded to face their guarantors. It now suggested

> a cash deposit from the guarantors, of an amount sufficient to cover the cost of repatriation if called upon within a period of two years, at the expiation of which period the guarantor could reclaim payment of the deposit – but full release from the guarantee would only be granted after a period of five years.

This was not a complete solution, but it could 'have a safeguarding effect, as the guarantors would probably not be so ready to do this as they would to sign the present form of guarantee'. It agreed that the numbers involved were comparatively small in so vast a population as that of London, but it was 'the high proportion of Cypriots who appear to drift into either undesirable callings or environment, that makes the question a serious one, quite apart from the disease and illness to which they seem to succumb so readily'. The Society argued that it was

> unfair that this country should be burdened with people of this type, even though it may mean that Cyprus has fewer destitute and able-bodied out-of-work people, even assuming that they are able-bodied when they leave their native Isle.[129]

The Colonial Office did not want to prolong the correspondence with the Society, yet it did think worth considering that guarantors pay actual cash deposits.[130] Storrs, who was in London, thought it was practicable, although it would not prevent destitution in the UK.[131] Then he changed his mind. While in London he came to believe that it was the grants from the Society which caused destitute Cypriots to reject repatriation.[132] Back in Cyprus, Storrs agreed to the idea of a cash deposit so long as it was applied to all emigrants irrespective of their destination, because those intending to go to England would conceal their intention and, after securing a passport for some other country, apply to a consul for the extension of its validity to England, something that was commonly successful. Such a requirement would probably lead to the end of emigration, since it was unlikely that a guarantor could, let alone would, provide the funds, therefore the advantage in restricting emigration to the UK would be 'counterbalanced by the corresponding restriction of desirable emigration'. He reiterated that the policy would not prevent Cypriots from becoming destitute in England nor would the handouts from the Society stop, and 'the prospect of unassisted destitution would soon overcome the emigrants' alleged fear of their guarantors', as had been the case in countries other than England.[133] For the Colonial Office this meant that Storrs was 'dead against the suggestion' and the Colonial Office would not force it upon him. The Society was told that the current system would remain and that they and other charities should refuse assistance to destitute Cypriots to force them to take up repatriation and face their guarantors'.[134] As for placing restrictions on those with venereal disease from emigrating, it was determined that this was a matter for the immigration authorities in England and not for the Cypriot authorities.[135]

As shown in a recently published article, restrictions were introduced in 1935 along the lines suggested in 1931, that is, that to obtain a passport to travel to the UK, Cypriots had to pay a bond (to cover repatriation if that need arose) and to provide proof of employment in the UK.[136] Although restrictions had been debated for many years, it was only after George Poulia advised the government to act that it did. Poulia recommended strict departmental instructions to all district commissioners and for them to carefully enquire into every passport application, to ascertain whether (a) the applicant does really possess sufficient funds for the journey and for a stay abroad for two months; (b) whether they are skilled, i.e. craftsman, artisan, labourer; (c) whether they know English; (d) whether they have a definite offer of employment; (e) what is the purpose of their travel; and (f) whether all things considered the applicant stands a good chance of employment.[137] When the Cypriot authorities discovered that many emigrants circumvented these restrictions by obtaining a passport to first travel to another country before making their way to the UK, further restrictions were introduced in 1937, namely that they had to prove that they could speak English (not as vigorous, but still inspired by the Australian dictation test), paid a £30 bond, and had an affidavit showing they had employment in the UK. The situation had considerably worsened between 1931 and 1934 as the perceived criminality of the Cypriots (Cypriots committed four murders between 1931 and 1934, but there was also claims of organised crime) and their communist activity, in conjunction with the destitution, forced the hand of the British authorities to introduce these restrictions at the port of departure.[138]

CONCLUSION

Cypriots were highly mobile, migrating to various places, especially to the USA, Australia and the UK from around 1910s through to the 1930s. Owing to their lack of skills and the lack of work for unskilled labour who had limited English many became destitute. The USA and Australian authorities were very quick to impose restrictions on the entry of Cypriots. The USA limited their departure through various mechanisms before doing so more formally through their restrictive quota system. The Australia government restricted Cypriots at both the port of departure and the port of entry. The policies and procedures were selectively applied at the port of entry, yet both together seemed to work in limiting numbers. Meanwhile, the British delayed in doing anything. The Cypriot community, particularly in London, grew substantially as the restrictions in the USA and Australia meant fewer options. The British authorities simply pushed the problem onto local non-government authorities, while the Cypriot government was forced to absorb the costs of repatriation as they could not easily recoup funds from guarantors or from those repatriated. As the Great Depression hit the problem of destitute Cypriots also grew and debate on what to do did not see further restrictions in the early 1930s, until the problem of destitute Cypriots grew into a wider problem of criminality and communism, and restrictions were finally introduced in 1935.

The Cypriots, like the Maltese, occupied a liminal space in British imperial thought and administration, particularly concerning their movement across the British Empire and other settler colonies, such as the USA. After 1915, Cypriot migrants were both colonial subjects, yet European, but were treated differently from other colonial subjects from South Asia and Africa, but also treated differently from other European aliens, such as those from Eastern and Southern Europe. Throughout the first four decades of the twentieth century, Cypriot migrants were seen largely as 'undesirable' by the British authorities, but it was found that controlling their movement was difficult, especially at port of entry. The British had restricted European migrants via the Aliens Acts and Indian migrants via legislative controls at port of departure on the subcontinent—two options that seemed unavailable for preventing Cypriots from coming to the UK. Both the USA and Australia made increasingly less of a distinction between Cypriots and other Mediterranean migrant groups, subjecting them to restrictions much earlier than the British did. Particularly concerned about destitute Cypriots in London, the British used a variety of informal means to discourage the migration of Cypriots and to repatriate those who were thought to be a nuisance, although trying to do so without drawing on government funds. The British authorities eventually felt this was inefficient to deal with the 'problem' of Cypriot migrants in London and from the 1930s onwards, imposed restrictions at the port of entry upon those coming from the island.

The restrictions placed upon Cypriots coming to Britain and the attempts to control their movement across the British Empire demonstrates the processes of the border control system acting as a filter to differentiate between 'desirable' and 'undesirable' migrants. As a number of scholars have shown,[139] the settler colonies, including Australia and the USA, established strict regulations upon who could enter the country from the end of the nineteenth century and the filtering of migrants became highly refined in the interwar period. The British, on the other hand, developed an ad hoc border regime between 1905 and 1948 determined by the competing interests of social control, economic imperatives and imperial administration. This meant that while the British border control system was used to try to filter out and expel 'undesirable' Cypriots from the imperial metropole, the effectiveness of these discriminating practices was often limited, eventually leading to harsher restrictions in the 1930s.

NOTES

1. This research was funded by the Australian Research Council as part of the ARC Discovery Project 'Managing Migrants and Border Control in Britain and Australia, 1901–1981' (ARC DP 180102200).
2. CO67/223/14, Australia House to Dominions Office, 25 July 1928; Amery to Storrs, 30 August 1928; Storrs to Amery, 11 January 1928.
3. CO67/223/14, Stonehaven (recipient not clear), 4 October 1927.
4. CO67/223/14, Australia House to Dominions Office, 26 January 1928; Amery to Storrs, 29 February 1928.
5. CO67/223/14, note, Dawe, 18 February 1928.

6. Robin Oakley, 'The Cypriot Migration to Britain' (ed.), Verity Saifullah Khan, *Family, Kinship and Patronage*, Macmillan, London, 1979, 13–34; Floya Anthias, *Ethnicity, Class, Gender and Migration: Greek-Cypriots in Britain*, Ashgate, Aldershot, 1992; and Panikos Panayi, 'Cypriots in Great Britain Since 1945' (eds.), K.J. Bade, et al., *The Encyclopaedia of Migration and Minorities in Europe*, Cambridge University Press, Cambridge, 2011, 301–302.
7. Nicolas Manitakis and Michalis N. Michael, 'Cypriot Emigration to the United States of America (1910 to 1930)', *Chronos*, 30, 2014, 99–143.
8. Robin Oakley, 'The Control of Cypriot Migration to Britain Between the Wars', *Immigrants & Minorities*, 6(1), 1987, 30–43; Robin Oakley, 'Cypriot Migration to Britain Prior to World War II', *Journal of Ethnic and Migration Studies*, 15(3), 1989, 509–525; Rolandos Katsiaounis, 'Η Κυπριακή Παροικία του Λονδίνου και το Αρχιεπισκοπικό Ζήτημα της Κύπρου, 1928–1936', *Annual of the Centre for Scientific Research* (Nicosia), 22, 1996, 521–556; John Solomos and Stephen Woodhams, 'The Politics of Cypriot Migration to Britain', *Immigrants & Minorities*, 14(3), 1995, 231–256; Rolandos Katsiaounis, 'Τα Πρώτα Βήματα της Επιτροπής Κυπριακής Αυτονομίας', *Annual of the Centre for Scientific Research* (Nicosia), XXVI, 2000, 263–287.
9. Evan Smith and Andrekos Varnava, 'Creating a "Suspect Community": Monitoring and Controlling the Cypriot Community in Inter-War London', *English Historical Review*, 132(558), 2017, 1149–1181.
10. Alison Bashford and Catie Gilchrist, 'The Colonial History of the 1905 Aliens Act', *Journal of Imperial and Commonwealth History*, 40(3), 2012, 409–437.
11. Stephanie J. Silverman, '"Regrettable But Necessary?"A Historical and Theoretical Study of the Rise of the UK Immigration Detention Estate and Its Opposition', *Politics & Policy*, 40(6), 2012, 1131–1157, 1136.
12. Panikos Panayi, *An Immigration History of Britain: Multicultural Racism Since 1800*, Longman, Harlow, 2010, 23.
13. See: David Saunders, 'Aliens in Britain and the Empire During the First World War', *Immigrants & Minorities*, 4(1), 1985, 5–27; Robert Winder, *Bloody Foreigners: The Story of Immigration to Britain*, Abacus, London, 2006, 211–251.
14. Becky Taylor, 'Immigration, Statecraft and Public Health: The 1920 Alien Order, Medical Examinations and the Limitations of the State in England', *Social History of Medicine*, 29(3), 512–533; L. Tabili, *'We Ask for British Justice': Workers and Racial Difference in Late Imperial Britain*, Cornell University Press, Ithaca, NY, 1994.

15. Callum Williams, 'Patriality, Work Permits and the European Economic Community: The Introduction of the 1971 Immigration Act', *Contemporary British History*, 29(4) (2015), 508–538.
16. Smith and Varnava, 'Creating a "Suspect Community"'.
17. Marilyn Lake and Henry Reynolds, *Drawing the Global Colour Line: White Men's Countries and the Question of Racial Equality*, Melbourne University Press, Melbourne, 2008, 150–157; David C. Atkinson, *The Burden of White Supremacy: Containing Asian Migration in the British Empire and the United States*, University of North Carolina Press, Chapel Hill, NC, 2016, 19–48.
18. Michele Langfield, '"White Aliens": The Control of European Immigration to Australia, 1920–1930', *Journal of Intercultural Studies*, 12(2), 1991, 1–14; Gianfranco Cresciani, *The Italians in Australia*, Cambridge University Press, Cambridge, 2003, 43.
19. Gerhard Fischer, *Enemy Aliens: Internment and the Homefront Experience in Australia, 1914–1920*, University of Queensland Press, St Lucia, 1989; James Jupp, *Immigration*, Oxford University Press, Oxford, 1998, 58; and Jürgen Tampke, *The Germans in Australia*, Cambridge University Press, Cambridge, 2006.
20. Langfield, 'White Aliens', 2.
21. See: Karen Agutter, '"Italians Deported—Australians Next": Italians, World War I and the Labour Movement' (eds.), Phillip Deery and Julie Kimber, *Fighting Against War: Peace Activism in the Twentieth Century*, Leftbank Press, Melbourne, 2015, 157–176; Andonis Piperoglou, 'Greeks or Turks, "White" or "Asiatic": Historicising Castellorizian Racial-Consciousness, 1916–1920', *Journal of Australian Studies*, 40(4), 2016, 387–402; and Joy Damousi, '"This Is Against All the British Traditions of Fair Play": Violence Against Greeks on the Australian Home Front During the Great War' (eds.), Michael J.K. Walsh and Andrekos Varnava, *Australia and the Great War*, Melbourne University Press, Melbourne, 2016, 128–145.
22. Langfield, 'White Aliens', 4–5.
23. *Report of the Royal Commission on Alien Immigration*, HMSO, London, 1903, 15–16.
24. Aliens Act 1905, s.1(3)(a).
25. Raminder K. Saini, '"England Failed to Do Her Duty Towards Them": The India Office and Pauper Indians in the Metropole, 1857–1914', *Journal of Imperial and Commonwealth History*, 46(2), 2018, 226–256.
26. Rozina Visram, *Ayahs, Lascars and Princes: The Story of Indians in Britain, 1700–1947*, Routledge, London, 2015, 51.
27. Saini, 'England Failed to Do Her Duty Towards Them', 228.
28. Ibid., 243.

29. Ibid., 245.
30. Ibid., 246–249.
31. FO 83/2070, Parish of Liverpool to Local Government Board, 7 December 1904.
32. FO 83/2070, Downing Street to Local Government Board, 7 January 1905.
33. FO 83/2070, Local Government Board to Vestry Clerk, Liverpool, 19 January 1905.
34. CO 67/250/7691, Treasury, Bermuda, to Colonial Secretary, 4 December 1911.
35. FO 83/2070, 'Repatriation of Distressed British Subjects', 21 February 1905.
36. Ibid.
37. See T1/11678.
38. T1/11678, Treasury Chambers to CO, 5 September 1911.
39. Ibid.
40. Laura Tabili, '"Keeping the Natives Under Control": Race Segregation and Domestic Dimensions of Empire, 1920–1939', *International Labor and Working Class History*, 44, 1993, 64–78; Jinny Prais, 'Imperial Travellers: The Formation of West African Urban Culture, Identity, and Citizenship in London and Accra, 1925–1935', University of Michigan, Unpublished PhD thesis, 2008, 110–112.
41. Marika Sherwood, 'Race, Nationality and Employment Among Lascar Seamen, 1660 to 1945', *Journal of Ethnic and Migration Studies*, 17(2), 1991, 229–244, 235.
42. David Byrne, 'Class, Race and Nation: The Politics of the "Arab Issue" in South Shields 1919–1939', *Immigrants and Minorities*, 13(2–3), 1994, 89–103.
43. Anne Dunlop and Robert Miles, 'Recovering the History of Asian Migration to Scotland', *Immigrants & Minorities*, 9(2), 1990, 145–167, 155.
44. Ibid., 156.
45. Immigration Restriction Act 1901 (Cth), s3(b).
46. A1 1907/9742, NAA Canberra, Circular from Department of External Affairs, 1 October 1907.
47. Tom Vickers, 'Migration, Political Engagement and the State: A Case Study of Immigrants and Communists in 1930s South Tyneside in the UK', in Mehmoona Moosa-Mitha (ed.), *Reconfiguring Citizenship: Social Exclusion and Diversity Within Inclusive Citizenship Practices*, Routledge, London, 2016, 58.
48. D. Garland, *The Culture of Control: Crime and Social Order in Contemporary Society*, Oxford University Press, Oxford 2001.

49. Evan Smith and M. Marmo, *Race, Gender and the Body in British Immigration Control: Subject to Examination*, Palgrave Macmillan, Houndmills, 2014, 49–50.
50. Ibid.
51. Andrekos Varnava, *British Imperialism in Cyprus, 1878–1915: The Inconsequential Possession*, Manchester University Press, Manchester, 2009, 163–165, 294–296.
52. HO334/253/2169, 17 May 1938, Costas Demetriou Xytta, born Baindirion, Ottoman Empire, 17 November 1907; HO334/255/3110, 16 May 1942, Nicolas Constantinou Soupides, born Cairo, Egypt, 30 March 1900; HO334/255/3436, 27 July 1945, Pantelis Ioannou Sarafis, born Symi, Dodecanese, Ottoman Empire, 20 May 1893; HO334/255/3447, 18 September 1945, Gabriel Alexander Gabrielides, born Mersin, Ottoman Empire, 18 February 1910; HO334/255/3463, 7 November 1945, Theodore Costa Papaloizou, born Cairo, Egypt, 8 February 1923; and HO334/255/3462, 7 November 1945, George Kyriacou Michaelides, born Cairo, Egypt, 11 August 1919.
53. HO334/253/2324, 19 December 1938, Yiangos Christou Antoniou, born Khartoum, Sudan, 7 January N/A; HO334/255/3391, 6 April 1945, Costas Charalambous Symeonides, born Port Sudan, 14 July 1914; HO334/255/3413, 24 May 1945, Themistoclis Constantinou Mitsingas, born Tanga, Tanganyika, 3 November 19??; HO334/255/3418, 22 May 1945, Aristides Constantinou Mitsingas, born Tanga, Tanganyika, 24 September 1917; HO334/255/3421, 21 May 1945, Kimon Constantinou Mitsingas, born Tanga, Tanganyika, 5 May 1920; HO334/255/3433, 25 July 1945, Christos Costa Philippides, born Chungking, China, 11 June 192?; HO334/255/3441, 25 August 1945, George Evgenios Petrides, born Trieste, Italy, 7 February 19??; HO334/255/3452, 29 September 1945, Anna Savva, born Dire-Dawa, Abyssinia, 17 July 1917; and HO334/255/3862, 6 May 1947, Fofo Stephani (formerly Antoniou), born Khartoum, Sudan, 31 January 1925.
54. SA1/1272/1915, telegram, McMahon to Clauson, 23 October 1915.
55. SA1/1272/1915, A.M. Fleury, Acting Commissioner, Paphos, to Chief Secretary, undated.
56. SA1/1272/1915, Clauson to Chief Secretary, 23 October 1915.
57. SA1/1272/1915, Clauson to McMahon, 25 October 1915; Ibid., Bolton, Limassol, to Chief Secretary, 28 October 1915.
58. Andrekos Varnava, 'Recruitment and Volunteerism for the Cypriot Mule Corps, 1916–1919', *Itinerario*, 38(3), 2014, 79–101; Andrekos Varnava, *Serving the Empire in the Great War: The Cypriot Mule Corps, Imperial Loyalty and Silenced Memory*, Manchester University Press, Manchester, 2017.

59. SA1/1083/1916/1, General Agent Cyprus, Elias Papadopoulos, advertisement, 17 October 1916; Ibid., Carauna Fils to High Commissioner of Australia in UK, 24 September 1916; Ibid., Caruana Fils to Secretary of Emigrants' Information Office, London, 24 September 1916; Ibid., T.C. MacNaghten, Chairman, Emigrants' Information Office, to CO, 11 October 1916; Ibid., Bonar Law to Clauson, 19 October 1916; Ibid., CO to Chairman, Immigrants Information Office, 19 October 1916; Ibid., Clauson to Bonar Law, 6 November 1916; Ibid., HM Consul, Lyons, to Clauson, 19 October 1916; Ibid., ACSC to HM Consul, Lyons, 8 November 1916; Ibid., Caruana Fils to CSC, 1 September 1919.
60. SA1/1083/1916/1, Clauson to Bonar Law, 6 November 1916; WO95/4790, WDSA, Long, DSTS, 1 November 1916.
61. *The Cyprus Gazette*, 1252, 24 October 1916. Passports already issued had to be returned.
62. SA1/1083/1916/1, telegram, Hearn, British Consul Paris, to Chief Sec, Cyprus, 10 May 1917.
63. See CO67/204/46764; and CO67/207/19844, Stevenson to Churchill, 14 April 1922, containing Annual Report for 1922 by J.M. Ellis, Assistant Secretary, Chief Secretary's Office.
64. League of Nations, *Summary of Annual Reports for 1922, received from governments, relating to the Traffic in Women and Children*, Geneva, March 1924, 16.
65. SA1/1083/1916/1, Stevenson to The Administrator, German East Africa, 23 October 1919; SA1/1083/1916/1, Stevenson to The Administrator, German East Africa, 6 January 1920; and SA1/1083/1916/1, The Administrator, German East Africa, to Stevenson, 23 January 1920.
66. SA1/1083/1916/1, Ioannis Vassiliou and 7 others from Koma tou Yialou, to chief secretary, 5 May 1920; G. Wilson, American Consular Agent Cyprus, to Chief Sec, 22 May 1920; G. Wilson, American Consular Agent Cyprus, to Chief Sec, 4 June 1920.
67. SA1/1083/1916/1, F.S. Moon, US Consular Agent, to Chief Sec, 11 October 1920; Moon to Chief Sec, 4 December 1921; chief secretary, notice, 6 December 1921; CO to FO, 23 February 1922.
68. SA1/1083/1916/1, FO to Stevenson, 6 September 1924; *Statistical Abstract of the United States*, Washington, DC. Government Printing Office, 1929, 100.
69. Oakley, 'Cypriot Migration to Britain Prior to World War II', 513; For 1921, the number of Cypriots is given as 334 in Vic George and Geoffrey Millerson, 'The Cypriot Community in London', *Race & Class*, 8, 1967, 277–292, 277.
70. CO67/237/7, Storrs to Passfield, 9 April 1931.

71. Katsiaounis, 'Η Κυπριακή Παροικία του Λονδίνου και το Αρχιεπισκοπικό Ζήτημα της Κύπρου, 1928–1936', 521; Manitakis and Michael, 'Cypriot Emigration to the United States of America (1910 to 1930)'.
72. In the report of the Committee on Distressed Colonial and Indian Subjects from 1910 seamen from Cyprus 'appear[ed] to present no problem' compared to Maltese seamen in Britain. *Report of the Committee on Distressed Colonial and Indian Subjects*, 9.
73. Oakley, 'Cypriot Migration to Britain Prior to World War II', 515–516; Panikos Panayi, *Spicing Up Britain: The Multicultural History of British Food*, Reaktion Books, London, 2008, 10, 17, 34, 78, 130, 157–161, 161, 166–168, 179, 215.
74. Smith and Varnava, 'Creating a "Suspect Community"'.
75. Australian Government, Department of Immigration and Citizenship, 2014, accessed at https://www.dss.gov.au/sites/default/files/documents/02_2014/cyprus.pdf.
76. FO371/1053, 49979, British Consulate-General San Francisco to FO, 14 February 1917; FO371/1053, 49979/344/T, FO to Alex C. Ross, San Francisco, 12 March 1917.
77. FO371/1053, 36092, HO to CO, 13 February 1917; FO 371/1053, 36092, FO, to CO, 10 March 1917; FO 371/1053, 55818/8330/1917, CO to FO, 14 March 1917; FO371/1053, 55818/344/17/T, FO to CO, 9 April 1917; FO371/1053, 83945/18438/1917, CO to FO, 24 April 1917; FO371/1053, 83945/324501/5, HO to CO, 30 March 1917; FO371/1053, 83945/344/T, FO to CO, 4 May 1917; FO371/1053, 98835, 23347/1917, CO to FO, 15 May 1917; FO371/1053, 98835, 344/17/T, FO to CO, 25 May 1917; FO371/1053, 99482, 272337/14, HO to CO, 15 May 1917; FO 371/1053, 120800; FO371/1053, 237596, 27 November 1917 Order in Council.
78. CO67/200, 'Issue of passports', memo, 12 February 1920.
79. CO67/200, British Embassy, Washington, to Passport Office, 29 December 1919.
80. CO67/200, CO to FO, 12 February 1920.
81. CO67/200, FO, 'Memorandum', 11 February 1920; CO67/200, FO to CO, 19 February 1920.
82. CO67/200, Timbrell & Deighton Solicitors (London) to Foreign Office, 22 January 1920.
83. CO67/200, FO to CO, 3 February 1920; CO67/200, 'Case of Mr M.S. Theodossiades', 4 February 1920.
84. CO67/200, minutes on Theodossiades case, 5 February 1920.
85. CO67/200, CO to FO, 11 June 1920.

86. CO67/200, CO to FO, 11 September 1920.
87. CO67/200, British Embassy, Washington, to New York Consulate, 10 August 1920.
88. Manitakis and Michael, 'Cypriot Emigration to the United States of America (1910 to 1930)'.
89. CO67/201, Note on Lozios Papa Michailides, June 1920.
90. CO67/203, Stevenson to Crown Agents, 18 May 1921; CO67/203, telegram, Stevenson to CO, 12 May 1921.
91. CO67/213, John Christopher to Secretary of State for the Colonies, 29 January 1924.
92. CO67/213, John Christopher to Secretary of State for the Colonies, 29 January 1924.
93. CO67/213, memo on Mr. Christopher, 29 January 1924.
94. CO67/213, note, 1 February 1924. There does not seem to have been any issues when repatriating Socrates Argyrides from London early in 1924 for £5. See SA1/1247/1923, Treasury, Nicosia, 26 February 1924.
95. *Census of the Commonwealth of Australia*, 2–3 April 1911, Part II Birthplaces, 116; *Census of the Commonwealth of Australia*, 30 June, 1933, Part X Birthplace, 732; National Archives Australia (NAA), B2455, file on Michael George, born Arodes, Cyprus, No. 545; file on John Cecil Wortabet, Nicosia, Cyprus, No. 1625; file on Peter Constantine, both in Hirokitia, Cyprus, No. 6738; file on George Henry Nahos, Nicosia, Cyprus, No. 19267; and file on George Orphanz, Cyprus, No. 77561.
96. *Census of the Commonwealth of Australia*, 3–4 April 1921, Part II Birthplaces, 49.
97. CO 67/214, Stonehaven to Amery, 15 March 1925.
98. CO 67/214, Handwritten note on accompanying minute, 26 March 1925.
99. CO67/223/14, Stonehaven (recipient not clear), 4 October 1927.
100. CO67/223/14, Governor General Stonehaven to Colonial Office, 4 October 1927.
101. CO67/223/14, Storrs to Amery, 11 January 1928.
102. CO67/223/14, note, Dawe, 18 February 1928.
103. Varnava, 'Recruitment and Volunteerism for the Cypriot Mule Corps, 1916–1919'. For more detail see, Varnava, *Serving the Empire in the Great War*, 85–92.
104. CO67/223/14, typed note, 22 February 1928.
105. CO67/223/14, Amery to Storrs, 29 February 1928; V.C. Duffy, Australia House, to DO, 26 January 1928.
106. CO67/223/14, typed note, 4 August 1928; CO67/223/14, Australia House to DO, 25 July 1928.

12 DEALING WITH DESTITUTE CYPRIOTS IN THE UK AND AUSTRALIA ... 309

107. CO67/223/14, Amery to Storrs, 30 August 1928.
108. SA1/504/1924, Bolton, District Commissioner of Limassol, to Chief Secretary, 1 February 1924; Acting Colonial Secretary to all commissioner except Kyrenia, 20 March 1928. See SA1/504/1924 for individual stories.
109. CO67/235/14, Acting Governor of Cyprus to CO, 13 August 1930.
110. CO67/235/14, minute, 'M' Department, Crown Agents to CO, 1 October 1930.
111. CO67/235/14, Storrs to Lord Passfield, 5 November 1930.
112. CO67/235/14, Crown Agents to CO, 4 December 1930; CO67/235/14, Dawe minute, 8 December 1930.
113. CO67/235/14, note, Under Secretary of State for Colonial Office, 27 December 1930.
114. CO67/235/14, Dawe minute, 8 December 1930.
115. CO67/235/14, minute, 'M' Department, Crown Agents to CO, 23 December 1930.
116. Panikos Panayi, *German Immigrants in Britain during the Nineteenth Century, 1815–1914*, Berg, Oxford, 1995.
117. CO67/237/7, Storrs to Passfield, 9 April 1931.
118. CO67/237/7, note, 24 April 1931.
119. CO67/237/7, Reply to above note, 24 April 1931.
120. CO67/237/7, note, 27 April 1931.
121. Andrekos Varnava, 'The Origins and Prevalence of and Campaigns to Eradicate Venereal Diseases in British Colonial Cyprus, 1916–1939', *Social History of Medicine*, forthcoming 2019.
122. CO67/237/7, Secretary of Society of Friends of Foreigners in Distress to CO, 12 May 1931.
123. Ibid.
124. CO67/237/7, note, 15 May 1931.
125. CO67/237/7, Constantinidis to W.J. Cable, 22 May 1931.
126. CO67/237/7, Secretary of Society of Friends of Foreigners in Distress to H.R. Cowell, 27 May 1931.
127. CO67/237/7, note, 6 June 1931.
128. CO67/237/7, Bevir to Secretary of Society of Friends of Foreigners in Distress, 13 June 1931.
129. CO67/237/7, Secretary of Society of Friends of Foreigners in Distress to Anthony Bevir, 19 June 1931.
130. CO67/237/7, note, 27 June 1931.
131. CO67/237/7, CO note, 25 July 1931; CO67/237/7, Storrs to Lord Curzon, 19 August 1931.
132. CO67/237/7, note, 1 October 1931.
133. CO67/237/7, Storrs to J.H. Thomas, 12 October 1931.
134. CO67/237/7, note, 15 October 1931.

310 A. VARNAVA AND E. SMITH

135. CO 67/237/7, Typed note, 28 October 1931; CO 67/237/7, note, 30 October 1931.
136. Smith and Varnava, 'Creating a "Suspect Community"', 1173–1176.
137. SA1/756/35, George E. Poulia to Colonial Secretary, 26 October 1935.
138. Smith and Varnava, 'Creating a "Suspect Community"', 1173–1176.
139. Lake and Reynolds, *Drawing the Global Colour Line*; Atkinson, *The Burden of White Supremacy*; Jeremy C. Martens, *Empire and Asian Migration: Sovereignty, Immigration Restriction and Protest in the British Settler Colonies, 1888–1907*, UWA Publishing, Perth, 2018.

REFERENCES

Agutter, Karen, '"Italians Deported—Australians Next": Italians, World War I and the Labour Movement' (eds.), Phillip Deery and Julie Kimber, *Fighting Against War: Peace Activism in the Twentieth Century*, Leftbank Press, Melbourne, 2015, 157–176.

Anthias, Floya, *Ethnicity, Class, Gender and Migration: Greek-Cypriots in Britain*, Ashgate, Aldershot, 1992.

Atkinson, David C., *The Burden of White Supremacy: Containing Asian Migration in the British Empire and the United States*, University of North Carolina Press, Chapel Hill, NC, 2016.

Bashford, Alison and Catie Gilchrist, 'The Colonial History of the 1905 Aliens Act', *Journal of Imperial and Commonwealth History*, 40(3), 2012, 409–437.

Byrne, David, 'Class, Race and Nation: The Politics of the "Arab Issue" in South Shields 1919–39', *Immigrants and Minorities*, 13(2–3), 1994, 89–103.

Cresciani, Gianfranco, *The Italians in Australia*, Cambridge University Press, Cambridge, 2003.

Damousi, Joy, '"This Is Against All the British Traditions of Fair Play": Violence Against Greeks on the Australian Home Front During the Great War' (eds.), Michael J.K. Walsh and Andrekos Varnava, *Australia and the Great War*, Melbourne University Press, Melbourne, 2016, 128–145.

Dunlop, Anne and Robert Miles, 'Recovering the History of Asian Migration to Scotland', *Immigrants & Minorities*, 9(2), 1990, 145–167.

Fischer, Gerhard, *Enemy Aliens: Internment and the Homefront Experience in Australia, 1914–1920*, University of Queensland Press, St Lucia, 1989.

Garland, D., *The Culture of Control: Crime and Social Order in Contemporary Society*, Oxford University Press, Oxford, 2001.

George, Vic and Geoffrey Millerson, 'The Cypriot Community in London', *Race & Class*, 8, 1967, 277–292.

Jupp, James, *Immigration*, Oxford University Press, Oxford, 1998.

Katsiaounis, Rolandos, 'Η Κυπριακή Παροικία του Λονδίνου και το Αρχιεπισκοπικό Ζήτημα της Κύπρου, 1928–1936', *Annual of the Centre for Scientific Research* (Nicosia), 22, 1996, 521–556.

Katsiaounis, Rolandos, 'Τα Πρώτα Βήματα της Επιτροπής Κυπριακής Αυτονομίας', *Annual of the Centre for Scientific Research* (Nicosia), XXVI, 2000, 263–287.

Lake, Marilyn and Henry Reynolds, *Drawing the Global Colour Line: White Men's Countries and the Question of Racial Equality*, Melbourne University Press, Melbourne, 2008.

Langfield, Michele, '"White Aliens": The Control of European Immigration to Australia, 1920–30', *Journal of Intercultural Studies*, 12(2), 1991, 1–14.

Manitakis, Nicolas and Michalis N. Michael, 'Cypriot Emigration to the United States of America (1910 to 1930)', *Chronos*, 30, 2014, 99–143.

Martens, Jeremy C., *Empire and Asian Migration: Sovereignty, Immigration Restriction and Protest in the British Settler Colonies, 1888–1907*, UWA Publishing, Perth, 2018.

Oakley, Robin, 'The Cypriot Migration to Britain' (ed.), Verity Saifullah Khan, *Family, Kingship and Patronage*, Macmillan, London, 1979, 13–34.

Oakley, Robin, 'The Control of Cypriot Migration to Britain Between the Wars', *Immigrants & Minorities*, 6(1), 1987, 30–43.

Oakley, Robin, 'Cypriot Migration to Britain Prior to World War II', *Journal of Ethnic and Migration Studies*, 15(3), 1989, 509–525.

Panayi, Panikos, *German Immigrants in Britain during the Nineteenth Century, 1815–1914*, Berg, Oxford, 1995.

Panayi, Panikos, *Spicing Up Britain: The Multicultural History of British Food*, Reaktion Books, London, 2008.

Panayi, Panikos, *An Immigration History of Britain: Multicultural Racism Since 1800*, Longman, Harlow, 2010.

Panayi, Panikos, 'Cypriots in Great Britain Since 1945' (eds.), K.J. Bade, et al., *The Encyclopaedia of Migration and Minorities in Europe*, Cambridge University Press, Cambridge, 2011, 301–302.

Piperoglou, Andonis, 'Greeks or Turks, "White" or "Asiatic": Historicising Castellorizian Racial-Consciousness, 1916–1920', *Journal of Australian Studies*, 40(4), 2016, 387–402.

Prais, Jinny, 'Imperial Travellers: The Formation of West African Urban Culture, Identity, and Citizenship in London and Accra, 1925–1935', University of Michigan, Unpublished PhD thesis, 2008.

Saini, Raminder K., '"England Failed to Do Her Duty Towards Them": The India Office and Pauper Indians in the Metropole, 1857–1914', *Journal of Imperial and Commonwealth History*, 46(2), 2018, 226–256.

Saunders, David, 'Aliens in Britain and the Empire During the First World War', *Immigrants & Minorities*, 4(1), 1985, 5–27.

Sherwood, Marika, 'Race, Nationality and Employment Among Lascar Seamen, 1660 to 1945', *Journal of Ethnic and Migration Studies*, 17(2), 1991, 229–244.

Silverman, Stephanie J., '"Regrettable But Necessary?"A Historical and Theoretical Study of the Rise of the UK Immigration Detention Estate and Its Opposition', *Politics & Policy*, 40(6), 2012, 1131–1157.

Smith, Evan and Andrekos Varnava, 'Creating a "Suspect Community": Monitoring and Controlling the Cypriot Community in Inter-War London', *English Historical Review*, 132(558), 2017, 1149–1181.

Smith, Evan and M. Marmo, *Race, Gender and the Body in British Immigration Control: Subject to Examination*, Palgrave Macmillan, Houndmills, 2014.

Solomos, John and Stephen Woodhams, 'The Politics of Cypriot Migration to Britain', *Immigrants & Minorities*, 14(3), 1995, 231–256.

Tabili, Laura, '"Keeping the Natives Under Control": Race Segregation and Domestic Dimensions of Empire, 1920–1939', *International Labor and Working Class History*, 44, 1993, 64–78.

Tabili, Laura, *'We Ask for British Justice': Workers and Racial Difference in Late Imperial Britain*, Cornell University Press, Ithaca, NY, 1994.

Tampke, Jürgen, *The Germans in Australia*, Cambridge University Press, Cambridge, 2006.

Taylor, Becky, 'Immigration, Statecraft and Public Health: The 1920 Alien Order, Medical Examinations and the Limitations of the State in England', *Social History of Medicine*, 29(3), 512–533.

Varnava, Andrekos, *British Imperialism in Cyprus, 1878–1915: The Inconsequential Possession*, Manchester University Press, Manchester, 2009.

Varnava, Andrekos, 'Recruitment and Volunteerism for the Cypriot Mule Corps, 1916–1919', *Itinerario*, 38(3), 2014, 79–101.

Varnava, Andrekos, *Serving the Empire in the Great War: The Cypriot Mule Corps, Imperial Loyalty and Silenced Memory*, Manchester University Press, Manchester, 2017.

Varnava, Andrekos, 'The Origins and Prevalence of and Campaigns to Eradicate Venereal Diseases in British Colonial Cyprus, 1916–1939', *Social History of Medicine*, forthcoming, 2019.

Vickers, Tom, 'Migration, Political Engagement and the State: A Case Study of Immigrants and Communists in 1930s South Tyneside in the UK' (ed.), Mehmoona Moosa-Mitha, *Reconfiguring Citizenship: Social Exclusion and Diversity Within Inclusive Citizenship Practices*, Routledge, London, 2016.

Visram, Rozina, *Ayahs, Lascars and Princes: The Story of Indians in Britain, 1700–1947*, Routledge, London, 2015.

Williams, Callum, 'Patriality, Work Permits and the European Economic Community: The Introduction of the 1971 Immigration Act', *Contemporary British History*, 29(4) (2015), 508–538.

Winder, Robert, *Bloody Foreigners: The Story of Immigration to Britain*, Abacus, London, 2006.

INDEX

A
Aboriginal (Indigenous Australians), 4, 5, 11, 93–97, 99, 104–110, 113, 114, 118, 232, 235, 271
Abyssinia, 284, 305
Adana, 284
Adelaide, 6, 8, 31, 33, 96, 101, 102, 119, 120, 123–127, 129, 131, 133, 136, 138, 139, 152, 153, 156, 158, 159, 162–164, 166–171, 173–176, 182, 208, 218, 222, 244
Agriculturalists, 277, 278, 292, 293
Albania/Albanians, 293
Alexandria, 284, 285, 289
Aliens Restriction Act 1914, 279, 283
Amalgamated Miners Association, 222
Amery, Leo, 277, 291
Angas, George Fife, 32, 36, 37
Anzac, 114, 230, 236, 237, 240–242, 244, 245, 247–249, 255, 268
Asia/Asian, 234, 238, 259, 279–281, 286, 291, 300
Atkinson, Meredith, 231
Atlantic, 3, 18, 257, 258

Australasian Institute of Mining Engineers (M.A.I.M.E.), 185, 186
Australia, 1, 2, 5, 6, 8–11, 14, 23–25, 28, 37, 46–50, 52, 55, 57, 58, 65, 95, 117, 120–122, 126, 127, 132, 140, 152, 153, 156, 157, 165–167, 171, 173, 176, 189, 192, 194, 196, 199, 201, 208–210, 212–214, 216, 217, 219, 220, 224, 229–233, 235, 237–239, 241–245, 247, 249, 255–261, 263, 265, 267, 268, 277–280, 283–285, 287, 290–293, 300, 301
Australia House, 277, 293
Australian Imperial Force (AIF), 231, 237, 241, 244, 245, 290, 291
Austria/Austrian, 158, 280

B
Barossa Valley, 187
Barrier Industrial Council, 223, 224
Bean, C.E.W., 230, 241

© The Editor(s) (if applicable) and The Author(s) 2019
P. Payton and A. Varnava (eds.),
Australia, Migration and Empire, Britain and the World,
https://doi.org/10.1007/978-3-030-22389-2

314 INDEX

Belfast, 155, 157
Bendigo, 186
Bentham, Jeremy, 50, 62
Bermuda, 282
Bible Christians, 219
Bolivia, 185
Booth, Mary, 8, 9, 229–237, 239–249
Boyd, William, 14
Brisbane, 9, 10, 127, 150, 253–255, 257, 258, 260, 261, 267, 268
Bristol, 32
British Empire, 1–3, 94, 229, 233, 243, 256, 258, 259, 264, 267, 268, 282, 288, 293, 300, 301
British Nationality and Status of Aliens Act (1914), 281
Broken Hill, 8, 162, 195, 215, 217, 223–225, 227
Bulgaria/Bulgarians, 280
Butcher, Eddie, 225

C
Cairo, 284, 286
Calais, 34
Canada, 3, 14, 21–23, 45, 46, 48–51, 58, 63, 169, 256–258, 278, 285
Catholic Seamen's Home and Institute, 289
Ceylon/Ceylonese, 269, 283
Chapman, Montague, 32, 35
China/Chinese, 33, 106, 122, 126, 130, 146, 158, 284
Chinese famine (1878), 122
Clauson, John, 284, 285
Coglin, Patrick Boyce, 125, 137, 149, 164
Colonial Office, 48, 50, 52, 63–68, 70, 82, 104, 117, 278, 281–283, 287–299
Coloured Alien Seamen Order in 1925, 279

Committee on Distressed Colonial and Indian Subjects (1909), 281, 282, 307
Commonwealth, The (British), 235
Constantinides, Michael, 296, 297
Cook, Joseph, 291
Coolgardie, 185, 186, 188, 197, 198
Cork, 35, 126, 143
Cornwall/Cornish, 2, 7, 8, 11, 17, 31, 32, 34, 37, 126, 144, 181–185, 188–199, 207–214, 216–220, 222, 224
Crimean War, 122
Crown Agents, 294, 295
Cumberland, 30
Curzon, Lord, 288
Cypriot Mule Corps, 285, 293
Cyprus/Cypriots, 10, 277–279, 284–301

D
Davitt, Michael, 157–159, 171, 172
Dawe, Arthur, 278, 292, 293
Deportation, 283, 290
Destitution, 10, 120, 123, 124, 277, 278, 283, 292–295, 298–300
Devlin, Joseph, 157, 173
Dodecanese, 284
Donovan, J.T., 157, 173
Dublin, 7, 29, 35, 120, 128, 129, 145, 155, 172, 179, 191
Dunedin, 22

E
Egremont, Earl (George Wyndham), 51
Egypt/Egyptian, 258, 259, 265, 278, 284, 285, 291
Ellis Island, 258

INDEX   315

England/English, 2, 18, 19, 24, 25, 29, 34, 36, 46, 54, 103, 128, 158, 166, 259, 285, 292, 293, 295, 299, 300
Esmonde, Thomas, 155, 157, 168, 177
Eugenics, 229–235, 241, 243, 245

F
Federation (Australia), 163, 279
Fishbourne, John, 234
Fitzgerald, J.D., 231
Foreign Office, 282, 287, 288
France/French, 18, 24, 34, 88, 158, 258, 278, 279, 285
Fraser, Malcolm, 186, 189, 190
Freeleagus, Christy, 10, 255, 260, 261, 263–265, 268

G
Gabi Gabi Tribe (Australia), 266
Galton, Francis, 232, 243
Galway, 37
Gawler, 8, 101, 129, 130, 146, 169, 173, 208
Geological Society of Australasia, 186
Geraldine, 7, 181–184, 197
Germany/Germans, 32, 33, 36, 158, 256, 279, 280
Glasgow, 283
Glen Osmond, 208, 212
Goderich, Viscount, 69, 70
Goold-Adams, Hamilton, 264
Gosport, 58
Gouger, Robert, 51, 52, 58, 59, 64, 65
Great Boulder, 186, 188, 194
Great Depression, 237, 294, 295, 300
Greece/Greeks, 10, 258–261, 263, 264, 267–269

Grey, Earl, 29
Gwennap, 208, 210

H
Hamburg, 36
Harcus, William, 36, 42
Hazleton, Richard, 157, 173
Healey, Pierce, 156, 162
Henwood, George, 210, 211
Hoover, Herbert, 7, 188, 189, 192–195, 198, 199, 203, 204
Hughes, Billy, 236
Hungary/Hungarians, 280

I
Immigration Act 1971, 279
Immigration Restrictions Act 1901, 279
India/Indians, 20, 33, 48, 58, 103, 106, 122, 126, 130, 133, 146, 156, 257, 258, 280–283, 297, 301
India Office, 281
Ionian Islands/Ionian, 253, 265, 267, 269
Ireland/Irish, 1, 2, 4–6, 10, 11, 15, 17–19, 21–39, 47, 70, 103, 119–133, 135–139, 143, 144, 146, 148, 149, 151–160, 162–176, 188, 191, 234, 279
Irish Famine, 119, 125, 129, 152, 155
Irish Home Rule, 151, 152, 155, 162, 169, 172–175, 177
Irish National League, 156, 163
Irish Parliamentary Party (IPP), 6, 151, 157, 158, 169–171, 174, 176
Irvine, Robert, 231
Isle of Man, 31

316 INDEX

Italy/Italian, 194, 199, 234, 258, 278, 279, 284

J
Jebb, Richard, 230
Jewish/Jews, 278, 279
Johannesburg, 189–191, 287

K
Kadina, 214, 219, 221–223
Kalgoorlie, 186, 188, 198, 256
Kangaroo Point, 9, 253
Kapunda, 32, 129, 130, 133, 134, 144, 173, 208
Kaurna, 96
Kimberly (WA), 150, 163, 183, 186
Kingston, George, 121, 126, 149, 156
Kyrenia, 294

L
Labor Party (Australia), 195
Laffan, J.J., 132, 133, 147
Lake, Octavius, 219, 220
Lambeth, 289
Lang, J.D., 75
Larnaca, 285
Latin America, 278
Levant, 259
Limassol, 305, 309
Liverpool, 281
London, 10, 19, 20, 31–34, 45, 54, 55, 58, 59, 71, 82, 124, 165, 189–191, 194, 198, 232, 244, 277, 278, 280, 281, 286–289, 291, 294, 295, 297, 298, 300, 301

M
Macedonian, 258, 285
Malta/Maltese, 265, 279, 282, 285, 292, 293, 300, 307
McMahon, Henry, 284
Melbourne, Viscount, 52
Menzies, Leslie Robert, 187
Merchant Shipping Act, 284
Mersin, 284
Mines/Mining, 7, 8, 34, 53, 59, 162, 181–195, 197–199, 201, 207–218, 220, 221, 223–225, 257
Mitchell, Samuel, 7, 183, 187, 193, 195, 196, 198, 200, 204
Montgomery, Michael Thomas, 119, 126
Moonta, 147, 193, 214–217, 219–223

N
Napier, Charles James, 50, 188
Native Title Act (1993), 97
New South Wales (NSW), 3, 4, 8, 9, 20, 45–49, 56, 57, 69, 70, 75, 77, 80, 82, 84, 103, 152, 153, 170–172, 174, 209, 213, 223, 230, 231, 234, 235, 239, 243, 249
New York, 3, 50, 56, 57
New Zealand, 14, 23, 171, 172, 279, 285
Ngadjuri, 96, 109, 118
Nicosia, 288
North Adelaide, 115, 129, 131, 146, 159, 160
Northampton, 181, 183, 193, 196, 197
Northern Territory, 235
Norway/Norwegian, 213
Nukunu, 96, 109

INDEX 317

O
Oats, William, 186–188, 195–198
Onkaparinga, 159, 160

P
Paphos, 285
Passfield, Lord, 294
Patagonia, 22
Peel, Robert, 52
Penhale Wheal Vor, 211
Pentonville, 297
Persia Famine (1871), 122
Perth, 185, 187
Peru, 22
Philhellenism, 256, 267
Piraeus, 258
Poor Law (UK), 219, 280–282, 297
Port Adelaide, 118, 129, 137, 148,
   149, 158, 160, 167, 171, 173
Port Augusta, 109, 129, 131, 133
Port Phillip, 48, 103
Port Said, 258, 291
Portugal, 18
Poulia, George, 299
Prisk, John, 220, 221

Q
Queensland, 9, 10, 156, 168, 171,
   172, 185, 219, 255, 256, 260,
   264–267
Quota (immigration), 22

R
Redmond, John, 157, 158, 163
Redmond, William, 136, 157, 173
Richards, Henry Charles, 189, 190
Royal Commission on the Basic Wage,
   231
Royal Phoenix Mine, 187
Rudd, Kevin, 97

S
Sandhurst, 186
San Francisco, 287
Scotland/Scottish, 2, 16, 19, 24–27,
   32, 39, 103, 142, 167
Scott, Ernest, 230
Simms, William Knox, 156, 163, 164
Smith, Edwin (E.T.), 6, 120, 126,
   127, 132, 140, 143, 156, 163
Socialism/Socialist, 167, 194, 196,
   199
Somerville, Phyllis, 218, 219
South Africa, 2, 7, 14, 21, 23, 49,
   189–191, 198, 216, 279, 285
South Australia, 3–6, 8, 14, 15,
   28–37, 45, 47, 50–59, 93, 95,
   99, 101–104, 106, 119–121,
   123–125, 127, 128, 131, 138,
   139, 151–159, 162, 164–176,
   182, 187, 189, 193, 207, 208,
   212–214, 216, 218, 219, 235,
   238
Spain, 18
Spence, W.G., 222, 223
Stevenson, George, 123
Stevenson, Malcolm, 287
Stonehaven, Lord, 278, 292, 293
Storrs, Ronald, 277, 292–296, 298,
   299
St. Petersburg, 22, 171, 172
Strangers' Home for Asiatics, Africans
   and South Sea Islanders, 281
Sudan, 284
Sussex, 30, 48, 51
Swan River, 46, 48, 49, 182
Sydney, 9, 70, 96, 97, 150, 165, 176,
   212, 229, 231, 236, 240, 242

T
Tanganyika, 284
Tasmania/Van Diemen's Land, 3, 45,
   46, 48, 57, 75, 103, 171

318 INDEX

Taylor, George, 231
Thorne, Serena, 219, 220
Tindale, Norman, 232
Torrens, Robert, 35, 47, 121
Transvaal, 190
Turkey/Turks, 280, 293
Twain, Mark, 131, 156

U
Ulster, 2, 16, 17, 19, 39, 168, 169
United States (US), 14, 21–23, 45–
    50, 57, 194, 229, 256–258, 269,
    278–280, 285–289, 300, 301

V
Vasyli, Hector, 9, 10, 253–256,
    258–261, 263–265, 267–269
Venereal disease, 107, 236, 243, 296,
    297, 299
Verran, John, 208
Victoria (Australia), 8, 9, 48, 122,
    127, 152, 167, 172, 182, 195,
    209, 213, 219, 230, 261
Vosper, Frederic Charles Burleigh,
    184–187, 195–198

W
Wakefield, Edward Gibbon, 30, 31,
    49, 50, 62
Wales/Welsh, 2, 16, 24, 25, 27, 170,
    286

Wallaroo, 129, 159, 160, 193, 214,
    215, 217–219, 221–223
Washington, 287, 289
Waste Lands Amendment Act (1869),
    106
Wellington, Duke of, 52
West, A.G., 244
Western Australia (WA), 7, 150, 163,
    181–195, 197, 198, 257
West Indies/West Indian, 280, 281
Westmeath, 35
White Australia Policy, 279
World War I/Great War/First World
    War, 9, 10, 25, 155, 229–231,
    237, 239, 244, 245, 254, 256,
    278–281, 285, 286, 289, 290
World War II/Second World War, 10,
    23, 237, 268, 278

Y
Yatala, 159, 160
Yemen/Yemenite, 283
Yorke Peninsula, 8, 107, 160, 161
Yugoslavia/Yugoslavs, 293

Britain and the World

Historical Journal of the British Scholar Society

Britain and the World focuses on Britain's global history in the modern era. The focus on the history of the 'British world' is unique amongst all journals concerned with British history.

EDITOR-IN-CHIEF
John MacKenzie

GENERAL EDITOR
Martin Farr

MANAGING EDITORS
John Griffiths
Juliette Desplat
Brandon Marsh

www.euppublishing.com/brw

Table of
Content Alerts

Free Featured
Articles

Free sample
issues

EDINBURGH
University Press

Printed by Printforce, the Netherlands